REEL TIME

Reel Time

MOVIE EXHIBITORS AND MOVIE AUDIENCES IN PRAIRIE CANADA, 1896 TO 1986

Robert M. Seiler and *Tamara P. Seiler*

AU PRESS

Published by AU Press, Athabasca University
1200, 10011 – 109 Street, Edmonton, AB T5J 3S8

ISBN 978-1-926836-99-7 (print) 978-1-927356-00-5 (PDF) 978-1-927356-01-2 (epub)

Cover and interior design by Natalie Olsen, Kisscut Design.
Printed and bound in Canada by Marquis Book Printers.

Library and Archives Canada Cataloguing in Publication

Seiler, R. M. (Robert Morris)
Reel time : movie exhibitors and movie audiences in prairie Canada, 1896 to 1986 / by Robert M. Seiler and Tamara P. Seiler.

Includes bibliographical references and index.
Issued also in electronic formats.
ISBN 978-1-926836-99-7

1. Motion pictures — Social aspects — Prairie Provinces — History.
2. Motion pictures — Economic aspects — Prairie Provinces — History.
3. Motion picture theaters — Social aspects — Prairie Provinces — History.
4. Motion picture theaters — Economic aspects — Prairie Provinces — History.
I. Seiler, Tamara Palmer
II. Title.

PN1995.9.S6S44 2013 302.23'4309712 C2012-901800-7

We acknowledge the financial support of the Government of Canada through the Canada Book Fund (CBF) for our publishing activities.

Canada Council for the Arts Conseil des Arts du Canada

Assistance provided by the Government of Alberta, Alberta Multimedia Development Fund.

Government of Alberta

To the memory of our parents

CONTENTS

ILLUSTRATIONS

ACKNOWLEDGEMENTS

Many people helped us prepare this volume. First, we acknowledge our huge debt to Charles R. Acland, Deborah Carmichael, Howard Lichtman, Janet MacKinnon, George Melnyk, Paul S. Moore, Donald B. Smith, Charles Tepperman, Donald G. Wetherell, and Maurice Yacowar for sharing their expertise with us and nurturing our work. The illuminating conversations we had with these scholars helped us focus our investigation and sharpen our arguments.

We are also indebted to those individuals who provided us with information about various aspects of movie exhibition. We thank Mrs. Ethel Allen, Helen Atnikov, Cheryl Baron, Cleo Barron and the late Bob Barron, Dick Barron and Jean Barron, the late Joe Brager, Charles Brawn, Bruce S. Elliott, Barry Elmer, Iona Fraser, Lloyd Hamilton, Irene Theodore Heinstein, Alan Hustak, Karen Marks, Ruth Millar, Arthur Osborne, Marty Rothstein, Pat Ryan, Harry Sanders, Reg Skene, Syd Sniderman, Greg Stoicoiu, Jack Stothard, Linda Wakefield, and Stan Winfield.

We are also grateful to all those individuals who helped us track down and access materials that were crucial to our research. We extend our sincere thanks to the librarians at the Cinémathèque Québécoise library and at Concordia University Library, in Montréal; to Justin Gauthier, Ginette Godward, Sophie Tellier, and Anne-Catherine Toulmonde, reference archivists in the Client Services Division, Library and Archives Canada; to the librarians in the Ottawa Room of the

Ottawa Public Library; to Donna Bernardo-Ceriz, assistant archivist at the Ontario Jewish Archives; to Julie Holland, archives assistant, and Michael Moir, archivist and head, at Clara Thomas Archives and Special Collections, Scott Library, York University; to Heather Wilson, research specialist at the Toronto Reference Library; to the librarians at the Robarts Library, University of Toronto, and at Ryerson University Library, also in Toronto; to Denise Kirk, local history librarian at the Brantford Public Library; to Giles Bugailiskis, D. M. Lyon, and R. R. Rostecki, of the Planning, Property, and Development Department, City of Winnipeg; to Alta Carter, librarian at the Winnipeg Public Library; to Anne Morton, of the Research and Reference division of the Hudson's Bay Company Archives; to archivists Irma Penn and Sharon Segal, at the Jewish Heritage Centre of Western Canada, in Winnipeg; to Christy M. Henry and S. J. McKee, archivists at the Archives and John E. Robbins Library, Brandon University; to Jonathan Hill, administrative assistant, Heritage Resources Department, City of Brandon; to archivists Cheryl Brown, Dorothea Funk, and Elaine Kozakavich, in the Local History Room of Saskatoon Public Library; to the Architectural Heritage Society of Saskatchewan, in Saskatoon; to Kenneth G. Aitken, prairie history librarian at the Regina Public Library; to Carey Isaak, librarian at the City of Regina Archives; to archivists Tim Novak, Paula Rein, and Bill Wagner, in Reference and Outreach at the Saskatchewan Archives Board; to the librarians at the Urban Planning Division, City of Regina; to Pat Ryan, researcher with Past Relations, in Regina; to archivist Pam Albert, of the Archives Department, Moose Jaw Public Library; to Graham G. Hall, artistic and executive director, and Judy Casey, business manager, at the Moose Jaw Cultural Centre; to Paula Aurini-Onderwater, Sherry Bell, Bruce Ibsen, and Kathryn Ivany, of the City of Edmonton Archives; to Shannon Vecchio, business manager, Archives Store and Client Services, Provincial Archives of Alberta; to Matthew Wangler, director of the Historic Places Designation Program, Alberta Culture and Community Spirit, Historic Resources Management Branch, Edmonton; to the archivists at the Calgary Land Titles Office, in the City of Calgary Assessment Department; to Jennifer Bobrovitz, local historian, at the Calgary Public Library; to Darryl Cariou, of the Heritage Advisory Board, City of Calgary; to Doug Cass, archivist at the Glenbow Archives,

Calgary; to Linda Fraser, archivist and chief curator of the Canadian Architectural Archives at the University of Calgary; to JoAnne Houston and Evelyn Ward, librarians at the W. R. Castell Central Library, in Calgary; to Laurie Leier, director of marketing and development at the EPCOR Centre for the Performing Arts; to Sharon Neary, data librarian at the MacKimmie Library, University of Calgary; to the late Jack Switzer, formerly of the Jewish Historical Society of Southern Alberta, in Calgary; to the librarians at Simon Fraser University Library, in Burnaby, British Columbia, and at the Vancouver Public Library; and to the librarians at Cleveland Public Library, in Cleveland, Ohio; at Northwestern University Library, in Evanston, Illinois; and at the University of Nevada Library, in Reno, Nevada.

The value of this work rests in large part upon the materials supplied by these various institutions.

We are indebted to the University of Calgary for granting us Sabbatical Research Fellowships, a Killam Research Fellowship, and administrative leave, which enabled us to undertake extensive research and prepare the manuscript.

Finally, we thank all our friends and colleagues for their stimulating conversation and moral support, in particular Linda Anton, Frances Batycki, Lee Carruthers, Sarah Carter, Janice Dickin, Marianne Fedori, R. Douglas Francis, the late Albert W. Halsall, Rick Horsley, Irene Karshenbaum, the late Henry C. Klassen, Irene Kmet, Clyde McConnell, Sue McConnell, Roderick McGillis, Brian Pleet, Anthony and Beverly Rasporich, R. Bruce Shepard, and Bob Shiell.

We presented parts of this book in the form of conference papers at a meeting of the Canadian Association for the Study of Rhetoric, in Halifax, on 29 May 2003; at meetings of the Southwest Texas Popular Culture Association/American Culture Association, held in Albuquerque, New Mexico, on 15 February 2002, 13 February 2003, 12 February 2005, and 10 February 2006, and in San Antonio, Texas, on 9 April 2004: and at a meeting of the Film Studies Association of Canada in Winnipeg on 2 June 2004. Parts of chapter 1 were previously published as "Movie Exhibition in Manitoba: The Case of J. A. (John) Schuberg," *Manitoba History* 58 (June 2008): 11–18. Parts of chapters 2 and 4 appeared as "Movie Exhibition on the Prairies: The Case of the Allens, 1910–15," *Prairie Forum* 31, no. 1 (Spring 2006): 71–84. Sections of chapter 5 appeared as "Nathanson, Zukor, and Famous Players: Movie Exhibition in Canada, 1920–1941," *American Review of Canadian Studies* 36, no. 1 (Spring 2006): 59–80.

We extend a special thanks to Walter Hildebrandt and his colleagues at Athabasca University Press, including Pamela MacFarland Holway, Megan Hall, Peter Enman, and Connor Houlihan, who shepherded the manuscript through the editing and production stages with enthusiasm and perspicacity. They provided the assistance every author hopes for. We also thank the anonymous reviewers for their valuable comments and suggestions. Of course, we take responsibility for any errors or omissions.

We are grateful to our children and their spouses, Tanya Palmer and James Maciukenas and Mark Palmer and Melanie Palmer, whose patience and understanding sustained us throughout the project.

Robert M. Seiler and Tamara P. Seiler
15 November 2011

REEL TIME

INTRODUCTION

Reel Time charts the growth of movie exhibition as a business venture and, by extension, documents the conditions of moviegoing as a social practice in the Canadian prairies, primarily during the heyday of the indoor, single-screen facility. We focus on selected entrepreneurs and on some of the more important facilities they operated in the region's major cities. We place movie exhibition and moviegoing in the context of spectator-oriented leisure-time pursuits, framing them with reference to the factors that determine the nature of the leisure-time activities that people in particular localities engage in.[1] Operators of amusement venues played a key role in defining as well as controlling the leisure-time activities of working-class and middle-class people across North America, contributing significantly to the emergence of mass culture in the first half of the twentieth century. We tell the story of those entertainment entrepreneurs who established movie exhibition as a legitimate business in prairie Canada, responded to campaigns to reform the industry, designed safe and comfortable facilities, and founded the national movie theatre chains, namely, Allen Theatre Enterprises, Famous Players, and Odeon Theatres. *Reel Time* thus examines such topics as theatre design, programming strategies, seating arrangements, pricing policies, marketing schemes, and expansion, with a view to illuminating the centralizing and standardizing processes at work in the commercialization of public leisure-time activities in general and in moviegoing in particular.[2]

THE PRAIRIE WEST

We argue that the dynamics that shaped the development of the prairie West and propelled it quite rapidly into the modern era also shaped movie exhibition. In doing so, we invoke a modified version of the "metropolitan-hinterland thesis," one that de-emphasizes the environmental determinism running through historian Frederick Jackson Turner's analysis, in 1893, of the development of American institutions.[3] At the same time, we acknowledge the interpretive power in Canadian cultural history of the north-south forces of geography and culture, particularly of north-south metropolitan influences. The backdrop of our study, the broad expanse of prairie and steppe extending from Lake Superior to the Rocky Mountains and from the low Arctic to the 49th parallel, is a continuation of the Great Plains, which covers much of the central United States and Mexico. As such, the region has much in common with its American counterpart, the histories of both having been similarly shaped by their roles as hinterlands to different but interrelated eastern metropolitan centres and thus by a complex relationship between similar as well as different north-south and east-west influences. As a far greater magnet for diverse European settlers than was Canada from the earliest days of European settlement, the United States developed earlier than Canada, the western regions of the latter attracting few settlers until the "closing" of the American frontier in the 1890s. Until then, western Canada was inhabited by only a relatively small number of settlers, primarily of British heritage and often from central Canada. In the late 1890s, however, immigrants from other nations, primarily European ones, began to move into the region. Following World War II, significant changes to Canada's immigration policy gradually opened the doors to settlers from non-European countries. These changes, along with expanding economic opportunities, meant that the West increasingly became home to people from around the world, as well as all across Canada.[4] Different areas of the prairies have generated different cultural and political formations, depending upon patterns of settlement and major economic activities. Unique political formations, albeit ones that have much in common with populist movements south of the border, have emerged in the prairie West. "Protest movements," such as the Winnipeg General Strike of 1919 and the rise of the United Farmers of Alberta, have been linked to the region's hinterland positioning and to consequent feelings of alienation from federal decision-making processes.

The idea that the frontiers of settlement have played a crucial role in shaping North America — the "Turner thesis"— has influenced the writing of Canadian history. Celebrated historians such as A. S. Morton and A. R. M. Lower emphasized the power of the environment in the settlement of the prairie West. However, what has come to be loosely called the "metropolitan thesis," as developed especially in the work of J. M. S. Careless, has arguably been more influential in Canada.[5] In the United States, the influence of Turner has also waned, with proponents of the "new Western history" arguing that too much has been made of the power of the frontier to "transform."[6] Growing out of the work of Careless and that of his predecessors, Harold A. Innes, author of *A History of the Canadian Pacific Railway* (1923) and *The Fur Trade* (1930), and Donald Creighton, author of *The Commercial Empire of the St. Lawrence* (1937) and *Dominion of the North* (1944), the metropolitan thesis, though nuanced differently by its various proponents, explains Canadian development in terms of geography and commerce.[7] Lower explained that, far from being independent and self-sufficient, the frontier is dependent, constantly requiring metropolitan aid and control, and he paid attention to the power wielded by such metropolitan centres as Montréal and Toronto economically and Ottawa politically. This perspective emphasizes that the investments, markets, transportation routes, and cultural patterns of the hinterland are affected by the interests of the metropolitan centre. Proponents of the metropolitan approach say that Canada pioneered not "frontier" democracy but a combination of public and private mechanisms to overcome the problems created by a harsh environment. The institutions and the practices developed sought to organize communications systems and to extend commerce.[8] Manifestations of metropolitan influences include the building of transcontinental railways and the designing of the policies of economic nationalism.[9]

In annexing the North-West Territories in 1870, the government of John A. Macdonald turned the region into a hinterland or "investment frontier," the burden of which the rest of Canada accepted. Gerald Friesen points out that, because expansion had previously led to an economic boom, the commercial and financial interests in central Canada decided to turn the territories into such a hinterland, thereby opening the North-West and benefitting themselves at the same time. The territories attained limited self-government, by way of an advisory Legislative Assembly, but the federal government retained possession of the public lands and the natural resources so that it could implement policies that facilitated the rapid settlement of the West.[10] Translating this plan into action meant, for example, building a transcontinental railway that would transport agricultural machinery west and agricultural products east. As well, the government planned to assert Canada's sovereignty in the face of American competition by sending a police force, the North-West Mounted Police (NWMP) to the territories. Economist V. C. Fowke explains that, in developing "an integrated economy on a national basis," the federal government in fact centralized power in Montréal and Toronto.[11] However, with its staples-based economy, its small and thinly scattered population, and its continuing need for various forms of outside investment, Canada itself has been a kind of hinterland, first to Great Britain and later to the United States. The history of film exhibition in Canada generally illustrates these relationships very clearly, while the history of film exhibition on the prairies arguably provides a case study of double metropolitan dominance — from the east as well as from the more powerful south, although the story is not without examples of locally shaped practices, influences, and resistance.

The First Phase of Urbanization

As urban historian Gilbert Stelter puts it, metropolis-hinterland dynamics shaped the first phase of urbanization in western Canada, which extended from the 1870s to the recession of 1913.[12] Attracting as well as retaining immigrants was a challenge. Approximately 2.5 million people emigrated from Europe between 1853 and 1870: 61 percent settled in the United States, 18 percent in Australia, and the remainder in countries like Brazil and Argentina; only a small percentage settled in Canada. Moreover, a number of eastern Canadians moved to New England to find work.[13] Shortly after Confederation, in 1870, John A. Macdonald launched a massive advertising campaign to attract hard-working farmers living in Great Britain and Europe. The results were less than impressive. Historians have blamed the poor results on such factors as the attractiveness of the United States as a place to settle, the haphazardness of the campaign, the inaccurate information circulated by foreign newspapers, and the economic depression that struck North America and Europe in 1873. In an effort to bolster settlement, the federal government encouraged ethnic and/or religious settlers to move to the region.

Frustrated by the slow progress of settlement, the federal government opened the western region of the North-West Territories (what is now Alberta) to cattle ranching, enacting, in 1881, legislation enabling entrepreneurs to lease up to 100,000 acres for up to twenty-one years at a yearly rental of one cent per acre.[14] However, mass immigration to the western interior of Canada did not begin until the late 1890s, when the westward expansion in the United States neared completion. The Liberal government of Wilfrid Laurier, elected in June 1896, decided to become proactive in the agricultural settlement of the prairie West, convinced that the region played a vital role in Canada's economic development.[15] Clifford Sifton, the new minister of the interior, proclaimed that settling the West was a national enterprise, akin to building an all-Canadian transportation system. He reorganized the Department of Immigration, with a view to making it easier for people to acquire free land grants, and pursued a policy of selective immigration, encouraging the settlement of experienced farmers from Great Britain, the United States, and Europe, and by the same token discouraging the settlement of others who were widely regarded as "undesirable," such as blacks, Italians, Jews, "Orientals," and urban Englishmen, who in the end (he believed) would settle in the cities. Nevertheless, he is credited with championing the settlement of agriculturalists from eastern Europe, such as Poles and Ukrainians from what was then the Austro-Hungarian empire, the "men in sheepskin coats with stout wives" who, he believed, could be counted on to stay on the land. He also believed that these new immigrants would eventually assimilate to a British-Canadian norm. The department employed a variety of methods to attract settlers, such as paying agents a commission for securing immigrants, flooding the agricultural communities in selected countries with promotional literature, in the form of pamphlets and brochures extolling the virtues of "The Last Best West," and taking selected journalists on tours of the region, so that they could write favourable accounts on their return. The department also devoted much time and effort to recruiting in the United States; in 1896 six agents and in 1899 three hundred agents recruited Americans, who had the capital needed, owned the equipment, and had experience farming on the prairie. Significantly, the number of Americans who settled in the West increased from 2,400 in 1897 to 50,000 in 1902.[16]

The influx of immigrants from eastern Canada, Great Britain, the United States, and eastern and central Europe transformed the whole region: between 1901 and 1911, Manitoba's population grew from 255,000 to 456,000, Saskatchewan's from 91,000 to 294,000, and Alberta's from 73,000 to 375,000. Despite the emphasis on agriculture, increasingly these people settled in urban centres. For example, in 1901, urban dwellers made up 25 percent of the population of western Canada; by 1911, they made up 35 percent. By 1951, almost half the population (49 percent) lived in urban centres.[17] Four factors explain this massive flow of people to western Canada: the Canadian government had in fact established an effective recruiting campaign; circumstances in the United States, Great Britain, and Europe had changed, favouring recruiters; the situation of the prairie agricultural frontier had changed, thanks to more advanced farm machinery and the development of hardier crops; and the agricultural boom had stimulated booms in other industries, such as coal and lumber, thereby creating a variety of jobs.[18]

In short, during the first period of urbanization, commercial elites established the network that defined the region, including five cities, each with a population of more than 12,000, that became major urban centres.[19] During this phase, the development of the cities was tied to the development of agriculture: every rural community needed a town or a city that served as a collection and distribution point for disseminating agricultural machinery and collecting agricultural products for shipping east. Such factors as advantageous location, the external demand for staples, especially wheat and beef, the development of agricultural and transportation technology, deliberate federal policy with regard to the West, and general economic conditions determined the pace and the contours of western urban development.[20]

Ultimately, individuals and groups, via their capability and initiative, turned opportunity into reality, negotiating the possibilities and the problems as they arose. Business and civic leaders in the region's emerging towns and cities practised a policy of "boosterism," signifying something more than "supersalesmanship" and less than "a precise ideology." Most boosters were white, Anglo-Saxon Protestants, such as Senator James Lougheed, discussed in chapter 3, who believed that growth was desirable and that material success was important. Accordingly, they took up the challenge of turning the undeveloped prairies into "a prosperous, populous, dynamic region as quickly as possible."[21] This meant achieving legal city status early, securing railway connections and attracting industry, and expanding civic boundaries, thus increasing the municipality's borrowing power and widening the tax base so that the community could undertake huge public works projects, such as urban transportation, power development, and water and sewer works, with a view to attracting more immigrants and more investment. In this way, civic boosters, dominating the decision-making process, sought economic advantage and prestige for their communities — and the possibility of winning status as the provincial capital and/or the home of the provincial university.[22] Interestingly enough, these boosters often pointed to the establishment of the movie theatre as a sign of progress toward the all-important goal of being recognized as a major metropolitan centre, able to boast of amenities as good as those in the cities of eastern Canada and in the United States. By the outbreak of the great recession of 1913, civic elites had, as mentioned above, presided over the creation of five cities that served as dominant centres: Winnipeg, Regina, Saskatoon, Calgary, and Edmonton, because they had negotiated external and internal circumstances effectively. (We discuss these communities in more detail when we talk about specific movie theatres.)

Friesen writes that the communities of the Canadian prairies were becoming similar to other urban communities in the capitalist world. One feature of the homogenization process at work was "the creation of a comparable urban social structure: it comprised a large working-class, a professional service-class, and the business leaders. The many elements ignored by this simplistic design, such as the thousands of small merchants, salesmen, and clerks, found their place by choosing the social identity to which they were most closely allied."[23] Nor was this process of homogenization limited to the urban centres. Small towns also followed predictable patterns, depending upon their economic base. Friesen points to the remarkable sameness of coal mining towns; whether situated in the landscapes of southern Saskatchewan, the Badlands of central Alberta, or the majestic valleys of the Rocky Mountains, all were dominated by the fortune and the routine of the mine. The hours of the shift work, the prices of the goods at the store, the conditions of the bunkhouse, and the quality of the school: all were determined by "the company."[24]

The Second Phase of Urbanization

During the second phase of urbanization, which started with World War I, communities experienced several decades of slow or declining growth. Many confronted continual economic crisis, especially during the 1930s. According to political scientist and urban historian Alan Artibise, new approaches were needed to meet the new challenges, especially the complex problems that were generated by World War I, the Great Depression, and World War II.[25]

Corporate capitalism replaced boosterism. Socialist and labour organizations challenged the conventional, booster-oriented style of leadership. The development of corporate capitalism after the turn of the century was accompanied by the creation of bureaucratic forms of organization, the growth of a managerial elite, and the emergence of trained experts. Small family-run businesses or partnerships of the 1870s gave way to joint-stock companies, owned by anonymous stockholders and impersonal directorates and managed by career executives. Whereas the proprietors of family firms located their operations in small towns and cities, the corporate industrialists moved to the biggest cities, such as Montréal and Toronto. Regional elites had quite distinct origins and tastes; thanks to their business interests, they were, by the twentieth century, coming together in boardrooms and exclusive social clubs in what can be described as an integrated national system. Increasingly, during the first half of the twentieth century, the provinces curtailed the autonomy of the municipalities, many of which were moving closer and closer to bankruptcy, by expanding their statutory control over municipal government, instituting a range of administrative and regulatory conditions over municipal government, decreasing municipal powers of taxation, and introducing a system of conditional grants, which standardized the services that were delivered.[26]

Responding to these developments, in the years after 1910, the more successful family business operations, for example, the Allens (discussed in chapters 3 and 5), began establishing branch offices in other cities, and entrepreneurs hitherto concerned about the future of their own community adopted a broader perspective on economic conditions. In some cases, western firms became national firms. Evidence of this shift of power can be seen in the fact that national and international firms financed and controlled the rapid growth of the oil and gas industries in Alberta during the 1940s and the 1950s. Gradually, entrepreneurs realized that corporations have no loyalty to place.[27] Western cities, Calgary and Edmonton in particular, entered a third phase of urbanization in the 1960s, when new industries related to energy and mineral resources began to have a significant impact on the region.

The population of the prairies became increasingly diverse and mobile and, particularly after World War II, increasingly urban. Prairie people kept moving — from farm to city, from construction camp to coal mine, from homestead on the southern prairie to homestead on the northern parkland. Many thousands left the region altogether, abandoning their farms during the drought after 1917, migrating to the Pacific coast, to the United States, or back to Europe.[28] Of the 2 million immigrants who originally settled in western Canada, about 40 percent remained by 1931. By 1940, five residents in ten would trace their paternal origins to non-British countries; two would trace their origins to eastern Europe; another two would trace their origins to western Europe; and one might trace his or her origins to Great Britain. A rough calculation, based on the federal 1941 census, suggested that 60 percent of Scandinavians, 70 percent of French and Germans, and 80 percent of Slavs (including 94 percent of Ukrainians) in north-central Saskatchewan still spoke their mother tongue at home.[29] Establishing and maintaining social cohesion in this highly diverse and mobile population was a challenge indeed. Local, regional, and national institutions, including schools, clubs, and political parties, worked directly and indirectly to this end, but so too did emerging mass cultural institutions, many of them based in the United States, and, during the period we focus on, none more than the movie industry.

Understandably, the ways people in the prairie West spent their leisure time changed radically during the late nineteenth and early twentieth century, thanks to the introduction of new technologies, such as electricity, telephony, the motion picture, the automobile, radio, and television. Initially, the street railway system and the automobile encouraged people to spend more time away from home, where traditionally they had amused themselves by reading, making music, drawing and painting, and mounting amateur theatricals. They visited amusement parks, dance halls, legitimate theatres, movie theatres, opera houses, skating rinks, and vaudeville houses. Like American cultural historian Gregory A. Waller, we are fascinated by this rich moment in the history of popular culture, and *Reel Time* examines how it was experienced in prairie Canada by exploring such interrelated questions as how selected entrepreneurs packaged, promoted, and exhibited commercial entertainment and how selected audiences consumed this entertainment during this period of massive change.[30] Central to this study are questions about how people embraced or resisted the mass culture that was emerging, and how (if at all) the public discourse of the day reflected a concern for the decline of provincialism and the increase in standardization.[31]

OUR PROJECT

Scholarly interest in commercial entertainment in general and motion pictures in particular developed slowly. Sensitivity to movie exhibition as a subject worth studying dates from the early 1960s, when people across North America noticed that developers were knocking down many of the picture palaces built during the 1920s in order to make way for urban renewal. A handful of enthusiasts, starting with the American theatre historian Ben Hall, launched a movement not only to preserve these historic sites but also to study the architectural design and the social function of these unique buildings, as illustrated in the work of Tino Balio, Charlotte Herzog, and Maggie Valentine.[32] Still, scholars have expressed regret that movie exhibition has not attracted the critical attention it rightly deserves, particularly in Canada, pointing out that we actually know very little about exhibition at the national level, and even less at the local level. In formulating our project, we take our cue from the pioneers in this relatively new field of research into how commercial entertainment in various locales or regions has been packaged, promoted, and consumed, particularly Robert C. Allen and Douglas Gomery, who challenge researchers to undertake empirical studies of such topics as moviegoing in their own communities. Gomery examined the development of movie exhibition in the United States from the nickelodeon period to the multiplex era, while Waller documented the emergence and the reception of commercial entertainment in general, and motion pictures in particular, in Lexington, Kentucky, from 1896 to 1930.[33] We proceed from a cultural studies perspective, regarding cultural artifacts, such as movie theatres, as oblique representations of their temporal and spatial circumstances. Like Fredric Jameson, we believe that the analyst's responsibility is not simply to illuminate an artifact's aesthetic qualities but also to lay bare its roots in social, economic, and political conditions and to explain how these roots have been obscured.[34] We thus situate our work in this emerging tradition of interdisciplinary scholarship and build on existing research on the movie industry in Canada, including that of Manjunath Pendakur, Charles Acland, Paul S. Moore, and the late Peter Morris.[35] As well, our project is deeply embedded in the interdisciplinary tradition of western Canadian studies scholarship that has emerged over the past decades. We have drawn on a number of works across a range of disciplines that explore the social, economic, and cultural forces that shaped life in Canada's prairie provinces, and we hope that our work will contribute to the collective effort to illuminate the history of this region.

We have sifted through a wide variety of primary and secondary materials. City and business directories, which list alphabetically and provide a street-by-street inventory of residences and commercial establishments, plus the names and street addresses of the owners and the managers of movie houses (and, for some periods, those of distributors and producers), proved useful for reconstructing the layout of a business area. In addition, we examined public records (such as building permits, fire insurance maps, property tax assessments, building evaluations, and demolition fire reports), corporate records (including annual statements, reports to stockholders, official opening-day programs, investment circulars, and press releases) and architectural plans and building reports. We also consulted newspapers and motion picture trade papers, which report on the week-by-week operation of movie theatres and movie theatre chains, in terms of box-office receipts, advertisements for up-and-coming movies, marketing strategies, and major renovations to, or the closing of, existing facilities. These sources were supplemented by local and regional histories, memoirs, interviews, and photographs.[36] In constructing this historical narrative, we employed qualitative as well as quantitative methods of research. These include:

(1) *critical political economy,* that is, examining film exhibition in the prairie West within the context of the high-risk, vertically integrated movie industry as a whole, which in practice has meant situating movie theatres (and their owners and patrons) in their social, economic, and political circumstances so as to identify the commercial imperatives at work in the industry[37]

(2) *stylistic typology,* that is, examining the variations in the architectural design and decoration (exterior and interior) of the exhibition space, as leading theatre architects adapted to specific aesthetic and functional imperatives, with a view to appreciating how the movie theatre developed into a unique type of building designed and equipped to meet the varying requirements of a new kind of entertainment[38]

(3) *discursive analysis,* that is, analyzing the various discourses — conveyed by media texts such as news reports, interviews, and letters to the editor — that structured the way people in the prairie West, in particular, and in Canada generally understood leisure-time activities, with particular reference to Michel Foucault's insights into the operation of knowledge and power, for the purpose of evoking the lived experience of both the impresarios who owned the theatres and the patrons who visited them.[39]

We present our findings in a chronological narrative that focuses on the development of film exhibition in the prairie West as a commercial enterprise, throwing light on where people went to the movies and (wherever possible) what they made of this new form of entertainment. We start with an overview of the innovations that made the screening of motion pictures possible. In chapter 2, we examine the efforts of entrepreneurs to establish movie exhibition on the prairies as a legitimate business venture during the period from 1896 to 1904. In chapter 3, we focus on the efforts of selected entrepreneurs to establish permanent exhibition sites during the store theatre era, from 1905 to 1913. We highlight the efforts of the Allen family, who developed business and programming strategies to enhance the moviegoing experience, in terms of the comfort and the safety of their facilities and the quality of the motion pictures they screened, thus persuading patrons from the emerging middle class to develop the moviegoing habit. The movie exhibition business quickly evolved into a multi-million dollar industry, creating a number of serious problems along the way, and from the 1890s to the 1920s, the heyday of the Progressive Era, social reformers urged governments to monitor the new enterprise. We consider (in chapter 4) the impact of the social reformers who urged governments at all levels to establish building codes and fire-safety laws, to ban Sunday screenings, and to censor movie content, limiting the (presumed) negative impact of motion pictures on attitudes and actions, particularly for young viewers. In chapter 5, we turn to the period from 1914 to 1932, which we designate the picture palace era, during which exhibitors and the architects they hired developed buildings expressly designed for showing feature films. We concentrate on the Allen family, who established the first made-in-Canada chain of movie theatres, and Nat Nathanson, who established the Famous Players chain, which, in 1923, acquired thirty-five of the largest Allen theatres when the circuit went bankrupt. In chapter 6, we continue the story of Nathanson's campaign to establish a made-in-Canada chain of movie theatres. Unhappy with essentially playing the role of manager of a branch plant, Nathanson left Famous Players and in 1941 established Odeon Theatres, thereby creating the "duopoly" that dominated movie exhibition in Canada for many years. In chapters 7 and 8, we offer more evidence of the centralizing and homogenizing processes at work during the 1950s and 1960s, noting that, increasingly, film exhibition in prairie Canada and film exhibition in the rest of North America became indistinguishable. We end by reflecting on moviegoing in the age of the multiplex. This means charting the rise and the fall of Cineplex Odeon, a story that offers more evidence of the increasing control that American interests have exerted on movie exhibition in Canada in general and prairie Canada in particular, and, in the postscript, musing on the digital revolution and its impact on moviegoing in the twenty-first century.

1

PIONEERS

A system of inventions — all patented by Thomas A. Edison — made the screening of motion pictures possible: the Kinetograph, the Kinetoscope, and the Vitascope.[1] Encountering the work of Eadweard Muybridge, the English-born, San Francisco–based photographer who focused on capturing animal and human locomotion, may have intensified Edison's resolve to develop his own motion picture system. On 25 February 1888, Muybridge gave a lecture in West Orange, New Jersey, very likely demonstrating his Zoopraxiscope, an apparatus that projected stop-motion images in a sequence (affixed to a glass disc) in rapid succession onto a screen, thus producing the illusion of motion. Edison's laboratory was located in West Orange, and Edison and one of his most talented employees, W. K. L. Dickson, a French-born Anglo-Scots photographer and inventor, may well have attended the lecture. Two days later, Muybridge and Edison met at the laboratory, where Muybridge proposed that they collaborate, combining the Zoopraxiscope and the Phonograph, thereby creating a mechanism that would produce sounds and images concurrently.[2] This collaboration never materialized. In an attempt to protect his future inventions, Edison filed a preliminary claim (known as a caveat) with the United States Patent Office in October 1888 outlining his plan to create a device that would do "for the eye what the Phonograph does for the ear" — that is, record and reproduce objects in motion. What Edison had in mind was an audiovisual system that would enable one to see and to hear (say) "a whole opera as perfectly as if [he or she were] actually present."[3] He filed another caveat in March 1889, proposing to develop a motion picture viewing device called the Kinetoscope, taking the name from the Greek words *kineto*, meaning "movement," and *scopos*, meaning "to view."[4]

Edison ran his laboratory on a collaborative basis, initiating experiments and involving himself in projects when he thought it necessary; ultimately, employees did much of the work, and in the end he claimed the credit for the products they created. In June 1889, he asked Dickson to take on the task of turning his concept into reality. The researchers progressed haltingly. Taking their cue from Edison's conception of the Phonograph cylinder, they tried to record tiny photographic images onto a specially treated cylinder, with the idea that, when rotated, the images would generate the illusion of motion.[5] The plan was to record images onto one cylinder and sounds onto another, and to replay the cylinders synchronously.

Meanwhile, Edison went to Europe to assess the progress that was being made in the field of chronophotography.[6] A number of innovations on exhibition at the 1889 World's Fair, held in Paris from 6 May to 31 October, piqued his interest. These included the Chronophotographic Gun, a portable camera developed by Étienne-Jules Marey, a French physiologist, which used a strip of flexible film and employed the principle of intermittent movement, capable of capturing images in sequence at a rate of twelve frames per second.[7] Edison was also intrigued by the Tachyscope, a device developed by Prussian photographer Ottomar Anchütz, capable of projecting moving images by means of an intermittent electrical flash, and by the Praxinoscope, a mechanism developed by Charles-Émile Reynaud, a French inventor, that employed a strip of flexible, perforated film and was capable of projecting animated drawings onto a screen.[8]

Edison corresponded with the laboratory, and Dickson and his colleagues revised their approach on the basis of the reports he provided. They experimented with sheets of emulsion-coated celluloid.[9] Wrapping a sheet of this material around a cylinder provided a superior base for recording photographs. Taking his cue from Muybridge, Dickson also experimented with recording photographs onto a disc. In due course, they abandoned the attempt to synchronize recordings of sounds and images. During August, the researchers experimented with strips of celluloid (Dickson had cut sheets into strips) in a prototype viewing machine.[10]

Edison returned to West Orange, believing that the development of a motion picture camera, as well as a mechanism for viewing the products of that machine, depended upon the production of flexible film of sufficient length and durability and the creation of a stop-and-go mechanism.[11] On 2 November 1889, he filed a caveat describing a device (the Kinetoscope) that utilized a strip of flexible (perforated) film and a sprocket-based mechanism that advanced the film smoothly and reliably.[12]

By early 1891, Dickson and his colleagues had developed a functional film-strip-based viewing system. The mechanism, housed in a wooden cabinet, included a loop of horizontally configured 19 mm film perforated on one side and running around a series of spindles; an electrically powered sprocket wheel moved the film beneath a magnifying glass, and an electric lamp illuminated the films from below. To the viewer, the series of still frames appeared to move. As well, Edison's researchers developed a motor-powered motion picture camera, the Kinetograph, capable of shooting with the new perforated film.[13]

On 24 August 1891, Edison filed three patent applications, two for a motor-powered camera, the Kinetograph, capable of shooting the new 35 mm perforated film, and one for an apparatus for exhibiting moving pictures, the Kinetoscope, allowing for the possible use of a cylinder.[14] During the spring of 1892, the researchers made coin operation, via a slot at the top, an essential part of the mechanics of the viewing system.

By the autumn of 1892, the peephole viewing machine, measuring 18 inches by 27 inches by 48 inches, was complete.[15] One inserted a coin into the slot, put one's eye to the eye piece, and watched (through a magnifying glass) a strip of perforated (on both sides) 35 mm film about fifty feet in length that moved along a bank of spools. An electrically driven sprocket at the top of the box moved the film between an electric light and a revolving shutter with a narrow slit. As each frame passed under the lens, the shutter permitted a flash of light so brief that the frame appeared to be frozen. The viewer looking into a peephole at the top of the cabinet would see the image move. On 21 February 1893, Edison secured a patent for the system that governed the intermittent movement of the film.[16]

During the winter of 1892–93, Edison built a studio (designed by Dickson) behind his laboratory in West Orange, knowing that a steady supply of new films would be needed to make his invention popular. The Black Maria, as it was called, resembled a police patrol wagon.[17] Mounted on a pivot and black inside and out, it could be positioned (the roof could be opened) in order to take advantage of the sun. The camera was mounted on steel tracks inside the studio. Dickson began making short non-fiction films in January 1893 (historians call the films produced by European and American filmmakers during the first ten years of the moving picture industry "actualities" because they focused on noteworthy persons, places, and events that would interest a general audience), taking as his subjects vaudeville performers who demonstrated their special talents. These films fell into two groups: the world of masculine sports, including cock fighting, boxing, and jousting, and visual excerpts of American performance culture, including serpentine and skirt dancers, Annie Oakley and bronco busters from Buffalo Bill's Wild West, scenes of Broadway shows, and trained animals. Over the course of 1894, Dickson (the director) and William Heise (the camera operator) made more than seventy-five films at the Black Maria studio, each running about twenty seconds.[18]

For a variety of reasons, the plan to introduce the Kinetoscope at the Chicago Exposition of 1893 was abandoned. The first "official" demonstration of the machine was held on 9 May 1893 at the annual meeting of the Department of Physics at the Brooklyn Institute of Arts and Sciences.[19] Some reports suggest (erroneously) that "one machine made its way to the fair, and before the season closed was installed on the second floor of the Electricity Building for all and sundry to see."[20]

Normally, Edison hired independently financed entrepreneurs to market his inventions. In this case, he contracted with the Kinetoscope Company, a consortium that included Norman C. Raff and Frank R. Gammon, who served as the managers, together with Andrew M. Holland and Alfred O. Tate, Edison's former business manager, to market the Kinetoscope as well as movies for the peephole viewing system. Raff and Gammon planned to sell the territorial rights to exhibiting the Kinetoscope, again following the pattern Edison had designed for merchandising the Phonograph.

Figure 1. A Phonograph and Kinetoscope parlour, San Francisco, ca. 1895. Thomas Edison National Historical Park, West Orange, New Jersey (National Park Service, U.S. Department of the Interior). Edison and Motion Pictures, photo no. 6.

Meanwhile, Andrew M. Holland and his brother, George C. Holland, Ottawa-based entrepreneurs, opened the first Kinetoscope parlour at 1155 Broadway, New York City, on 14 April 1894.[21] The sons of William L. Holland, an Irish-born merchant who had immigrated to Canada with his family in 1827, eventually settling in the Ottawa Valley, the Holland brothers succeeded at a variety of enterprises. They trained as reporters, learning Pitman shorthand: Andrew wrote for newspapers in Ottawa and George wrote for newspapers in Ottawa and Toronto and then in several American cities, including Chicago. From 1872 to 1875, they also served as joint owners and managers of the *Ottawa Citizen*. In 1875, George secured a contract to report and to publish the debates in the House of Commons, introducing the innovation of making typewritten transcripts from shorthand notes, and two years later he and Andrew secured a contract to report and to publish the debates in the Senate, again making typewritten transcripts from shorthand notes. From their offices on Elgin Street, the brothers championed a range of new technologies which would, they believed, propel Ottawa, and Canada, into the twentieth century, marketing, for example, the (Charles)

Sorley storage battery, introduced in 1884, and the Smith Premier (later the Smith-Corona) typewriter, introduced in 1889. Their entrepreneurial vision was truly international: for example, in 1892, Andrew helped establish the Canadian-Australian Steamship Company, which offered service from Vancouver to Sydney. Importantly, the Holland brothers recognized the commercial potential of Edison's inventions, and from 1891 served as agents for the Phonograph, the Kinetoscope, and the Vitascope, selling territorial rights and equipment to potential exhibitors and opening parlours themselves.

The Holland brothers acquired ten machines from the Kinetoscope Company at a cost of $250 apiece and the films at $10 apiece; they set the machines up in rows of five in the centre of the space and erected an office at the back and a box office at the front, near the entrance.[22] Staff running the enterprise included a manager, a technician, who installed and later repaired the films, and a female ticket taker. The machines exhibited different movies, spliced end to end to form a continuous band and each running from twenty to thirty seconds. For twenty-five cents (the price of admission to a vaudeville house), a customer could view the movies in one row; for fifty cents, a customer could view the movies in both rows. The Holland brothers opened the doors at one o'clock that Saturday afternoon and ran until one in the morning, taking in $120.

The Kinetoscope parlour was a huge success. The Holland brothers opened a parlour with ten machines in Chicago in May and one with five machines in San Francisco in June. Later, they opened one in Atlantic City and one in Ottawa on 3 November 1894. They opened another Kinetoscope parlour in Ottawa on 2 November 1895.[23] Soon, entrepreneurs around the country were operating Kinetoscope parlours and arcades.

Over fifty weeks of operation, the Holland brothers' New York City Kinetoscope parlour generated, on average, a weekly revenue of $1,400.[24] The demand for the machine then dropped. Clearly, the peephole machine had a serious limitation: only one person at a time could view the film.[25] Accordingly, in April 1895, Edison introduced the Kinetophone, which proposed to make talking motion pictures a reality: the customer looked through a peephole viewer of the Kinetoscope and listened to a soundtrack conveyed through ear tubes that were attached to a Phonograph in the cabinet. The device did not provide exact synchronization, and ultimately faded into oblivion.

EXHIBITING MOTION PICTURES FOR A LARGE AUDIENCE

Entrepreneurs as well as machinists vied for the honour of being the first to take motion pictures out of the peephole machine and put them on the screen. Shortly after visiting the Kinetoscope parlour in the summer of 1894, Otway Latham and his brother, Grey Latham, formed the Kinetoscope Exhibition Company (which included Samuel L. Tilden, Jr., and Enoch Rector) with a view to exhibiting fight pictures (in large-capacity machines built by Edison) at their own parlour, at 83 Nassau Street, New York City.[26] They soon realized that exhibitors could generate more revenue by projecting images onto a wall. With his sons, Otway and Grey, Woodville Latham formed the Lambda Company for the express purpose of developing their own motion picture system. Eugène Lauste, who had worked on the Edison Phonograph, served as their machinist, and W. K. L. Dickson, key to the development of the Kinetoscope, served as their consultant. By March 1895, the Lathams had developed a movie camera and a movie projector, the Eidoloscope. Utilizing a band of 51 mm film that moved continuously and employing the "Latham Loop," which prevented the tearing of the film, the camera could photograph four rounds of a contest or eight minutes of action. The Lathams demonstrated their system prematurely on 21 April 1895 with mixed success (the pictures flickered). The Eidoloscope never achieved the success anticipated, thanks to underfinancing and to competition from technically superior machines. Business collapsed in 1898, and the Latham patents passed into the hands of others.

Meanwhile, two Washington-based inventors, C. Francis Jenkins and Thomas J. Armat, joined forces with a view to developing a machine that would project motion pictures onto a screen.[27] Jenkins focused on creating a camera and Armat focused on creating a projector. The latter introduced a mechanism similar to the "Latham Loop" so that the stop-and-go motion would not tear the unwinding film. Armat funded the project. In due course, they created an efficient, portable machine, the Phantoscope, that projected moving pictures onto a screen, and demonstrated it for a paying audience at the Cotton States Exposition, Atlanta, in September 1895. Attendance was poor. They subsequently had a falling-out, each claiming sole credit for the invention. During the winter of 1895–96, Raff and Gammon acquired the rights to the machine from Armat, hoping to revive their failing motion picture business. They secured Edison's blessings, renamed the Phantoscope the "Edison Vitascope," and, faced with foreign and domestic competition, formed the Vitascope Company to market the machine. They sold exclusive marketing rights for specific territories across North America, just as they had done for the Kinetoscope.

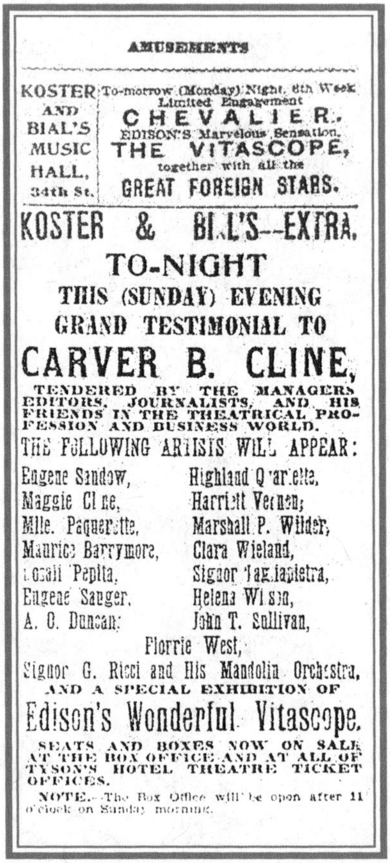

Figure 2. Advertisement for an exhibition of Thomas Edison's Vitascope at Koster & Bial's Music Hall. New York Times, 23 *April* 1896, 11.

Raff and Gammon mounted the first exhibition of moving pictures as a commercial enterprise at Koster & Bial's Music Hall, located at 315 West 34th Street, New York City, on 23 April 1896.[28] Selling this new kind of entertainment meant screening a selection of Edison films as part of that week's vaudeville program, which included a Russian clown, an "eccentric" dancer, two "gymnastic" comedians, and a singer of "coster" songs. Armat supervised the installation of two projectors at the centre of the balcony; at the appointed time, the manager turned the lights off, and the projectionist, Edwin S. Porter, turned the first machine on, projecting the first of five films onto a 12-by-20-foot screen and set in a gilded frame hanging from the proscenium arch. Armat spliced the films end-to-end to form a continuous band, so that Porter could screen each film six times before showing the next film on the other machine. According to a correspondent for the *New York Times*, an appreciative crowd of well-to-do customers (wearing frock coats and top hats) watched the films with great excitement, marvelling at the movement of the lifelike figures.[29] The writer noted that "a view of an angry surf breaking [on the pier at Dover] amazed spectators. The waves tumbled in furiously and the foam of the breakers flew high into the air." Film historian Terry Ramsaye argues that, by organizing a program of films into a theme, the Koster & Bial demonstration set the pattern for motion picture exhibition for the next ten years.[30]

EARLY PRODUCTION COMPANIES

As we have seen, Raff and Gammon encouraged Edison to launch the Phantoscope as the "Edison Vitascope," the Edison Manufacturing Company producing the projectors and the films needed.[31] They formed the Vitascope Company to market the machine across North America. By October 1896, the company had encountered difficulties; the Edison Manufacturing Company had become dissatisfied with Raff and Gammon, and other entrepreneurs had started to introduce their own machines. Here, we consider the major entrepreneurs in this contest, focusing on the technological innovations they introduced and the business strategies they employed in trying to take control of the new industry.

Figure 3. Interior of Koster & Bial's Music Hall, New York City. From The New Metropolis, *edited by E. Idell Zeisloft (New York: D. Appleton & Co., 1899), 351.*

The Cinématographe System

Antoine Lumière, the founder of a Lyon-based photographic business, visited a Kinetoscope parlour in Paris in September 1894, and encouraged his sons, Auguste and Louis, to develop an apparatus that would take and project motion pictures.[32] Within a few months, Auguste and Louis had developed the Lumière Cinématographe, a machine that used a sprocketed film-transport mechanism to advance 35 mm film. On 28 December 1895, the brothers launched their apparatus at the Grand Café in Paris, where, for the price of one franc, patrons could watch a program of films lasting about twenty minutes, featuring images of everyday life. The Lumière brothers decided not only to sell Cinématographe projectors but also to dispatch operators to various parts of the world to photograph events. They soon introduced their system internationally: at the Royal Polytechnic Institution in London on 21 February 1896, at the Palace Theatre, Montréal, on 27 June, and at B. F. Keith's Union Square Theatre, New York City, on 29 June. The exhibition in Montréal marked the first screening of films in Canada.[33] Keith not only booked the projector for his vaudeville circuit, but also acquired the US rights to the machine. Early in November, the Lumière company opened an agency in New York City, offering to sell territorial rights or to lease its machines. It serviced the American market well. Agents arranged exhibitions, scheduled tours, and provided a selection of films, a projector, and a projectionist; these self-contained units travelled the circuits more easily than an acrobat or a juggler.[34] Initially, audiences were impressed by the motion pictures they screened. A number of features gave the Cinématographe an edge over other machines: first, it was compact, weighing a little over sixteen pounds; second, it relied on hand-cranking rather than electricity for its power; and third, it operated as a camera, a printer, and a projector. Thus, the operator could take the machine into the streets by day to shoot local scenes and incorporate them into the evening's performance. However, in the spring of 1897, the Lumière company withdrew from the American market due to the growing importance of the American Mutoscope Company and possible legal action by the Edison company.[35] By 1905, the Lumières had abandoned the movie business, focusing instead on photographic colour processes.

The Biograph System

W. K. L. Dickson resigned from the Edison Manufacturing Company in April 1895, and with inventors Herman Casler, Harry Marvin, and Elias Koopman formed (in December) the American Mutoscope Company (later the American Mutoscope and Biograph Company), with a view to manufacturing and distributing the Mutoscope, a peephole viewing machine that featured a variety of flip-card movies, thereby challenging the pre-eminence of Edison's Kinetoscope. In light of the growing interest in projection technology, the group shifted their focus, and developed their own projector, one that used large-format (68 mm) film, thus avoiding Edison's patents, employed friction feed, as opposed to the Vitascope's sprocket feed, and exposed film at thirty frames per second, double the speed of the Vitascope.[36] They premiered their system, which produced a vivid image, at Hammerstein's Opera House, New York City, on 12 October 1896. As Charles Musser puts it, the company developed a film that other exhibitors could not use and screened its own productions (along with those of sister companies overseas) as main attractions at first-class vaudeville houses.[37]

Figure 4. New releases from the American Mutoscope and Biograph Company, New York City. Moving Picture World, *9 January 1909, 27.*

Initially, the company produced actualities, including, in 1898, films of approximately two minutes about events in the Spanish-American War. Dickson produced five train films that tapped into North Americans' love of steam engines, including *Empire State Express* (1896). In this case, he placed the camera next to the tracks and directed it at the train, which came toward and then passed the camera. The film was a great hit.[38] Very quickly, Biograph challenged the Edison studio for pre-eminence in the motion picture business. After 1903, the company produced narrative films. In 1908, Biograph joined Edison in forming the Motion Picture Patents Company (MPPC), a consortium (popularly known as the "Edison Trust") the goal of which was to control the motion picture industry and to shut out smaller filmmakers.

Biograph's star reached its zenith in the years between 1908 and 1913, when D. W. Griffith, a former stage actor and writer, directed hundreds of one- and two-reel comedies, fairy tales, gangster films, romances, and westerns for the company. He established his own stock company at Biograph, comprising, at various times, such actors as Harry Carey, Lionel Barrymore, Lillian and Dorothy Gish, Florence Lawrence, Mae Marsh, Mabel Normand, Mary Pickford, and Mack Sennett. Inspired by the work of Edwin S. Porter, and with the assistance of such cinematographers as Arthur Marvin and G. W. (Billy) Bitzer, Griffith developed filmic techniques — lighting, camera placement (such as the establishing shot, the tracking shot, the close-up, the medium-shot, the fade, and the iris shot), editing (such as cross-cutting and the flashback), and acting — with a view to creating the conventions of narrative filmmaking.[39] Unhappy with the company's opposition to making big-budget, feature films and giving him and his actors on-screen credit, in 1913 Griffith joined the Mutual Film Corporation, for which he made a number of films, including the twelve-reel blockbuster *The Birth of a Nation* (1915). Biograph ceased operation in 1928.

The Pathé Frères System

Charles Pathé entered the amusement business in 1894, exploiting Edison's phonograph at fairs around Paris.[40] The profits he earned enabled him to establish a shop in Vincennes, where he sold imitation Kinetoscopes and photographic equipment. In September 1896, Charles, with his brothers, Émile, Théophile, and Jacques, formed Société Pathé Frères, which would soon become the world's largest manufacturer of film equipment, including the Pathé Cinématographe projector, which handled the Edison-sprocketed film, and phonograph records. Pathé may well have started exporting films to United States later that year. Émile handled the phonograph side (which contributed about 90 percent of the revenue), and Charles handled the technical and the marketing side, dealing with problems involving cameras, projectors, and film stock. Determined to create a worldwide empire, Charles took the company public in 1897; he acquired the Lumière brothers' patents and handled the work of Georges Méliès, among others, in 1902. The company established offices in Moscow, New York City, and Brussels in 1904; in Berlin, Vienna, and St. Petersburg in 1905; and in London in 1906. Reports suggest that the Pathé catalogue for 1904 featured over a thousand titles.

The company had introduced important elements of the studio system by 1906, including a stock company of actors and multiple production units. By October of that year, the company was exporting as many as twelve films per week on a variety of subjects, and seventy-five copies of each to the United States, including chase comedies like *The Policeman's Little Run* (1907), crime stories like *The Female Spy* (1907), and historical dramas like *The Venetian Tragedy* (1906). The company was responsible for over one-third of the films screened in the United States in 1907.[41]

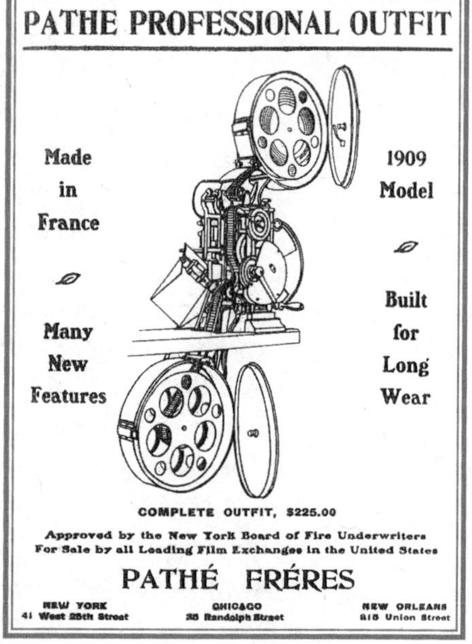

Figure 5. Advertisement for the Pathé motion picture projector. Moving Picture World, 15 *May* 1909, 619.

In 1908, Pathé Frères launched the newsreel as a vehicle for satisfying the public's insatiable curiosity about the details of daily life in far-flung parts of the world. Soon, exhibitors everywhere screened Pathé newsreels before they screened the feature film. Pathé produced a number of films at their New Jersey studios, starting with the suspense serial (twenty episodes) called *The Perils of Pauline* (1914), which was directed by Donald Mackenzie. This serial tells the story of Pauline (played by Pearl White), who evades various attempts on her life by assorted villains, including pirates, gypsies, and her dastardly guardian (played by Crane Wilbur). The company began renting films in 1909, thus becoming one of the first vertically integrated film corporations. World War I stopped Pathé Frères in its tracks, allowing American movie moguls to copy the company's operations carefully.[42] Pathé split into two divisions after the war, one devoted to phonograph records and the other devoted to producing film stock.

The Selig Polyscope System

William N. Selig, a Chicago-based vaudeville performer, entered the movie business after visiting a Kinetoscope parlour in Dallas, Texas in 1894.[43] Selig returned to Chicago and opened a photography studio, with a view to making his own motion pictures. By chance, he met a machinist who had duplicated a Cinématographe for a Lumière employee, and the two created the Selig Standard Camera and the Selig Polyscope Projector, basically a Cinématographe projector with sprockets that handled Edison film. In 1896, he formed the Mutoscope and Film Company (later the Selig Polyscope Company), producing actualities, slapstick comedies, and travelogues, exhibiting them in vaudeville houses in and around Chicago. In addition, he made industrial films for Chicago businesses, including films about Armour and Company, the largest food processing enterprise in the world at the time, including *Entrance to Union Stockyard* (1901). One of his first films — and first successes — was *The Tramp and the Dog* (1896), a comedy about a tramp who, looking for a handout, is pursued by a vigilant bulldog. In 1898, he made films about the Spanish-American war, photographing mock battle scenes at Camp Turner in Springfield, Illinois. As well, he manufactured equipment, supplying several Midwestern vaudeville chains with projectors and selling projectors via the Sears and Roebuck mail-order catalogue.

Avoiding litigation was a constant concern. Selig's operation caught Edison's attention, and in February 1906 the latter sued the filmmaker and exhibitor for copyright infringement. As Musser puts it, changes in film practices and the legal expenses incurred in fighting Edison's patent suit pushed the Selig Polyscope Company close to bankruptcy; Philip D. Armour, founder of Armour and Company, prevented this disaster by providing Selig legal support.[44] Selig joined, with some reluctance, the MPPC in 1909. He completed *The Count of Monte Cristo* (1908) in southern California and set up a studio at 1845 Allesandro Street, now Glendale Boulevard, Los Angeles.

Here, Selig made a variety of films, including jungle films, nature films, historical dramas, and westerns. A number of stars, including Roscoe Arbuckle and Tom Mix, worked at his studio. In 1913, Selig purchased thirty-two acres of land near Los Angeles to accommodate the seven hundred animals that appeared in his films. Selig made one of the first cliffhanger serials, *The Adventures of Kathlyn* (1913–14), starring Kathlyn Williams, and one of the first feature films, *The Spoilers* (1914), starring William Farnum and Kathlyn Williams. The nine-reel production (set in the 1898 gold rush in the Yukon) opened on 11 April 1914 at the Strand Theatre in New York City, the first purpose-built cinema for new releases. World War I adversely affected business, and Selig retired in 1918, closing his film production company.

The Vitagraph System

The Edison Manufacturing Company filmed J. Stuart Blackton and Albert E. Smith, Anglo-American entertainers, at various venues in the summer of 1896. These sleight-of-hand performers offered audiences a routine that included "lightning sketches," caricatures produced rapidly on an easel, which appeared to come to life, with a steady stream of talk, delivered rapidly, and magic tricks.[45] The films were later screened at F. F. Proctor's Pleasure Palace and Proctor's 23rd Street Theatre, leading New York City vaudeville houses, to great acclaim. Encouraged by this publicity, Blackton and Smith acquired an Edison projector and a number of Edison films, determined to incorporate motion pictures into their act. In March 1897, they formed the Edison Vitagraph Company for this purpose.

During the theatrical off-season, Blackton and Smith dabbled in advertising, making slides and films that promoted the services and products of a number of New York City stores. Soon, they had an advantage over many of their competitors: Smith turned a projector into a camera, enabling them to make their own films, and modified a Projecting Kinetoscope by adding a framing device, enabling them to project a steady image.[46] This enterprise, called the American Vitagraph Company, made actualities, for example, photographing events in the Spanish-American war. As well, Blackton hit upon the idea of photographing events especially arranged for the camera, such as *Battle of Manila Bay* (1898), which he produced by re-enacting in miniature (using cutout photographs) Commodore George Dewey's crushing victory over the Spanish fleet in the waters west of Manila on 1 May 1898. These and other war-related productions earned the team a spot at Proctor's

23rd Street Theatre and his Pleasure Palace. Hungry for first-hand accounts of the Cuban Crisis, people started thinking of the cinema as a "visual newspaper."

The partners avoided prosecution by becoming Edison licensees and by making films on a royalty basis for the Edison Manufacturing Company. In September 1898, William T. Rock, an experienced exhibitor, became the third partner in the American Vitagraph Company, increasing their capitalization. Blackton prepared the programs and made the films, Smith served as the bookkeeper, and Rock booked their exhibitions into theatres. They produced quality motion pictures, experimenting with a number of genres, including trick films and comedies, such as *The Vanishing Lady* (1898), starring Smith as the magician, and *The Burglar on the Roof* (1898), starring Blackton as the burglar. In producing "trick films," they worked in the tradition established by Georges Méliès, which meant stopping the camera for a moment, changing some aspect of the scenery, and then running the camera again, thus making objects appear and disappear. (Blackton thus developed the basic concepts of animation.) They exhibited these films at Proctor's theatres and Edison later copyrighted them.

The Vitagraph company expanded enormously during the first decade of the twentieth century, striking out on its own and challenging Edison and Biograph for control of the motion picture industry. In 1904, the company built a studio in the Flatbush area of Brooklyn, increased its roster of players, directors, and technicians, and in 1905 became the Vitagraph Company of America. The company launched such up-and-coming actors as Florence Lawrence, Florence Turner (the "Vitagraph Girl"), Gladys Hulette, and Clara Kimball Young. Blackton produced other important documentaries, including films of the aftermath of the San Francisco earthquake, comedies, such as *Humorous Phases of a Funny Face* (1906), and narrative films based on classical themes, including *Romeo and Juliet* (1908), which he shot in Central Park, New York City, and *The Life of Moses* (1909), a five-reel film that ran for ninety minutes. About the time it became a member of the MPPC in 1908, Vitagraph was producing eight films per week and operating offices in London, Paris, and Berlin. In 1910, the company opened a studio in California, and initiated a monthly current events newsreel. World War I marked the beginning of the end for Vitagraph; the number of the company's foreign distributors dropped and the number of major production-distribution companies increased. Warner Bros. acquired Vitagraph in 1925, plus the research unit it had organized in order to enter the field of sound.

The Cineograph System

In June 1896, Sigmund Lubin, a Polish-American optician, visited William T. Rock's Vitascope parlour in New Orleans, where he studied the projector and watched the movies.[47] He opened an optical shop in Philadelphia, with a view to developing his own motion picture projector. He contacted C. Francis Jenkins, and together they developed the Cineograph, a combination camera and projector, and formed a company to manufacture the projector and to distribute it and various movie supplies.

Early in 1897, Lubin launched a marketing campaign, placing advertisements in newspapers and circulating brochures, alerting managers of vaudeville houses and travelling exhibitors that he was now selling movie supplies, including projectors, song slides, screens, tents, tickets, and so on, at bargain prices. For a while, he served as an agent for Edison films.

Lubin then built production facilities and formed the Cineograph Service, planning to exhibit films at vaudeville houses. Initially, Lubin made actualities, recording newsworthy events or photographing reenactments, such as battles that took place during the Spanish-American War and events that occurred during the Boxer Rebellion in China.[48] He also made facsimile reproductions of dozens of fights, starting with the Corbett-Fitzsimmons heavyweight championship boxing match.[49] In this case, he hired two freight handlers from the Pennsylvania Railroad (he dressed them to look like champions) and many ordinary people from the neighbourhood to act out the drama, a round-by-round description of the original fight serving as the scenario. In order to produce the sharpest image possible, he condensed the action and decreased the camera speed. Lubin released *Reproduction of the Corbett-Fitzsimmons Fight* (1897) one week before the Veriscope Company premiered their official version of the fight; it generated a mixed response, but (Musser writes) was immensely profitable, serving as the poor man's way of seeing a widely publicized event.

Eager to create a vertically integrated operation, Lubin expanded the exhibition side of his business, building, in 1899, the first of the many theatres he operated along the East Coast. He added a distribution side in 1903, when he opened the first of a number of exchanges he eventually ran in Philadelphia, Cincinnati, and Norfolk. He also began duplicating movies made by other filmmakers, starting with two Edison pictures, *Uncle Tom's Cabin* (1903) and *The Great Train Robbery* (1903): his versions were titled *Uncle Tom's Cabin* and *The Bold Bank Robbery* and were made in 1903 and 1904, respectively. By September 1907, the Lubin Manufacturing Company was producing three titles per week, offering the public pictures that were sensational in both subject matter and treatment.[50] For example, he made *The Unwritten Law: A Thrilling Drama Based on the Thaw-White Tragedy* (1907), while the murder trial was still in progress. Mixing sex and violence and revealing decadence among the wealthy, Lubin's film also suggested that the killing was condoned by an unwritten law, namely, the right of a wronged husband to defend his wife's honour — an idea that fascinated some and scandalized others.

Lubin reorganized his business in 1909, calling it Lubin Manufacturing Company, Inc., and over the next half-decade operated four studios, located in Betzwood, Pennsylvania, Jacksonville, Florida, and Los Angeles and Coronado, California, introducing a number of up-and-coming actors, including Arthur Johnson, Marie Dressler, and Oliver Hardy. In 1908, Lubin joined the MMPC, hoping that this would put an end to his legal problems, but circumstances conspired against him. In 1914, a fire at the Philadelphia studio, coupled with the outbreak of World War I, which dramatically reduced the European market for his films, pushed Lubin into bankruptcy.

VAUDEVILLE

The movie producers discussed above introduced their projectors in vaudeville theatres during the 1896–97 season; these theatres (and to some extent legitimate theatres) across North America served as the primary site for commercial movie exhibition for the next decade.[51] As Robert C. Allen puts it, vaudeville managers valued movies because they helped satisfy audiences' appetite for visual novelty, and movie producers valued this venue because vaudeville theatres enabled them to reach an enormous middle-class audience, possibly more than one million spectators per week. Moreover, vaudeville provided the nascent industry a measure of stability during a period of uncertainty, generated in large part by the many patent infringement suits Thomas A. Edison launched against his rivals.[52] Movie producers benefited greatly from this arrangement: they did not have to risk spending huge sums of money on building exhibition facilities. Equally important, the expansion of major vaudeville circuits to the major cities throughout the United States and Canada served as the model for the development of the movie exhibition business.

A handful of savvy theatre entrepreneurs with an eye on the direction popular entertainment was taking during the last decades of the nineteenth century transformed the bawdy acts seen in the penny arcade, the dime museum, and the saloon into vaudeville, the family-oriented entertainment that predominated until the advent of radio and talking pictures. In doing so, they signalled the start of entertainment as big business, dependent upon the skills of white-collar workers and the tastes of an emerging middle class. Here, we consider the entrepreneurs who had the greatest impact on movie exhibition in the prairie West.

The Keith Circuit

B. F. Keith began his career in Boston, where he operated the Hub Museum, founded in 1883, which offered the public "freak" attractions. In 1886, with partner E. F. Albee, he opened the Bijou Theatre, a 900-seat venue located next door to the Hub that featured dramatic productions. These facilities served as the nucleus of the powerful Keith Circuit, which extended along the northeastern United States. To compete with such successful vaudeville managers as Tony Pastor and F. F. Proctor, they implemented two policies: to present top-notch entertainment in an environment that was attractive as well as safe and to offer patrons "continuous performances" from 10:30 a.m. to 10:30 p.m. every day of the week, encouraging them to enter the theatre at any time and to stay as long as they liked.[53] Encouraged by the success of these operations, in 1887 they opened a dime museum in Providence, Rhode Island, followed, in 1893, by the Union Square Theatre in New York City, a 1,300-seat facility presenting "high-class" vaudeville for admission prices between fifteen and fifty cents, and then, in 1894, by the New Theatre in Boston, a luxurious facility that could accommodate 3,000 patrons. In 1896, Keith sailed to Great Britain, where he visited music halls looking for talent, and in Paris secured the rights to show the Cinématographe. Keith and Albee renovated their Providence Theatre in 1898, giving it a capacity of 1,500, and in 1900 built the Philadelphia Theatre, a 2,300-seat facility located in the city's shopping district that attracted upper-class patrons. During its heyday, the Keith Circuit controlled theatres in a number of cities in Canada, including Montréal, Ottawa, Toronto, and Hamilton. Keith and Albee exhibited Biograph films from 1896 and Edison films from 1905. In 1906, the Keith and the Proctor chains merged, and in 1909 Keith turned his business activities over to his son.

The Orpheum Circuit

On the East Coast, vaudeville grew out of liquor-free entertainment found in circuses and dime museums, whereas on the West Coast vaudeville grew out of the variety performances found in smoke-filled German beer halls and gardens. Gustav Walter, a German emigré, opened three of these facilities, in 1879, 1882, and 1884. The second of these was the Vienna Gardens, located at Sutton and Stockton streets in San Francisco. Hoping to attract women and their children, Walter advertised the Vienna Gardens as a "Picturesque Family Resort" and scheduled matinees on Wednesday, Saturday, and Sunday. He set ticket prices at twenty-five cents for adults and ten cents for children. The house orchestra played concerts, a stock company put on short sketches, and variety artists performed their acts. These three facilities served as the cornerstone of the Orpheum Circuit, which at its peak extended throughout the West Coast and into the Midwest.[54] Morris Meyerfeld, a shrewd businessman, became a major partner in 1893; Martin Beck, a former member of a theatrical troupe in his native Austria, became the booking agent in 1895 (he had an uncanny ability to find new talent) and the general manager in 1899. When he took over (Walter had died in 1898), Beck devoted his time and effort to bringing high culture to the vaudeville stage — at prices ordinary people could afford.

In order to attract top-notch performers from Europe and the East

Coast, the company offered performers extended periods of work — and in order to do that the company had to expand its circuit. Accordingly, the firm opened Orpheum vaudeville theatres in such metropolitan centres as Los Angeles (in 1894), Kansas City (in 1898), and Denver (in 1899). During 1911 and 1912, Beck also acquired theatres in Winnipeg, Calgary, Edmonton, Vancouver, and Victoria, which meant that performers could tour theatres stretching from the Ohio Valley to the Pacific Coast and from central and western Canada to the Gulf of Mexico. In 1913, Beck built the luxurious, 1,717-seat Palace Theatre on Broadway, between 46th and 47th streets in New York City, thus precipitating a war with the Keith circuit. (The latter eventually secured 51 percent of the theatre's stock.) Beck, determined to bring high-class vaudeville to audiences, booked Sarah Bernhardt and her company for a period of twenty-four weeks, at a cost of $7,000 per week.[55] The Palace featured established and up-and-coming performers, including Charlie Chaplin, Buster Keaton, the Four Marx Brothers, Douglas Fairbanks, and Will Rogers.

The Sullivan and Considine Circuit

In 1904, John W. Considine, a Seattle-based entrepreneur, and his partner, Timothy D. Sullivan, a New York City-based lawyer, transformed a chain of cabarets that featured gambling and drinking, plus "dance hall girls," into the Sullivan and Considine Circuit, a chain of vaudeville houses. The cleansing process took place quickly. By 1906, the partners operated thirty-two theatres, in such centres as Denver, Salt Lake City, Butte, Tacoma, Spokane, Portland, Seattle, Sacramento, San Francisco, and Vancouver. Considine booked some of the biggest names of the stage, including Charlie Chaplin, Will Rogers, and Marie Dressler, paying them high salaries. By 1911, the Sullivan and Considine Circuit stretched from one coast to the other.[56] At its peak, the circuit controlled theatres in such centres in western Canada as Winnipeg, Regina, Saskatoon, Calgary, Edmonton, Vancouver, and Victoria. Timothy Sullivan suffered a mental breakdown in 1913, making it impossible for him to raise money or to exert his political clout to arrange for good theatre sites; Considine arranged to sell his theatre interests to the Orpheum Circuit in 1914, but the deal fell apart, thanks to the outbreak of war. Alexander Pantages picked up the pieces.

The Pantages Circuit

An enterprising Greek immigrant, Pantages settled in San Francisco in 1885 and discovered the financial possibilities in commercial entertainment. Piqued by the Yukon Gold Rush, he moved to Dawson City, where he managed variety shows. He moved to Seattle in 1902 and opened a number of small theatres, programming a mixture of variety acts and moving pictures and charging patrons ten cents admission. These sites formed the nucleus of the Pantages Circuit, which at its peak during the 1920s formed a crescent, extending from Winnipeg through western Canada to Seattle, down the Pacific Coast to San Diego, and then eastward to Chicago.[57] Interestingly, he leased and built a number of facilities in western Canada, controlling theatres in Winnipeg, Brandon, Regina, Saskatoon, Moose Jaw, Calgary, Edmonton, Vancouver, and Victoria. In 1914, he opened the luxurious Pantages Theatre, located at 180 Market Avenue East, in Winnipeg, which served as the starting point of all Pantages tours: if a show fared well in Winnipeg, he judged, it could move on to major urban centres across western Canada and the United States. Despite the fact that he had no formal education, Pantages took a personal interest in all aspects of his theatrical business, stressing that he provided patrons the best service at a reasonable price. At the peak of its power, the Pantages organization conducted its business in offices in New York City, Chicago, and Los Angeles and owned or controlled more than seventy vaudeville theatres, offering performers contracts for fourteen weeks of work. (In exceptional cases, contracts were extended to between thirty-two and fifty weeks.) In 1929, he sold his theatrical holdings to the Radio-Keith-Orpheum Corporation (RKO). Dozens of his theatres still stand, including the Pantages Playhouse Theatre in Winnipeg.

Transforming crude variety acts into vaudeville meant programming family-oriented, variety entertainment in a modular format, offering patrons from eight to ten unrelated acts, each lasting about twenty minutes, organized with an eye to balance and diversity and performed sequentially. Vaudeville managers featured a wide variety of talented performers during the 1890s, including singers, dancers, comics, acrobats, jugglers, animal trainers, readers of inspirational texts, and Broadway actors who offered condensed versions of popular plays.

The goal was to ensure that all patrons, working-class as well as middle-class, would find something of interest.[58] The second strategy was to present this entertainment in strategically located, luxurious facilities, in terms of architectural design and decoration, that rivalled the appeal of legitimate theatres, based on the understanding that the more affluent patron felt more at home in a carefully planned and ornately decorated theatre. The third strategy was maintaining a competitive pricing policy, ensuring that most patrons could afford to attend performances now and then.

Initially, vaudeville managers screened a selection of films, usually actualities, as one "act" on the program (actualities accounted for about half of the films presented). As we have seen, early film producers catered to the interests of vaudeville audiences, covering, for example, the Spanish-American War, because viewers were particularly fascinated by the visual documentation of important current events. Audiences discovered that films had the power to help them view the familiar afresh and to become familiar with places they had never seen before. Travelogues that created the illusion of being in the path of an object (a locomotive, say) travelling through space generated great excitement. When public interest in the Spanish-American War waned around 1900, filmmakers realized that they were handicapping themselves by relying on topical subjects. Many, including Sigmund Lubin, determined that by substituting the events of fictional narrative for the events of everyday situations they would gain much more control over motion picture subject matter and production than they had with the topical film.[59] They started producing comic and dramatic narratives, and these took up more and more of the vaudeville programs, accounting for about half of the films screened between 1904 and 1906.

Vaudeville entrepreneurs demonstrated that succeeding in the entertainment business meant pleasing the audience, and in this case pleasing the audience meant featuring top-notch performers from Europe and the East Coast. Succeeding also meant expanding their operations as widely as possible, so that they could offer performers work for many weeks. In short, they demonstrated the economic advantages of vertical and horizontal integration: establishing chains of theatres — not as family operations but as corporations — enabled them to exploit economies of scale; and centralizing such important functions as management, booking, and accounting enabled them to minimize expenses and to maximize profits.[60] As we will see in the following chapters, movie entrepreneurs in the prairie West put these lessons to good use.

MOVIES IN THE AMUSEMENT PARK

Vaudeville theatres offered movie entrepreneurs access to a huge audience, but eventually it became apparent that what they needed was a permanent site of their own. In the meantime, entrepreneurs tried a number of venues, including penny arcades and amusement parks. The latter, which were usually located at the end of trolley lines in major cities, offered them the possibility of attracting a large audience. However, this meant screening films during the summer months only. The disadvantage here was that films functioned as just another attraction in a mix of popular attractions.

Douglas Gomery writes that, on 26 June 1896, an entrepreneur opened a Vitascope Hall in West End Park, New Orleans, offering the first true movie show in the community and possibly the first in the South.[61] The operator of this open-air facility was William T. Rock, the entertainment impresario (mentioned above) who operated a penny arcade in New York City and who had recently obtained the Vitascope territorial rights for Louisiana. Judging by newspaper reports, Rock screened films every night, from 8:30 p.m. until 10:00 p.m., featuring them not as fillers for regular band concerts but as the evening's main entertainment. An admission fee of ten cents entitled customers to watch a selection of Edison films. West End Park reopened in May 1897 and again featured Vitascope movies, along with vaudeville attractions and open-air concerts.[62] Advertisements in the local newspapers suggest that the entertainment included classic circus acts, such as high-wire performers, tightrope walkers, gymnasts, and clowns. The movies were shown between performances of music and vaudeville acts. Up to twelve different films were shown each week, and often local newspapers advertised them as special attractions.

Word of Rock's success spread, and amusement park operators in other cities began screening movies. Gomery offers us an overview of their operations in these venues (they usually featured such amusements as rail rides, roller coasters, and ferris wheels), including Luna Park in Coney Island, New York City, White City Amusement Park in Syracuse, New York, Riverview Park in Baltimore, Maryland, the Athletic Park in Montgomery, Alabama, the Woodland Park in Lexington, Kentucky, and the Riverview Park in Chicago, Illinois. Typically, local street railway systems organized special services, thus promoting the park and the picture show.

An expanding entertainment industry that organized in the United States during the 1890s moved northward, shaping business opportunities in the prairie West. We have outlined some of the social, economic, and technological forces that converged during the development of motion pictures and the industry that soon grew up around producing, distributing, and exhibiting them. In the chapters that follow, we chart the development of movie exhibition as a business venture and, by extension, document the conditions of moviegoing as a social practice in the prairie West from 1896 to 1986.

2

INTRODUCING CINEMA TO PRAIRIE CANADA: MOVIE EXHIBITION, 1896 TO 1904

From the middle of May 1896, when the Edison Manufacturing Company completed its first batch of Vitascopes, entertainment entrepreneurs across North America began premiering the projectors.[1] Agents responsible for marketing the Vitascope in the United States unveiled the machine in such centres as Boston (on 18 May), Atlantic City (23 May), Philadelphia (25 May), Buffalo (8 June), San Francisco (8 June), St. Louis (15 June), New Orleans (28 June), Detroit (1 July), Los Angeles (5 July), Chicago (5 July), and Milwaukee (26 July).

Local entrepreneurs faced a number of technical challenges, however.[2] First, the Edison Manufacturing Company initially shipped the Vitascope in parts, without benefit of a user's manual, forcing exhibitors to assemble and then learn to operate the machine on their own. Second, in an era when currents and voltages varied from region to region, securing the electrical power needed to run the machine was sometimes a problem. Third, films, which cost about US $12.50 per print, often wore out quickly. In addition, entrepreneurs attempting to expand into rural regions had difficulty attracting audiences. The residents of such areas tended to be suspicious of big-city entertainment and thus responded to the advent of the Vitascope with little enthusiasm. Finally, as we have seen in chapter 1, competition soon became intense, as a variety of production companies sought to control the exhibition as well as the manufacture of their films. Here, we consider the organizations that introduced cinema to the prairie West, assessing the impact the new technology made on the public.

EDISON'S VITASCOPE ARRIVES IN WINNIPEG

Andrew M. Holland and George C. Holland, agents who marketed the Vitascope in Canada, premiered or took responsibility for premiering the machine in the major metropolitan centres across the country. They very likely provided the equipment that enabled entertainment entrepreneurs R. A. (Richard) Hardie and F. H. (Fred) Wall to introduce cinema to prairie Canada (if not all of English-speaking Canada) when they exhibited the Vitascope in Winnipeg from 18 to 25 July 1896.[3] Hardie and Wall had made a name for themselves presenting phonograph "concerts" and stereopticon "exhibitions," reproducing, among other things, recordings of famous American brass bands and casting "living pictures" onto a screen, including still images of British infantry, marines, and artillery, scenes from the life of Queen Victoria, and images of Canadian voyageurs in their canoes. They chose to premiere Edison's movie projector in Winnipeg, hoping to take advantage of the crowds of people who were flocking to the city to participate in the wide variety of "holiday" events taking place during July. These events included two American three-ring circuses — arguably the most exotic and spectacular form of entertainment available to North Americans at the time — evening entertainment at Fort Garry Park and at River Park, and the annual Winnipeg Industrial Exhibition.

Winnipeggers had incorporated their settlement (with a population of 1,869), located at the confluence of the Red and Assiniboine rivers, as a city in November 1873; as historians point out, for almost two hundred years the site had served as an important collection and distribution point.[4] Prior to the arrival of the Canadian Pacific Railway (CPR) in 1881, city merchants maintained commercial ties almost entirely with American merchants, especially with those located in such centres as Duluth and St. Paul, in Minnesota. Routing Canada's first transcontinental railway through Winnipeg increased east-west commerce, however, and generated a massive migration to the prairie provinces. The arrival of the CPR, together with the policies developed by Sir Wilfrid Laurier's Liberal government, elected in 1896, paved the way for a massive influx of settlers to the prairie West, North America's last agricultural frontier, leading to the emergence of Winnipeg as the region's major metropolitan centre. News that Winnipeg was becoming the "Gateway to the West" generated a heady real estate boom, and the population increased from 42,340 in 1901 to 163,000 in 1916.

Initially, business and civic leaders, who typically shared a language (English), the Protestant religion, and British heritage, focused on the construction of grand buildings and the expansion of the city's electric railway, the paving of roads, and the installation of sewer and water mains. In 1882, they formed the Winnipeg Electric Street Railway Company, with a view to operating a street railway system.[5] They regarded their community as the "Chicago of the North" and invited Chicago-based architects to design and to erect major buildings. Winnipeg was indeed similar to Chicago in the degree to which it was becoming an "immigrant city," characterized by an increasingly diverse population. Business and civic leaders located the central business district on Main Street, just north of its intersection with Portage Avenue, eventually calling it the "Exchange District," after the Winnipeg Grain Exchange, which opened in 1887. Via the Grain Exchange, speculators linked up to their counterparts in other major financial centres, such as Montréal and Toronto, New York City and Chicago, and London and Liverpool.

Between 1885 and 1900, Winnipeg consolidated its position as the industrial, financial, and cultural centre of western Canada by coming to control all government-regulated aspects of the western grain economy and by serving as the principal wheat marketing centre after the founding of the Winnipeg Grain Exchange. By 1900, Winnipeg-based firms dominated the Canadian wholesale trade from Lake Superior to the Pacific Coast.[6] Two additional transcontinental railways — the Canadian Northern and the Grand Trunk Pacific–National Transcontinental — were built between 1900 and 1915, both routing their main lines through Winnipeg and building their freight terminals and repair shops there. This gave Winnipeg the distinction of being the only major prairie city on the main line of both transcontinental railways between Windsor and Vancouver that acted as a terminus for American railways. Despite the removal of discriminatory freight rates between 1907 and 1909, Winnipeg's control of the western grain economy was augmented by the strength of its financial concerns, including banks, insurance companies, investment brokers, and (to a lesser extent) the Winnipeg Stock Exchange, which was formed in 1903.

Winnipeg's business and civic leaders projected the sophistication of their community by establishing various cultural institutions, among them newspapers. These included the liberal *Manitoba Free Press,* launched in 1872, the conservative *Winnipeg Telegram,* first published in 1876, and the independent *Winnipeg Tribune,* which began publication in 1886. Importantly, the provincial university was built in the city.[7] In addition, middle-class Winnipeggers (especially those of British origin) formed a variety of amateur athletic organizations and cultural groups, which flourished in churches, schools, and social clubs. Business and civic leaders also created three parks: Assiniboine Park in 1904, Kildonian Park in 1910, and St. Vital Park in 1933. With a grant from the American philanthropist Andrew Carnegie, they built the Winnipeg Public Library, which opened in 1905. Five theatres offered Winnipeggers professional and amateur productions: the Winnipeg Theatre (built in 1897), the Dominion Theatre (1904), the Walker Theatre (1907), the Orpheum Theatre (1911), and the Pantages Theatre (1914).

Of course, a great many citizens (immigrants in particular) had neither the time nor the money to take in leisure-time activities. In 1913, social reformer J. S. Woodsworth conducted a study of what constituted "a normal standard of living" in Winnipeg, claiming that an average family needed an income of $1,200 a year to survive. Woodsworth concluded that "it is difficult to find an actual working man's budget that maintains a normal standard. Large numbers of workmen are receiving under $600 per year, many under $500, half of what is necessary."[8] Many immigrants were forced to take drastic measures to survive. Families often broke up; mothers and their children went to work to supplement the incomes of their husbands and fathers. Many immigrants were demoralized by the conditions of life in Winnipeg, especially the low wages they earned.

Such was the increasingly complex metropolis that was emerging when, in the summer of 1896, Hardie and Wall "planted" a number of notices about the Vitascope in the *Winnipeg Tribune* before the

Winnipeg Industrial Exhibition got underway.[9] The statements convey the message that the Vitascope was no mere novelty but represented one of the latest advances of science. They stress the fact that the Vitascope threw "a stereopticon picture" onto a canvas screen, endowing it with realistic movement and expression.

Hardie and Wall deployed a two-pronged approach to exhibiting the Vitascope in Winnipeg. During the day, Wall managed the presentation at the Exhibition Grounds on Selkirk Avenue and Sinclair Street. According to newspaper reports, a steady stream of people passed through Wall's tent, inspecting Edison's inventions with great interest. Wall screened a variety of films produced by the Edison Manufacturing Company.[10] These may have included *Sandow* (1894), featuring Eugene Sandow, a.k.a. Friedrich Muller, known as the strongest man in the world; *Carmencita* (1894), featuring the Spanish dancer going through the routine she had made famous since 1890, when she first performed at Koster & Bial's Music Hall; *The Leonard-Cushing Fight* (1894), featuring an actual six-round contest between Mike Leonard, the "Beau Brummel" of pugilism, and Jack Cushing; *Buffalo Bill* (1894), featuring the famous army scout in an exhibition of rifle shooting, along with a rider and a horse from Buffalo Bill's Wild West; *The Execution of Mary, Queen of Scots* (1895), featuring a representation of the beheading of the queen; and *Herald Square* (1896), featuring pedestrians and trams moving through Herald Square, New York City, at noon. Meanwhile, Hardie managed the exhibition in the committee room of the Honourable Joseph Martin's campaign office, located in a building next to the Queen's Hotel, at 223 Portage Avenue, offering the public continuous exhibitions every evening. According to reports, Hardie exhibited a variety of Edison films (including those mentioned above) that reproduced "every appearance of life."

Hardie and Wall introduced motion pictures to the people of Manitoba at a time when, as we have seen, entertainment entrepreneurs generally competed fiercely for audiences; however, it would seem that they attracted only a modicum of critical attention. In their reports on entertainment in the city, correspondents for the *Manitoba Free Press* and the *Winnipeg Tribune* focused on the annual Winnipeg Industrial Exhibition, declaring it to be a success in every sense of the word.[11] They reported that forty thousand visitors attended the event, noting that the vast majority of them enjoyed the livestock, agricultural, and machinery displays. They praised the organizers for bringing some of the most exciting vaudeville artists of the age to Winnipeg, including the jugglers, the comedians on roller skates, the high-wire divers, and the trapeze artists. Some commended the organizers for including a travelling art exhibition, which had been mounted by the Ontario Society of Arts, and the Vitascope. However, only three journalists declared that the Vitascope, on exhibition "in the same tent as Mr. Wall's excellent Phonograph," was one of the most interesting items.[12] One noted that the prizefight appeared remarkably lifelike. Clearly, it would take some time for the general public to appreciate the significance of the Vitascope and the potential of moving pictures as a new form of entertainment.

OTTAWA'S WEST END PARK

A few days after Hardie and Wall exhibited the Vitascope in Winnipeg, the Holland brothers premiered the invention at West End Park, in Hintonburg, a suburb of Ottawa, from 21 July to 28 August 1896. A thriving manufacturing and administrative centre (with a population of 37,269) located at the confluence of the Ottawa, the Gatineau, and the Rideau rivers, Ottawa was acquiring a character (to paraphrase George Nader) commensurate with its status as a national capital.[13] Civil servants as a community were engendering a conservative atmosphere that largely submerged the "hurly-burly" boisterousness of its lumbering past.

Fur traders travelling the Indian trade route that passed through the Ottawa Valley had established the first settlements in the area. During the early nineteenth century, the rich timber resources of the region served as the foundation for what became the major industry in the valley. As John H. Taylor points out, Bytown sprang up around the construction, in 1826 to 1832, of the Rideau Canal, which linked Kingston and Ottawa. In 1855, business and civic leaders incorporated the community as a city, calling it Ottawa, after the Odawa First Nations people of the area, and in 1857 Queen Victoria selected it as the capital of the newly created Dominion of Canada. Ottawa expanded rapidly, growing from a population of about 8,000 in 1855 to 14,669 in 1861 to

44,154 in 1891. By the 1880s, sawmills replaced pulp and paper plants, attracted by the availability of cheap hydro-electric power.

Ottawa offered the entertainment entrepreneurs several important attractions.[14] To begin with, the city projected a progressive attitude; that is, it featured an infrastructure that included electric street lights and a street railway system, thanks to Thomas Ahearn and Warren Soper, who in 1881 had formed an electrical contracting firm that grew into a network of companies controlling the utilities offered in Ottawa.[15]

Initially, the Ahearn and Soper company erected telegraph and telephone transmission lines in eastern Canada. In 1882, Ahearn and Soper formed the Ottawa Electric Company, installing the country's first hydraulic generator at Chaudière Falls and 165 carbon arc street lamps on the streets of Ottawa, and the Ottawa Telephone Company, setting up a telephone service for Parliament Hill and various government offices. In 1887, Ahearn and Soper installed thousands of light bulbs on the Parliament Buildings, providing illuminations to mark Queen Victoria's Diamond Jubilee. In 1891, they formed the Ottawa Street Railway Company, installing the first electric streetcar system in Canada, and the Ottawa Car Company, designing, manufacturing, and servicing streetcars for the Canadian market.

Second, by the 1890s Ottawa had become relatively sophisticated, offering residents a wide variety of leisure activities.[16] From October to May, these activities included dramatic productions, educational and literary meetings, concerts, photography exhibitions, scientific conferences, roller skating, and sporting events, and from June to September they included band concerts, games, and circuses, which were held at amusement parks.[17] Several family-oriented performances visited Ottawa during the summer of 1896, including daily performances of the Norris Brothers' Company of one hundred dogs and ponies in a tent (seating 1,500) on Nepean Street, and bicycle races on Thursday nights under electric lights at the Metropolitan Grounds.[18]

Third, the Holland brothers had a vested interest in West End Park, an amusement park located on the property of the Ottawa Land Association (OLA) in Hintonburg, a village of about five hundred families, just west of the city, which was incorporated in 1893.[19] This land of natural beauty (the Holland family had once owned it) featured a large grove of beech and maple trees, judged to be suitable for picnicking and a variety of sporting events. The OLA investors, including the Holland brothers, Thomas Ahearn, and Warren Soper among others, believed that adding moving pictures to the program of high-class entertainment (such as band concerts) would encourage middle-class citizens of Ottawa to travel by streetcar to the amusement park and in turn encourage some to buy property in Hintonburg.[20] They reasoned that cheap land and lower taxes would appeal to many residents in Ottawa. Accordingly, they installed arc lamps and benches, a merry-go-round (which had been operating in Rockliffe Park, located on the east side of Ottawa), "electric swings," linking them to an organ, and an enclosure seating between 800 and 1,000 patrons, and an outdoor stage. The park opened in the spring of 1896. Patrons entered the grounds free of charge but paid an admission of five cents to attend the entertainment.

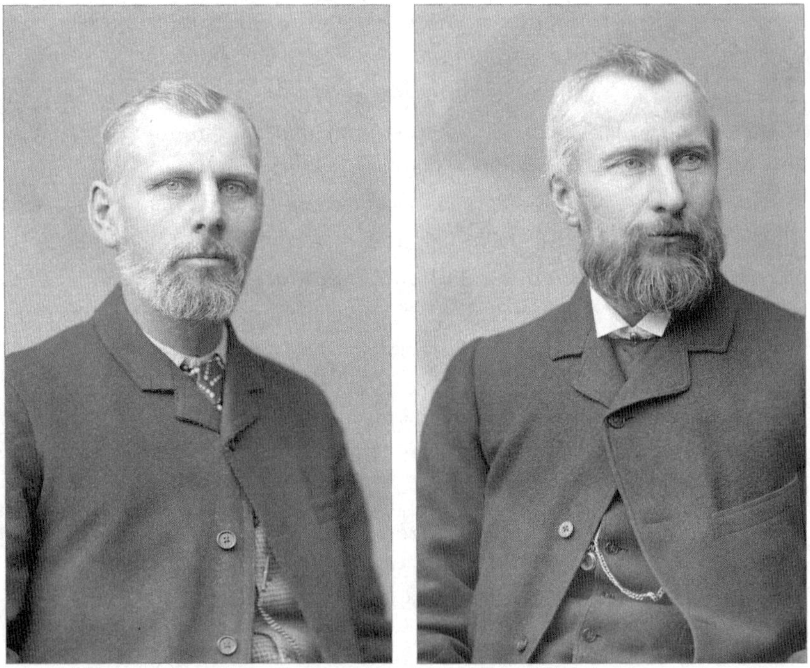

Figure 6. Ottawa-based entrepreneurs Andrew M. Holland and George C. Holland, 1888. Library and Archives Canada, negative no. PA-208770 (accession no. 1936-270 NPC; Mikan no. 3449587) and negative no. PA-206311 (accession no. 1936-270 NPC; Mikan no. 3449583), respectively.

The managers of the entertainment at West End Park took responsibility for the publicity, and the Holland brothers took responsibility for screening the films. The former invoked Ottawa's cosmopolitan aspirations in their advertisements, noting that the Vitascope, recently on exhibition in New York, London, and Paris, had attracted huge crowds. They observed that citizens of Ottawa should feel proud to be the first Canadians to see Edison's latest invention in action. (As we have noted, Hardie and Wall, under the auspices of the Holland brothers, introduced moving pictures to English-speaking Canada.) A journey of merely fifteen minutes by streetcar would get people to West End Park. "Selling" the new entertainment meant screening films as part of a variety program that included John C. Green, known professionally as "Belzac, the magician,"[21] who had delighted audiences in the United States and elsewhere in Canada, James Hardy, the high-wire walker who had recently (on 4 July 1896) crossed Niagara Falls, and a brass band, which provided musical accompaniment. Admission prices were set at ten cents for adults and five cents for children.

Judging by reports in the newspapers, the films screened during the first two weeks were very similar to those screened elsewhere.[22] The Governor-General's Foot Guard provided a musical accompaniment. Presumably, the exhibitors — like those at Koster & Bial's Music Hall — spliced the films from end to end and screened them about six times. Most commentators found

Edison's Vitascope

AT

West End Park

BIG ATTRACTION FOR THIS WEEK

The machinery for the vitascope arrived by express to-day, and the first exhibition in Canada of this latest marvel of Edison's will be given at West End Park to-morrow, Tuesday night. It is safe to say that nothing has been brought out in the nineteenth century that has created anything like the enthusiasm caused by Edison's success in bringing the vitascope to perfection. Railway trains in motion, th falls of Niagara incoming ocean vessels,' the ocean surf breaking on the shores, etc., are thrown upon the canvas with a distinct realism. In New York, Paris and London, where the vitascope has been on exhibition for several weeks, the interest continues unabated, and the theatres in which it is exhibited are crowded nightly. The sole right for exhibting the vitascope in Canada has been secured by the Holland Bros. with whom the Electric Railway Co. made arrangement for the first exhibition to take place in Ottawa.

The Electric Railawy Co. have also engaged for th week Belsac, the magician, who has been startling the American and Canadian cities during the past year. The press of every city in which he has appeared speaks in the highest praise of his performance and states that many of his tricks are without any possible explanation.

The vitascope will be exhibited and Belsac will perform at the West End Park every night this week, commencing to-morrow, Tuesday night.

Admisison, 10 cents. Children half price. Reserved seats, 10 cents extra. Round trip tickets including car fare both ways, admission and reserved seat, may be secured at Ahearn and Soper's office, 56 Sparks street.

Figure 7. Advertisement for an exhibition of Edison's Vitascope on 21 July 1896 in Ottawa's West End Park. Ottawa Journal, *20 July 1896, 1.*

it difficult to talk about what they were looking at; a few identified the subject matter of the films (they ran with no titles) and described the action; many reiterated the statement that the Vitascope reproduced action in a lifelike manner. As well, reporters provide little information about the makeup of the audiences in terms of class, gender, or ethnicity, or how audiences responded to moving pictures. Encouraged by the steady attendance — between 600 and 800 attended the show on the 21 July, 1,600 on 23 July, and 1,100 on 31 July — the managers of West End Park extended the run for a total of six weeks, featuring new performers and films. From the second week, commentators focused on the headline acts, including James Hardy, who performed on a wire stretched over the stage, the Diantes Brothers, musical and acrobatic clowns; the Tukushimas, a troupe of Japanese acrobats; Bartell & Morris, instrumentalists; and Baldwin & Daly, comedy acrobats.[23] Arguably, the Holland brothers took a loss exhibiting the Vitascope for the sake of selling property in Hintonburg and along the railway line.[24]

Figure 8. The stage at the Ottawa Electric Railway Park. Library and Archives Canada, negative no. PA-027261 (accession no. 1936-270 NPC; Mikan no. 3381031).

THE SPREAD OF CINEMA IN MANITOBA

While the second exhibition of the Vitascope in Canada took place in Ottawa, the third took place in the prairie West. Following their premiering of the Vitascope in Winnipeg, Hardie and Wall travelled to Brandon, an important economic and political centre in southwest Manitoba, 124 miles west of Winnipeg, planning to premiere the machine at the Brandon Summer Exhibition, to be held on 28 and 29 July 1896. Their plan was to take advantage of the crowds of people from all parts of the prairie West who were travelling to the city to attend the event.

Brandon, a community with a population of roughly 1,500, was incorporated as a city in 1882, and thanks to the construction of railways in the region and the boom in the wheat economy, the new city expanded quickly.[25] People from Ontario and the United States poured into the region, and between 1891 and 1911 the population jumped from 3,778 to 13,839.[26] Whenever they had the chance, boosters promoted Brandon as an important metropolis, emphasizing its cultural institutions as well as its economic potential.[27] These included the City Hall and Opera House, a two-storey structure erected in 1892 on the property between 8th Street and 9th Street on Princess Avenue, which served as the centre of Brandon's cultural life. Over the years, the Opera House hosted a wide variety of touring organizations, including Shakespearean companies from Great Britain, the Dixie Jubilee Singers (who performed plantation songs), and Pollard's Lilliputian Opera Company (a company of Australian child actors), plus local groups such as the Brandon Light Opera Company, the Schubert Choir, and the Brandon Little Theatre. In due course, entertainment entrepreneurs offered the citizens of Brandon a wider range of amusements, starting with the activities associated with the city's agricultural fairs, including grandstand shows and midway rides and games, and branching out to include roller skating at the Roller Rink during the summer, ice skating at the exhibition arena during the winter, and dancing at the Imperial Dance Gardens.

According to reports, the directors of the Brandon Agricultural Society resolved in 1895 to produce the best exhibition to that point.[28] The Exhibition Committee launched a campaign to attract more exhibits than ever before; the Buildings Committee refurbished the buildings, the grandstand, and the dining hall; and the Grounds Committee improved the exhibition grounds. The Special Attractions Committee organized a brass band competition and sporting events. Moreover, the board secured nearly all of the New York City–based attractions that had appeared at the Winnipeg Industrial Exhibition.

Hardie and Wall planted a notice in the *Brandon Sun* announcing that among the "most interesting things" currently on exhibit in the city was "one of the latest inventions of the fertile mind of Thomas A. Edison."[29] Wall demonstrated the Vitascope during the day at the exhibition grounds, located at what today is the corner of 10th Street and Victoria Avenue, and Hardie demonstrated it in a vacant store on Rosser Avenue during the evening.

Commentators declared the exhibition to be an unqualified success, praising the organizers for orchestrating the various activities.[30] They deemed that the event had attracted an audience of twenty thousand, five times the population of the city. They called attention to a number of outstanding displays that represented the latest developments in agriculture and manufacturing and special attractions, including the polo match. A writer for the *Winnipeg Tribune* noted that Edison's Vitascope and Phonograph attracted much attention.[31] A writer for the *Brandon Sun* invited the people of Brandon to watch Thomas A. Edison's latest invention in action, "one of the latest advances of science," which "throws stereopticular pictures on a canvas with all the movements and expressions of life."[32]

Meanwhile, back in central Canada, the Holland brothers travelled to Toronto, Halifax, and Montréal, where they premiered the machine on 31 August 1896, 10 September 1896, and 28 September 1896, respectively.[33] Ultimately, however, Andrew found the prospects of the motion picture business in Canada disheartening; he complained about the quality of the films that were available, the great distances between major urban centres, and the varying electrical systems they encountered in their travels.[34] By the end of 1896, the Holland brothers had abandoned the motion picture business.

Others refused to write off the economic potential of film exhibition. For example, the Cosgrove family amusement company (comprising up to ten performers), managed by J. Cosgrove, toured the prairie West during the late 1890s and the early 1900s, staging variety entertainment in such centres as Rat Portage, Winnipeg, St. Paul, Minneapolis, Duluth,

Fargo, and Grand Forks under the auspices of various social, religious, and cultural institutions. His troupe went through a number of configurations, depending upon the kind of entertainment the public desired.

The Cosgrove Musical Company (as it was then called) played at the Grand Opera House in Winnipeg from 24 to 29 May 1897. They charged an admission ranging from twenty-five to fifty cents evenings and between twenty-five cents (children) to thirty-five cents (adults) afternoons for a variety program that included the Animatograph and Phonograph. Presumably, the company used the "Theatrograph," which had been designed and manufactured by R. W. (Robert) Paul, a London-based electrician, instrument maker, and film producer, to run films produced by the Edison Manufacturing Company.[35] The machine, often called the "Anamatagraph," had played with great success at the Bijou Theatre in Toronto for the month of December.[36] One commentator noted that the machine projected "animated" pictures onto a large screen that were life-sized and true to life.[37] The writer described the films — presumably produced by the Edison Manufacturing Company — as the New York Fire Brigade responding to a call, the cavalry on parade, the New York Central flyer travelling at sixty mph, and several rural and seaside sites. It is likely that the films Cosgrove screened included *Going to the Fire* (1896), featuring a fire brigade (led by the chief) responding to an alarm; *Knights of Templar Parade* (1896), featuring the Knights Templar on parade in New York City; *Fast Train* (1896), featuring an express train of the Hudson River and New York Central Railroad passing around a curve in the picturesque Mohawk Valley at high speed; and *Sea Beach Scene* (1896), featuring a group of people under umbrellas at Asbury Park or Atlantic City, New Jersey.[38] The commentator did not describe the various sounds that were reproduced by the phonograph. Apparently, the Cosgroves played to full houses.

THE WESTWARD EXPANSION OF CINEMA

The Royal Animatograph Company brought cinema to Regina on 16 and 17 August 1897, when members of the group included motion pictures in the variety program they offered the public in the auditorium on the second floor of the City Hall, a wooden structure built in 1886 on the northeast corner of Scarth Street and 11th Avenue.[39] For a number of years, officials rented City Hall Auditorium — a space measuring 28 feet by 52 feet — to local amateur groups at a rate of $5 per evening and occasionally hosted travelling companies, which produced melodramatic spectacles, comic operas, and incipient vaudeville.[40] The flow of professional performers across the region during the Golden Age of theatre in Canada was controlled (as we will see in chapter 3) by C. P. Walker, the Winnipeg-based theatre impresario.

Regina matured slowly, becoming an important metropolitan centre after a period of twenty years.[41] Three decisions affected the community's development: its designation as a divisional point on the transcontinental railway in 1882, as the headquarters of the NWMP in 1885, and as the capital of the province of Saskatchewan in 1906. In 1883, business and civic leaders incorporated the hamlet as a town, at which point it became the capital of the North-West Territories. It was incorporated as a city in 1903, when its population stood at 2,249. Immigrants flowed to the region, and the population climbed to 30,213 in 1911. As Nader points out, four economic activities have been central to Regina's growth: public administration (the provincial government accounted for most of public administration employment); marketing and distribution services to the agricultural community of southeast Saskatchewan; wholesale services to the southern half of the province; and financial services to the whole province.

Important cultural and recreational institutions sprang up after the turn of the century. These included the opening in 1904 of the Auditorium Rink, which operated as a skating rink and a theatre, and the founding of the Regina Orchestra Society by Frank L. Laubach; the founding in 1908 of the Regina Symphony Orchestra and the opening of the new City Hall Auditorium; the construction in 1910 of the Regina Theatre, an 800-seat facility that served as the home of the Regina Operatic Society and the Regina Orchestra Society, and the Roseland Theatre, a 600-seat facility that featured stage productions as well as movies; and the construction in 1911 of the Regina Public Library, with the assistance of a grant from Andrew Carnegie.

Reginans expressed their sophistication in terms of the newspapers they published. The earliest were two weekly papers, the *Regina Leader*, first published in March 1883, and the *Regina Journal*, founded in 1886. In 1895, a third weekly, the *West*, was added to the list, followed by the

Standard, a daily paper that began publication in 1904, and the *Leader*, which appeared as a morning newspaper from 1905 to 1910, when it became an evening paper.

A writer for the *Regina Leader* for 19 August 1897 noted that the Royal Animatograph Company, comprising Will McLeod, Barney and Grace Flynn, Miss Doyle, and a young (female) pianist, played to full houses, offering a varied program: Kinetoscope motion pictures (films featuring, e.g., prizefights and fire brigades in action, and bathing scenes), comic songs, dances, and skits.[42] People liked some parts of the program but disliked others. According to the writer just mentioned, people were impressed by the images the machine projected onto a screen, finding them to be a "sort of magic lantern exhibition of Kinetoscope pictures — photographs of motion." All the writer says about the films themselves is that they were "a novelty and very entertaining." By the same token, people liked the performers, finding the young pianist "quite proficient," but disliked the solo singing of Grace Flynn.

On 10 September 1897, Hardie screened a selection of motion pictures at a "private" event held in Winnipeg, possibly organized by William Whyte, the general-manager of the CPR, for the purpose of introducing films that might be utilized in a campaign to promote emigration to the prairie West.[43] Invited guests included Thomas Greenway, the premier of Manitoba, Charles Mickle, a provincial cabinet minister, and W. F. (William) McCreary, the mayor of Winnipeg. On a Projecting Kinetoscope, Hardie screened several films depicting life on the prairies that he himself had made, including views of Greenway working on his farm and a CPR train speeding down the tracks, as well as films he had acquired, such as scenes of a procession marking Queen Victoria's Diamond Jubilee. The former were possibly the first moving pictures produced in Canada by Canadians.[44] A correspondent for the *Manitoba Free Press* noted that members of the audience were delighted with what they saw, adding that several films, especially those showcasing life on a Manitoba farm, would offer people abroad a "correct impression" of the region.[45]

Meanwhile, the Cosgrove company travelled westward to Calgary, north to Strathcona, and by ferry across the North Saskatchewan to Edmonton, where they performed at Robertson's Hall on 15 and 16 October

1897. According to one newspaper report, the company included moving pictures in the vaudeville programs they offered audiences.[46]

Edmonton was, at this time, maturing socially, economically, and culturally, thanks in part to a number of major developments: the completion in August 1891 of the CPR branch line from Calgary to the south side of the North Saskatchewan River; the shift in immigration policy after the general election of 1896, boosting the population of the city from 4,176 in 1901 to 31,821 in 1911; and the discovery in April 1897 of gold in the Klondike, encouraging business and civic leaders to promote the city as "the poor man's route to the Yukon."[47]

Edmonton had been incorporated as a town (with a population of 700) in 1892, and Strathcona as a town (with a population of 650) in 1898. Canadians in general and Edmontonians in particular were confident that Edmonton would have a great future. Forward-thinking entrepreneurs, such as W. S. (Scott) Robertson, judged that the time was indeed ripe to build facilities that would accommodate the productions of the vaudeville and the light opera companies that were touring the prairie West in growing numbers.[48] Born in Saint John, New Brunswick, Robertson settled in Edmonton in 1882, eventually serving the community as an auctioneer and as sheriff. He quickly developed a wide range of commercial interests, not to mention a passion for the theatre. Accordingly, in 1892, he built a wooden frame, two-storey multi-purpose complex at the south side of Jasper Avenue, at the foot of 97th Street, where the Edmonton Convention Centre now stands.[49] Robertson Hall served as an important social, cultural, and political centre for more than a decade.[50] Interestingly, *The Danites*, an anti-Mormon play written by Joaquin Miller and produced by McKee Rankin, an American touring stock company, was the first play to be presented (on 2 August 1894) at the hall.[51]

A correspondent for the *Edmonton Bulletin* wrote that the Cosgrove Company played to good houses at Robertson Hall.[52] The writer — who identifies neither the entertainment in general nor the films in particular — noted that the audiences expressed every mark of approval. Just how big those audiences were, however, is a matter for speculation. Presumably, many Edmontonians, caught up in the frenzy of the gold rush, had little time to think about the significance of Edison's movie projector.

The Cosgrove Family Vaudeville Company (as they called themselves) travelled to Calgary, where they appeared at Hull's Opera House on 25 and 26 October 1897. According to newspaper reports, the company included Edison's movie projector, billed as "the greatest wonder of the age," on the program of musical novelties they offered the public.[53]

Calgary had expanded considerably in size and significance since 11 August 1883, when CPR locomotive No. 87 reached the settlement of tents and shacks on the piece of flat land at the juncture of the Elbow and the Bow rivers.[54] The arrival of the first train set the stage for the rapid development of what is now southern Alberta. Business and civic leaders incorporated the community (with a population of 506) as a town on 7 November 1884; boosters spoke of Calgary as another Chicago.[55] Business and civic leaders incorporated the community (with a population of about 3,900) as a city on 16 September 1893. The expansion of the cattle industry was launched in 1881 by the Conservative federal government with the express purpose of enabling British subjects to lease up to 100,000 acres of land for twenty-one years at a rate of one cent per acre. Soon, the railway line to Edmonton and on to Athabasca Landing, which was completed in 1891, and the line to Fort Macleod and on to the international boundary, completed in 1892, gave Calgary the four-way rail traffic it needed to dominate the region. By 1897, two metropolitan centres dominated the prairie West: Calgary and Winnipeg.

Many people living in the region surrounding Calgary were ranchers, former officers of the North-West Mounted Police (many of them born in eastern Canada) who had decided to stay in the West, and, to a lesser extent, people who were born in Great Britain; all were instrumental in making ranching commercially viable. Ranching capital was key to establishing the first manufacturing enterprises in the city, including the Calgary Brewing and Malting Company, organized in 1892 by A. E. Cross, W. R. (Roper) Hull, and John Lineham.[56] The situation changed after 1905, the year the federal government created the provinces of Alberta and Saskatchewan. The agricultural industry expanded enormously, thanks to changes Minister of the Interior Clifford Sifton had made to immigration policy, as well as to developments in farming practices and in farming machinery generally. Immigration figures for the area indicate that during the last two decades of the nineteenth century Anglo-Saxons outnumbered Europeans by a ratio of seven to one. The majority of Calgary's business and social leaders claimed

British ancestry: most were born in eastern Canada, especially in Ontario; some were born in Great Britain; almost all were Protestant.[57] They constituted a landed aristocracy, which increased significantly in number during the years leading up to World War I; they organized charitable and benevolent organizations, including the St. George societies, the Sons of England Benevolent Society, and the Daughters of England, which sponsored annual dances and dinners and held polo and cricket matches, epitomizing the traditions of a privileged class.

Calgary's cultural life dates from the arrival of the CPR, when a former NWMP officer, Captain Boynton, built Boynton's Hall, the community's first performing arts venue.[58] Amateur musical and theatrical organizations, including brass bands, church choirs, dramatic groups, and operatic societies, performed at Boynton Hall during the late 1880s and the early 1890s. In 1882, W. R. Hull, a Devonshire-born rancher, entrepreneur, developer, and philanthropist, decided to build a venue that would attract some of the road shows that were touring Canada.[59] He commissioned Child and Wilson, a local firm of architects and surveyors, to design a two-storey, brick-and-sandstone performing arts complex, located at the southeast corner of Centre Street and 6th Avenue. The management opened the facility on 22 March 1893, and for the next thirteen years it served as an important social and cultural centre.[60] For example, Harold Nelson and his stock company played at Hull's Opera House in May 1903, presenting *Hamlet*, *Taming of the Shrew*, and *Othello*.

Interestingly, the J. Cosgrove company advertised extensively to call attention to their various specialists, including "character" vocalists and elocutionists, plus Edison's improved Kinetoscope, the greatest wonder of the age.[61] They set admission prices at twenty-five, fifty, and seventy-five cents for the two hours of entertainment. According to reports, the Cosgrove company played to packed houses. A correspondent for the *Calgary Herald* reported that audiences enjoyed the company's musical skills, which were manifested in the rendering of "character songs" and the playing of bells, glasses, and xylophones.[62] The writer noted that the greatest novelty on the program, however, was the Kinetoscope, which projected a variety of films onto a screen vividly and realistically. These films included the New York Fire Brigade responding to a call, a stable on fire, a troop of cavalry in action, a train travelling at great speed, soldiers going to war, Queen Victoria's Diamond Jubilee procession, and Thomas Greenway, the Premier of Manitoba, at work on his farm in Brandon Hills, south of Brandon, stooking wheat and riding his horse, presumably the film that Hardie had made and exhibited in Manitoba.[63] The writer judged the show to be one of the best ever presented in Calgary.

Despite the positive responses to their presentation, the manager of the Cosgrove company judged that their visit to Calgary was not as profitable as it should have been. In a letter to the *Calgary Herald*, J. Cosgrove claimed that Calgary's city council was driving away business by levying an uncommonly high tax on public performances, thus adding $10 to the expenses they incurred in bringing the show to the city.[64] During the two days the company stayed in Calgary, he pointed out, the performers put no less than $84 into the tills of local businessmen, purchasing, for example, clothes and chemicals for the Kinetoscope. This is "the straw that breaks the camel's back; companies won't come here," he declared. Why not tax the venue, he asked, at the rate that other city councils tax entertainment venues in their jurisdiction? For example, in both Winnipeg and Toronto, city councils levy theatres and opera houses an annual tax of $100. Calgary is the only place of any pretensions to being a city, he concluded, "where companies are confronted with a policeman threatening to stop the performance unless an exorbitant license fee is handed over."

Arguably, the Millar Vaudeville Company brought cinema to Saskatoon when, on 29 and 30 September 1903, the group celebrated the opening of Cairns' Hall, with a program of films and comic songs.[65] Located on 2nd Avenue, in the second floor of a wooden structure built by entrepreneur J. F. (James) Cairns, for years Cairns' Hall served as the community's social and cultural centre. The performers timed their stay with a view to taking advantage of the crowds that were flowing into the city to attend the annual fair.

Saskatoon dates from 1882, when Methodists from Toronto tried to establish a "dry" community on land on both sides of the South Saskatchewan River, at the heart of Saskatchewan's agricultural region.[66] The experiment failed, but the settlement grew nevertheless, the settlers believing that eventually the community would play an important role as a supply and service centre to its regional hinterland. The North-West

Rebellion of 1885 adversely affected immigration, and the completion in 1890 of the railway from Regina through Saskatoon to Prince Albert had less impact than anticipated; however, the community grew rapidly during the first decade of the twentieth century, thanks to the general boom in immigration from eastern Canada and the British Isles and eastern Europe to western Canada.

Born in Québec and educated in Ontario, Cairns taught at the Chatham Collegiate Institute, edited a cycling magazine, and managed opera houses in Chatham and London.[67] In October 1902, he and his wife moved to Saskatoon. He opened a bakery in December and soon became an important member of the community, helping establish the Board of Trade, serving as its secretary and president, and undertaking a number of community-oriented activities. By the same token, Cairns' Hall prospered, featuring such performers as E. Pauline Johnson, Walter Jackson, and T. H. (Thomas) Marks.[68]

Employing a tactic common at the time, the boosters of the community incorporated it (with a population of 544) as a town in 1903, and (with a population of 3,011) as a city in 1906, so that they could increase the municipality's borrowing power and therefore build the infrastructure needed to attract more investment. Saskatoon failed in 1906 to become the site of the provincial capital but succeeded in 1909 in becoming the site for the University of Saskatchewan. By this time, the city had developed the functions that subsequently formed the basis of its economic growth, namely, as a distribution, marketing, and administrative centre for the agricultural community of central Saskatchewan and as an educational centre for the whole province.[69]

Like many western cities, Saskatoon experienced a real estate boom from 1910 to 1913, when the population reached 12,004. Commercial lots on 3rd Avenue sold for about $200 in 1907, for $4,000 in 1910, and for $15,000 in 1912; realtors turned 2nd Avenue into a kind of "Broadway of the prairies," with lots selling for $1,600 per foot of frontage, prices never equalled again.[70] The city grew in importance, thanks to the energy and the ambition of its leading citizens.[71]

One could see signs of civic pride everywhere: the *Saskatoon Phoenix* began publishing in 1902; the Saskatoon Choral Society was founded in 1903; the Saskatoon Philharmonic Society gave its first concert in 1909; the Orpheus Society organized its first performances of opera in 1910, the year builders began work on the University of Saskatchewan; the Saskatoon Oratorio Society gave its first concert in 1913; the Saskatoon Little Theatre Club organized its first sessions in 1922 for reading, studying, and producing plays; the Saskatoon Arts and Crafts Society began sponsoring local artists in 1923; and the Saskatoon Public Library opened its doors in 1928.

According to reports, the people of Saskatoon, accustomed to creating their own entertainment, flocked to the seventeenth Exhibition of the Central Saskatchewan Agricultural society, which had attracted more entries in all categories than ever before, and to Cairns' Hall.[72] One writer noted that people were impressed by the design and the decoration of the opera house, adding that Cairns should be commended for "giving Saskatoon one of the best opera houses in the country." Apparently, they responded enthusiastically to the comic illustrated songs the group presented, applauding repeatedly; surprisingly, the writer did not identify the films the group screened or describe how people responded to them. Interestingly, the manager announced that lovers of high-class music would enjoy seeing the Cosgrove Concert Orchestra, who would appear at the hall during the last week of October 1903, marking the group's first visit to the city.[73] Again, the writer does not say whether or not the group would add motion pictures to their program.

THE TRAVELLING EXHIBITOR

As we have seen, amusement parks and vaudeville houses provided temporary venues for exhibiting motion pictures. However, in spite of the massive urbanization that was taking place in the late nineteenth and early twentieth centuries, many people in the United States and Canada still lived in small communities with fewer than three thousand residents, places that usually had no such amenities. One way to bring motion pictures to people in the rural areas was to follow the example of nineteenth-century entertainers and to travel, working a circuit of sites within a given territory.[74]

Entering the itinerant movie exhibition business was one thing; prospering at it was another.[75] From 1898, a number of ambitious individuals — possessing some mechanical ability and some showmanship skills — obtained the equipment required from any number

Figure 9. Film exhibitor John Schuberg, ca. 1940. More than anyone, it was Schuberg who brought the movies to prairie Canada. Manitoba Free Press, *27 February 1960, 20.*

of suppliers. For example, as Kathryn Fuller notes, they could purchase Edison Kinetoscopes from Edison Manufacturing Company outlets in New York City, Chicago, and San Francisco for US $135. They could also buy this equipment from Sigmund Lubin or Sears, Roebuck, and Company, the Chicago-based mail-order retailer, which had just launched a department called "Public Entertainment Outfits and Supplies." Taking advantage of the increasing interest in motion pictures, Sears, Roebuck, and Company supplied the would-be exhibitor with all the equipment needed to enter the business, including stereopticons, moving picture projectors, motion pictures, and phonographs, plus lecture scripts, sets of slides, records, advertising posters, and rolls of tickets.[76] The firm supplied instruction manuals explaining how to handle the machinery, how to secure the venues, and how to advertise. Equipped with these materials, the exhibitor would travel the country, visiting such venues as churches, town halls, theatres, and opera houses. Many travelled to fairs, where they erected temporary canvas theatres for staging vaudeville shows and exhibiting their movies.[77]

In rough-and-ready venues, audiences sat in makeshift seats or stood during the show, which lasted fifteen or twenty minutes. The first projectors were noisy and produced flickering images. The itinerant exhibitor would show a program of movies until the audience lost interest, and then move on to another locale. To turn his program into a "special event," the showman adopted some of the techniques that managers of vaudeville theatres employed, including arranging short films to evoke a theme or featuring a lantern show or securing a lecturer who talked throughout the movies, commenting on or clarifying the action.[78]

This was the context in which J. A. (John) Schuberg operated as an exhibitor. It can be said that Schuberg brought motion pictures to western Canada.[79] What set him apart from his colleagues was his resourcefulness, especially his strategy of designing "thematic" programs of short films, thereby intensifying the moviegoing experience.[80]

WINNIPEG THEATRE
C. P. WALKER, Manager
TWICE TO-DAY Mat. 2:30 Night, 8:30.
The Volunteer Organist
Popular Prices
Evenings, $1 to 25c. Matinee, 50c and 25c
3 Nights Beginning Thursday, October 13
SATURDAY MATINEE
Over 300 Nights at Terry's Theatre, London

THE INTERNATIONAL, LIVE FOREVER SUCCESS
MRS. WIGGS OF THE CABBAGE PATCH
Liebler & Co., Managers
Evenings, $1.50 to 50c Matinee, $1.00 to 25c.
Coming—DEWOLF HOPPER

The Walker CANADA'S FINEST THEATRE
ADVANCED VAUDEVILLE
Eve. 15 to 75c Mat. best seats 25c
WILL VAN ALLEN
Musical Comedian
DIAMOND COMEDY FOUR
Real Singers and Comedians
THREE SISTERS MACARTE
"The Land of the Lotus."
NELLIE LYTTON
Singing Comedienne
HIGBY BROTHERS
High-Class Instrumentalists
MILDRED & LESTER
Singers and Dancers
Direct from his London run
GERMAIN—The Wizard

Dominion
Week of MONDAY, OCT. 10
Matinees, Tue., Thur., Sat
PERMANENT PLAYERS IN
Shall We Forgive Her?
Evenings, 15 to 50c.. Best Matinee Seats, 25c.
Next Week—Brewster's Millions

Bijou THEATRE
HAPPY JACK GARDNER & CO.
In the Roaring Comedy
"Close Call."
3 NATIONAL COMIQUES
GEORGE YEOMAN
WARD BROS.
BIG EXTRA FEATURE.
Fred Eckhoff and Anna Gordon.
THE MUSICAL LAUGHMAKERS
MOTIOGRAPH

DREAMLAND
ENJOYMENT
TO-DAY
GRAND
All-Round
PROGRAMS
Special Features
AMUSEMENT
STARLAND

ROLLER SKATING
ARENA RINK
Every Afternoon and Evening
Afternoon session 2.30 to 5.
Evening session 8 to 10.
Popular Prices. Band.
Phone Main 4514.

Figure 10. Advertisements for theatres, some of them operated by John Schuberg. Manitoba Free Press, 12 October 1910, 9.

The son of Swedish immigrants, Schuberg grew up in Minneapolis. A showman at the age of thirteen, he worked at Kohn and Middleton's Dime Museum, learning how to perform sleight-of-hand tricks and to operate a Punch and Judy Show. Billed as "Johnny Nash," he toured with the John T. Robinson Circus, travelling across Oregon, California, Arizona, New Mexico, Texas, and Louisiana. When he was nineteen, in 1894, he struck out on his own, moving to Winnipeg, where he worked for Fred Burrows, who operated a circus. He played fairs and carnivals during the summer and freelanced during the winter, travelling as far east as Montréal. In 1898, he married Nettie, Burrows's youngest daughter, and the couple travelled to Vancouver, where they spent their honeymoon.

Schuberg decided to settle in Vancouver, planning to open an umbrella repair shop. Business prospered, but he longed for the excitement of show business. Learning that a merchant in Seattle was selling an Edison projector, he resolved to become a movie exhibitor. He bought the machine for US $250, along with a number of Edison films, including *The Wreck of the Battleship "Maine"* (1898) and *Burial of the "Maine" Victims* (1898), as well as a number of stereopticon slides that featured the major news item of the day, the Spanish-American War.[81] His timing was perfect.

Schuberg rented a large building on West Cordova Street, located in the central business district of Vancouver, a city of about twenty-five thousand people at the time. He set up the equipment near the front and hung a screen at the back, providing no chairs because his program of films would run for only thirty minutes. He opened the doors of the theatre to the public on 15 December 1898, charging patrons ten cents to watch a program of selected movies and slides of the Spanish-American War, which he called "The War Show." At first, people stayed away. Some were likely preoccupied with the Klondike Gold Rush, which overnight had almost transformed Dawson City into the largest city west of Winnipeg; others were suspicious of the latest showman's "gimmick." To pique people's interest, he promoted his show as if it were a sideshow. This meant beating a bass drum, rattling a large sheet of metal to suggest thunder, and firing two pistols loaded with blank cartridges, so as to "add some realism" to the program.[82] He left the front door open, so that people on the street could hear the sound effects; this manoeuvre caught their attention, and soon he was playing to full houses.

Naturally, Schuberg resolved to exploit the commercial possibilities of this venture. Like other showmen across the continent, he had only one set of films, so two weeks later he moved on, looking for new audiences. The Schubergs concluded that this would mean showing films in a black-top tent at fairs and carnivals, which were becoming popular, and so decided to return to Winnipeg, where during the winter they could design such a facility.

On their way back to Winnipeg in 1899, they stopped at small communities along the CPR line to put on movie shows; however, business proved to be uncertain. For example, the electrical power in Ashcroft was insufficient for running the projector. The light was rather poor, so Schuberg stopped the show and refunded patrons' money. In Kamloops, he mounted a show in a hall over a printing shop. When no one showed up, he decided to attract attention by moving the projector to the balcony, where he ran the machine and lectured to an imaginary audience. People who had seen this charade soon packed into the hall.

In Winnipeg, Schuberg and his father-in-law designed a black-top canvas tent measuring 20 feet by 60 feet that seated two hundred people. Hilary Russell writes that the facility contained an inner tent of black cotton, which kept the sun out on bright days. At the end of a show, the exhibitor raised the "sidewall" so that the audience could cool off. In addition, the exterior featured a marquee-like banner on poles and rather lurid paintings or posters advertising the movie inside.[83] Schuberg called this facility the "Edison Electric Theatre."

In May 1899, Schuberg erected his black-top tent in a vacant lot on the west side of Main Street, about one hundred yards north of Logan Avenue. At the time, the Winnipeg and the Grand theatres offered the public such fare as the James Neill (stock) company and the Metropolitan Opera Company, respectively. In addition, Elm Park offered such variety entertainment as band concerts. Schuberg presented "The War Show," presumably to take advantage of the crowds that had gathered for the Empire Day Celebration on 23 May 1899. He later recalled that the money came in so fast that it almost turned their heads.[84] During the summer months from 1899 to 1902, they played fairs and carnivals in Manitoba, North Dakota, Minnesota, Wisconsin, Illinois, and New

Mexico.[85] In the spring of 1900, he obtained copies of George Méliès's films, *A Trip to the Moon* (1902), based on Jules Verne's famous novels *From the Earth to the Moon* (1865) and *The First Men in the Moon* (1901), and *The Eruption of Mt. Pelée* (1902), which captured the devastation caused by the eruption of Mt. Pelée on the French Caribbean Island of Martinique. These films, played in Winnipeg's River Park, generated much excitement. Exhausted by travelling constantly, the Schubergs returned in 1902 to Vancouver with a view to setting up a permanent facility for screening movies. It seems that they were the first of the travelling showmen in Canada to do so.[86]

While in Los Angeles, in the summer of 1902, Schuberg visited Thomas L. Tally's "permanent" facility, the Electric Theatre, located at 262 South Main, opposite 3rd Street.[87] He may have noticed the advertisement in the *Los Angeles Times* describing Tally's penny arcade as "a new place of amusement" that featured "up-to-date high-class moving picture entertainment, especially for ladies and children."[88] Tally screened such films as *Capture of the Biddle Brothers* (1902) and *New York City in a Blizzard* (1902), charging adults ten cents and children five cents admission.

Taking his cue from Tally, Schuberg rented an empty store at 38 Cordova Street, Vancouver, where in October 1902 he opened the Edison Electric Theatre. He charged customers ten cents to watch a program of vaudeville acts and movies. The response to the program, which included two films, Méliès's *The Eruption of Mt. Pelée* and Edison's *The Great Train Robbery* (1903), as well as illustrated songs, was enthusiastic.[89] Schuberg printed a program (dated 16 February 1903) in which he announced that the Electric Theatre catered to "the refined" and that an usher would help ladies obtain desirable seats.[90]

Meanwhile, Schuberg and Burrows formed an amusement company geared to operating movies-and-vaudeville theatres in Winnipeg. Schuberg and Burrows opened the Unique, located at 529 Main Street, late in 1903; Schuberg then sold the Electric Theatre in Vancouver to Fred Lincoln, later associated with the Sullivan and Considine vaudeville circuit. They opened the Dominion, located at 175 Portage Avenue, in 1904, and the Bijou, located at 498 Main Street, in 1905, attracting much attention by screening *The Great Train Robbery*. They arranged with a distributor in Minneapolis for one reel of film and three vaudeville acts per week. Business prospered, and they opened the Dreamland, located at 530 Main Street, in 1909, and the Province, located at 209 Notre Dame Avenue, in 1910. As a correspondent for the *Canadian Film Weekly* notes, the Dreamland was the first dedicated movie theatre in Winnipeg.[91] These theatres formed the nucleus of the Nash Theatre Chain, which eventually included theatres in Manitoba, North Dakota, Minnesota, and Wisconsin.

Over the years, Schuberg employed a number of performers who later became movie stars. In 1906, he booked Al Jolson and Charlie Chaplin at the Winnipeg Bijou. Chaplin and his troupe of about twelve players appeared in an act called Karno's "A Night in an English Music Hall." Schuberg booked these acts through the International Booking Office in Chicago, and later through the Sullivan and Considine Circuit in Minneapolis, which charged a booking fee. Schuberg, an independent operator, understood the advantages of having his own booking office, so he opened one in the Tribune Building in Chicago. This was short-lived, as Considine bought Schuberg's circuit for $100,000.[92]

In 1914, Schuberg and W.P. deWees, a Vancouver-based exhibitor, formed a partnership. In 1916, they opened the Rex Theatre in Vancouver and in 1917 secured the First National Exhibitors' Circuit franchise.[93] Schuberg served as the president and DeWees as the general manager of the exchange. They hoped that this arrangement would give them a distinct business advantage.

At this time, securing a steady supply of desirable films on favourable terms could be a challenge. The major moviemakers employed a national producer-distributor marketing system known as "block booking," devised by Paramount Pictures, an early champion of feature films.[94] Under this system the exhibitor contracted in advance to lease a determined number of films, many of which were to be made within a definite period of time. If the exhibitor accepted the all-or-nothing package, he or she signed a contract and made a payment on account. Initially, the system worked to everyone's satisfaction. The exhibitor preferred patronizing a single company that supplied at least two motion pictures of uniform quality weekly to dealing with various exchanges on a weekly basis, devising programs on the fly. By the same token, the producer found the scheme a source of stability, ensuring a steady flow of films to exhibitors and a steady flow of production financing. Later, the system was abused, whereby poor films were sold on the strength of good films. The owners of twenty-eight of the largest theatre chains across the United States (led by Thomas L. Tally and J. D. Williams) controlling over one hundred theatres, thirty of which were first-run houses, formed (on 25 April 1917) the First National Exhibitors' Circuit expressly to counter this controversial system of marketing. These exhibitors (many had been Paramount clients) pooled their resources so that they could produce and distribute their own films, supplementing this supply with films made by independent producers. First National prospered under the management of Williams, signing such directors as D. W. Griffith, Louis B. Mayer, and Joseph Schenck, and "stars" such as Charlie Chaplin, Mary Pickford, Lillian Gish, and the Talmadge sisters, awarding them enormous salaries.

Thanks in large part to his First National connection, Schuberg became, in under two decades, the leading theatre chain operator in western Canada. Schuberg and Burrows owned and operated a sizable number of theatres in Manitoba, including three first-run theatres in Winnipeg, and controlled eleven theatres in British Columbia, including two first-run theatres in Vancouver and two first-run theatres in Victoria. However, in June 1919, Schuberg sold his exhibition and distribution interests to the Allen organization for close to $1 million (see chapter 5). He had suffered financial losses at the box office, thanks to the closure of the theatres during the influenza epidemic of 1918 and to the Winnipeg General Strike, which affected unionized projectionists and musicians during the spring of 1919. Schuberg was also concerned about the labour unrest that was sweeping across Canada. He took up ranching in the state of Washington, but two years later he was back in the exhibition business, running the Strand Theatre in Vancouver. In 1924, he sold his theatre interests to Famous Players, agreeing to stay out of the moving picture business for ten years. He tried ranching again, but movie exhibition was in his blood and he returned to Winnipeg, where he ran the Province and the Bijou for a number of years.[95]

Travelling exhibitors such as Tally and Schuberg took moving pictures to audiences, experimenting with such venues as the black-top tent, and penny-arcade owners, who had earned a good living with their peepshow cabinets (among other amusements), tried converting the back section of their parlours into small auditoriums, equipping this space with chairs, a screen, and a projector. Interestingly, Tally charged patrons ten cents admission, less than the admission vaudeville operators charged, and to reassure those people who avoided "darkened, partitioned" public spaces and who doubted that a real movie show would be offered at such a low price, he cut a hole in the partition so that they could see that his offer was genuine. The manoeuvre worked and news of the scheme spread quickly.

DEMAND GROWS: THE ADVENT OF FILM EXCHANGES

As we have seen, despite a mixed response to initial demonstrations of the Vitascope, rapid improvements in exhibition practices spurred a steadily growing demand for motion pictures. As Lewis Jacobs writes, entrepreneurs, seeing opportunities for getting rich quickly by exploiting the novelty, leapt into the growing trade; however, as Tino Balio explains, "distribution" was the major factor inhibiting the development of the business.[96] Despite the growing popularity of motion pictures, they were not readily available before 1903. Companies such as Biograph, Edison, Lumière, Lubin, Selig, and Vitagraph focused on providing vaudeville operators a complete motion picture service — they supplied projectors, operators, and (their own) motion pictures. Initially, only Raff and Gammon sold films on the open market, but they concentrated on selling territorial rights, not motion pictures. Exhibitors obtained prints from producers, paying about $50 for a title, which they exhibited until the prints fell apart. This mode of distributing films did little to encourage the expansion of the industry. Exhibitors found a temporary solution to the problem in trading films with other exhibitors. Conditions changed in 1903 when Harry J. Miles and Herbert Miles organized the first film exchange in San Francisco. Their organization served as a broker between producers and exhibitors, buying prints from the former and leasing them to the latter for 25 percent of the purchase price. Film exchanges thus fuelled the rise of the narrative film and the nickelodeon boom.[97]

By 1907, between 125 and 150 exchanges located in major metropolitan centres served much of North America. Thanks to film exchanges, exhibitors cut their costs, enabling them to change their programs frequently — so as to encourage the moviegoing habit and thus create audiences for their product. Operators of exchanges liked this method because they could rent films long after they had recovered their purchase costs. The method benefited producers least. Eventually, producers discovered that exhibitors were willing to pay more for new releases because new subjects had a greater drawing power. They charged exchanges more for new releases — a cost distributors passed on to theatre operators.

Throughout this turbulent period, the major influences shaping the emergence of film exhibition in Canada were already moving from south to north and were already revealing the overwhelming importance of economies of scale. Moreover, prairie Canada's rapidly growing cities, Winnipeg and Calgary especially, were important exhibition sites during the early stages of this evolving narrative. In the chapters that follow, we consider the business strategies that the Allen family — based in Calgary from 1910 and in Toronto from 1915 — employed in establishing and maintaining a made-in-Canada, coast-to-coast chain of film exchanges and movie theatres.

3

MOVIE EXHIBITION DURING THE NICKELODEON ERA, 1905 TO 1913

The increased output of production companies, sparked by the increasing popularity of narrative films, along with the expansion of the exchange system of distribution, quickened the development of the motion picture business. As the demand for movies intensified, activities evolved into three distinct industries: production, distribution, and exhibition.[1] Initially, exhibition drove the enterprise.

Two entertainment entrepreneurs, Harry Davis and John P. Harris, established one of the first permanent (that is, non-travelling) motion picture theatres when they converted an empty building at 433–35 Smithfield Street, Pittsburgh, into a venue devoted solely to the exhibition of movies. This meant mounting a linen sheet at one end of the space and installing a motion picture projector at the other, arranging ninety-six discarded opera chairs in rows facing the screen, and adding fittings, also from an opera house. Davis and Harris marked the opening of their storefront theatre on 15 June 1905 with a screening of *The Great Train Robbery* (1903).[2] They called their theatre the "Nickelodeon." (The Greek word *odeon* means "theatre," and "nickel" indicated the price of admission.) The business flourished, and within two weeks they were running shows of fifteen minutes continuously from early morning until late at night, generating a profit of nearly $1,000 a week. A correspondent for the *Moving Picture World* explained that Davis, who served as the manager, knew how to cater to the public and how to treat (and retain) employees: he renovated the building, installing a new front at a cost of $7,000, instituted daily matinees, and hired pianist Harry Carroll to provide a musical accompaniment.[3] Davis recognized the commercial possibilities in screening movies and within two years was operating theatres in a number of metropolitan centres.

News of the "Pittsburgh experiment" spread rapidly, and from 1905 to 1913 entrepreneurs in major urban centres across North America sought out empty buildings, preferably located in the central business district, such as banks, cigar stores, pawn shops, and restaurants, with a view to converting these commercial spaces into storefront theatres.[4] Commentators have suggested that, by the end of 1906, three thousand storefront theatres were in operation in the United States, and that, by the end of 1910, when the craze reached its peak, ten thousand makeshift moving picture theatres were in operation, attracting twenty-six million Americans every week, just under 20 percent of the national population, and generating $91 million annually.[5] The proliferation of storefront theatres was one aspect of the expansion of cheaply priced public entertainment generally, including the rise of "ten cent" vaudeville, inaugurated by, for example, Sullivan and Considine, thanks to the economic prosperity that defined the period from 1897 to 1907.[6] Gradually, this prosperity filtered down to the working class, as did an increase in leisure time; between 1850 and 1900, the average work week for non-agricultural industries in the United States declined an average of 3.17 percent for each decade; between 1890 and 1910, the average non-agricultural work week declined from 57.1 to 50.3 hours, a decrease of 10.01 percent.[7] By 1909, immigrants from southern and eastern Europe constituted one-third of the labour force of the principal industries of the United States. In 1911, the Russell Sage Foundation released a report indicating that, in New York City, blue-collar workers made up 2 percent of the audiences of live (dramatic) productions and 75 percent of moving picture audiences at moving picture shows.[8] According to Roy Rosenzweig, the people who flocked to the early nickelodeons simply transferred their allegiances from existing cheap entertainment, such as amusement parks and dime museums; after all, gallery seats at a theatre sold for twenty-five cents, whereas all seats at the nickelodeon sold for five cents.[9]

Looking to profit from this trend, entrepreneurs hired architects and builders to prepare the facilities they had rented. According to the prevailing wisdom, the key to success lay in attracting middle-class customers, who patronized vaudeville houses and legitimate theatres, and to this end exhibitors refurbished their venues, trying to meet the public's demand for comfort and safety and for technical sophistication (in presentation).[10] As Charlotte Herzog points out, entrepreneurs designed and decorated the exterior of their buildings so that they attracted attention — and inspired confidence in the product for sale.[11] To begin with, the builders removed the glass front and the framing for the door and the window and pushed the entrance back from the sidewalk about six feet, creating a recessed exterior vestibule, where they installed a box office or ticket seller's booth and, on either side of this structure, entrance and exit doors. The recessed vestibule — combining the open front of the penny arcade and the enclosed front of the vaudeville theatre — offered customers shelter in inclement weather. They covered the façade with pressed tin, painted it in pastel colours, and installed a version of the triumphal arch or the "Coney Island front," which gave the building a monumental presence. In addition, large letters mounted above the entrance or electric lights arranged in some decorative scheme announced the name of the movie theatre. Some gave their venues names such as "Dreamland," "Starland," or "Wonderland" to suggest that the entertainment was magical or fantastic or mysterious; others gave their venues such names as "Monarch," "Palace," or "Rex" to suggest that the entertainment was refined.[12] Colourful posters mounted in glass cases in the vestibule announced up-and-coming attractions.

By contrast, exhibitors turned the interior, which was typically long and narrow (perhaps 80 feet by 25 feet), into a simple auditorium, not much more than a screening room. They decorated the foyer with items such as glass mirrors, artistically framed lithographs, and potted plants.[13] A linen bedsheet, mounted on the wall at the front, served as a makeshift screen. The "screen" was often enclosed in an elaborate frame and covered by a curtain. On each side of the screen, fans were installed to provide ventilation, although this was often inadequate: buildings could be excessively warm in the summer (as well as very cold in the winter). By way of seating, exhibitors arranged straight-backed kitchen chairs or wooden benches in straight rows facing the screen, with an aisle in the middle. In this period, most American entrepreneurs installed no more than 299 seats because, according to civic regulations, operators of facilities for three hundred or more had to obtain an amusement license, which could easily cost $500 per year.[14] A small "projection booth," often no more than 5 feet square, was was set up near the entranceway and was surrounded by fire-resistant material, usually tin. This space had to accommodate the equipment, which generally consisted of two projectors (one might break down), one stereopticon, and possibly two coloured spotlights, along with its operators. The control panel, from which the manager signalled the operator and rang for the singer, was usually located near the ticket seller's booth. Between the screen and the first row of chairs, enough space was left for a piano or a small ensemble to provide musical accompaniment. Starting in 1912, exhibitors began to install indirect or shaded lighting to banish the gloom of the interior.[15]

The staff running these establishments generally included the manager, two projectionists, one of whom operated the lantern slide projector, a cashier (usually a young woman), a door keeper, a pianist, a singer, a caretaker, and a barker. In due course, the barker, who targeted passersby, beckoning them to buy a ticket, was replaced by a gramophone. Managers considered a variety of factors when planning programs, including the number and kinds of films to be screened and the total length of the films.[16] Taking their cue from vaudeville managers, they arranged their programs in a modular fashion, the better to manipulate the expectations of the audience, featuring announcement slides, followed by the first film and then an illustrated song, then the second film and a second song, and finally the third film, after which came a series of illustrated advertisements. Initially, a singer started the song and the audience sang the chorus. A pianist provided an appropriate musical accompaniment, drowning out the noise of the projector, and a lecturer identified the people and the places in the films screened. Illustrated songs (deriving from the dime museum and the vaudeville theatre) were quite popular, especially when they told a story and/or related to one of the films screened. Programs were initially quite short — about fifteen minutes in length in 1907 — but ran to about sixty minutes by 1911.

Figure 11. A typical nickelodeon: Calgary's Bijou Theatre, ca. 1913. Glenbow Archives NA-1469-11.

Figure 12. Interior of Edmonton's Bijou Theatre, 1912. Glenbow Archives NC-6-21.

Beginning in 1907, innovative managers added vaudeville to their programs, compensating for the proliferation of nickelodeons in major urban centres and the paucity of new films, with a view to attracting middle-class patrons and extending their programs without adding more films. As we will see, sustaining this new mode of movie exhibition (called "small-time" vaudeville) demanded a new set of business strategies. Adding vaudeville to programs resulted in increased operating costs, and running fewer but longer programs meant a reduction in audience turnover and revenue generated. With costs increasing and revenue declining, many operators moved to larger buildings, but this meant increasing ticket prices. Soon, badly managed and badly located theatres were forced out of business.[17] From 1907 onwards, entrepreneurs found running storefront theatres uneconomical and by 1910 were starting to erect purpose-built, strategically located theatres that accommodated between 500 and 1,000 customers.[18]

THE FIRST PICTURE PALACE

Harry Marvin launched the picture palace era (see chapter 5) when, in 1913, he built the Regent Theatre, an opulent, five-storey, 1,800-seat facility at the corner of 116th Street and Seventh Avenue in New York City. Henry Marvin believed that moving pictures warranted "high-class" treatment, meaning that they should be screened in a magnificent environment. He hired Thomas W. Lamb, an up-and-coming theatre architect, to design the luxurious venue, widely regarded as the first deluxe theatre built expressly for screening moving pictures.[19] Lamb gave the exterior an Italian Renaissance treatment. The façade, clad in white terracotta tiles, with green accent, featured two loggia at the corners of the upper level and an ornamented arched entrance on the ground level, flanked by an arcade of storefronts reminiscent of the Palazzo del Consiglio in Verona or the Palace of the Doges in Venice. He gave the interior a Spanish-Moorish treatment, providing a colour scheme of gold, blue, and red. The lobby featured two large marble staircases (one on either side) leading to the luxurious balcony. Marvin installed a Wurlitzer Organ and hired more than a dozen musicians to provide musical accompaniment. Claude Tally, the manager, opened the doors of the Regent Theatre in February 1913, offering the public a program that included five reels of first-run films, changing the bill three times per week. Business fell off gradually, apparently because patrons were somewhat baffled by the opulence surrounding something as seemingly trivial as moving pictures.

By October 1913, Marvin had installed S. L. (Roxy) Rothafel as manager; he was making a name for himself as an impresario who could reverse the fortunes of a failing theatre. Rothafel believed that the key to success in presenting feature films in the picture palace lay in enriching the moviegoing experience, that is, giving the public much more than they expected, a view he had outlined in a series of articles he had written for *Moving Picture World*.[20] He closed the Regent to make a number of changes. First, he moved the projection booth from the balcony to the rear of the orchestra floor, correcting the distortion produced by projecting movies from a great angle. As well, he modified the interior in subtle ways, framing the stage with an ornate stage set, installing a velvet curtain (which closed after screenings) and new stage lighting, and fitting the stage with an electric fountain, illuminated by a variety of coloured lights, and potted plants. He installed rose-tinted light bulbs, so as to illuminate the auditorium during shows. Importantly, he modified the prevailing practice of providing musical accompaniment, with a view to "interpreting" the action taking place on the screen. Finally, he hired a staff of young people — from cashiers to ushers — who were able to project the esprit de corps of the organization, training them with great care, dressing them smartly, and holding frequent "pep" talks so that they provided the courtesy and the service demanded. Rothafel reopened the Regent Theatre on 8 November 1913 to great acclaim, offering the public a multimedia program that included a screening of *The Last Days of Pompeii* (1913), a colour-tinted and colour-toned black-and-white film, 88 minutes in length. Soon, he featured programs that were the talk of New York City, ultimately spawning imitators across the continent, including the Canadian prairie West, and thereby established a template for film exhibition.

As we show in this chapter, the vertical integration of production, distribution, and exhibition was underway during the first decade of the twentieth century, and increasingly movie theatre chains such as the one established by the Allens controlled much of exhibition, hiring professional managers and well-disciplined staff who (following Rothafel's example) imposed order and discipline on their theatres, turning moviegoing into a predictable, disciplined experience.[21]

ALLEN THEATRE ENTERPRISES

The Allen family introduced the deluxe movie theatre to communities across Canada, and in under fifteen years created a large movie theatre chain, with plans to expand into the United States, Great Britain, and Russia. In the process, the Allens initiated millions of Canadians into the moviegoing habit and provided impresarios in the industry with important lessons in the management of a theatre chain.[22] They championed the design of structures built expressly for screening movies, emphasizing comfort and safety. They built an empire in a short period of time — a story that has been described as one of vision, aggressiveness, and concentration.[23] It begins with Bernard (Barney) Allen and his wife, Goldie Allen, Russian-born Jews who, in the early 1880s, settled

Figure 13. Publicity for Calgary affiliates of Allen Theatre Enterprises. From The City of Calgary Yearbook *(Calgary: Albertan Job Press, 1919), 147. Glenbow Archives* NA-7891-53.

in Bradford, McKean County, a major industrial region of northwestern Pennsylvania.[24] Here, Barney set himself up as a jeweller, and with his wife raised a family of four boys, Jule, Jay J., Herbert, and Sol, all of whom joined the family movie business when they grew up.[25]

The Allens prospered, and eventually Jule (b. 1888) and Jay (b. 1890) developed an interest in business.[26] Jule left high school at seventeen, and moved to Charleston, West Virginia, where he worked as a shoe salesman; Jay left high school and moved to Rochester, where he worked as a clothing salesman. Jay probably stayed with his uncle, H. J. (Harry) Allen, and his family. Later, Jule and Jay worked as managers of general stores for a company that operated in the mining communities of West Virginia. However, they found life in this region difficult and returned to Bradford with a view to rethinking their prospects with their father.[27]

In September 1906, Barney and his sons held a meeting to consider the line of business the latter should take up. Inspired by the entrepreneurs who were opening up storefront theatres in the area, Jule and Jay said that they could make a good living as movie exhibitors, a new kind of profession requiring little technical training and a relatively small amount of capital. The experience they had gained as merchants, in terms of developing an insight into public taste (and sensitivity to the aspirations of other immigrant and working-class families) and devising marketing strategies to respond to swings in the market, stood them in good stead.[28] A major concern was locating a town that didn't have a theatre. Jay later recalled that, on a visit to Hamilton, a booming industrial city of about sixty thousand on the western end of Lake Ontario, he had not seen a nickel theatre. Hamilton enjoyed great prosperity during the last two decades of the nineteenth century, thanks in part to the construction of the national railway.[29]

Barney advanced his sons the money they needed to open a storefront theatre, and sent Jule north to Hamilton to find a suitable location. Jule searched the city, but learned that he would have to wait at least thirty days to rent a store; as it happened, the general contractors could not keep up with the demand for commercial space. Not prepared to wait that long, he travelled twenty-five miles west to Brantford, an industrial city of fifteen thousand southwest of Hamilton, near Niagara Falls, where he located an empty store at 43 Colborne Street, one of the main thoroughfares. Soon, Barney and Jay joined Jule, and over a period of ten days they set up their first theatre, mounting a white cotton sheet in a frame at one end of the building, arranging 150 kitchen chairs to face the screen, and setting up the Edison movie projector they had brought with them at the other end, the lot representing an investment of approximately $400. They hired two showmen with experience as travelling exhibitors, Clair Hague and B. J. (Ben) Cronk, to work as manager and projectionist, respectively, and opened the Theatorium on 10 November 1906, running a program of films (each lasting about fifteen minutes) throughout the day. On the first day, two thousand people paid five cents admission to see their moving pictures.

Although Jay had assumed at the time of their venture that moving pictures had not yet invaded Canada, in fact, two entrepreneurs had already built permanent facilities in the country: L. E. (Ernest) Ouimet, who, in January 1906, had opened the Ouimetoscope, a 600-seat theatre located at the corner of St. Catherine and Montcalm streets in Montréal, and John Griffin, who had opened the Theatorium, a 150-seat nickel theatre located at 183 Yonge Street, Toronto, in March 1906.[30]

Encouraged by the success of their first project, the Allens rented another empty store, located at 21 George Street, Brantford, and transformed it into "a comparatively high-class theatre" called the Wonderland.[31] They hired Hague and Cronk to manage the theatre and to operate the projector, and then spent $2,000 decorating the front of the building, ordering specially made chairs and mounting a phonograph over the ticket-seller's booth, positioning the horn to face the street, into which they broadcast the popular melodies of the day in the hope that they would attract the attention of the townsfolk whose curiosity might have waned. Finally, they hired Harry de Kane, a Detroit-based entertainer, to sing illustrated songs at a salary of $35 per week.[32] They circulated announcements saying that the theatre would open on Saturday night, but when the chairs arrived late Saturday morning Barney suggested that they postpone the opening. Jule and Jay disagreed, and on Saturday afternoon they installed seats in one-half of the building.[33] This arrangement was not unusual at the time; many exhibitors installed a brass rail down the middle of their storefront shows, with seats on one side only, thereby forcing "latecomers" to stand.[34] This gamble paid off handsomely: people flocked to the theatre, and in a few weeks the venture was generating from $30 to $35 a day.

Now clearly in the movie business, Barney closed his jewellery store and moved the rest of the family to Brantford, making Canada their new home. They made many friends in Brantford, including the Rosenfeld family, who had recently moved there from Barrie. Jule later married into the Rosenfeld family.[35]

Figure 14. Advertisement for the Laemmle Film Service, an independent film exchange that operated in Winnipeg, Montréal, and other cities. Moving Picture World, *1 May 1909, 538.*

Soon, the Allen organization was operating a chain of nickel theatres in such cities as Kingston, Berlin (renamed Kitchener in 1916), and Chatham. When, in September 1908, a natural gas explosion destroyed the Theatorium, they opened the Gem, located at 87 Colborne Street, Brantford.[36] This facility, a combination vaudeville house and motion picture theatre (accommodating 400 people) featured a sloping floor, a "good" stage, and some fine dressing rooms.[37]

In 1909, the Allens reviewed their position as exhibitors, and after some reflection sold their theatres, deciding to take up another kind of business altogether.[38] First, they were concerned about the reports denouncing motion pictures as a negative influence on young people.[39] Second, they were worried that, in cultivating "stars" as drawing cards, Carl Laemmle was pursuing a course of action that would push salaries through the roof — and ultimately ruin the industry.[40] Third, they were anxious about the depression that had hit the region, driving attendance down sharply.

Finding no line of work more rewarding, however, the Allens returned to the moving picture business and, acting upon Jule's advice, opened a film exchange called the Canadian Film Exchange.[41] It had become obvious that they could earn more by buying and renting (popular) films than by simply exhibiting them. Soon, Jule secured the rights to distribute films made by Biograph, Pathé Frères, and Independent Motion Picture Company (IMP),[42] which was headed by Laemmle, who was on his way to becoming a major figure in the emerging motion picture industry.

Suffice it to say that Laemmle, the Jewish German-American movie pioneer, began his career as a movie exhibitor in Chicago.[43] Laemmle opened his first nickel theatre in February 1906. Sensitive to the growing concern about the effects of movies on audiences, especially children, and the unsavoury conditions under which movies were generally exhibited, he focused on family-oriented entertainment, emphasizing personal service and customer satisfaction.[44] Unhappy with existing distribution services, which he deemed chaotic and unreliable, he formed (in November 1906) the Laemmle Film Service, thereby becoming a distributor. He pursued a policy of providing "the best goods on the best terms." The service grew apace, and by 1909 was arguably the largest on the continent, with branches in Montréal and Winnipeg.

Laemmle left the Motion Picture Patents Company (MPPC) and led the campaign to abolish the Trust (see chapter 1), declaring it to be a conspiracy of monopolists devoted to stifling competition and raising prices. In advertisements placed in trade papers, he projected an image of himself as an honest, "independent" operator, a friend of the "little guy." Faced with a declining supply of quality, family-oriented films, Laemmle decided to become a producer; in June 1909, he formed the Independent Motion Picture Company of America (IMP) and opened a studio in New York City. In order to improve the quality of his movies, he attracted important stage performers and spirited talented screen actors from competitors, featuring them as IMP "stars," including Florence Lawrence and Mary Pickford in 1910 and 1911, respectively. He knew that, increasingly, moviegoers wanted to know the names of their favourite actors (by contrast, Edison maintained that the names of actors should be concealed).

About this time, the Rosenfelds helped their cousins from Smolensk, Louis Shalit and his wife, settle in Brantford. Learning that Smolensk, a city of eighty thousand people, had no movie house, Jay borrowed $3,000 from the family and travelled to Smolensk to open a movie theatre.[45] Jule recalled that this project failed because Jay could get an upstairs location only and because he could not speak the language. Jay (not yet twenty) returned to Ontario broke. He spent some time in Kingston, where he and Rae Abrahamson were married, and in Brantford, where Jule and Sara Rosenfeld were married.[46] Jule and Sara announced that they would be travelling west on their honeymoon, spending three months in Calgary and Vancouver, before returning to Brantford.

CALGARY BECOMES THE CENTRE OF CINEMA

The Allens sold their movie interests, with a view to moving not to Toronto or to Winnipeg, communities seemingly overrun with nickel theatres, but to Calgary. It is tempting to think that they were in part motivated by the report that the Winnipeg-based American consul general sent in December 1909 to *Moving Picture World* to the effect that the prairie West constituted a market waiting to be exploited by enterprising moving-picture exhibitors: "It would be profitable for the manufacturers of moving picture machines to send a representative through western Canada to exploit the field. In Winnipeg this form of amusement only became popular during the past year, and the promoters are now reaping a fine business as a result of their enterprise. The people soon acquire a fondness for this form of amusement, and willingly pay ten cents for admission. In this new country, where all forms of amusement are scarce, moving pictures are welcomed, and there is no reason why manufacturers of the United States should not control this business."[47] These words would be more prophetic than the writer could have imagined.

This time, Jay served as the Allen family's emissary. He arrived in Calgary in July 1910 and, after determining that business prospects in the West were as good as he had expected, leased office space at 134 8th Avenue East, in the heart of Calgary's business district. The press referred to the structure as a "skyscraper," a sign of the city's great prosperity.[48] Phil Kaufman managed the Canadian Film Exchange, utilizing some of the Brantford exchange films, including the IMP movies the family had purchased.[49] In addition, Jay soon secured the exclusive rights to distribute Universal films.[50]

In 1912, Laemmle's company, IMP, merged with several other firms to form the Universal Motion Picture Manufacturing Company, in order to challenge the Mutual Film Corporation for domination of the independent sector of the motion picture industry.[51] At first, Universal was a loose confederation, but via a number of battles with other executives Laemmle gained control, signalling that the company would challenge the MPPC for pre-eminence. Universal handled the films of such up-and-coming directors as George Lane Tucker, who made *Traffic in Souls* (1913), a sensational motion picture (six reels) about a young woman (played by Ethel Grandin) who was rescued by her fiancé (played by Matt Moore) from a gang of white slavers. Along the way, Laemmle discovered the box-office value of sex.[52]

In addition, the Allens formed the Theatre Amusement Company, Limited, to acquire and then to renovate theatres with potential and to build luxurious theatres in all the ideal locations.[53] In this way, they became inextricably bound up in the dynamics that shaped business opportunities in the continental entertainment industry.

AN EXPANDING ENTERTAINMENT INDUSTRY

At this time, an expanding east-west trade system shaped most business opportunities in western Canada. Tariffs levied against American manufacturers and suppliers ensured that eastern-Canadian enterprises dominated the lucrative market that had been created by the rapid development of the region.[54] By contrast, an expanding entertainment industry that originated in the United States and moved northward shaped opportunities in the entertainment business in the Canadian West. Supplying the new market with entertainment meant transporting performers, not to mention props and sets, by train from St. Paul, Minnesota, to Winnipeg, the northernmost point on the continental system. The system of tariffs just mentioned did not apply to "show business."

We can see the opportunities and the constraints created by this situation in the business strategies of two major theatrical entrepreneurs who, years before the Allens settled in the region, set out to profit from improving the cultural life of the prairie communities they settled in. In doing so, they forged important links with the American entertainment industry and forged a template for prairie movie exhibitors such as the Allens who followed them. C. P. Walker, who settled in Winnipeg, built the Walker Theatre in 1907, and, in 1912, Senator James Alexander Lougheed, who settled in Calgary, built the Sherman Grand Theatre, each venue serving as the centre for its community's social and cultural life for several decades. These entrepreneurs championed live, "highbrow" entertainment, but added movies to their programs as the new mode of entertainment increased in popularity.

C. P. Walker

Corliss Powers Walker grew up in Rochester, Minnesota, where he apprenticed as a printer.[55] With his brothers, he set up a printing firm in Fargo, North Dakota, which became the largest in the state. All the while, his passion for the theatre intensified, and by the late 1890s he had acquired a number of venues in the area. He leased the Bijou Theatre in Winnipeg in 1897 and, with his wife Harriet (Anderson) Walker (a former actress), moved to the city, planning to take advantage of the business opportunities there. The Walkers worked as a team: he managed the facility and booked the productions and she produced publicity materials and wrote reviews.[56] Walker remodelled the Bijou and reopened it as the Winnipeg Theatre (1897) in September to much acclaim.[57]

Figure 15. C. P. Walker, manager of Winnipeg's Walker Theatre, as pictured on the cover of the program for the theatre's official opening, 1907. Provincial Archives of Manitoba, WinnipegTheatresWalker, P 2184-A.

Walker realized that the key to success lay in allying himself with the Theatrical Syndicate, which had been formed in 1896 by a group of New York City theatre magnates, including Charles Frohman, A. L. Erlanger, and Marc Klaw, to standardize booking interests and to organize the theatres they controlled into a national chain.[58] The syndicate soon dominated the theatrical world, valorizing theatrical contracts and normalizing booking arrangements. Walker prospered from his connection with the syndicate and soon ran a chain of theatres located in Fargo, Grand Forks, and Grafton, North Dakota; Crookston and Fergus Falls, Minnesota; and Winnipeg, Manitoba. These theatres were situated on the Northern Pacific Railway route, Winnipeg serving as the northern terminus. He signed up New York City productions (plays and operas) soon after their runs on Broadway, and featured them on his circuit twelve months a year.

Productions got bigger and bigger, and it became obvious that the Winnipeg Theatre could not handle the large shows that touring companies wanted to stage. Many Winnipeggers campaigned to close the theatre, claiming that fire-safety violations made the place dangerous. Concern for safety in public buildings had intensified after 1903, when a fire at the Iroquois Theatre in Chicago in December of that year claimed the lives of 605 moviegoers (a tragedy we discuss in chapter 4). Walker managed to keep his license, promising to build a new theatre as soon as he could.[59]

The Walkers resolved to build the most comfortable, the most convenient, and the safest theatre possible, one that brought together "the advantaged and the disadvantaged in the common enjoyment of [high] culture."[60] Walker visited a number of newly built theatres in the northeastern United States to get ideas for the project, and commissioned Howard G. Stone, an American-born architect, to design the new facility. Ultimately, Walker and Stone took their cue from the Auditorium Building (1889), a multi-storey, multi-purpose commercial building comprising a hotel, an office building, and a theatre located at 430 South Michigan Avenue, Chicago.[61] This limestone-clad, seven-storey structure, designed by Dankmar Adler and Louis Sullivan, housed a 400-room, first-class hotel, a 4,200-seat auditorium (designed for the production of Grand Opera) at the centre of the building featuring perfect acoustics and sightlines, and a fifteen-storey office tower including a reservoir for storing water to operate the water hydraulic piston in driving the stage hydraulic machinery.[62]

The contractors erected the Walker Theatre in 1907, part of a seven-storey complex, at 364 Smith Street, in the heart of Winnipeg's commercial district.[63] However, they completed only part of the complex, because Walker failed to persuade investors to support the non-theatrical parts. Passersby could see those sections of the structure that should have been concealed, namely, the large seven-storey block housing the theatre and, set at a right angle to it, the short, narrow, four-storey projection housing the entrance and the box office.[64] The stone-clad façade featured (at street level) a trio of double doors set inside a three-storey glazed arch, elaborately carved keystones, an ornamental iron-and-glass marquee suspended over the entrance, which extended over the sidewalk, and a bracketed cornice separating the third and fourth floors.

According to reports, patrons found the interior of the building "monumental." The vaulted ceiling was ornate, the proscenium arch and the sounding board were immense, and the side boxes were elegant. The curve of the proscenium arch and the sounding board was repeated over and over again through higher and higher bands, giving the impression that the architect had designed a huge megaphone, the stage forming the small end (this design resulted in excellent acoustics).

An ocean of seats ascended to a height of seven storeys. The orchestra floor featured 594 red plush orchestra chairs. The orchestra pit, at the front of the stage, was sunk below the floor, deep enough to separate the musicians from the audience. The balcony accommodated 573 patrons (the supports were situated behind the last row of seats in the auditorium). The gallery accommodated 575 patrons.

Figure 16. View of the Auditorium Building, Chicago, from Michigan Avenue, 1890. Library of Congress, Prints and Photographs Division, Washington, DC, HABS ILL, 16-CHIG, 39-75.

Figure 17. Construction of the Walker Theatre, Winnipeg, 1907. Provincial Archives of Manitoba, WinnipegTheatresWalker, negative no. 13270.

Figure 18. Interior of the Walker Theatre, Winnipeg, 1907. Provincial Archives of Manitoba, WinnipegTheatresWalker, item 9, negative no. 13272.

The management marked the opening of the Walker Theatre on 18 February 1907 with a gala celebration that included a spectacular production — staged in English by the Henry W. Savage English Grand Opera Company — of Puccini's *Madame Butterfly*, a work that had opened in La Scala, Italy, three years before.[65] Inspired by their grand venue, the Walkers embraced the task of "bringing culture" to the city, and from 1907 to 1914 ran the Walker twelve months a year, featuring big American and British shows during the winter, under the auspices of the Theatrical Syndicate, and repertory companies during the summer.

Walker broke with the Theatrical Syndicate in 1910, however, and allied himself with the Shubert brothers, three Syracuse-based theatre magnates who, with John Cort, a Seattle-based theatre owner, had recently formed the Independent National Theatre Owners' Association, which included many former syndicate theatre owners. The Shubert brothers had achieved great success as, among other things, producers of operettas, introducing many stars to the public. For example, they persuaded Sarah Bernhardt to perform in their theatres across the United States. In this way, Walker allied himself with operators of other regional chains in the northwest and the southwest United States, becoming a key figure in the North American theatre business.[66] Soon, he had a monopoly over booking and theatre management in the region.[67] Tours would start in Winnipeg and visit Regina, Saskatoon, Calgary, Vancouver, and Victoria.

Gradually, Walker modified his business strategies and programming policies, responding to the shifting dynamics of the entertainment business. Increasingly, vaudeville and motion pictures satisfied the entertainment needs of the new immigrant working class. While they hoped to reach a broad audience, the Walkers nevertheless concentrated primarily on serving the social and the economic elite, but this group did not grow in numbers.[68] The speculative boom peaked in 1912 and then petered out when, in August 1914, Great Britain (of which Canada was a part) declared war on Germany. Increasingly, vaudeville chains challenged the syndicate's near-monopoly on presenting highbrow entertainment, offering audiences big stars of the legitimate stage without the support of the companies they normally played in. As the popularity of movies increased, Walker screened, dating from 16 October 1909, more and more films he thought would attract an audience.[69]

Figure 19. Advertisement for a screening of D. W. Griffith's Intolerance *(1916) at the Walker Theatre.* Manitoba Free Press, *17 April 1917, 12.*

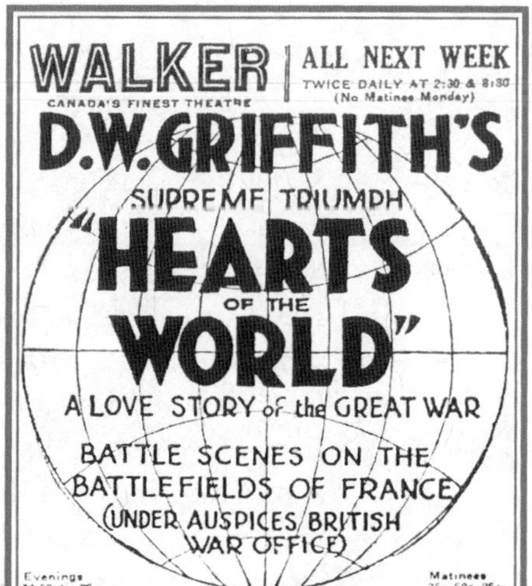

Figure 20. Advertisement for a screening of D. W. Griffith's Hearts of the World *(1918) at the Walker Theatre.* Manitoba Free Press, *4 December 1918, 9.*

James Lougheed

Figure 21. Senator James Alexander Lougheed, builder of Calgary's Sherman Grand Theatre, ca. 1911. Glenbow Archives NA-3918-14.

Senator James Lougheed grew up in Cabbagetown, a district in the east end of Toronto.[70] He studied law at Osgoode Hall, becoming a solicitor in 1881, and, inspired by the "National Policy" of Sir John A. Macdonald's Conservative government, decided to exploit the business opportunities that were opening up in the West.

Lougheed travelled west in 1882, stopping at Winnipeg and then at Medicine Hat, to undertake legal work. He secured employment as the Fort Calgary–based solicitor for the CPR, and in August 1883 travelled to the hamlet, reaching the new community days before the first train arrived. He cemented his position as an elite member of the community by becoming an astute businessman (he made a fortune by speculating in real estate),[71] and by marrying Belle Hardisty, the daughter of William Hardisty, a Hudson's Bay Company chief factor. The quintessential "booster," Lougheed supported western interests, believing that Calgary would become a major metropolitan centre.

Lougheed's legal practice, not to mention his business ventures, prospered, and by 1889 reporters noted that his net worth was $70,000. Sir John A. Macdonald rewarded his unquestioning support of the Conservative Party in 1889 by appointing him to the Senate, at the age of only thirty-five. Lougheed served as leader of the Conservatives in the Senate from 1906 to 1931, and to replace himself in the courtroom the senator formed a partnership with R. B. Bennett. By 1910, the firm of Lougheed and Bennett represented such major firms as the CPR, the Bank of Montreal, the Bank of Nova Scotia, the HBC, Massey-Harris, and Manufacturers Life Insurance.

Lougheed erected a number of commercial buildings in Calgary, including two small vaudeville houses in the central business district, which he both built and operated.[72] The Lyric Theatre, which opened in 1904, featured performers on the Seattle-based Sullivan and Considine vaudeville circuit,[73] and the Empire Theatre, built in 1908, featured performers on the Chicago-based Orpheum circuit. In 1905, he leased the Lyric to W. B. (Bill) Sherman, a flamboyant, Ohio-born theatre impresario who had worked with a variety of circuses and a small vaudeville company as an actor-manager.[74]

Late in 1910 or early in 1911, Lougheed decided to build a first-rate legitimate theatre, which he called the Sherman Grand, named after the first manager of the facility. Lougheed, like many of his fellow boosters, believed that, with a bit of a nudge, Calgary would become the Chicago of the north. Like C. P. Walker, he looked to the tall, multi-use buildings that were being built in Chicago, in particular the Auditorium Building, as models for his project.[75] The senator argued that a tall, multi-use, steel-and-concrete commercial structure containing a theatre would enhance the cultural life of Calgary enormously — while enabling him to diversify his sources of income and diminish his risk.[76]

Lougheed hired L. R. (Len) Wardrop, a Utah-based theatre architect, to build the structure at the corner of 1st Street and 6th Avenue West.[77] Wardrop's plan called for an L-shaped multi-purpose complex comprising retail stores on the ground floor, along the street, and along the avenue, offices on the second, third, and fourth floors, and luxury apartments on the fifth and sixth floors, that enclosed (on the south side) a shoebox-shaped theatre, the two structures sharing a wall. Wardrop located the entrance to the theatre at 608 1st Street West, requiring patrons to pass through a lobby or a long hallway which actually ran through the Lougheed Building.

By early 1912, the builders completed the theatre and most of the Lougheed Building. By any measure, the design and ornamentation of the building, inside and out, were impressive.[78] The brick-and-sandstone façade featured five rows of eight windows on the street side and five rows of thirteen windows on the avenue side; three brick balustrades on the street side and five brick balustrades on the avenue side separated the windows into sections; every window (they were the same size) featured a sandstone sill

Figure 22. Flamboyant Calgary theatre impresario Bill Sherman and his wife, ca. 1915. Glenbow Archives NA-460-7.

Figure 23. The Lougheed Building, looking southeast, featuring the slender sign for the Sherman Grand Theatre, 1912. Glenbow Archives NA-4385-3.

Figure 24. The lobby of the Sherman Grand Theatre, September 1912. Glenbow Archives NA-1469-30.

and lintel. A concrete cornice, trimmed with tin, extended beyond the building slightly, and a sign about two storeys high, hanging above the entrance, identified the facility lodged within, the word "SHERMAN" running vertically and the word "GRAND" running horizontally.

Patrons made their way to the theatre through a long hallway, which featured a tiled floor and marble wainscotting. From the lobby, patrons walked up two gently inclined ramps (these doubled back twice) to the balcony, which featured twelve loges (each with a seating capacity of six). Altogether, the balcony accommodated 685 theatregoers.

Inside the auditorium, patrons admired the domed ceiling, which featured elaborate plaster work and a massive chandelier. Two wide aisles separated the 685 opera chairs — upholstered in green leather and offering theatregoers plenty of legroom and an unobstructed view of the stage — into three sections.

Sherman organized a gala celebration to mark the opening of the theatre on 5 February 1912. Commentators writing for the *Calgary Albertan* and the *Calgary News-Telegram* described the facility as "the finest and most modern theatre in the Dominion," exceeding the Walker Theatre in all important dimensions, and the opening as "the most brilliant event ever held in this city."[79] Ticket prices ranged from $1 to $5, about 50 percent higher than ticket prices in Toronto. The highlight of the evening was the production of Jerome K. Jerome's allegorical play *The Passing of the Third Floor Back* (1911), which had run for three hundred performances in London and over two hundred performances in New York City. The play tells the story of a Christlike figure (played by Johnston Forbes-Robertson) who checks into a Bloomsbury rooming house and changes the lives of the people living there.

Sherman offered Calgarians a spectacular first season, which included Cecil B. DeMille's mammoth production of *Stampede*, and Sophie Tucker and Fred and Adele Astaire in the vaudeville show called *California*.[80] The solution to the booking problem lay in contracting (in May 1912) with C. P. Walker of Winnipeg and John Cort of Seattle to form a circuit, enabling travelling stock companies to play at approximately two hundred playhouses across western Canada and the Pacific Northwest.[81] Sherman was determined to offer Calgarians a wide variety of sophisticated amusements. From Monday to Wednesday, the Sherman Grand featured American and British performers, who appeared in dance, drama, and music productions, and from Thursday to Saturday, variety theatre performers signed with the Orpheum Vaudeville circuit.[82] Martin Beck, the managing director of the circuit, visited Calgary in October 1912, with a view to judging the facilities at the Sherman Grand. Fred and Adele Astaire appeared again in October 1912 and Lillie Langtry appeared in December 1912.[83]

Figure 25. Advertisement for a screening of Edison's "Talking Motion Pictures" at the Sherman Grand Theatre, Calgary, sponsored by Orpheum Shows. Calgary Herald, *26 April 1913, 10.*

Sherman inaugurated the policy of exhibiting films on 24 April 1913, featuring Thomas A. Edison's latest invention, the Kinetophone.[84] This apparatus, provided by the Orpheum circuit, offered the audience a crude version of "talking pictures" (this meant synchronizing a film with a phonograph record). Thanks to Walker, and later thanks to Jeff Lydiatt, who visited movie distributors in New York City, the Sherman Grand featured a program of "high-class" motion pictures (some were hand-painted) with suitable music and stage settings, a strategy that enabled the latter to keep the Grand running continuously.[85]

THE ALLENS' BUSINESS STRATEGY

For about a decade, many exhibitors regarded motion pictures as a passing fad, and thus (as the Allens put it) took people's money and ran.[86] From the outset, though, the Allens organized their business activities as a "serious" enterprise, determined to give their customers value for their money, thereby building up a satisfied clientele.[87] As Barney Allen put it, "Anticipate the wants of the public and give them more than they expect."[88]

In developing their movie exhibition and distribution enterprise, the Allens combined show-business flair with sound business sense. Barney, even-tempered and unassuming, served as president; Jay J., boisterous and adventurous, served as vice-president, revelling in planning big projects; and Jule, quiet and cautious, served as secretary-treasurer, relishing the job of taking care of the details; this included visiting every new theatre whenever possible. According to industry analysts, a spirit of co-operation permeated every aspect of the brothers' work, and they made every decision jointly.[89]

The Allens recruited talented people and rewarded them for performing well.[90] Harry Allen, Max Allen (Harry's son), and Ben Cronk joined the organization in 1911. A commercial high school graduate and a former employee of Eastman Kodak (Rochester), Harry helped Jule manage the family's film distribution company, the Canadian Film Exchange. Harry later served as Manager of the Western Division of Allen Theatres Limited, taking charge of building theatres in all key centres on the prairies. Max managed the Gem, the Monarch, and the Allen in Edmonton.[91] Ben Cronk, the Allens' Brantford projectionist, managed the Monarch, the Rex, and the Allen theatres in Calgary. Louis Rosenfeld, Jule's brother-in-law, joined the organization in 1910, working as an usher at the Gem Theatre in Brantford. Herbert Allen also joined the organization at this time, working as a shipper in the film service.

Like many families of the period who owned and operated businesses, the Allens resolved to control every aspect of their operation, and so turned their profits back into the business and, importantly, financed parts of projects by floating shares locally as popular investments, thereby raising from as little as $40,000 at first to as much as $260,000 later on to build a new facility or to renovate an existing one.[92] However, investment banking practices would soon change, and they would find it difficult to keep up with rivals who were supported by international capitalists.

During the decade before World War I, the forces of standardization and centralization, pursued in the interest of increased productivity and efficiency, transformed manufacturing and retailing across North America. These forces redefined the notion of "management." The work of Frederick W. Taylor, a mechanical engineer, who conducted time-and-motion studies at the Bethlehem Steel plant in 1898, was central to this movement. In *Principles of Scientific Management* (1911), based on these studies, Taylor claimed that managers' central task was to organize work into patterns better suited to the new machines and in the process gain better control over the workplace and the workers.[93]

Henry Ford utilized Taylor's principles to great effect in perfecting the assembly line, a version of which had been used by Chicago packers in dressing beef. Managing directors of manufacturing and retailing organizations, such as Woolworths, employed these principles to reduce expenses and maximize profits. They learned that running a national business from a "rational" perspective meant setting up a central office from which to maintain records and to control inventory for all the outlets, standardizing products and functions, training employees in tasks that advanced the goals set for the departments in which they worked, increasing the volume of business, and speeding up the delivery of service. In short, they learned that they could keep their costs low by taking advantage of economies of scale, spreading fixed costs over more and more operations, and by buying in bulk, at lower-than-normal unit prices.

Movie exhibitors, like their colleagues in other industries, took the next step in expanding their businesses — exploiting the national market — when they located their head offices in major metropolitan areas and employed college-trained staff to run individual theatres according to directives.[94] "Rationalizing" their operations included, for example, renting films for all their theatres. The Allens realized the merits of this approach, and during the years they were located in Calgary, they incorporated elements of it into their plan for establishing a made-in-Canada chain of movie theatres; however, they also realized the importance of maintaining local connections. They developed a business strategy that combined key principles of scientific management with an emphasis on the role Allen Theatre Enterprises played in "building" the communities in which they operated.[95] Their strategy can be summarized as follows:

(1) *Locate movie theatres strategically.* The Allens deemed it crucial to build theatres in ideal locations, preferably in an urban community's central business district, where, thanks to public transportation, workers, shoppers, and amusement-seekers congregated in great numbers. According to conventional thinking, people who shopped downtown were inclined to spend time relaxing in movie theatres and restaurants. The Allens courted middle-class patrons, especially women, many of whom had jobs outside the home. They planned to offer these women and the many who shopped in the area with their children a secure environment in which to relax.

(2) *Build attractive movie theatres.* The Allens concentrated on developing the deluxe movie theatre, thereby persuading the public generally that the new medium of film should be taken seriously.[96] Believing that the show began at the sidewalk, the Allens hired architects who regarded the movie theatre itself as a "production."[97] Combining architectural features of palaces, opera houses, and temples of Renaissance Italy and eighteenth-century France, these architects built theatres that exuded character inside and out. The thinking was that, by virtue of their design and decoration, these buildings would encourage passersby to visit the box office. Accordingly, they gave Allen theatres eye-catching façades

that incorporated such classical forms as the triumphal arch, the Palladian window, the Corinthian column, and the pediment, to which they added an octagonal ticket office, a marquee that extended to the sidewalk, and a vertical sign (outlined in light bulbs) that identified the facility.

(3) *Offer the public painstaking service.* The Allens believed that the key to building a satisfied clientele lay in providing "a painstaking and courteous service."[98] After all, what they as entertainment entrepreneurs had to offer the public as a corporate "product" was service. Developing efficiency in all aspects of theatre operation meant, among other things, hiring and training employees who would treat patrons as if they were royalty, and establishing a variety of basic services, over and above luxurious restrooms for men and women, for example, equipping theatres with telephones. Ultimately, ushers and usherettes, serving as ambassadors of the firm, interacted with patrons from the time they entered the facility to the time they left, attending to a variety of important tasks, such as guiding the very young and the elderly to their seats. Jule later told the press that the public must be satisfied, no matter what the trouble or the expense.[99]

(4) *Subordinate all elements to the entertainment.* The Allens promised to offer the public quality entertainment at popular prices. They sought family-oriented motion pictures of the highest quality, including the films distributed by Paramount Pictures, Artcraft Pictures (formed in 1916 to distribute the Mary Pickford Film Corporation pictures), Select pictures, and Goldwyn pictures. (Artcraft soon became a production brand name of the Famous Players–Lasky Corporation.) They installed the best pipe organs and hired the best musicians available, with a view to offering the public a rich sensory experience.[100] Allen theatres offered moviegoers a continuous program of first-run films from 11 a.m. to 11 p.m., changing programs Monday and Thursday. Attempting to cater to local audiences, the Allens featured, whenever possible, fledgling British and Canadian films.[101]

In the next section, we consider how the Allens implemented this business strategy, which enabled them to achieve great success in a short period of time. We consider how they programmed and marketed motion pictures on the one hand and how the community responded to the new form of entertainment on the other. Experience would quickly show these exhibitors that the right to the first showing of a film would ensure great earnings at the box office.[102]

BUILDING THEATRES EXCLUSIVELY FOR SCREENING MOVING PICTURES

When the Allens began, in Calgary, to create their movie theatre empire, they built on the work of other entertainment entrepreneurs. As mentioned in chapter 2, the Cosgrove Family Vaudeville Company had premiered the Vitascope in Calgary in 1897, but interest in moving pictures in the city developed gradually, intensified in large part by the managers of vaudeville houses, who, starting in 1905, added films to their programs.

Bill Sherman may well have inaugurated the process. Sherman acquired the Lyric Theatre in 1905 and reopened it as the Sherman Lyric Theatre, offering the public "high-class" entertainment at reasonable prices. His strategy for creating "Calgary's premier place of amusement" was to book first-class touring stage productions and add the latest moving pictures to his program.[103] Sherman featured a selection of moving pictures in March 1906; Sigmund Lubin's *The San Francisco Disaster* (1906) on 28 May 1906; and more of "the latest moving pictures" in July, all obtained directly from producers in New York City.

Other entrepreneurs developed a similar strategy. Early in 1906, officials at the Starland Theatre Company, a Winnipeg-based entertainment firm, decided to open a vaudeville theatre in Calgary, believing that the city — boasting a population of 14,216 — could support yet another facility.[104] The Starland Company, managed by Paul LeMarquand, made documentaries on western Canadian topics and operated a chain of theatres (at its peak, just before World War I, the firm would control a circuit of more than a dozen facilities). They hired W. B. (William) Dodd, an Ontario-born architect, to transform the commercial space in a building at the corner of 8th Avenue and

2nd Street East into the Starland Electric Theatre. The management, including J. W. McDonald, the manager, opened the Electric Theatre for business on 25 June 1906.[105] They celebrated the event with a program of "Continuous Vaudeville," featuring performers directly from New York City, including Ali Zada, "The Great Magician," the Sherrahs, who performed a "Buck and Wing Dance," the Merritt Sisters, contortionists, and a number of illustrated songs.

Apparently, McDonald found the competition stiff, for in July 1906 he told reporters that the proprietors of the Starland Electric would alter their entertainment policy, focusing on providing "clean, moral, and refined vaudeville" at "moderate" prices. His program for 5 July 1906 featured the performers mentioned above, plus a singing comedian named Harold Price, who had "won a deserved reputation for himself at the Louisiana Purchase exhibition." McDonald indicated that the Electric would also present the "Best of Moving Pictures" available.[106] Two weeks later, McDonald introduced another innovation, a daily "Ladies' Matinee," with admission prices of ten and fifteen cents, respectively.

The Sherman Lyric and the Starland Electric were not the only competitors in this business. Nine vaudeville houses in the city included moving pictures in their program during the period from 1905 to 1910, when the Allens settled in Calgary. The Starland group took over the Arcade Picture Parlor, located at 116A 8th Avenue West, increasing their presence in Calgary.[107] They renovated the facility and reopened it as the Starland Theatre on 23 November 1909, promoting it as "A Motion-Picture Theatre for Ladies and Children as well as Gentlemen." The strategy of attracting women and children indicated a desire not only to expand the audience for the entertainment product on offer, but also to "discipline" that audience; that is, advertisements suggest that women and children would feel at home in the respectable atmosphere of these venues, thereby signalling to potential customers the kind of behaviour that would be expected of them. They also promised to present the "greatest" motion pictures and the "latest" illustrated songs.

The Starland group set a high standard, programming quality events, starting with *The Lion Tamer* (1909–10), a one-reel film produced by the Selig Polyscope Company, and charging reasonable admission prices.

Figure 26. The Starland Theatre, Calgary, 1909. Glenbow Archives NA-909-1.

They organized their programming with an eye to those Calgarians who had come from Ontario or Great Britain, roughly 80 percent of the city. For example, the Starland featured a selection of horse-racing films for the period from May to July; documentaries on the Grand National, which had taken place the previous April at Aintree, Lancashire; the Ascot Races, which had taken place the previous May at Ascot, Berkshire; and the Epsom Derby, which had taken place the previous June at Epsom Downs, Surrey.[108]

Sometime in 1910, presumably before the Allens launched their exhibition and distribution businesses, the Starland group announced that they were going to build another venue in Calgary, the Empress Theatre, which opened in 1911. The Allens responded to this challenge by building the Monarch Theatre the same year. To create their theatre, the Starland group decided to transform the commercial space at the west end of the Co-Operative Block, located at 219–221 8th Avenue East, into the Empress Theatre. They hired Harry S. Burroughs and J. Bernard Richards — architects who had begun their careers as draughtsman for Dodd and operated as a partnership from 1910 to 1915 — to create an entrance and to erect a 425-seat auditorium at the back of the structure.

Burroughs and Richards gave the exterior of the brick-clad Empress a neoclassical look.[109] Four pilasters separated the red-brick façade into three bays: two glass-fronted stores and a terracotta arch dominated the first level and nine arched windows (three per bay) dominated the upper level. A decorated pediment, situated at the centre, plus two small sandstone urns, one located on each corner, crowned the structure. A sign hanging vertically above the entrance spelled out the name of the theatre in capital letters: EMPRESS.

Patrons entered the Empress via the triumphal arch, buying their tickets at the three-sided box office, located at the back of the external vestibule. A reporter for the *Calgary Herald* predicted that Calgarians would regard the Coney Island front as one of the building's most attractive features. Pressed tin covered the ceiling, and pilasters divided the side walls into large panels, decorated in gilt and green. The floor of the auditorium was "raked," ensuring that all patrons had a good view of the stage and the screen.

Figure 27. The Wright Block, featuring, on the right, the Empress Theatre, Calgary, ca. 1916. Glenbow Archives NA-3795-2.

Figure 28. Interior of the Empress Theatre, Calgary, ca. 1920. Glenbow Archives NA-5416-2.

Figure 29. The Elma Block, with the Monarch Theatre on the right, Calgary, 1915. Glenbow Archives NB-16-361.

Figure 30. Interior of the Monarch Theatre, Edmonton, 1917. Glenbow Archives NC-6-3119.

Not to be outdone, the Allens hired James C. Teague, the American-born, Calgary-based architect, to transform commercial space at 134 8th Avenue East into the Monarch Theatre, a facility that accommodated 480 patrons, complete with sandstone arch.[110] Teague gave the façade a recessed vestibule, which featured a five-sided ticket booth, with glass on three sides, and two sets of doors, each fitted with a large oval window. Electric light bulbs adorned the underside of the arch. Two classical figures in relief, one on each side, and lettering in relief on the sign-band (located just below the windows on the second level) spelling out MONARCH THEATRE dominated the façade.[111]

The Allens advertised the facility as the "Theatre Beautiful," emphasizing the effort they had made to appeal to patrons' demand for comfort and safety: several advertisements carried the phrase "We guarantee to please." Teague fitted the auditorium with large, upholstered chairs in green leather, arranging them in two sections, providing one aisle for patrons to enter and leave. The projection room — lined with asbestos and metal — was equipped with two projectors, ensuring that patrons did not have to wait between movies.

The Allens organized a gala celebration to mark the official opening of the Monarch on 21 January 1911. The event, which included speeches, music making, and motion pictures, served as the facility's "grand entrance," anticipating the flamboyant premieres of a later era, starting with the gala opening in 1922 of Sid Grauman's Egyptian Theatre in Hollywood and the first screening of *Robin Hood* (1922), starring Douglas Fairbanks. These events would become important rituals in the movie business, valued for the promotional opportunities they afforded and for their power to highlight the contribution movie theatres made to the community. A writer for the *Calgary News-Telegram* remarked on 21 January 1911 that patrons "had nothing but praise" for the beautiful building and the quality movies offered. Norman J. Holmes, formerly a vocalist at a leading motion picture theatre in New York City, sang the illustrated songs that pleased audiences.

Business prospered. Reporters remarked during the first months of the theatre's operation that the "cosy" theatre had become a "popular" place indeed, thanks to the high-quality moving pictures and illustrated songs offered by the Allens. Operating from 11 a.m. to 11 p.m., the Monarch featured Reliance and IMP films, supplied by the Canadian Film

Exchange, and music, provided by a three-piece orchestra, all for an admission ranging from ten cents for adults to five cents for children.

Maverick journalist and newspaper publisher R. C. (Bob) Edwards offered a contrasting perspective on the Monarch. In the 16 September 1911 issue of the *Eye Opener* newspaper, Edwards turned his attention to the dangers posed by the new form of entertainment, claiming that "an awful responsibility" rested on the shoulders of the city officials who licensed this "death trap."[112] He reminded readers of the disaster that had occurred the previous month when, in a moving picture show in Canonsburg, Pennsylvania, the film exploded, killing twenty-six people and injuring over sixty, mostly women and children who were rushing to the doors. After all, he pointed out, the building is long and narrow, extending 125 feet from the street to the alley, with only one aisle running down the centre. Edwards went on to say that one Sunday evening he "attended a religious service in the building — the time the Baptist real estate divine was holding forth — and at the close of the proceedings it took all of fifteen minutes for the congregation to get out of the building. Imagine a packed house, he added, made up of women and children, trying to get out of this place in the event of a panic." He urged city officials to take action, before an appalling number of people were "crushed, trampled on." The Allens very likely reflected on these remarks when they planned their next facility.

Meanwhile, the Starland group celebrated the opening of the Empress Theatre on 4 March 1911, offering patrons a special program of moving pictures and illustrated songs. A correspondent for the *Calgary Herald* noted on 25 February 1911 that hundreds of people were unable to obtain tickets; those who could praised the appointments, especially the plaster screen, and the performances (apparently, patrons judged the acoustics to be perfect). The opening program included a variety of moving pictures, including *The Cigarette Maker of Seville* (1910), an Edison production, with musical accompaniment. Reporters predicted that the Empress would become "one of the most popular moving picture resorts in the city."[113]

By early 1913, the Allens had established, despite the competition, the nucleus of what would become a national chain of movie theatres, including three theatres in Calgary, two in Edmonton, one in Regina, and one in Winnipeg.[114] This brought the number of seats under their control in the prairie West to 5,232. They had planned to build a deluxe, 910-seat facility in Moose Jaw, hiring James C. Teague to design the building, which would cost $100,000 to erect. As well, they had organized the Monarch Theatre Company of Moose Jaw and offered the public $40,000 in stock at $10 a share, estimating a dividend of 40 to 50 percent. Construction had started on 1 August 1913, but they abandoned the project a few months later; they completed the theatre in 1916.

Figure 31. The Allen Theatre, Calgary, ca. 1913. Glenbow Archives NA-1469-10.

Figure 32. Postcard showing the auditorium of the Allen Theatre (later the Strand), as seen from the balcony, Calgary, ca. 1930.

Given the success of the Monarch, the Allens decided to erect another facility in Calgary, namely, the Allen Theatre at 119 8th Avenue East, one of the first luxurious theatres in Canada devoted exclusively to exhibiting movies.[115] They commissioned James C. Teague to create another unique building. Commentators noted with pleasure that, in terms of financing and construction, this was a made-in-Calgary project. The Allens spent $200,000 acquiring the property at the heart of Calgary's business district and another $125,000 erecting the two-storey building, which was completed in 1913. In order to raise a portion of the capital required to erect this elegant structure, which would accommodate 840 patrons, they formed the Allen Theatre Company, offering the public $50,000 in stocks at $10 a share.

A correspondent for the *Calgary News-Telegram* for 7 November 1913 described the Allen — again, in the language of the booster — as one of the "masterpieces" of movie theatre construction on the North American continent. The façade suggested the frontispiece of a Venetian palazzo.

A highly decorated semicircular pediment, just above the central pilasters, crowned the roof, and an arrow-like sign conveying the letters THE ALLEN hung vertically from the centre of the pediment. Four onyx balusters separated the lower façade into three bays; two businesses occupied the two outer bays.

Passing through the main lobby, patrons climbed one of two marble staircases and entered the balcony, or passed through double doors and entered the auditorium. Plaster mouldings, such as rectangular borders, vases, and garlands, covered the ceiling and the walls; Axminster carpets covered the floor. Large opera seats, upholstered in red velour, formed four sections. The auditorium featured an 18-by-13-foot "bowed" screen, a pipe organ designed for use in theatres, built at a cost of US $15,000 by W. W. Kimball of Chicago, builders of the mammoth organ in the Mormon Tabernacle in Salt Lake City, and a Mason and Risch grand piano.

The colour scheme throughout the Allen Theatre — and throughout the other theatres in the Allen chain — was ivory, gold, French Grey, and old rose.

The management organized a gala evening to celebrate the opening on 15 November 1913. Dignitaries included Harry Allen, the regional manager of Allen Theatre Enterprises, local manager Carl G. Milligan (formerly the manager of the Pantages Theatre, San Francisco), and Meyer Cohen, the Allens' publicity agent. The Allen Theatre Orchestra, under the direction of John Switzer, performed a variety of compositions, including marches and waltzes. The initial program consisted of talks, one on boosterism by a local advertiser and another on the evolution of the motion picture by the Alberta censor; a short piano recital and three films: *The Dramatic Story of the Vote* (1913), telling (with organ accompaniment) the story of the suffragette movement in Great Britain; a Universal newsreel (with orchestra accompaniment) describing the events of the week; *His Hour of Triumph* (1913), a Universal picture (directed by George Lane Tucker and starring William E. Shay, Jane Gail, and William Welsh) telling the story about the difficulties of producing a play; and a comedy.

Fortunately, for all exhibitors, most patrons of the period were more enamoured with the moviegoing experience than Bob Edwards was. It had become clear to all that movies were not only here to stay but were also becoming the most popular form of entertainment. It was also becoming clear that lavish theatres built purposely to screen films were fast becoming a ubiquitous feature of cities across North America.

In little more than a decade, then, the Allens had parlayed their growing knowledge of the evolving business of film exhibition into the nucleus of a national theatre chain. They attracted and retained an increasing number of patrons, exploiting the connection between film exhibition and distribution. The Allens operated, in addition to their expanding list of theatres, distribution offices in the major urban centres across the country, namely, Montréal, Toronto, Winnipeg, Regina, Saskatoon, Calgary, Edmonton, and Vancouver.[116] They realized that the key to success in the distribution and the exhibition branches of the industry lay in securing franchises from top-notch producers; thus, eventually, distribution became a major part of the Allen business. They secured in 1914 the exclusive rights to distribute Paramount movies, for years the industry leader, and changed the name of their exchange to the Famous Players Film Service.[117] They sold their Universal franchise to Carl Laemmle, believing that Adolph Zukor would soon offer them a more attractive supply of films.[118] In chapter 4, we consider the campaigns to reform and regulate urban amusements in general and movies in particular, and in chapter 5 we consider the strategies the Allens employed to establish a chain of sixty movie theatres stretching across the country, thereby dominating the market, not only in the prairie West but across Canada.

4

REFORMS AND REGULATIONS: MOVIE CENSORSHIP IN THE PRAIRIE WEST

Entrepreneurs involved in the three branches of the growing motion picture industry developed ways to maximize profiting-making opportunities by integrating and regularizing a range of business practices. As we have seen, in 1908 the Edison Manufacturing Company and the American Mutoscope and Biograph Company formed a cartel called the Motion Picture Patents Company (MPPC) in order to control the production, the distribution, and the exhibition of films, bringing order to an industry that had been characterized by fierce competition and endless litigation over patents. The trust included Essanay Film Manufacturing Company, Kalem Company, Lubin Manufacturing Company, American Pathé, Selig Polyscope Company, and Vitagraph Company of America.[1] In order to limit competition, that is, to check the operations of other (independent) companies, and to increase profits, the members of the trust bought and pooled their major patents (on cameras and projectors, for example) and drafted an exclusive agreement with the Eastman Kodak Company for the supply of new, less inflammable film. This agreement conferred on members the exclusive right to produce, distribute, and exhibit motion pictures in the United States; the trust charged rental fees and imposed specific conditions on other companies for producing, distributing, or exhibiting movies. In this way, the members of the trust hoped to reduce foreign imports, fight movie piracy, protect film copyrights, reduce the power of emerging distributors, and drive rival companies out of business.

General Film Service is the magnet that draws the crowds

WHEN you were a kid you had a magnet. Every youngster had. You marveled at the way objects of steel were attracted to it. You didn't worry much about the principle of the thing or attempt to analyze why they fairly jumped at the magnet. They did — and that was enough.

General Film Service is the magnet of the exhibiting business. It draws the crowds right in your door. The reason is easily explained; but here again you needn't worry. The continued popularity of General Film Service is dependent upon our maintaining its present high standard. And that standard will be maintained so long as motion pictures are exhibited. We put the stuff in our programs that insures the success of your show. About all you have to do is arrange for the service.

Just the other day an exhibitor in Kansas said: "We have tried out other services, but the General beats them all." His case is not unusual by any means. The staunchest friends General Film Service has to-day are exhibitors who first tried some other service, and, in some cases, several others! Why not investigate now?

We have printed a little booklet that we'd like you to have. It's a concise review of the things that stamp General Film Service as superior. The colored cover alone is worth the stamp it will cost you to get it. Mention the World when you write.

General Film Company

200 Fifth Ave., New York Distributing offices everywhere

Figure 33. Advertisement for the General Film Company, a distribution firm formed in 1910 by the Motion Picture Patents Company. Moving Picture World, *3 May 1913, 455.*

The MPPC imposed a number of conditions on business activities, including limiting the length of films made to one or two reels, charging royalties on exhibitors using their equipment ($2 per week), refusing to give screen credits to players, and establishing a standard price of half-a-cent per foot for film prints that were to be rented on a weekly basis.[2] In addition, the trust threatened to bring sanctions against producers who rented non-trust cameras and used non-trust stock, distributors who handled non-trust films, and exhibitors who rented non-trust projectors and screened non-trust films. In 1910, the MPPC formed the General Film Company, with a view to managing the distribution of the members' films and eliminating unlicensed independent operators. By 1911, the MPPC had constructed the first example of effective vertical integration in the film industry. Eventually, however, independent producers, distributors, and exhibitors organized themselves in response to the MPPC monopoly. Charges of antitrust violations were filed in 1912 against the MPPC by the U.S. Department of Justice, and in 1915 the MPPC was ordered to break up.

THE REFORMERS SPEAK UP

Clearly, the stakes for all players in this fast-moving enterprise were high. The motion picture business evolved into a multi-million dollar industry rather quickly, generating much opposition along the way. During the Progressive Era, from the 1890s to the 1920s, evangelists, social workers, anti-vice crusaders, and feminists in the United States and Canada urged governments to enact legislation to regulate the new enterprise. Public anxiety over the movies, which many people thought damaged the minds of young people, and movie theatres, which were located in working-class neighbourhoods, was part of a much larger anxiety over the proliferation of urban amusements generally, including cabarets, saloons, dance halls, and vaudeville houses, where men and women mingled freely; a great many activists felt that, in these "unsavoury" establishments, men forced young women into lascivious behaviour, including prostitution. As Lary May puts it, reformers focused on the ill effects of industrialization and (by extension) the mass consumption of goods and services, especially popular amusements, through the lens of the Victorian family.[3] They concluded that the dynamics of modern life threatened the family (the force that shaped society), thanks to the routine of assembly line work, which alienated the labourer from the product made; ongoing labour-management conflict; class conflict; unregulated immigration; and the proliferating urban amusements of the "lower orders." Consequently, they campaigned to bring about social, economic, and political reform via democratic means in order to restore the family. Such reforms included regulating business practices and making businesses more accountable; cleaning up corrupt municipal governments; improving working conditions, increasing wages, and reducing the work week, so that workers could be better providers; improving living conditions in slum neigbourhoods, where new immigrants settled; enforcing compulsory education and child labour laws, to keep the young off the streets and away from vice; extending the franchise to women, so that they could bring their "maternal" influence to the public sphere; and reducing the evil effects of drinking to excess. Without entirely rejecting the assumptions of big business, progressive reformers reasoned that citizens might be inspired to save the one interest everyone holds in common: by creating a state that served as a "good" parent, governments would "humanize" society; that is, the state would rescue the family by means of social welfare legislation that regulated business practices.[4]

Two of the figures involved in the campaign to "cleanse" the movies, Jane Addams and Frederic C. Howe, were associated with the Settlement Movement. In the late nineteenth century, reformers had established settlement houses, starting with Toynbee Hall (1884) in East London and the Neighborhood Guild (1886) in the Lower East Side in New York City, as a means of translating "Social Christianity" into action. This meant transforming a large building into an institution that featured living space for residents, an auditorium, a gymnasium, classrooms, and meeting halls, and mounting a variety of programs that fit the needs of the residents and the people living in the area, including adult education classes, kindergartens, recreational activities, legal aid, and employment centres. Addams founded one of the most famous of these institutions in 1889 when she and Ellen Gates Starr created Hull House, located on the west side of Chicago. Addams also published eleven books on topics related to her activities as a social worker, including *The Spirit of Youth and the City Streets* (1909), in which she reflects on the new medium of film and its impact on young people. Like other reformers, she believed that movies, as the most powerful form of communication, could have a positive influence if they were subject to a great deal of control. Interestingly, she set up a nickel theatre (seating 300), complete with an electric sign, in Hull House to test her ideas. She opened the movie theatre to the public in June 1907 with a program that ran from 6 p.m. to 11 p.m. every evening and all day on Saturday and Sunday. The plan was to operate the theatre for three months, screening literary adaptations, such as *Uncle Tom's Cabin* (an Edison film made in 1903), and travelogues. The supervisor of the project, Gertrude Howe Britton, hoped to augment the movies with short lectures about the films shown. Unfortunately, as Kathleen McCarthy points out, residents and neighbours did not find the films lively enough; one evening, only thirty-seven people attended a screening, the potential audience being siphoned off by theatres in the neighbourhood that featured such films as *The Life of an American Cowboy* (1906). Addams closed the theatre, admitting that she was not prepared to screen the films people wanted to see, and shifted her efforts to helping the Juvenile Protective Association.[5]

Howe had trained as a lawyer, but made his mark as a social worker, a municipal reformer, and an administrator. In 1894, he joined the Cleveland law firm of Harry Garfield and James R. Garfield, sons of the former American president, where he specialized in tax questions and also worked at a settlement house in New York City, justifying his training and developing a sense of "responsibility to the world." During this period he published his manual of reform; in *The City: The Hope of Democracy* (1905), he outlines a vision for economic, cultural, and moral improvement via municipal planning and activist city government. He retired in 1910, so that he could concentrate on social work, municipal reform, and administration.[6] From 1910 to 1915, Howe served as the director of the People's Institute in New York City, which initiated and administered a number of experiments in cultural reform, including the National Board of Censorship, which (as discussed later in this chapter) played a key role in legitimizing the movies.

Reformers intent on improving the moviegoing experience focused on the physical safety of patrons. Initially, nitrate film stock, a highly inflammable substance, and early projector lamps made movie exhibition a hazardous undertaking. (During the 1930s, manufacturers introduced "safety film," a cellulose triacetate plastic base.) It should be remembered that, at this time, most North Americans were particularly fearful of the destruction of life and property that fire causes, especially in buildings full of people. One of the disasters that haunted people across the continent for decades was the fire that broke out at the Iroquois Theatre in Chicago on 30 December 1903, causing the death of hundreds of patrons (mostly women and children) who were attending the matinee.[7] The Iroquois Theatre, a six-storey palace of marble and mahogany — which had been open for only five weeks — had been advertised as "absolutely fireproof." Patrons were told that the theatre had been equipped with an asbestos curtain, which could be lowered to separate the audience from any fire that might break out on stage. On the day in question, 1,900 people packed into the 1,724-seat facility to see vaudeville stars Eddie Foy, Annabelle Whitford, and a troupe of five hundred, in *Mr. Bluebeard*, the musical. About 3:15 p.m., just as the second act was starting, a bit of the canvas brushed against a hot reflector behind a calcium arc spotlight and burst into flames. Within seconds, everything combustible ignited, and the audience bolted for the twenty-seven exits, only to find that many of the gates covering them were locked. Many moviegoers were trampled and crushed against the doors by the onrush of humanity. According to the report in the *New York Times*, 578 people died in the theatre and about 27 more died from their injuries. With 605 casualties, the Iroquois fire was the deadliest blaze in Chicago history, including the Great Chicago Fire of 1871, which had taken the lives of 250 people. Survivors said that the screams of children for their mothers and mothers for their children would haunt them to their dying day. Ironically, the theatre itself sustained only light interior damage; it was repaired and reopened less than a year later as the Colonial Theatre, which was demolished in 1926 to make way for the Oriental Theatre.

Not surprisingly, reformers urged municipal governments to enact legislation requiring entertainment entrepreneurs to "fireproof" their facilities, in terms of building codes and procedures in the event of a fire. Boyd Fraser outlined in a 1912 article some of the measures reformers hoped could be put in place.[8] To begin with, Fraser observed, the facility should be free-standing; where the facility was part of a commercial structure, the walls dividing the spaces should be covered with such fire-resistant material as metal or plaster. Most importantly, the walls, the ceiling, and the floor of the auditorium (as a self-contained unit) should be made of fire-resistant materials; the auditorium should also feature exits on both sides of the proscenium, leading out to a street or an alley, plainly labelled with electric signs. Throughout the nickelodeon period, reformers pressed for these and other regulations, such as those requiring entrepreneurs to fireproof projection rooms, provide a fire-resistant curtain to separate the stage (and the scenery on it) from the audience, and install lighting and windows that provided adequate light at all times.[9] The authorities in New York City passed an ordinance in 1913 governing the construction and the operation of open-air theatres and motion picture theatres with fewer than six hundred seats; the ordinance specified that, among other things, such facilities should be provided with separate restrooms for men and women, and that the environment should be neither too hot nor too cold, meaning the temperature should not be less than 62 degrees or not more than 70 degrees Fahrenheit and the relative humidity not less than 50 and not more than 75 percent.[10] Across the continent, reformers pressed for similar reforms, often finding that city officials were not willing to enforce measures that would hamper the growing business of movie exhibition.[11]

In addition, Gregory A. Waller writes, the country-wide crusade to pressure local governments to ban Sunday screenings, like the ongoing campaign to censor the content of movies, was part of the larger question of how to manage leisure time in a society invaded by mass entertainment.[12] In fact, reformers called for the closing of all forms of amusement on the Sabbath, including skating rinks, movie theatres, dance halls, and so on, arguing that these activities destroyed the sacredness of the day. In one of a series of editorials on the "Sunday Problem" that appeared in *Moving Picture World*, W. Stephen Bush advised exhibitors to screen only educational and religious motion pictures on that day, claiming that "nothing would add more dignity to moving pictures, nothing would secure more respect for motion pictures from the better classes" of patrons.[13] In making the case that motion picture theatres should be closed on Sunday, reformers thought of women and children, who were visiting movie theatres in increasing numbers on the Sabbath.

Reformers also focused on the psychological well-being of patrons, urging government to institute censorship as an apparatus for limiting the (presumed) negative impact motion pictures had on attitudes and actions, particularly of young viewers. Interestingly, officials in the United States tended to regard the demands for censorship more favourably than the requests to enforce the laws regarding Sunday closing (the so-called "blue laws"). Sunday crowds accounted for almost 15 percent of an exhibitor's weekly box office; Sunday closing was in fact costlier than local censorship.[14] The initiatives to "censor" the movies date from the first public screenings of motion pictures.[15] From this period, Garth Jowett explains, the motion picture industry devoted much effort to resisting these threats of censorship and legal actions.[16] Standards of morality and cultural values were shifting during this period of urbanization and industrialization, and many people were reluctant to relinquish control over their lives and over the lives of their children. Many individuals and groups resisted the medium's pervasive influence; collectively, they pursued one aim: to exercise greater control over content, at the local, the state, and the federal levels.

Many attempts were made at the local and the state levels to pass legislation regarding the inspection and the licensing of films that were screened, and these efforts usually involved the chief of police, who judged whether or not a film was "immoral" or "obscene." Ultimately, censorship campaigns conducted at the federal level produced the most effective results.[17] Arguably the earliest case of censorship was the incident documented in the *Newark Evening News* of 17 July 1894, which involved Senator James A. Bradley, a New York City businessman who in 1871 had founded a resort called Asbury Park. Bradley condemned as offensive to public taste a Kinetoscope moving picture called *Carmencita* (1894). This film, one of the many W. K. L. Dickson produced at Edison's West Orange studio, features Carmencita, a Spanish dancer, performing a butterfly dance, during which she exposes her undergarments — and her ankles.[18] The first official case involving a movie was *People v. Doris* in 1897, in which the presiding judge ruled that the pantomime of a bride's wedding night was "an outrage upon public decency."[19] Many reformers denounced fight films — which featured the prizefighters of the day — as degrading entertainment. The *New York Times* and the *New York Tribune* ran articles and editorials conveying this sentiment.[20] The *Chicago Tribune* ran an editorial on 13 April 1907 attacking the nickelodeons of Chicago, suggesting that the city enact a law forbidding a boy or a girl under eighteen from entering a "five-cent" house, unless accompanied by an adult. At this time, there were 116 nickelodeons, 18 ten-cent vaudeville houses, and 19 penny arcades showing motion pictures with titles such as *Gaieties of Divorce* (made in 1906), *Cupid's Barometer, Old Man's Darling, A Seaside Flirtation,* and *Beware, My Husband Comes* (all made in 1907). On any given day, 100,000 people visited these theatres.[21] On 2 May 1907, Jane Addams, then active at Hull House, presented a resolution to Chicago city council advocating regulating rather than suppressing motion picture theatres, but without success. On 24 December 1908, George B. McClellan, the mayor of New York City, issued a proclamation revoking the licenses of all five hundred movie houses in the city, claiming that these cramped venues, these "unclean and immoral places of amusement," were safety hazards.[22] Only decisive action by several prominent showmen who obtained a temporary injunction prevented the exhibitors from losing their box-office revenue for the holiday.[23]

The most significant consequence of Mayor McClellan's attack on the movie industry was the creation of a national board of censors.[24] Charles Sprague Smith, formerly a professor of romance languages and comparative literature at Columbia University, founded (in 1897) and served as the director of the People's Institute of New York, a citizen's bureau of social research located in the Jewish and Italian section of lower Manhattan. Smith conducted a study of the situation, and together with representatives of the motion picture industry, formed a citizen's committee in 1909 called the National Board of Censorship (NBC) for the express purpose of previewing all motion pictures before they were shown in New York City theatres. As it happened, researchers had discovered that a great many "impressionable" boys and girls were part of the 250,000 people in New York City who daily visited the city's 700 moving picture theatres.[25] In this undertaking, the board (made up of nine civic and social reformers) was guided by the example of the City of Chicago, where in 1908 the police department started previewing pictures.[26] Smith died in March 1910, and, as we mentioned, Frederic C. Howe served as the director of the institute and executive chairman of the NBC from 1910 to 1915. His approach was simple: the motion picture screen has a right to the same First Amendment freedom accorded to all the other media. Apparently, a subcommittee of the board (made up of four to ten members) processed about 600 films every month; as exponents of "public opinion," the members censored "offensive" material, including depictions of violence, crime-for-crime's sake, suicide, and lascivious behaviour. For example, during October 1914, the board reviewed 571 films, eliminating 75 scenes, cutting 10 reels, and rejecting 3 films altogether.[27] Producers found in the board a "prestigious" mechanism for legitimizing the movies. In 1915, the board changed the name of the organization to the National Board of Review, thereby distinguishing itself from advocates of legalized, state censorship.[28] The board changed its focus from "reviewing" or "censoring" to co-operating with all interests in promoting the artistic, moral, and social improvement of the movies. Since 1919, the National Board of Review has chosen the ten best English-language movies of the year and the ten best foreign films of the year.

After World War I, reformers intensified their campaigns, urging state legislatures to enact legalized censorship. In 1921, the New York state legislature passed the Lusk-Clayton Motion Picture Censorship Bill in order to remedy what was widely perceived to be "a very great evil." This bill established a Motion Picture Censorship Commission of three people, appointed by the governor, who would review all movie theatres and movies in New York City, with a view to eliminating "indecency." Realizing the futility of opposing the demand for a legal censorship body, the motion picture manufacturers established a self-censoring body in March 1922 called the Motion Picture Producers and Distributors of America (MPPDA), installing William H. Hays, the former postmaster general, as its president.[29] This measure concluded the board's experiment in motion picture censorship and deflected interest away from state censorship campaigns. Most North Americans applauded the industry's effort to adopt a self-censorship plan based on the ideal of common decency.

SAFEGUARDING THE SOCIAL GOOD

As we have seen, the motion picture business quickly evolved into an international industry, generating serious problems in Canada as well as in the United States. Social and radical reformers across Canada urged governments to regulate the new medium, which, they believed, exerted a negative impact on the attitudes and the actions of viewers, especially those of young spectators, thereby threatening the basis of social authority, the family.[30] Anxiety over the movies was, as we have noticed, part of the concern over the proliferation of commercial amusements in general, regarded by many activists as evils of industrial capitalism. That is, the censoring of movies in the prairie West was part of the larger story outlined in the last section, reflecting the influence of developments in Canada and the United States, and the censorship practices employed in prairie Canada were similar to those employed elsewhere. Second, the characteristics of the region, including its strong link to the reformist movement in the early years of the century and the degree to which it attracted immigrants connected with conservative religious movements, such as Doukhobors, Hutterites, Mennonites, and Mormons, arguably made the region particularly sympathetic to censorship.[31]

During the heyday of the Social Gospel movement, roughly from the 1890s to the 1930s, western Canadian reformers, like their colleagues to the south, attempted to apply Christian doctrines to the social ills of industrializing and urbanizing society.[32] Methodist, Presbyterian, Congregationalist, Baptist, and Anglican churches predominated, all concerned with the quality of human relations in society. Two Methodist ministers, S. D. Chown and J. S. Woodsworth, figured prominently in the attempt to turn the Social Gospel into a form of liberal progressivism.[33] The Social Gospel represented a shift in emphasis from individual sin and salvation to the environment in which the individual was required to make his or her way. The movement exerted a major influence on life in the prairie West, serving as "the driving force in the development of a distinct western Canadian mission," that of rebuilding Canada.[34] Believing that "they lived in a democratic, malleable community and thus could effect significant social change,"[35] western Canadian reformers urged government to enact legislation that would transform the country. They sought to alter the political system as a whole, so as to break the stranglehold that old-time political parties had on the country and weaken the control that politicians, manufacturers, and bankers in eastern and central Canada exercised over the political process, thereby subverting the will of the people. This campaign included the creation of a western Canadian liberal party, which would redress prairie farmers' grievances, as well as plans to extend the franchise to women, who would purify politics. In addition, reformers aimed to ameliorate the Canadian capitalist system, in order to reduce the growing danger of the concentration of capital in fewer and fewer hands. In practice, this would mean moving capital from the central Canadian heartland to the periphery, effecting a kind of "regional justice," and giving workers a greater share of the wealth they produced and a greater voice in the management of industry. Added to these political and economic goals was a platform of social change: eliminating the slum areas of cities, monitoring immigration, improving the educational system, eradicating prostitution, and combatting the evils of excessive drinking. Social Gospellers believed that changes in the environment would lead to a "better" human being — and ultimately a "better" society.[36] The progressive movement remained a vital force in prairie provincial politics throughout the 1920s, surfacing in such institutions as wheat pools and consumer co-operatives.

As we have noted, the proliferation of commercial amusement facilities, thanks to the flow of people to the cities, worried reformers; accordingly, they urged governments to pass legislation controlling the building and the operation of these facilities, forcing entrepreneurs to take responsibility for the health and the safety of their customers. For example, early in 1911, police chiefs across Alberta reported to the attorney general that, while most movie theatres were safe, some were dangerous, owing to such hazards as insufficient lighting, narrow aisles, poor ventilation, and too few exits.[37] These concerns converged with those of the proponents of the urban planning movement, which swept across North America during the early decades of the twentieth century. Many civic and business leaders now believed that cities should be hospitable places, not just centres of commerce, and resolved to exercise control over development, tackling such issues as sanitation, health, and poverty, together with such attendant social problems as illiteracy, excessive drinking, prostitution, and crime, and to promote efficiency, economy, and beauty.

To this end, in 1911 the Alberta government created the Department of Municipal Affairs, and in 1912 passed the Town Planning Act, thereby forcing municipalities to develop plans for orderly and planned growth.[38] The City of Calgary created a planning committee in 1911, and hired T. H. (Thomas) Mawson, the Liverpool-based landscape architect, to prepare a plan for directing the city's development. The members of the Institute of Western Canada Civic Building Superintendents held a conference in Calgary in 1912, with a view to creating a uniform building code for the prairie provinces. On the basis of these deliberations, the City of Calgary established a set of regulations in 1912 for designing and building structures in Calgary, including "Theatres and Picture Houses." Predictably, these efforts to promote urban planning became fodder for boosterism. For example, a correspondent for the *Calgary Albertan* described the building code "as the most advanced and practical legislation of the kind adopted by any community of the western world."[39] The building code required the basement walls of four-storey theatres to be 25 inches thick, the first- and second- storey walls to be 21 inches, and the walls of the third and fourth storeys to be 17 and 13 inches, respectively. All theatres and moving picture houses had to have exits measuring 22 inches for every 100 seats of capacity; that is, a house with a seating capacity of 1,000 had to provide emergency exits of a width of not less than 18 feet 4 inches. In addition, aisles had to measure a minimum of 2 feet 6 inches, increasing one inch in width for every 5 feet in length; an aisle of 60 feet in length would thus require a width of 3 feet 6 inches, and a 100-foot-long aisle would need to be 4 feet 2 inches wide. According to the code, not more than thirteen seats were permitted in any row between aisles, and stages had to be cut off from the body of the house by fireproof walls and asbestos curtains, which were periodically inspected. The code also stipulated that "theatres must not admit persons who have with them any article that might obstruct egress." This condition applied to carts, parcels, and so on.[40]

Predictably, "fight films" generated much debate, across Canada as well as across the United States. Commentators were concerned about the morality of these violent contests — and reports that women made up 60 percent of some audiences probably intensified their discussions. The example of Toronto, where concerned citizens urged the authorities to prohibit the exhibition of *The Corbett-Fitzsimmons Fight* (1897), which was being shown at the Toronto Opera House in August 1897, is representative. The city council held a special meeting on 9 August 1897 to consider passing a bylaw to this effect, because the existing bylaws offered police no power to ban the film.[41]

A decade later, in May 1907, a group of concerned citizens approached Toronto City Hall with a view to pressuring city councillors into establishing censorship over "the places of amusement known as five-cent theatres."[42] The five nickel theatres in question, each having a capacity of between 150 and 200, were attracting young boys and girls and women in great numbers. A reporter observed that this agitation represented the first public recognition of an enterprise that was beginning to exert a "disruptive influence" over the youth of the city. Meanwhile, on 7 May, the *Toronto News* reported that the city council had given the matter some thought and had promised to act, possibly when the Reverend Chown, a member of the special committee looking into the problem, returned from his trip through the United States and Great Britain, where he was collecting information about existing regulations governing motion picture theatres.[43] Later, in 1911, the Toronto city council attempted to prohibit all children under the age of fourteen from being admitted to moving picture houses after six o'clock in the evening, unless they were accompanied by their parents.

Similarly, in July 1910 the members of the Saskatchewan legislature considered censoring motion pictures. Like their colleagues in other parts of the dominion, they considered the growing number of reports about the negative impact of movies on the young. For example, according to a report originating in Pittsburgh, three youths held up a streetcar immediately after watching a moving picture about a train robbery and in the process shot a policeman. Apparently, the incident prompted Pittsburgh's director of the Department of Public Safety to notify exhibitors in the area that such pictures could no longer be exhibited.[44] Legislators focused on "fight films" because they were attracting much negative attention worldwide. The *Regina Leader* reported that, by virtue of an order-in-council, the province had prohibited the exhibition of all fight films, including the film of the Jack Johnson–Jim Jeffries heavyweight boxing match held at Reno, Nevada, on 4 July 1910 for the heavyweight championship of the world.[45] No fewer than nine camera operators from Essanay, Selig Polyscope, and Vitagraph production companies captured the action, whereby the black champion (Johnson) had defeated the "white hope" (Jeffries). A number of interested parties pressured the government to ban the *Jeffries-Johnson World's Championship Boxing Contest* (1910). The Reverend Chown, as

General Secretary of the Department of Temperance and Moral Reform, wrote to the premier, asking him to prohibit the showing of fight films because "they are universally acknowledged to be very demoralizing to the people, particularly the young."[46] J. G. Shearer, Secretary of the Social and Moral Reform League, claimed that "all moving picture representations of prize fights" were "offenses against decency and inevitably demoralizing."[47] The *Regina Leader* reported later that banning such movies appears "to be in line with the widely prevailing feeling that civilized society will no longer tolerate the prize-fight," a truly unwholesome spectator sport.[48] According to D. H. Bocking, these complaints ran to the centre of the issues that led to the systematic censorship of motion pictures in Canada. Critics and reformers recognized "the fact that the moving picture industry [had become] big business and that it [now] carried with it all the odium attached to that concept."[49] Not surprisingly, those who controlled the industry were concerned not so much with freedom of expression as with the disruption of business.[50]

From 1911 to 1913, four provincial legislatures in English-speaking Canada passed censorship laws and set up boards to apply them: Ontario, Manitoba, Saskatchewan, and Alberta. Québec passed censorship laws early in 1911. Moved by public opinion, on 24 March 1911 the Ontario legislature passed the Theatre and Cinematographs Act and then, on 27 June, set up a board of three censors, with George Armstrong as the chairman.[51] In due course, the Ontario Board of Censors developed close links with other boards, paying close attention to the weekly reports of the National Board of Review in New York City. In the early days, the Ontario board passed only about 25 percent of all films reviewed, although by 1919 it was approving more like 60 percent.[52] This was in part because the processes involved in censorship were becoming more streamlined. In addition, the film industry was shifting toward the production of films that reflected the growing status and centrality of moviegoing as a cultural activity. In other words, the industry was becoming more and more adept at catering to the expectations of a growing and increasingly middle-class audience as well as negotiating the constraints of regulation.

Interestingly, in 1920 the Ontario provincial government appointed the first woman to the board, Caroline Cassels.[53] In March 1920, the board issued a booklet outlining its standards and practices, promising to save as many pictures as possible by cutting offensive scenes; the censors claimed to be making judgments from the perspective of the average Ontario moviegoer, "excluding degrading, immoral, improperly suggestive, harmful, and indecent films." They declared that movies were not allowed "to show a successful balking of the law," although "the showing of certain good-natured comedies dealing with officials may not be regarded as attacks on law and order." The board also declared that there should be no "display of foreign flags, cruelty to animals, firearms, violence, crime, arson, insanity, murder, and suicide."[54]

By 1921, the Ontario Board of Censors was charging distributors $3 to review a reel of film. According to Malcolm Dean, Hollywood kept an eye on the Ontario censors, inviting them to tour studios and from time to time consulting with them about new products. The tenure of O. J. Silverthorne, who served as the board's chairman from 1934 to 1974, marked the period of "liberal" censorship in the province. Silverthorne presided over a major development in censorship when, in 1946, he instructed the board to "classify" films, introducing the "Restricted" category so that moviegoers could easily assess films from a moral standpoint.[55] In 1953, the province replaced the Theatres Act of 1911, experimenting with an "X" rating that would be applied to films that "do not permit of treatment without obvious mutilation of the subject matter."[56] With the arrival of the 1960s, film societies across the country began challenging the legitimacy of censorship.[57]

The evolution of censorship in the prairie provinces followed a similar trajectory. In March 1911, provincial legislators created the Manitoba Board of Censors and asked the City of Winnipeg — at the time, the only centre screening motion pictures on a regular basis — to serve as the first censoring authority. In making their decisions, city councillors took their cue from their colleagues in Toronto. By 1914, Manitoba and Saskatchewan were sharing this Winnipeg-based board of four censors, in large part because movie distributors were located there. In November 1915, the board examined D. W. Griffith's *The Birth of a Nation* (1915). A symphony orchestra of thirty players provided the appropriate music and sound effects. Critics praised the film, especially the "midnight" photography, which rendered some battle scenes particularly realistic.[58] Before passing the film, however, the board cut the scenes showing women in distress over the horrors of war.[59] Griffith's landmark film played at the Walker Theatre twice daily for the last two weeks of the month.

The two boards — one representing civic interests and the other provincial — separated in 1916. The provincial government then assumed control of censorship for Manitoba. For a variety of reasons, the Saskatchewan censors used the Manitoba facilities, probably viewing the same films at the same time. In 1919, the Manitoba board, chaired by T. A. D. Bevington, examined 5,462 reels of film, condemning 54 feature films. Censors objected to, among other things, the increasing presence of the American flag in newsreels and war films.[60]

In 1926, the Manitoba Board of Censors examined 782 films, banning 33; they also made over three hundred cuts to the films they passed for public exhibition.[61] (By this time, Manitoba boasted 59 movie theatres, 25 of them in Winnipeg.) In 1930, the Manitoba board, like the Alberta board, adopted a system of classification according to which films were categorized as "Universal" or "Adult," admission, the latter restricting admission to persons twenty-one years of age or older. They also continued to cut offensive scenes and to reject some films altogether. Each month, the board sent censors across Canada a list of films, indicating cuts and rejections. As Dean notes, the practice of restricting entertainment to adults was slow to gain ground, as censors felt that labelling a film adult-only would just pique the interest of the young. In 1954, the Manitoba board reported: "In censorship, our problem continues to be the adolescent reaction to films. Various women's organizations throughout the United States are protesting

Figure 34. Advertisement for a screening of D. W. Griffith's The Birth of a Nation (1915) *at Winnipeg's Walker Theatre.* Manitoba Free Press, 20 Novem*ber* 1915, 20.

strongly against the ever-increasing brutality, torture, and sex scenes in pictures released as suitable family entertainment." The proportion of "adult" films to the total output stood at 42 percent. The film industry faced serious difficulties in the postwar era as recreational activities proliferated and television became ubiquitous. The industry's response was to go where television could not go, that is, to make movies about previously forbidden subjects.[62] Interestingly, the Manitoba Board of Censors passed *Tom Jones* (1964), whereas other boards banned it.

In 1972, Manitoba's NDP government passed a new film classification bill, the Amusements Act, which removed the board's power to cut films and provided for the classification of films only. The debate that ensued highlighted the central issue: "Government control of the mind, implicit in any kind of censorship, is contrary to the very foundation of a free society."[63] When the Progressive Conservatives gained power in the province in September 1978, they fired the censorship board and appointed a new one, with Mrs. Hope Carroll as chairperson, empowering the new board to classify (as opposed to reject) all slides or films prior to exhibition anywhere in Manitoba and to regulate the advertising of these products. A former home economics teacher, Carroll told the press that she was shocked by the sex and violence in the films she had viewed; she added that the censor board would strive to be a reflection of the public.

The first move Saskatchewan made toward censorship came with the banning of the Johnson-Jeffries fight film. During the 1910–11 session, the provincial legislature passed a bill called "Egress from Public Buildings," providing for the licensing of motion picture machines, and on 3 November 1911 passed an order-in-council creating a board of censors for the purpose of examining (and stamping with an official seal) all films to be exhibited in the province. On 3 August 1912, the Saskatchewan government decreed "that no exhibition shall be permitted on the Lord's Day, except in connection with religious service by permit of the Provincial Secretary, and that no theatre will exhibit a picture depicting crime," nor could pictures featuring prizefights be shown. In addition, the decree empowered the provincial police to enforce the regulation.[64] The province passed the Theatre and Cinematographs Act in January 1913, creating a board consisting of a minimum of three censors, initially chaired by W. M. Omand, with the power to permit or to ban the exhibition of all films or slides.[65] Appeals had to be conducted under prescribed conditions.

Soon, the censors were rejecting and further cutting films that had already been censored by boards in New York, Ontario, and Manitoba, with a view to eliminating scenes featuring drunkenness, gambling, domestic infidelity, indecency, murder, suicide, insanity, burglary (where actual theft was shown), cruelty, poisoning, and brutal violence.[66] As mentioned earlier, the Saskatchewan and the Manitoba boards collaborated from 1914 to 1916, possibly as a result of pressure from the film exchanges, who hoped to reduce costs and red tape.[67] The joint board dissolved their agreement in 1916, possibly in a disagreement over standards. The Manitoba Board of Censors was prepared to accept *Damaged Goods* (1915), a film based on a play by Eugène Brieux about venereal disease, which had run on Broadway for sixty-six performances in 1913. The Manitoba board allowed the film to be shown to segregated audiences, whereas the Saskatchewan Board of Censors rejected it. As of 1 January 1917, Saskatchewan assumed responsibility for censoring films shown in the province. Samuel Clarke served as the censor from 1913 to 1916 and C. A. Robson from 1916 to 1923. Meanwhile, the Alberta and British Columbia censor boards tried — but failed — to join forces.

By 1920, the Saskatchewan board exercised jurisdiction over all advertising for films, and by 1921 the board was charging movies distributors $2 to review a reel of film. Determining standards represented an ongoing problem. In June 1919, the prairie censors met at the Palliser Hotel, in Calgary, to establish a list of criteria that would help censors make decisions and to establish a national board of censors, but this attempt failed. According to Bocking, the board rejected about 2.5 percent of the films they reviewed, largely because of sexual content.[68] In 1968, the province created a film classification board under the authority of the Theatres and Cinematographs Act, which empowered the censors to oversee commercial and public exhibitions of films, as well as to license distributors and projectionists and to maintain safety standards in theatres and drive-ins. This system categorized films as General, Adult, Restricted Adult, and Special X.

During the early twentieth century, business and civic leaders across Alberta regarded the movies as a serious threat to the province's social order, which was based on British standards and traditional institutions, especially the family. They were troubled by explicit depictions of sex, violence, and crime in movies, including portrayals of seduction, infidelity, and indecency, not to mention gunplay, burglary, and brutality, which, according to popular wisdom, encouraged young people to "experiment." In 1910, R. R. Jamieson, the mayor of Calgary, told reporters that films depicting violence of any kind, including robbery, murder, and the destruction of property, should be banned from the movie theatres of Calgary, and in 1911 a writer for the *Calgary Herald* claimed that movies depicting illicit sexual relations outraged common decency. The writer referred to a "disgusting" film called *The White Slave Trade* (1910), which had been on exhibition throughout southern Alberta. The film featured the interior of a brothel, where men and women ("in a state of deshabille") were drinking. Apparently, a lecturer explained these "filthy details" in the event that the audience failed to understand "what these sordid details meant." The writer added that he was shocked to discover that theatre operators allowed children to watch the film.[69] Reformers were also concerned about the invasion of American propaganda, for example, flag waving. In 1912, police departments across Alberta expressed their views on the matter, saying that depictions of sex and violence made censorship necessary. They also complained that the movies on exhibition conveyed far too few scenes of Great Britain or Canada to develop patriotism in the audience.[70] These concerns culminated in a proposal to enact legislation that would monitor the exhibition of movies in the province. Following the example of the Ontario legislature, on 13 February 1912 the Alberta legislature passed an act to regulate theatres, entertainment halls, and cinematographs. The act stipulated that, as of 13 February 1913, a board of censors would be empowered to examine and to affix a stamp of approval on all 35 mm films deemed fit for exhibition.[71] R. B. Chadwick, the chief censor from 1913 to 1916, and his two colleagues initially reviewed films at a movie theatre in Edmonton because government facilities were not yet in place. Howard Douglas, a Methodist from Ontario, served as the chief censor from 1916 to 1928.

The belief that censorship was key to protecting the morality of the province was based on the understanding that the social environment influenced human behaviour. As Donald Wetherell and Irene Kmet explain, the prevailing thinking was that since the mind was impressionable, and since the mind of the child was highly impressionable, some mechanism was needed to control the content of visual messages. At a meeting in 1913 of the Naomi Mothers' Society in Calgary, the Reverend A. D. McDonald, a member of the board of censors, claimed that young boys take up smoking and drinking after watching motion pictures, many of which encourage "reckless" behaviour.[72] In his 1927 report to the provincial government on juvenile delinquency, Gerald Pelton, a Calgary lawyer, observed that movies filled the minds of children with "suggestions." He said that if a child saw a hero "getting away" with a crime and being applauded for his "success in eluding detection," the child would become convinced that a crime was not a crime "unless you get caught." The problem was more than mere "emulation." In Pelton's words, "every act of every individual is the expression of a corresponding thought." Pelton noted that movies serve as a poignant case, given their powers of depiction; the depiction of "unwholesome mental impressions" in any form is "inimical to the young mind."[73]

Linked to the determination to censor movies that might have a negative impact on behaviour was the desire to make leisure useful and socially productive. This issue was pressing because movie theatres were open to everyone, young and old, sophisticated and unsophisticated. Proponents of censorship believed that universal entertainment had to be "shaped," turned into a force that would educate as well as entertain. Some people put movies in the same category as card playing, dancing, and vaudeville, that is, frivolous and morally corrupting.[74] Reformers argued that censorship should promote films "which have an educational function" and "obliterate" those which would disturb "the morals of the population in any way." In 1922, the Alberta censor remarked that the province should protect the integrity of movie entertainment, just as it should protect the integrity of churches and schools.[75]

Predictably, establishing criteria proved to be a difficult task. Censors relied on their perception of what the public regarded as acceptable in terms of morality and behaviour. Different censors from different provinces defined the problem in different ways. As we mentioned above, provincial censors met in 1919 and drew up a list of criteria that would help censors "condemn" or "disapprove" films. The targets for censorship included a whole range of sexual topics, such as "white slavery" (unless the film conveyed a good moral lesson), seduction, common-law relationships, and abortion; depictions of violence, for example, violent death, and exploitation of "notorious characters"; and scenes of drunkenness, especially if women played a part in the scene.[76] The targets for disapproval included such topics as "the drug habit" and depictions of women smoking, crime against property, "gangsterism," vulgarity, and the ridicule of religion.

In any event, the Alberta censor was able to review only a portion of the many films that entered the province. In 1920, 5,443 reels of film entered the province, and the censor reviewed 3,379, passing 2,064 without examination. On the one hand, the films passed by other boards in Canada could be exhibited automatically without further examination; on the other, films that had been condemned by other boards in Canada had to be examined by Alberta censors.[77] Provincial censorship may or may not have been consistent; it is difficult to determine, given the number of films reviewed and the breadth of the standards applied. By 1921, the censorship board was charging movie distributors $1 to review a reel of film. In 1922, the Alberta censor condemned eight films for depicting "lawlessness" (including murder), thirteen for immorality, eight for vulgarity, eight for being suggestive, and three for presenting a travesty of religion.[78]

The coming of the "talkies" complicated censorship considerably. Censors now felt obliged to scrutinize dialogue closely, to cut "double meanings" that could be deemed risqué. In some cases, dialogue made it past the censors, only to be cut after the film's release because members of the public identified "the objectionable side of the statement."[79] The problem was more than the use of objectionable words. In 1932, Robert Pearson, a Methodist minister who served as chief censor from 1928 to 1946, observed that "the coming of the talking picture has made possible the producing on the screen of a large number of rather sophisticated plays that have run successfully on Broadway, but which deal with problems of life that are not always acceptable as entertainment to the family trade that frequents theatres in Alberta."[80]

In reality, censorship was a pragmatic enterprise, a function of the censor's interpretation of what the public regarded as acceptable morality and behaviour and the pressures that special interest groups throughout the province brought to bear on the censorship of particular films. Indeed, the success of any particular campaign represented a measure of the group's status. Some people demanded the banning of films they had never seen — or films that had never been released in Alberta — because they had read about these movies in American magazines.[81] In 1932, the Calgary Board of Trade demanded that the censor ban all gangster films because they "glorified" crime and corrupted the youth of Alberta. In 1934, the Alberta Association of Registered Nurses campaigned to have a representative of their profession review all pictures "featuring nurses so that pictures which are distasteful to the nursing profession may be banned."[82] This campaign failed. The same year, the Roman Catholic Church tried to persuade the censor to ban all scenes or films featuring divorce, but since most Protestants were happy with the standards of censorship in the province, this campaign too failed.[83] In 1937, the National Council of Women and the Alberta Women's Institute campaigned to have all scenes featuring liquor cut from movies, but prohibition sentiment had waned and so the censor could ignore the request.[84]

Clearly, censorship by itself could not render every movie suitable for every viewer, regardless of age. As J. R. Boyle, the attorney general of Alberta, observed in 1919, some films are perfectly acceptable for adults — and unacceptable for children. The problem was exacerbated by the fact that movie theatres admitted children "indiscriminately," and "it was especially bad for them to see certain kinds of rough play which might contain a moral for adults" but not one that children would notice or comprehend. The solution to the problem seemed to be to prevent children from seeing some films altogether; a writer for the *Edmonton Journal* explained that it would be better if films were banned altogether than to "have them under the present circumstances" of unrestricted admission.[85]

A number of reformers took part in the debate over age classification. The Calgary Council on Child Welfare, together with its parent organization, the Canadian Council on Child Welfare, presented a petition calling for restricted admission based on age.[86] Howard Douglas opposed classification by age, arguing that filmmakers had found children's movies unprofitable, as the market was too small. The Canadian Council on Child Welfare drew up monthly lists of films that had no "objectionable" material, and he advised parents to consult these lists, rather than rely on a state-devised system of classification.[87]

Although the advocates of classification agreed that parents were required to supervise their children's moviegoing habits, they felt that voluntary control was insufficient. Mrs. Riley of the Calgary Council on Child and Family Welfare argued in 1928 that movies were "often destructive in the character building of children, and even if they are chaperoned, this form of amusement often becomes harmful."[88] Eventually, the provincial government brought in by order-in-council a system of classification, one of the first in the country; this measure stipulated that films classified as "Passed U" were suitable for "universal exhibition" as "family pictures." In addition, it stipulated that no child under the age of fourteen could attend a film that was not classified as "U," except for news films, unless accompanied by a parent or a "bona fide guardian."[89] Given the censor's concern that identifying films as "adult only" would serve to advertise films as risqué, it's not surprising that only the "U" classification was advertised and that all others were automatically defined as "adult." In 1941, the censor refined this system, introducing two slightly different classifications: the "Passed" classification indicated films for adults and the "Passed U" classification indicated films for families and children. In the late 1940s, the Alberta Board of Censors began to use the "Adult Passed" classification instead of the "Passed" classification to indicate movies that were "too tense, [and] too emotional."[90]

The campaign to promote British standards and institutions included promoting British-made films and (especially during World War I and the 1930s) urging theatre managers to display patriotic symbols and to encourage audiences to sing "God Save the King." These measures represented a conscious attempt to counteract the American domination of the movie market. As we have seen, Hollywood entrepreneurs regarded Canada as part of the American domestic market in their arrangements for distributing and exhibiting movies. Between 1929 and the end of 1934, the Alberta censor reviewed 10,594 films; of these, 10,337 were American, 249 British, and 8 "foreign."[91] In 1930, Pearson noted that 90 percent of the films screened in Canada were American.[92] He noted that he had to go "further" than censors in many parts of North America — because of the special nature of Alberta society."[93] Pearson countered this neglect of Canadian sensibilities by promoting, whenever possible, British- and Canadian-made films, to keep Canada a "strong and energetic nation." In practice, film distributors in Canada rarely imported British films, arguing that these films were poor in quality and that, generally speaking, they were unpopular with audiences. Actually, few British or Canadian films were available. In 1926, only thirty-nine British films were available.[94] As Peter Morris notes, Ontario, Alberta, and British Columbia enacted legislation "permitting the establishment of a quota for British films" but took no concrete steps to implement these quotas.[95]

The second measure represented the province's conscious attempt to promote British standards and institutions. In 1932, the National Council of Women demanded that the Union Jack be displayed prominently and that the audience sing "God Save the King" "during at least one performance in each theatre each day." As Wetherell and Kmet explain, only the American-owned Famous Players chain of theatres (the subject of chapter 6) screened a trailer featuring the King during the playing of the national anthem. At one time, managers of Famous Players theatres played the national anthem "in the middle of the evening performance," but people resented being disturbed in the middle of their visit to the theatre, preferring to rise at the close. By 1934, most urban theatres ran a patriotic trailer at the end of the last show of each day.[96]

Concern about the left-wing messages conveyed in films dates from just before World War I, and it intensified during the interwar period. Anxious about propaganda, the censor closely scrutinized films that were made in Germany. In 1924, the provincial cabinet decided to ban a film made in Russia, in part because it promoted communism, arguing that "we should not encourage any organizations, communistic or otherwise, outside of our own state, to manufacture and send into Canada films intended solely for political propaganda."[97]

Later, alarm spread throughout the film industry when executives watched censor boards across North America indulge in "anti-Communism." This meant (to paraphrase Russell Merritt) that the pressure to produce "popular" movies was offset by the pressure to produce "respectable" movies, that is, movies that were not made under the influence of "Communist thought."[98] In March 1946, the Alberta legislature advised the board of censors that one of their major political responsibilities would be "to see that those films shown [in the province] are in keeping with good democratic principles."[99] P. J. A. Fleming served as chief censor from 1946 to 1964, gaining a reputation for his old-fashioned attitude toward censorship; during his tenure, Fleming banned nearly one hundred films (more than any other provincial censor) and made more than four thousand cuts from others. Fleming believed that censorship was designed to protect "the recognized moral code."[100] In 1965, the Calgary Film Society presented a brief to the province's Special Committee on Boards and Tribunals, calling for the activities of the Alberta censors to be restricted to the simple classification of films. In November 1972, the legislature of Alberta converted the censorship system into a classification system (almost identical to the system employed by the province of Manitoba), empowering the board to categorize some films "X" because of violent and sexually explicit content.[101]

As we have seen, censorship in Canada became — as it has remained — a provincial matter. Policymakers regarded the cinema as an entertainment industry, the objective of which was to make money, and motion pictures as property; accordingly, the provinces took responsibility for its trade.[102] Thanks to the political nature of censorship, the first Canadian censors found themselves playing the role of guardians of national public morality and identity, with an anti-American emphasis.[103] They noticed that the vast majority of American films featured the Stars and Stripes flag, ignoring the Union Jack, which they declared was almost invisible; they urged filmmakers to produce films that featured British and Canadian heroism, which would have a significant impact on Canadian children.[104] Concern about American influence intensified in 1913, when censors objected to what they saw as the flag waving that characterized American films.[105] During World War I, they were concerned that American films played up the American war effort while downplaying that of the British. In addition, they were concerned that Canadian women "seeing men fall on the field of battle [would] raise their feelings to such an extent that the necessary consent of a wife to allow her husband go to the front, or of a mother her son, [would] not be obtainable."[106]

About this time, censors found themselves in the middle of a moral dilemma, one demanding nothing less than public acknowledgement. During and after the war, "thousands of its troops were bringing back socially reprehensible souvenirs."[107] As early as 1916, a furor erupted when the Ontario censor banned the film *Damaged Goods* (1915), which the Manitoba censors had passed, as had censors in the United States. On 20 January 1916, the makers of the film, the Mutual Film Company, arranged a private test screening in Toronto. According to a writer for the *Toronto Telegram*, the select audience (mostly women) approved of what the film depicted, explaining that it had great educational value, whereas the censor judged that the public generally would find the material offensive.[108] Interestingly, the federal government was so concerned about an epidemic of venereal disease after the war that in 1919 it initiated a conference with the provinces, prior to setting up VD clinics across the country.[109]

CHANGING ATTITUDES

For more than three decades, censors across Canada — like their colleagues elsewhere — provided what was widely regarded as a "public service." On the one hand, operating behind closed doors, they cut and sometimes banned films on the grounds that such actions were necessary to protect the commonweal.[110] With an eye on British standards, they excised scenes that depicted "cruelty to animals, 'indelicate' sex relations, scenes disparaging public figures and institutions, the *modus operandi* of criminals, misrepresentation of police methods, offensive vulgarity and impropriety in conduct or dress, nudity, the use of drugs," and so on.[111] On the other hand, they and the regulatory process they constituted implicitly ensured that the police would not seize films and thereby disrupt the exhibition business.

However, simmering dissatisfaction with this arrangement gradually increased, crystallizing during the late 1940s, when a growing number of people inside as well as outside the movie industry began to chafe under systems they regarded as overly bureaucratic, political, puritanical, and ultimately self-serving. In 1946, Canadians had every reason to feel that they were over-regulated, in censorship and other regimes, a situation confirmed by the statistics. In the United States, six state-supported censorship boards served 141.4 million people; in Great Britain, a single board served 49.2 million. Canada, with a population of only 12.3 million, had eight censorship boards.[112] Many industry analysts called for one national board of censors, although they generally acknowledged that Québec would never subscribe to a national system of censorship. Major figures inside and outside the industry claimed that the time had come to fight censorship; after all, they argued, Canada was vast in size and diverse in culture and religion. Reports in the *Canadian Film Weekly* show that distributors and exhibitors focused on three grievances. First, all too often local interest groups won censors' attention and were able to influence their judgments. Second, representatives of the industry were rarely, if ever, permitted to sit on censorship boards. Third, what had originally been intended as a public service had become a money-making operation. Industry analysts noted that, in 1946, it cost distributors in Great Britain $10 to have a reel of film reviewed, where exhibitors operated 4,850 movie theatres; in Canada, where exhibitors operated only 1,640 theatres, it cost distributors $33 to have the first reel reviewed.[113] One argument, advanced by opponents inside as well as outside the industry, was that film censorship violated democratic freedoms. Another was that the Motion Picture Production Code of 1930, a set of guidelines introduced by Will H. Hays to govern the content of motion pictures, should render censorship unnecessary.

Many early reformers had regarded moviegoing as a violation of the Sabbath, and thanks to effective lobbying on the part of an alliance of church and labour groups they had succeeded in pressuring the Dominion government to pass the Lord's Day Act. These lobbyists argued that "uninterrupted toil was brutalizing" and that people needed a day of rest so that they could devote time to their spiritual, moral, and physical development.[114] Taking effect in 11 July 1906, the Lord's Day Act restricted trade, labour, and recreation on Sunday, with the result that games of chance organized for gain, not to mention public performances and public meetings for which the public paid an admission fee, were prohibited.[115] Interestingly, in 1913 the Methodist Church proposed to establish a chain of movie theatres in every large city in the Dominion of Canada with a view to public uplift. The movement, which started in Vancouver, planned to screen films that would deal with church work being carried out in congregations throughout the world. As Wetherell and Kmet put it, sabbatarians understood leisure not as rest or enjoyment but as useful and morally improving activity, that is, as a means of living a personal and social life of "quality."

In the wake of the Lord's Day Act, popular secular activities such as baseball games and dances, which would have been held on Sundays before 1907, were thus gradually replaced by church services and private pursuits such as reading the scriptures or undertaking charity work. The law clearly prohibited the screening of movies. Some exhibitors attempted to circumvent the Lord's Day Act by continuing to screen films on Sunday but free of any formal charge. Instead, patrons were asked to put whatever they regarded as an appropriate donation onto a plate; many donated nothing at all, however, and such efforts proved fruitless.[116] It was not until 24 April 1985 that the Supreme Court of Canada finally struck down the Lord's Day Act, arguing that its provisions violated freedom of religion as guaranteed by the Charter of Rights and Freedoms.[117]

During the period following World War II, attitudes became increasingly liberal. The development of television during the 1950s and the flood of sexually explicit and violent films during the 1960s marked the end of censorship as a secretive, arbitrary practice and its replacement by classification as a transparent one, undertaken expressly to provide a guide for film patrons. Television also reduced the number of children in attendance at movie theatres. Moreover, the CBC, not to mention television stations in nearby American cities such as Buffalo and Detroit, offered Canadians uncensored versions of films that had been cut or rejected by provincial boards.[118] During the 1960s, the campaign conducted by film societies across Canada to abolish censorship accordingly intensified.[119] Anti-censorship arguments exposed the subjective nature of censorship judgments and underscored the claim that censorship as it had traditionally operated was of limited practical value.[120] One by one, the provinces followed Québec and transformed "censorship" boards into "classification" boards.[121]

The censors' response to *Tom Jones* (1963), which toured the prairies in 1964, signalled that the old system was no longer tenable. This lavish, freewheeling adaptation of Henry Fielding's eighteenth-century picaresque novel depicts a young man's bawdy experiences. Tom Jones, an abandoned orphan raised by aristocrats, is a devilishly good-looking young man who has a way with women, although he loves only one, Sophie Western. Tom's attempts to woo Sophie and the many adventures that befall him, including a sword fight in the forest and bedroom romps, lead him to London, where a duel with a jealous husband lands him in prison waiting to be hanged. The secret of Tom's birth is eventually revealed, his life is saved, and he secures Sophie's love. The film, with its *carpe diem* theme, extended the limits of artistic expression and marked a watershed in British cinema, winning Oscars for Best Picture, Best Director, Best Adapted Screenplay, and Best Score.

P. J. A. Fleming, the Alberta censor, viewed the film in January 1964 and judged that seventy seconds had to be cut before Albertans could see it. Fleming liked to boast that Alberta's censorship board was the "toughest in Canada."[122] Henry Beissel, the president of the Edmonton Film Society, created a fuss when he publicly challenged censorship in general and Fleming's arbitrary decision in particular. As a result of the debate in the legislature and in the press, in May 1964 the Alberta cabinet approved an "Adults Only" category for the film, ten years after Ontario pioneered this innovation. The Saskatchewan censors examined the film about the same time, finding it immoral; in particular, they were offended by the scene that featured Tom Jones in bed with a woman, which violated the prevailing sense of cinematic decorum, and demanded that it be cut. Eventually, though, the Saskatchewan censors approved a version of the film for exhibition to adults only. In contrast, the Manitoba censors liked the film, declaring that they "couldn't wait to see it again," although they likewise gave it a "Restricted" rating, albeit without proposing cuts.[123] Similarly, Ontario censors, who viewed the film in August, enjoyed it immensely and refused to cut a single scene.[124]

Arguably, these rather diverse responses to *Tom Jones* are indicative of the social changes that took place during the post–World War II period — cultural dynamics that shaped the evolution of film censorship throughout North America. For half a century, motion picture censorship had served as "a repressive mechanism," representing a broadly based cluster of attitudes toward behaviour and discourse. As historian David C. Jones aptly puts it, the notion underlying the principle of censorship, and the decisions reached by censorship boards, was that too much reality could be harmful.[125] One might also see the movement to censor movies as a product of local resistance to the enormous expansion of the movie industry and its growing influence during the first half of the twentieth century on cultural practices throughout the United States and Canada. While prairie elites might welcome certain elements of this industry — namely, those that confirmed their community's status as a bona fide metropolis, such as elegant theatres and the availability of "the latest" popular entertainments — they might also denounce those elements they saw as potential threats to the social and moral order of their world. Like their counterparts elsewhere, film exhibitors in the prairie West were obliged to negotiate these ambivalent and shifting attitudes in order to stay in business.

5

GRAND ENTERTAINMENT: MOVIE EXHIBITION DURING THE PICTURE PALACE ERA, 1914 TO 1932

On 4 December 1915, the Allen family formed a holding company called Canadian Paramount Pictures Corporation Limited, consolidating the nine theatres they operated and their film exchanges, including Famous Players Film Service, and shortly afterwards moved their headquarters to Toronto. It should be said that they relocated their organization at a critical time.[1] The city of Toronto grew enormously in the late nineteenth and early twentieth centuries, increasing from a population of 181,215 in 1891 to 521,893 in 1921, thanks to the flow of migrants from rural areas and small towns and to the influx of immigrants from overseas. By 1918, Toronto had established itself not only as the second largest city in Canada but also as one of the major economic and cultural centres of North America. About 80 percent of the population had British ancestry and more than 75 percent were Protestant, mainly Anglican, Presbyterian, and Methodist.[2]

Toronto's boom was conspicuous in the pace of building construction and in the rapid expansion of civic services, such as electricity, telephone, paved roads, water works, sanitation, and the street railway system.[3] As Patricia McHugh points out, the city offered spectators a twentieth-century cityscape that included the Provincial Parliament Building (completed in 1892), Massey Hall (1894), the City Hall

(1899), and the Royal Alexandra Theatre (1907).[4] One could also see the city's affluence in recent cultural and recreational developments, such as the founding of the Toronto Symphony Orchestra, the building of the Mutual Street Arena, and the construction of a new Central YMCA. Plans for the establishment of the Art Gallery of Ontario, the Royal Ontario Museum, and a zoo (in Riverdale Park) were well under way. In addition, the city boasted three morning papers, the *Globe*, the *Mail and Empire*, and the *World*, with a combined circulation of over 150,000, and three evening papers, the *News*, the *Star*, and the *Telegram*, with a combined circulation of 190,000.[5] In short, Toronto had become the largest market in Canada for commercial entertainment, including the movies, so it is not surprising that the Allens saw it as the logical place from which to oversee the national chain of theatres they had established while they were located in Calgary.[6] Jule moved first and Jay followed.

This relocation took place during the first years of World War I, which adversely affected the flow of movies into Canada and required exhibitors to develop some new strategies, as well as to demonstrate their willingness to contribute to the war effort.[7] The Allens supported the war effort in a number of ways. For example, the managers of their theatres collected money for the war chest. As well, they sent S. W. (Sam) Smith, an associate of Lord Beaverbrook, to Great Britain to acquire films, because, as we have seen, patrons and exhibitors alike, especially in Ontario, objected to the preponderance of American films being screened, particularly those that displayed "American self-glorification."[8] Jay wanted to satisfy the demand for British films; however, it was difficult to sell British films to Canada directly, because British producers wanted to distribute their work in the United States.[9] They purchased a number of films that became big money makers, including *The Battle of the Somme* (1916). They also distributed propaganda films or dramatized newsreels; indeed, Canada became one of the first countries to use motion pictures in the war effort. The Dominion government realized that, when left to distributors, propaganda films received poor distribution; consequently, in 1917, W. J. Hanna, the government's Food Controller, authorized the formation of the Motion Picture Committee (MPC) of the Food Controller, charging it with the task of promoting the special films made by the department to inform the public on the important war measure of food control.[10] Leading members of the movie industry, including Jule and Jay Allen and Clair Hague, served on the committee.[11] Other departments, such as the Dominion Victory Loan Committee (DVLC), sponsored films encouraging Canadians to buy war bonds.[12] Most of these films were produced by Famous Players–Lasky Corporation and featured a variety of stars, including Mary Pickford, Douglas Fairbanks, and Charlie Chaplin, but in fact they were adaptations of the US Liberty Loan films.[13]

After the war, Jule and Jay created British Films Limited, a company geared to meeting "the ever-increasing demand of the patriotic people of Canada for the display of British films on the Canadian screens."[14] In light of this demand, the Allens wanted to import, distribute, and screen the leading photoplays telling stories about life in Great Britain and Canada. Accordingly, they travelled to Britain and purchased through their London office a wide variety of British films, including *The Better 'Ole* (1919), a comedy inspired by a Bruce Bairnsfather cartoon. The Allens screened the film in all their theatres; it played at the Allen Theatre in Calgary during the last week of February 1919 and again during the third week of November 1921, generating considerable profit for their organization.[15] "Old Bill" also inspired a number of works. For example, Bairnsfather wrote and directed *Carry On, Sergeant* (1928), which depicted life in the trenches from the Canadian perspective. Produced by Canadian International Films studios in Trenton, Ontario, the film premiered at the Regent Theatre, Toronto, on 10 November 1928; it has been described as "the Canadian cinema's most expensive flop."[16] Other exhibitors expanded the market for British films by organizing weeks of all-British films, but these schemes had limited impact: exhibitors across Canada made little attempt to invest in the local production of films. Ultimately, Canadian exhibitors, even those who, like the Allens, were successful in creating regional, even national chains, and attempted to be sensitive to the preferences of local audiences and to engage local investors, did not contribute significantly to the development of a Canadian film industry; indeed, their success as exhibitors was largely dependent on the strength of their connections with the American film industry.

Figure 35. The Allen Theatre, a major feature of the Moose Jaw Cultural Centre. The theatre later became the Capitol and then, in 2003, the Mae Wilson. Photo by Robert M. Seiler.

Figure 36. Interior of the Allen Theatre, Moose Jaw. Photo by Bob Hoskins.

BUILDING CAMPAIGN, 1915–17

From 1915 to 1917, the Allens erected only three movie theatres, thanks to the seriously reduced availability of labour and building materials. They built Allen theatres in Moose Jaw, Brandon, and Toronto. In completing these projects under rather difficult conditions, they demonstrated not only their confidence in the Canadian economy and their commitment to developing the theatre as a unique space but also their policy of encouraging local entrepreneurs to become shareholders in the individual businesses they had created.[17]

In 1916, the Allens hired James C. Teague to revive a project they had abandoned at the start of the war, namely, building the Monarch Theatre at 51 Main Street in Moose Jaw, a fast-growing community nestled in the picturesque valley where the Moose Jaw River meets Thunder Creek. The community dates from 1883, when the CPR located its maintenance yards there, explaining that the site was ideally located in terms of its distance from other divisional points at Winnipeg and Calgary.[18] Rapid settlement of the area after the turn of the century ushered in a commercial and an industrial boom: between 1901 and 1911, the population of Moose Jaw increased from 1,558 to 13,823. The city became a wholesale distribution and industrial centre for a large area of the province. The optimism running through the community could be seen in a number of developments (when the community was incorporated as a city in 1903, officials described it as a city of "Pride and Promise"). The *Moose Jaw Times,* founded in 1889, became a semi-weekly in 1904, and the *Evening News* became a semi-weekly in 1906. Crescent Park, the site of a make-work project featuring paths, waterways, and a bridge, opened in 1906. The public library was built during 1912–13, at a cost of $110,000.

Teague modified the theatre plans slightly, and builders completed the structure, the steel beams of which had stood like a blot on the landscape. The building, now called the Allen Theatre, cost $135,000 and was completed in 1916. In true booster fashion, a correspondent for the *Moose Jaw Daily News* observed that the facility, the finest of its kind in the prairie West, could be called a "made-in-Moose Jaw building."[19]

The brick-clad exterior of the facility, like the exterior of the Allen Theatre built three years earlier in Calgary, resembled a Venetian palazzo. Four pseudo-pilasters, each topped with a terracotta mask of a mythological figure, separated the upper façade into three bays. Patrons entered the theatre via the middle bay, which featured a kiosk, set back from the sidewalk. The auditorium accommodated 500 patrons and the balcony another 410. A Chicago-based cathedral and theatre decorator, A. Jasinski, completed the ceiling and the walls, giving them quasi-classical designs, such as cherubs in bas-relief and the Allen Theatre crest.

As we have seen, the Allens concentrated on creating movie theatres that provided the best possible environment for screening and watching motion pictures. Characteristically, they installed the latest equipment, including projectors supplied by the Nicholas Power Company of New York City. They hired an eight-piece ensemble and installed a grand piano so that the musicians could provide an appropriate background for watching movies. The management marked the opening of the theatre on 19 August 1916 with a gala celebration.[20]

From 1916 to 1922, the Allens pursued a policy of continuous programming, screening quality movies, providing fine musical accompaniment, and reserving seats, all for an admission ranging from ten cents for children to fifteen cents for adults. They screened films at the Allen Theatre until October; during the full entertainment season, they hosted road shows, supplied by Winnipeg's Walker Theatre, and vaudeville acts, supplied by the Orpheum circuit. Churches and church societies used the theatre on Sundays, free of charge.

Just before moving their operation to Toronto, the Allens hired architect J. W. Kirkland to build a 700-seat movie facility in Brandon, Manitoba. A thriving transportation, distribution, and marketing centre, Brandon boasted four movie theatres at the time: the Arcade, built in 1905, the Starland and the Bijou, both dating to 1909, and the Princess, which opened in 1910.[21] All four featured a wide range of entertainment, combining movies and live productions, both professional and amateur, and charging admission fees that ranged from ten cents for children to fifteen cents for adults. In addition, two legitimate theatres operated in the town. The Empire, which opened in 1914, featured controversial speakers, while the Strand, built in 1916, featured "big names," including Fannie Ward, Billie Burke, and Francis X. Bushman, not to mention travelling and local stage productions.[22]

Figure 37. The Allen Theatre (later the Capitol), Brandon, ca. 1964. Photo by Arthur Osborne.

Figure 38. Postcard showing the interior of the Allen Theatre, Brandon, ca. 1920.

The Allen Theatre in Brandon opened in 1917, at 113 8th Street. We know that local firms supplied the labour and the materials for this made-in-Brandon facility, but otherwise details regarding its construction are scant.[23] Kirkland downplayed the exterior, focusing on the interior and attending to the decorative details that affected the moviegoing experience. The builders clad the façade with red bricks, laid in a pattern of interlocking diamonds, which moved upwards in columns. Four pilasters on the upper level separated the space into three bays, a single-hung window standing at the centre of each. Kirkland gave the interior, including the auditorium, which resembled a Roman amphitheatre, a Beaux Arts treatment. Large bowl-shaped chandeliers hung from the border at regular intervals. The manager organized a gala celebration on 14 July 1917 to mark the official opening of the new Allen Theatre, and according to a correspondent for the *Brandon Daily Sun*, people in formal attire packed the building.[24]

Over the years, the management of the Brandon Allen Theatre featured Paramount and Artcraft films, in addition to live performances, charging an admission of five cents for children and fifteen cents for adults for matinee performances and ten cents for children and fifteen cents for adults for evening performances. During the last week of September 1918, management screened *Hearts of the World* (1918), the controversial feature film D. W. Griffith made for the Artcraft Company.[25]

Business in Brandon, as elsewhere throughout their empire, faltered for the Allens during the Spanish flu pandemic of 1918–19, which reached Québec City on 8 September 1918, killing nine American soldiers, and moved westward on troop trains, reaching Winnipeg on 30 September, Calgary on 2 October 1918, and Vancouver on 5 October 1918.[26] Between thirty thousand and fifty thousand Canadians died during the epidemic. Reporters noted that the ban on holding meetings in public places would affect about 125 theatres across western Canada and North Dakota, including those in such centres as Calgary, Edmonton, Medicine Hat, Swift Current, Moose Jaw, Regina, and Winnipeg. The writer also highlighted the economic impact of these closures, noting that these theatres employed about six hundred people, whose weekly salaries totalled about $15,000. Apparently, the loss in rentals amounted to about $6,000 per week.[27]

DEVISING A TRANSCONTINENTAL ARCHITECTURE

The campaign to establish a made-in-Canada chain of movie theatres stretching from coast to coast had moved to another level in 1916, when the major exhibitors sought the services of the American architects who had pioneered the development of a building designed expressly for screening motion pictures. The Nathanson organization hired Thomas W. Lamb, the New York–based architect who had designed the 1913 Regent Theatre, a facility devoted exclusively to screening motion pictures, to transform the Majestic Theatre in Toronto into the Regent Theatre, a deluxe facility that opened in 1916 and became the nucleus of the Famous Players chain (as we will see in chapter 6). Not to be outdone, the Allen organization hired C. Howard Crane, a Detroit-based architect who had just designed the Majestic Theatre, a 1,651-seat facility that opened in 1915 at 4120 Woodward Avenue, in Detroit. Crane planned and built many deluxe movie theatres for Allen Theatre Enterprises; by and large, these represented variations on the organization and the ornamentation of the 1917 Allen Theatre in Toronto, which soon became the flagship theatre of their chain.[28]

By 1915, Crane had demonstrated an impressive ability to design elegant theatres of every scale and scope. Like Lamb, he deployed the "Adam" style, a school of design and decoration that can be traced to the work of Scottish architect Robert Adam (1728–92) and his brother, James Adam (1740–94), who ran a company that designed, built, and decorated mansions and upper-class country houses in England and Scotland.[29] Characteristically, the brothers Adam harmonized the exterior and the interior of their buildings, applying simple architectural elements to façades, such as pilasters or columns, Palladian windows, pediments, and portals, suggesting Roman triumphal arches, arranging these according to the principles of balance and symmetry and decorating the surface with balustrades and cornices. They covered the ceilings and the walls of the interiors with a variety of plaster bas-relief forms, such as circles, ovals, and rectangles, embellishing these with cartouches, garlands of leaves and flowers, medallions, ribbons, swags, and urns, painting these in elaborate colour schemes.

Fanciful yet linear, the Adam style predominated in England and Scotland up to the 1790s and across North America up to the 1830s.

Architects, artists, and designers rediscovered the work of the brothers Adam during the Beaux Arts period, roughly from 1880 to 1920. Crane ran offices in Detroit and Windsor, Ontario, out of which he handled his Canadian contracts. He earned much acclaim for the movie theatres he designed for William Fox, among other movie magnates, including his Byzantine masterpiece, the 5,000-seat facility in St. Louis called the Fox Theatre. Built in 1929, the theatre still stands.[30]

Modelling the Toronto Allen Theatre on the Detroit Majestic Theatre, Crane applied neoclassical principles to the design of the exterior of the facility, including symmetry and repetition. He deployed the straight line and the arch to great effect, suggesting the loggia of a Venetian palazzo.[31] Patrons entered the theatre via an outer lobby and a spacious foyer, and from there they walked through one of four archways to enter the auditorium, designed as a Roman amphitheatre and decorated in the Adam style, the colours old rose, ivory, and French grey predominating. The tiered seating was arranged into three sections, the first (the closest to the screen) being bowl-shaped; two cross-aisles separated the second from the third, which served as a balcony.

Figure 39. The Allen Theatre (later the Tivoli), Toronto, 1919. Photograph by Arthur Goss. City of Toronto Archives, fonds 1231, item no. 842.

Figure 40. Interior of the Allen Theatre, Toronto, 1917. City of Toronto Archives, fonds 251, series 1278, file no. 160.

The management, including Ben Cronk, who served as the local manager, pledged to offer the entertainment-seeking public "artistic, refined film productions," along with "painstaking and courteous service" and top-quality music. Admission prices for adults ranged from fifteen to twenty-five cents for matinee performances (with reserved seating at twenty-five cents) and from twenty-five to fifty cents for evening performances. Violinist Luigi Romanelli, who served as the Allens' music director, and keyboardist Roland Todd provided musical accompaniment.

Like their colleagues at other Allen theatres, the managers organized a gala evening on 10 November 1917 to mark the official opening of the Toronto facility. The event served as another demonstration of the skill with which exhibitors advertised their "product," not to mention the important role that the architectural features of "purpose-built" theatres played in legitimatizing motion pictures as an art form and moviegoing as a cultural practice. It also illustrated the competing cultural discourses — British and American, popular and elite — that converged at the Canadian movie theatre during this period. The Allen family, together with local business and civic leaders, attended the grand event, which included a screening of Cecil B. DeMille's *The Little American* (1917), a war film starring Mary Pickford, Toronto's favourite daughter, and two newcomers, Wallace Beery and Ramon Novarro.

The Toronto theatre served as the Allens' headquarters. According to Floyd S. Chalmers, who interviewed the Allens in 1920, every weekday Jule and Jay, responsible for selecting the films that were screened at Allen theatres across the country, convened a "miniature grand jury" at the theatre; Herb Allen and Ben Cronk, the supervisors of all the Toronto theatres, took part in these deliberations. Interestingly, on average 75 percent of the motion pictures screened at these meetings were rejected as being unsuitable for their clientele. Usually, a film deemed suitable was exhibited first at their main Toronto theatre. The "jury" believed that Toronto motion picture fans were "very, very critical" and that if these people approved of a film it was ready to tour the country.[32] They then purchased anywhere from three to eight copies of the film with a view to sending it to theatres across the country.

A SHIFTING CONTEXT AND THE BUILDING CAMPAIGN OF 1918–21

Despite the difficulties World War I created, the growing popularity of motion pictures translated into increasing profits, encouraging leading producers and distributors to expand their operations. With the outbreak of war, British and European production had virtually stopped, leaving the development of the art and the industry to American companies. From 1914 to 1924 American companies produced 90 percent of the films that were exhibited.[33] Vertically integrated motion picture companies, that is, those that oversee a product from the planning stage through the production and the distribution stages to the consumption stage, vied for pre-eminence.

Adolph Zukor, a Hungarian-born Jew, understood the importance of vertical integration early in his career as a movie impresario.[34] He began as the operator of a grand nickelodeon in New York City, convinced that motion pictures would become a major cultural force. In 1912, he secured the rights to distribute *The Loves of Queen Elizabeth* (1912), a French film starring Sarah Bernhardt, then billed as the greatest actress in the world. This venture was a huge success, and with the profits he organized Famous Players, a production company geared to presenting photographed versions of plays, including Edwin S. Porter's *The Prisoner of Zenda* (1913), starring James Hackett, and *The Count of Monte Cristo* (1912–13), starring Hobart Bosworth, a character actor with stage experience. Zukor soon realized that distributing his films was a major challenge.

Figure 41. Adolph Zukor, president of the Famous Players–Lasky Corporation. Photo courtesy of Photofest.

Meanwhile, in 1912, W. W. Hodkinson organized the merger of eleven rental bureaus to form Paramount Pictures, the first nationwide feature film distributor in the industry.[35] Hodkinson thought that Paramount would help producers finance their pictures by way of advance rentals from the exchanges; in return, the firm would charge producers a distribution fee of 35 percent of the gross to cover operating costs and to provide a built-in profit. Soon, the producers of the best films signed up, including Famous Players, Jesse L. Lasky Feature Play Company, Bosworth, and Oliver Morosco. Zukor chafed at the terms, however, and resolved to go into distribution himself. Via a set of intricate manoeuvres, including the June 1916 merger of Famous Players with Jesse Lasky's studio to form the Famous Players–Lasky Corporation, he emerged as the director of an integrated company, one that would serve as the model for the "studio system." Paramount Pictures became the (giant) distribution subsidiary of the new firm. Famous Players–Lasky, which was based in Hollywood, would go on to produce highly successful "family" pictures, seldom creating "deep" films but nevertheless providing agreeable light entertainment.[36] Controlling the best talent in the industry enabled Zukor to dominate the field. By 1918, Paramount was distributing 220 feature films.[37]

Figure 42. Advertisement for Adolph Zukor's Famous Players Film Company, which had just released The Prisoner of Zenda (1913). Moving Picture World, 25 *January* 1913, 331.

Zukor had learned an important lesson from the development of the First National Exhibitors' Circuit (see chapter 1). He resolved to enter the exhibition business — and to increase his company's revenue — because the cost of producing films kept going up, thanks to the price of screenplays and the salaries of stars.[38] Late in 1919, Zukor obtained a loan of $1 million from Kuhn, Loeb & Company, investment bankers on Wall Street, with a view to covering a stock flotation, and with this support he embarked on a massive campaign of theatre acquisition and construction, planning to operate first-run venues in all the major metropolitan centres. His representatives, known as "the wrecking crew" and "the dynamite gang," coerced independent exhibitors to lease Famous Players–Lasky Corporation films and to sell or to lease their facilities by threatening those who refused, telling them that their film service would be cut off and that Paramount would build or lease competing facilities nearby, tactics employed fifteen years earlier by Edison Trust agents.[39] By 1919, Zukor had acquired or built 303 first-run theatres, adding exhibition to his production and distribution activities. By 1921, he had acquired or built 400 theatres in the United States and Canada. First National executives followed his example, and (as we have seen) built a studio in Burbank, California. Zukor achieved a major victory in this campaign when in 1926 he acquired the controlling interest in the Balaban and Katz chain, comprising 93 theatres in and around Chicago. This chain had served as First National's major base.

In Canada, meanwhile, the Allens were enjoying great success. From 1918 to 1921, their business strategy had enabled them to dominate the market in the prairie West, challenging the opposition by building bigger movie palaces and acquiring more luxurious theatres. They believed that their business prospects looked good indeed. After all, young people in increasing numbers were flocking to movie theatres, in search of fun and excitement. Their latest expansion campaign included building deluxe facilities in urban centres across the country, including Montréal, Winnipeg, Calgary, and Vancouver. In 1919, Jay travelled to Europe, staying three months. He inspected motion picture production plants in Great Britain and France and talked to producers about the kinds of movies the Canadian public wanted to see.[40] As well, the Allens bought John Schuberg's chain of theatres and his First National franchise in 1919, spending about $1 million. As we have seen, Schuberg operated fourteen theatres, including three first-run movie houses in Winnipeg and three first-run houses in Vancouver. Thus, by 1920 the Allens ran the largest movie exhibition chain in Canada, operating sixty theatres in twenty-one Canadian cities, many having a seating capacity of over two thousand.[41] According to at least one report, these facilities represented an investment of $25 million.[42] Ultimately, their goal was to establish a worldwide circuit. As a columnist for the Cleveland *Sunday News-Leader* observed, they tried to expand into the United States, where they built a 3,400-seat facility in Cleveland, Ohio, and planned to build a 4,000-seat facility in Detroit.[43] In the United Kingdom, they acquired the most attractive property in London, the Empire Theatre and the Queen's Hotel, in Leicester Square, for a price of $4 million, with a view to opening a grand movie palace.[44] Plans for expansion also included the USSR, where the Allens aimed to build a deluxe movie theatre in Smolensk.

Not surprisingly, the Allens planned to open a third theatre in Edmonton. They already controlled the Gem, a 490-seat facility built in 1914, and the Monarch, a 600-seat facility that opened the following year. A correspondent for the *Edmonton Bulletin* noted that the new Allen Theatre would bring the number of theatres in the chain to thirty-two.[45]

Figure 43. The Allen Theatre, Edmonton, 1918. Glenbow Archives ND-3-1039.

Figure 44. Interior of the Allen Theatre, Edmonton, 1919. City of Edmonton Archives EA 160-272.

The Allens hired H. L. (Herbert) Gage to draw up the plans for the deluxe facility, to be built at 10065 Jasper Avenue, at the very heart of Edmonton's business district. The structure, modelled on the Toronto Allen, cost $150,000.[46] The Allens announced that, according to "policy," they would provide patrons with the best moviegoing experience that money could buy. By this, they meant building movie theatres in accordance with the latest principles of science and art. They called their facilities "Temples of the Silent Art."[47]

Characteristically, the architect downplayed the exterior, which, like the exterior of all their theatres, was meant to be dignified and unpretentious in appearance, and instead concentrated on the auditorium, where the real "show" would take place.[48] Clad in rough, terracotta-coloured brick, the façade featured (on the street level) a wide entrance, which was flanked by two retail spaces. Two signs identified the theatre: one consisting of the words "ALLEN THEATRE" stretched across the front, above the windows and below the balustrade, and a second, reading "ALLEN," hung vertically. A correspondent for the *Edmonton Bulletin* noted that patrons were impressed by the Adamesque finish of the facility, the graceful lines and soft tones of which pleased the eye.[49] The auditorium, again laid out as a Roman amphitheatre, featured seats that descended and sidewalls that curved inward toward the proscenium arch and the orchestra pit.

Commentators noted that the Allens had given the comfort and safety of moviegoers much consideration. Commenting on the theatre's state-of-the-art ventilating system, for example, a correspondent for the *Edmonton Journal* remarked that "influenza germs would stand but little chance in such a purified atmosphere as this."[50] The Allens' attention to providing patrons a memorable moviegoing experience was also apparent in the installation of a Hillgreen-Lane pipe organ, costing $15,000, and a Williams grand piano.

Max Allen, the manager of the Edmonton Allen from 1918 to 1924, implemented the Allen entertainment policy. That is, he screened quality motion pictures at reasonable prices, including Paramount, Artcraft, Select, and Goldwyn pictures, plus Roscoe "Fatty" Arbuckle comedies, Burton Holmes travelogues, and British weeklies, and featuring popular Paramount and Artcraft players.[51]

The ritualized gala opening on 2 December 1918 was attended by many dignitaries, including the lieutenant governor of Alberta, as well as by many business and civic leaders. The mayor of Edmonton read telegrams from various movie personalities and formally opened the facility, declaring that the event marked the dawn of an era of peace and prosperity. The popular *Hearts of the World* served as the main attraction.

STORM CLOUDS

The Allens also decided to build another theatre in Saskatchewan, a deluxe facility that opened in 1918 at 1801 11th Avenue, on the corner of 11th Avenue and Broad Street, in the heart of Regina's business district. The population of the city had grown from 6,169 in 1908, when builders began work on the legislative buildings for the new province of Saskatchewan, to 26,127 in 1916. This was enough to support two vaudeville houses, the Regina and the Sherman, and three movie theatres, the Rex and the Rose, both of which the Allens had operated for a number of years, and the Roseland. Economic prospects for the community looked good. Wheat prices were climbing, which they continued to do until 1920, when they began a collapse. Drought intensified the difficulties, and the years from 1920 to 1924 were marked by a serious economic recession.[52]

Again, the Allens hired Herbert Gage to design the 1,000-seat, brick-and-steel structure.[53] Gage added a number of novel features to the design, giving the brickwork on the exterior an embroidered effect and eliminating pillars and posts in the interior. Despite labour shortages caused by the flu epidemic, the general contractor completed this project in good time, at a cost of $85,000.

The two-storey, brick-and-steel building, clad in red brick, offered passersby two similar façades, one facing Broad Street and one facing 11th Avenue.[54] On the Broad Street side, shops occupied the bays in the middle and far end, and tall, narrow windows dominated the bays on the upper level; on the 11th Avenue side, rectangular patterns dominated the bays on the street level and on the upper level. A large "T" superimposed on an "A," the Allens' monogram, crowned each of the pilasters and stood at the centre of the bays on the 11th Avenue side.

Figure 45. The Allen Theatre, Regina, 1918. Saskatchewan Archives Board R-B13509.

Commentators praised the design as well as the ornamentation of the interior, especially the auditorium, which, like the Edmonton Allen, had been treated as if it were a Roman amphitheatre. Two wide aisles divided the seats into three sections. It featured a small stage and, in front of it, an orchestra pit, big enough to accommodate a concert grand piano and an ensemble of about six musicians. In their advertisements, the Allens promised to screen quality motion pictures at the new theatre, including the first releases of Artcraft, Paramount, Select, and Goldwyn production companies. Characteristically, the management organized a gala celebration on 30 December 1918 to mark the official opening. Again, the event included a screening of *Hearts of the World*. On this occasion, a symphony orchestra from New York City provided the musical accompaniment.[55]

Buoyed by the success of these projects, in 1918 the Allens asked C. Howard Crane to build a deluxe, 2,200-seat facility at 285 Donald Street, Winnipeg, east of Portage Avenue and just opposite the entrance to Eaton's.[56] The Allens already controlled forty-six theatres and, in addition to this project, were building or planning to build eleven more, including deluxe theatres in Vancouver, Montréal, and Calgary, many designed by Crane, including the 3,400-seat Allen Theatre in Cleveland, built in 1921. However, the Allens experienced several developments along the way that affected business negatively, including (as mentioned) the Spanish flu pandemic.

By May 1919, the Allens had completed their arrangements for building the Winnipeg Allen. Gage told the press that work on the Donald Street project would get underway in June, by which time the leases of a number of tenants occupying the property would have expired, and that workers would then demolish the buildings standing on the site. He predicted that the new Allen Theatre would be open for business on 1 December 1919. Soon, however, a major labour dispute forced the workers to put down their tools.[57]

When negotiations between management and labour in the building and metal trades broke down on 15 May 1919, the Winnipeg Trades and Labour Council called a general strike.[58] At issue were the principle of collective bargaining, better wages, and the improvement of often dreadful working conditions. Within two hours, about 30,000 workers left their jobs, turning the life of Winnipeg (a city of 170,000) upside down.

Figure 46. Architect's sketch of Winnipeg's Allen Theatre. Manitoba Free Press, 29 *November* 1919, 5. *Provincial Archives of Manitoba, Winnipeg–Theatres–Allen 2, negative no.* 9863.

Public-sector employees such as policemen, firemen, postal workers, streetcar workers, telephone operators, and employees of waterworks and other utilities joined the workers on strike in an impressive display of working-class solidarity. On 1 June 1919, 10,000 war veterans showed their support by marching on the provincial legislature. Before the strikers returned to work on 25 June 1919, the government had arrested ten leaders of the Central Strike Committee and members of the Royal North-West Mounted Police had charged into a crowd of strikers, resulting in thirty causalities, including one death.

As Kirwan Cox writes, the strike affected the Allen organization in three ways.[59] First, all theatre construction in Winnipeg came to a halt, meaning that the Allen Theatre was not going to be completed on time — or on budget. Second, the strike adversely affected attendance, a major source of the Allens' revenue. Projectionists walked out, forcing the managers to take over; backing the strike, patrons boycotted movie theatres. Third, convinced that the Bolshevik Revolution was going to sweep across Canada, John Schuberg (who had been losing money) sold his theatre holdings, including the best theatres in the city: the Province, the Bijou, and the Gaiety. As noted, the Allens acquired these theatres from Schuberg during the spring of 1919, plus the First National franchise, spending about $1 million.[60]

In the aftermath of the strike, the builders began this made-in-Winnipeg project on 5 July 1919 and completed the building in good time, despite an early snowfall that arrived just as the workers were putting on the roof. During the last weeks of the project, three crews worked eight-hour shifts around the clock to complete the interior decorations. They completed the project late in December.

The new "Temple of the Silent Art," as it was heralded in advertisements, bore a striking resemblance to the 1917 Allen Theatre in Toronto. Commentators remarked on the plain exterior, which they nevertheless found to be dignified and pleasing.[61] At the upper level, eight fluted Corinthian pilasters, standing on a massive lintel and supporting a massive frieze, separated the brick façade into seven bays, each featuring a Palladian window fitted with a wrought iron railing. At street level, large pillars separated the space into five bays: four shops (two on either side) flanking the wide entrance, at the centre of which stood a ticket office. A flat, metal marquee stretching across the entrance and extending out to the edge of the sidewalk protected moviegoers during inclement weather. Finally, a sign hanging vertically at the middle of the entrance identified the building: a circular section on the top carried the word "ALLEN," a narrow section carried the word "THEATRE," and a rectangular section at the bottom of the sign carried the word "PHOTOPLAYS."

Commentators praised the Adamesque design Crane gave to the interior, especially the enormous auditorium, which featured a 40-foot ceiling, plus a massive dome with a great crystal chandelier, elaborately decorated side walls curving toward the massive proscenium arch, (60 feet long and 40 feet high), and wave upon wave of large, padded seats, fourteen hundred altogether, which formed a semi-circle.[62] As in other Allen theatres, American decorator Theodore Jagmin designed the plaster work, which included figures and patterns in bas-relief.

Creating the appropriate "atmosphere" for watching movies — as the Allens explained in their advertisements — included providing the appropriate music and altering the lighting to complement the films being screened.[63] For this theatre, Crane designed not a conventional orchestra pit but a curved bandshell, which he located behind the proscenium arch; there, obscured by a small, artificial hedge, the orchestra of fifteen players produced music to accompany the films. The Allens also installed a Hillgreen-Lane concert pipe organ, imported from Alliance, Ohio, at a cost of $20,000, to the left of the pit.

Commentators described the richly furnished mezzanine, measuring 120 feet wide by 30 feet deep, as the most attractive feature of the interior.[64] The Allens furnished the area with richly upholstered chairs and settees, oak writing desks, and rose-coloured piano lamps. The gently sloping balcony accommodated about six hundred patrons. The fireproof projection room — the heart of the theatre — was located at the back of the balcony. The chief operator and two assistants operated the state-of-the-art movie projectors (installed at a cost of $15,000) and adjusted the colour and the brilliance of the house lights.

Figure 47. Interior of the Allen Theatre, Winnipeg, 1922. Provincial Archives of Manitoba, Winnipeg–Theatres–Allen, negative no. 9862.

The management, including manager Will N. Elliott, formerly the manager of the Regent Theatre, Toronto, and his staff focused on living up to the Allens' slogan, "Satisfaction in Excellence." Characteristically, Elliott organized a gala evening on 20 January 1920 to mark the official opening of what was the forty-seventh and to this point the largest theatre in the Allen circuit. Barney Allen travelled from Toronto to take part in the celebration.

Again, the Allens promoted this theatre as a made-in-Winnipeg project. This effort included inviting moviegoers via newspaper advertisements to invest in the Allens' Winnipeg Theatres, a thriving corporation controlling the principal motion picture theatres in the city: the new Allen, the Bijou, the Dominion, the Gaiety, the Province, and the Rex.[65] They urged members of the community to buy 7 percent cumulative preferred shares of $100 each at par, adding that acquiring this stock entitled each purchaser to a bonus of 25 percent of common stock.

In order to highlight the health of the industry, they reprinted a news report — which had been issued recently by Dow, Jones, and Company — stating that, in 1919, movie theatre operators across the United States had earned $800 million, as compared to $675 million for 1918.[66] They went on to say that the earnings of the six constituent theatres were in fact sufficient to pay the 7 percent interest on the entire amount of preferred stock (outstanding after the amalgamation) fully six times over. Edward Brown and Company, bond dealers, handled this offering.

However, developments, particularly in the realm of distribution, were afoot that would challenge the Allens' ability to deliver on all of these promises. In 1916, Adolph Zukor formed Artcraft Pictures Corporation expressly to distribute the movies of Mary Pickford.[67] As Tino Balio puts it, Pickford's movies "could no longer be sold as a series, but one by one, separate and apart from the Paramount program." Pickford became the first star to produce her own movies and to win a considerable degree of control over her work. In 1917, Artcraft's president, Walter E. Greene, signed Douglas Fairbanks, at a weekly salary of $10,000, and in 1918 contracted to release the movies of D. W. Griffith, starting with *Hearts of the World* (1918). The Allens' contract to distribute Paramount Pictures expired in September 1919. Contrary to their expectations, Zukor awarded the contract to the Nathanson group (see chapter 6).

The Allens were not entirely dependent on their Paramount contract, since in December 1918 they had secured the rights to distribute and to exhibit Goldwyn films.[68] Goldwyn Pictures had grown out of the partnership Samuel Goldwyn and his brother-in-law, Jesse L. Lasky, formed in 1913 to make a feature-length film. They hired Cecil B. DeMille, an aspiring playwright, to direct *The Squaw Man* (1914), an early Western about an Indian girl (played by Winifred Kingston) who saves the life of a British aristocrat (played by Dustin Farnum). The film was a huge success. Zukor was so encouraged by this project that he engineered a merger; as we have seen, they called the new company the Famous Players–Lasky Corporation. Preferring to work on his own, Goldwyn left, and in 1916 he formed his own production company, Goldwyn Pictures Corporation, which produced the films of such stars as Maxine Elliott, Mary Garden, Mae Marsh, Mabel Normand, and Will Rogers. His shares in Goldwyn Pictures were acquired by Metro, and via a succession of mergers, the studio known as MGM was formed. He became an independent producer, forming Samuel Goldwyn, Inc., and releasing his films through United Artists.

Nevertheless, the Allen enterprise remained vulnerable to the effects of shifting alliances in the realms of production and distribution. For example, in 1916, Lewis J. Selznick, the Russian-born Jewish-American movie impresario and father of David O. Selznick, the celebrated producer, was forced out of his position as general manager of World Pictures. Selznick took Clara Kimball Young with him and formed his own production company, Select Pictures Corporation; he leased the Solax studio in Fort Lee, Florida, making it the production centre for the Clara Kimball Young Film Corporation.[69] The following year, Selznick merged with Adolph Zukor, president of Famous Players Pictures, calling the new company Select Pictures, which handled the films of a number of up-and-coming stars, including Constance Talmadge, who appeared in such films as *Panthea* (1917), and Clara Kimball Young, who appeared in such films as *Eyes of Youth* (1921). The firm went bankrupt in 1923. As well, the First National Exhibitors' Circuit (as we saw in chapter 1) handled the films of Charlie Chaplin, Milton Sills, and Richard Barthelmess, among others. Clearly, being able to count on access to the films produced by competing production companies was crucial to an exhibitor's success. As the Allens would soon discover, such access became increasingly difficult to ensure.

Figure 48. Advertisement for Allen's Calgary Theatre's stock offering of $260,000. Calgary Herald, *19 March 1920, 31.*

FINANCIAL DIFFICULTIES

About the time they were planning the Winnipeg Allen, the Allens once again turned their attention to Calgary, hoping to build the sixty-first facility in the chain they ran in twenty-one Canadian cities. They hired C. Howard Crane to build a deluxe facility, which would seat 1,951 patrons, at 213 8th Avenue West, located at the heart of the city's financial district — a made-in-Calgary project that would cost the Allens over half a million dollars. In effect, this project marked the conclusion of the massive building program they had started in 1913 in Calgary.

Characteristically, the Allens financed the project in two ways. First, they secured a mortgage of $180,000 from the Minnesota Loan and Trust Company, with the National Trust Company as trustees, and, under the terms of the mortgage, sold bonds in Minneapolis. Second, Allen's Calgary Theatre, the company they formed to operate the theatre, offered entrepreneurs and moviegoers in Calgary $260,000 in preferred stock and common stock. Pursuing the strategy they had employed in Winnipeg, they presented themselves in advertisements as progressive "minds" making their way in "the world's fifth largest industry."[70] They encouraged local entrepreneurs and moviegoers to invest in Allen's Calgary Theatre, making the case that, thanks to the steady increase in theatre attendance generally and to the efficient management of the Allen theatre chain in particular, they could offer investors a dividend of at least 12 percent in the first year. In addition, they pointed out that "last year the number of people attending theatres in Calgary was enormous. More than 43 times the population of the city filled the theatres. This year, as the population increases, theatre attendance will also increase. Calgary will have good reason to be proud of the New Allen Theatre and Calgarians will patronize the beautiful movie house."[71]

Commentators, in booster fashion, described the Allen's Palace, thought to be the last word in movie theatre construction, as "the finest motion picture theatre in western Canada," noting that the exterior was also pleasing to the eye.[72] Predictably, many regarded the facility as the finest in the Allen chain. At the upper level of the exterior, fluted Corinthian pilasters, resting on a massive lintel and supporting an entablature, separated the brick-and-limestone façade into seven bays, the white limestone contrasting with the red of the tapestry bricks. Each of the central bays featured a circular stone decoration at the top and, at the bottom, a single-sash window topped with a low-pitched pediment. Four shops, two on either side, flanked the wide entrance. Above the entrance, a vertical sign outlined in light bulbs spelled out the name of the theatre, ALLEN'S PALACE, and at the entrance itself, a small marquee extended over the sidewalk, to protect incoming patrons. A series of floodlights illuminated the front of the building at night.

Figure 49. The Allen's Palace Theatre under construction, Calgary, 26 May 1921. Glenbow Archives PA-3537-1.

Figure 50. Interior of the Allen's Palace Theatre, Calgary, ca. 1925. Glenbow Archives NA-1178-2.

Commentators likewise described the interior of the new "Temple of the Silent Art" as striking. They praised such features as the massive marble staircases, which stood on either side of the foyer, the massive balcony, the thirty-foot ceiling of the auditorium, which featured a huge crystal chandelier and elaborate decorations in bas-relief, the orchestra pit, which accommodated the seven-piece band that provided musical accompaniment for the films, and the mass of upholstered seats, which were organized into five sections. Theodore Jagmin created the neo-classical designs and motifs called for by Crane's plans, and J. Davidson Company, Winnipeg, executed the plain and ornamental plaster work according to his directions. The Hillgreen-Lane organ was located next to the pit, and the front openings in the boxes concealed the pipes and the complex lighting system.

The staff, including J. F. Price, the general manager, organized a gala celebration on 25 October 1921 to mark the official opening. Invited guests included Alberta's Lieutenant Governor Brett and Calgary's Mayor S. H. (Samuel) Adams.[73] They screened "Allen Screen Magazine," a compendium of travel and world news events, "especially selected and edited for Allen's Palace patrons," and a comedy, *She Sighed by the Sea Side* (1921), featuring Ben Turpin, Billy Bevan, and Mack Sennett's "bathing beauties" as preludes to the feature film, which was Rupert Hughes's *Dangerous Curves Ahead* (1921), a comedy about married life.

The Palace would become an important social and cultural centre, although not without overcoming some difficulties. The management settled on a program, the specific items in which changed every Monday and Thursday, that comprised a feature film; a musical performance, such as an organ recital or an orchestral interlude; a vaudeville act or two (sometimes followed by a local performer); a documentary produced by the Allen cameraman; and a series of screen snapshots about the private lives of popular screen actors. The theatre also hosted the first radio broadcast in Calgary, which took place in 1922, when the *Calgary Herald* inaugurated its radio station, later known as CFAC. Three members of the Palace orchestra broadcast a performance from the station set up in the Herald Building; these signals were picked up and aired by the receiving set installed in the Palace. Despite the indistinct (scratchy) reception, the audience found this an "unexpected and novel experience."[74]

By 1921, the Allens had clearly became the major force in the motion picture business in Canada: they operated a chain of more than sixty movie theatres in twenty-one Canadian cities, many having a seating capacity of over two thousand. Moreover, they were expanding into the United States, Great Britain, and the USSR, building new theatres and taking over existing ones. They encouraged moviegoers across the country to regard Allen Theatre Enterprises was "an all-Canadian achievement, born of an acorn to hope, courage, and desire to serve, grown to a sturdy oak of more potential strength."

However, as we will see in the next chapter, the loss of the lucrative Paramount franchise in 1919 soon affected their business adversely. Undoubtedly, they sensed that their fortunes were about to take a turn for the worse: they placed a series of large, posterlike advertisements in Toronto newspapers, in which the development of Allen Theatre Enterprises was linked to the development of Canada as a nation. One advertisement features a tall ship resting at sunset in a harbour labelled "Success." The ship has just sailed through rough water filled with the rocks of "Financial Worries," "Building Difficulties," "Musical Perplexities," and "Picture Problems." The text reads: "From the days of the little Allen Nickelodeon, when the pictures shown might be properly described as 'shakin' pictures, until the present time, when Allen Theatres extend from coast to coast in Canada to the number of more than sixty, when Allen theatres become factors in the entertainment of the people in Great Britain and the United States — there has been the aspiration and the determination to sail a clearly-laid course to be ultimate in Allen achievement, with a Canadian craft and a Canadian crew."[75] Another (see figure 59) features a man with a magnifying glass in his hand, studying images of Allen movie theatres, and, to the side, a man with a view camera taking a photograph of a beaver cutting down a tree. The text reads: "They went over the ocean and secured theatre locations in the heart of the British Empire. And in the name of welcoming Canadian courage and enterprise, the British people show themselves ready to extend a crowning gesture. Although Allen Theatre Enterprises at home and beyond our border radiates the influence of an all-Canadian achievement, born from an acorn of hope, courage and desire to serve, grown to a sturdy young oak of more potential strength."[76]

Major storm clouds soon appeared, signalling serious trouble. In 1922 and in 1923, under the Tax Recovery Act, the City of Calgary placed caveats on the title of the Allen's Palace Theatre so as to recover property taxes. The Allens could not make their mortgage payments, and a foreclosure order was granted in October 1924, vesting the property in the Minnesota Loan and Trust Company for the bond holders. J. B. (Jack) Barron, the Allens' Calgary-based solicitor, formed the Palace Theatre Company, secured a second mortgage on the property, and leased it from the Minnesota Loan and Trust Company, hoping to recoup some of the money the Allen organization owed him.[77] (As we will see in chapter 7, Barron would later become an important theatre impresario in the prairie West.) The rosy pronouncements of lengthy newspaper advertisements notwithstanding, the Allen empire was about to fall.

6

FAMOUS PLAYERS CANADIAN CORPORATION LIMITED

N. L. (Nat) Nathanson, the Russian-born, Toronto-based movie impresario, "rationalized" movie exhibition in Canada, founding two national movie theatre chains, Famous Players and Odeon Theatres. In doing so, he created the duopoly that shaped movie exhibition in this country for more than half a century.[1] In this chapter, we examine Nathanson's initial attempt to create a Canadian-owned, Canadian-operated chain of movie theatres. This meant trying to dominate the market by forcing the Allens out of business and trying to wrest the control of movie exhibition from American interests. These were represented by Adolph Zukor, who exerted his influence from Broadway and Hollywood.[2] A belief that Canadians should control the Canadian movie exhibition industry shaped Nathanson's business strategies.[3] He brought British films to Canada and encouraged overseas production companies to make movies with Canadian settings. He hoped to create a chain of movie theatres that would span the British Empire, linking sites in Canada, Great Britain, South Africa, and Australia.

The chronicle of Nathanson's career reads like a Horatio Alger story. He started with little in the way of worldly goods, but via his ability, ingenuity, and perseverance rose to a position of considerable importance in the cultural life of Canada. Like the Allen brothers, he was the son of Russian-born Jewish parents, Benjamin and Yetta Nathanson. Benjamin and Louis, their eldest son, migrated from Taurage, Lithuania,

Figure 51. Nat Nathanson, managing director of Famous Players, Toronto, 1921. Cropped version of a photograph of the newly created Canadian Broadcasting Corporation's board of governors. Library and Archives Canada, negative no. C-045317 (accession no. 1971-271 NPC; Mikan no. 3380855).

to the United States in 1885, and Yetta and five children followed in 1889.[4] The family settled in Minneapolis, Minnesota, where they raised eight children. As a youth, Nathanson worked as a newsboy, enjoying the competition involved in selling papers, and after leaving school he worked as an agent selling railroad tickets for a cut-rate concern.

Eventually, this enterprise collapsed, and in 1907 Nathanson, then twenty-one, moved north, with a view to making his fortune in the entertainment industry of Toronto. At first, he worked for H. A. Dorsey, a genial Irish entrepreneur who ran amusement parks in a number of cities in eastern Canada; Nathanson managed the concession stands at Scarboro Beach, Toronto, and then at Dominion Park, Montréal. While managing the refreshment stands at Scarboro Beach, Nathanson introduced the "edible holder" we know as the ice cream cone.[5] He then worked as a salesman for the E. L. Ruddy Company, an advertising agency that made movie posters, billboards, neon signs, and marquees. He showed a knack for promoting goods and services, and in due course he and W. Rein Wadsworth set up their own poster advertising agency.

According to Hye Bossin, the editor of *Canadian Film Weekly*, Nathanson gravitated toward projects geared to the masses — and succeeded because he had an uncanny ability to conceptualize big projects and to see them through to completion. Friends and colleagues were impressed not only by his dynamic mind, but also by his gift for organizing material and non-material resources and for understanding the whims and the tastes of the public.[6] Bossin adds that Nathanson knew what people liked even before they did, and he gave it to them. Despite the fame and the fortune these abilities brought him, the movie mogul never forgot his origins; he would display one of his most cherished possessions on his desk: a 1902 photograph of himself as a cornet player in the *Minneapolis Journal*'s newsboys' band.

Nathanson pursued a variety of interests, over and above his business projects. For example, he served as a member of the Toronto Board of Trade and the CBC Board of Governors; he promoted horse racing and ice hockey; he supported a number of charitable organizations, such as the Canadian Red Cross. He married Violet Ruby Kuppenheimer in 1909, and sometime after their divorce in 1913 he married Irene Harris, the daughter of an Omaha newspaperman and later a Toronto theatre manager. Quite possibly, he became a Canadian citizen (and thus a British subject) shortly before 1926.[7] He died unexpectedly on 27 May 1943, at the age of fifty-seven, after a brief illness. Speaking at the funeral, Toronto, J. J. Fitzgibbons paid tribute to his predecessor at Famous Players with these words: "The industry has lost one of its most colorful characters. His opinions were used to the betterment of the motion picture industry, not only in Canada but also in the United States."[8]

THE REGENT THEATRE COMPANY

Nathanson developed an interest in moving pictures when he worked for the E. L. Ruddy Company. He told reporters years later that he sensed the great possibilities moving pictures represented — and noticed that exhibitors were overlooking a number of strategies for presenting their shows to greater effect. What he needed, he added, was an opportunity to test his ideas.[9] That came in 1916, when he and a group of financiers (J. P. Bickell, P. W. Cushman, E. L. Ruddy, W. J. Sheppard, and J.B. Tudhope) formed the Regent Theatre Company, Limited, with a view to acquiring and transforming the Majestic Theatre, located on Adelaide Street, Toronto, into the Regent Theatre, a deluxe movie theatre, often described as the first of its kind in Canada.[10] The Majestic, owned by J. Ambrose Small, had featured melodramas. Ruddy served as president, Nathanson as managing director, Bickell as vice-president, and Cushman as secretary-treasurer in this Canadian venture.

The Nathanson group purchased the property and the building for $300,000, and commissioned Thomas W. Lamb, the leading theatre architect, to erect a steel-and-concrete facility at a cost of $200,000.[11] The builders knocked down much of the building, save for the outside walls, replaced the two balconies with one having a gentle slope, constructed a huge mezzanine floor, featuring elegant restrooms and a club-like lounge, enlarged the stage, and rearranged the seating in the auditorium and in the balcony to accommodate a total of 1,475 patrons, ensuring that every padded-leather seat afforded an unobstructed view of the screen. The decorators finished the interior in the Adam style, producing attractive designs on the walls and the ceilings, and covered the floors throughout with red carpet. Lamb equipped this fireproofed building with a number of unique features, including a sophisticated lighting system that enabled the management to change the tones of light in the auditorium, thereby altering the atmosphere, and a powerful ventilating system.

In advertisements, Nathanson promised that the Regent would offer moviegoers high-calibre entertainment: first-run Paramount pictures, a playbill that changed three times per week, and competitive admission prices. The group also installed the latest Casavant concert organ at a cost of $11,000, and hired eminent musicians to provide an appropriate background for the films exhibited. They opened the "Picture Play Palace" to the public on 25 August 1916 and screened a romantic photo play called *Little Lady Eileen* (1916), featuring Marguerite Clark.[12]

The Nathanson group soon expanded their operations, acquiring several Toronto neighbourhood houses and building a few new theatres in small Ontario cities. In 1918, Nathanson, now the managing director of Paramount Theatres, Limited, as the company was now called, learned that the Allens, the holders of the much-prized Paramount franchise, had refused Zukor's offer to form a fifty-fifty partnership and resolved to secure the franchise for himself.[13] Upon hearing this, Nathanson then travelled to New York City with a proposition, offering Zukor a partnership in his theatre company, based on a fifty-fifty split of profits, in return for the exclusive rights to distribute Paramount pictures in Canada. Zukor replied that, in order to gain the franchise, the impresario would have to build additional movie theatres.[14]

In the meantime, Nathanson organized a film distribution company called Regal Films, Limited, installing his brother, H. L. (Henry) Nathanson, as the managing director, and acquired the rights to distribute the productions of Metro Pictures Corporation, Pathé Frères, and Triangle Motion Picture Company. With this arrangement in place, Nathanson intensified his efforts to expand their operation into a major chain of theatres.[15]

Figure 52. *Advertisement for the formal opening of the Regent Theatre, Toronto.* Toronto Mail and Empire, 25 August 1916, 6.

THE ALLENS FALTER

It was becoming obvious that Adolph Zukor had intensified his campaign of theatre acquisition and construction, determined that he would operate first-run theatres in all major markets.[16] Zukor's production company, Famous Players–Lasky Corporation, was producing between forty and fifty films per year, and he wanted to ensure that his films would be screened in his theatres. He planned to invade Canada, via a partnership with the Nathanson organization if not via the Allen organization. The Allens had benefited hugely from their contract with Paramount Pictures to screen Famous Players–Lasky productions, but Zukor refused to renew that contract when it expired on 1 September 1919.[17] As we have seen, the Allens nevertheless faced the future with optimism. On the one hand, they controlled movie exhibition in Canada, operating a chain of forty-five theatres.[18] On the other, their film exchange, Famous Players Film Service, a profitable part of their business, still had the rights to distribute the productions of Select, Goldwyn, First National (in western Canada), the latter thanks to the Schuberg deal, and access to Lord Beaverbrook films through Sam Smith, an associate of Lord Beaverbrook. Overproduction kept exhibitors busy. Producers in the United States made nearly nine hundred motion pictures in 1919; apparently, the market absorbed only 75 percent of these works.[19] However, the Allens could also see that raising capital locally, by floating shares in individual theatres, would not finance their building program at home and their expansion abroad. They would have to secure major financial support.

Accordingly, the Allens looked to William Maxwell Aitken, Lord Beaverbrook, the Ontario-born, London-based politician and newspaper tycoon. Lord Beaverbrook had moved in 1910 to Great Britain, where he had been elected Member of Parliament for Ashton-under-Lyne and had built up a chain of newspapers, including the *Daily Express* in 1915 and the *Sunday Express* in 1918, bringing them to unprecedented levels of circulation. He was appointed minister of information in Lloyd George's wartime cabinet and elevated to the peerage. In 1918, as Kirwan Cox puts it, Lord Beaverbrook sold his Montréal firm, Royal Securities, to his partner, I. W. Killam, and bought into both Provincial Cinematograph Theatres and Pathé Frérès in an attempt to ward off Zukor's expansion into Great Britain.[20] By the spring of 1920, Lord Beaverbrook controlled three hundred theatres, about 10 percent of the total number in Britain. He then thought about investing in theatres in the United States and Canada, declaring: "I have five million dollars to put into theatres in Canada."[21] Jay was visiting London at the time, seeking British capital, and apparently talked to Lord Beaverbrook, who offered the Allens $5 million for 50 percent of their holdings, which the latter would manage. However, the largest Canadian investors in Allen Theatre Enterprises, First National and the Bank of Commerce, wired Jule, telling him to reject the offer. This decision would prove disastrous to the Allens.[22]

In July 1920, the Allens "enrolled" each of their theatres in Associated First National Pictures, Inc., which was reincorporated in 1919, in order to ensure a steady flow of quality motion pictures. This arrangement enabled them to screen, starting in December, the films of such popular stars as Norma and Constance Talmadge, who had signed an exclusive contract with the association.[23] As well, because First National, one of the largest distributing organizations in the business at the time, handled independent films, the Allens were able to screen the work of such Canadians as Ernest Shipman when it became available.[24]

The Allens formed new companies for all their new theatres, offering shares to the public. As well, they consolidated all of their companies under a new holding company, Allen Theatres, Limited, capitalizing this firm at $5 million in preferred shares, which they offered to the public.[25] Edward Brown, a Winnipeg bond dealer, politician, and the treasurer for the province of Manitoba, underwrote the offering. The prospectus for the company, Cox writes, indicated that it was acquiring the entire assets of Jule and Jay Allen, including fifty-two theatres with a total seating capacity of 51,862, six theatres under construction with a total seating capacity of 13,200, three theatre sites, and a number of film exchanges. The prospectus also indicated that total earnings for the calendar year 1919 were $459,154.23 and that the earnings for the first four months of 1920 were $144,902.54. On paper, the Allens appeared to be in good shape.[26] However, Brown lost his cabinet position in the provincial election in 1922, and thus the underwriting failed.

Two economic developments exacerbated the situation for the Allens.[27] First, the depression of 1921–22, marked by the collapse of international wheat markets, led to a decline in movie attendance, which was the Allens' only source of revenue. Second, the federal government devalued the dollar 25 percent during the years 1920 to 1922. In response, Jay decided to make a short-term investment that would produce a quick profit: risking the money he owed creditors, he invested a fortune in the German mark, which was inflating at an astronomical rate, believing that the mark would hit bottom and then rebound.[28] However, the mark plummeted, and bankruptcy was certain.

NATHANSON FORMS FAMOUS PLAYERS

By the autumn of 1919, the Nathanson group operated a chain of sixteen movie venues in British Columbia and Ontario with a total seating capacity of fifteen thousand. Buoyed by this achievement, they formed, on 23 January 1920, Famous Players Canadian Corporation, capitalizing it at $15 million, with a view to seeking additional support.[29] Ray Lewis, the editor of *Canadian Moving Picture Digest*, later recalled that, in an interview with Nathanson, she mentioned that the Allens had rejected Lord Beaverbrook's offer and that the latter had declared that someone would get his $5 million for theatres in Canada.[30] In due course, Nathanson secured Lord Beaverbrook's financial support, but the details of the arrangement have remained vague.

Zukor, impressed by these initiatives, decided to form a partnership with the Nathanson group. On 5 February 1920, he invested $100,000 in Famous Players and granted the company the franchise for Paramount Pictures for a period of twenty years. A number of prominent Canadians became members of the board of directors, such as Sir Herbert Holt (Royal Bank), J. P. Bickell, W. D. Ross (Bank of Nova Scotia), and I. W. Killam (Royal Securities), who underwrote $4 million of the initial share offerings, which were listed on the stock exchanges in Toronto and Montréal. The board of directors included J. P. Bickell, H. D. H. Connick, I. W. Killam, N. L. Nathanson, W. C. Pitfield, W. D. Ross, W. J. Sheppard, J. B. Tudhope, and Adolph Zukor, with Zukor as the president and Nathanson the managing director.[31]

Armed with the most lucrative franchise of the day and supported by national and international capitalists, Nathanson turned his attention to establishing a chain of fifty movie theatres extending from coast to coast.[32] To this end, he employed a variety of business strategies to strengthen his position as an exhibitor — and to weaken that of his competitors, especially the Allens.

(1) *Locate theatres strategically.* Nathanson set out to acquire large, ideally located theatres with a view to refurbishing them. This meant forming affiliations with independent exhibitors. It has been said that he was heavy-handed in his dealings with independent exhibitors, "squeezing" them as he expanded his organization. Garth Drabinsky writes: "He would go into a town and say to an exhibitor: You're paying forty or fifty percent for pictures, what for? If you give me a partnership in your theatre, I'll give you Paramount pictures for only fifteen percent of the gross." It was hard to refuse such a deal since, as we have seen, Paramount produced what were widely regarded as the best pictures. If the exhibitor balked, he would employ Zukor's tactic of threatening to build a theatre right next door.[33] By means of such tactics, in four years he expanded the circuit from twenty-two to seventy theatres. Nathanson also planned to build large, luxurious movie theatres, locating them close to Allen theatres, and to buy choice real estate with a view to developing this property at the most appropriate moment.

(2) *Offer the public a new form of entertainment.* In press releases and newspaper advertisements, especially those circulated in the weeks leading up to the opening of a new theatre, Nathanson promised that Famous Players would revitalize the business of showing movies, that is, it would bring "a form of entertainment entirely new to western Canada," one which blended the arts of the moving picture, singing, dancing, and acting, and music making, all "synchronized" into the kind of program familiar to patrons in sophisticated metropolitan centres across North America.[34] Presumably, he referred to such elaborate and highly popular stage productions as well as the motion pictures presented by Barney Balaban and Sam Katz at their picture palaces in Chicago.[35]

(3) *Provide exceptional service.* Nathanson promised that all Famous Players theatres would provide exceptional service, asserting that

patrons who appreciated the entertainment and the service offered at a theatre would return, bringing their families and friends. According to reports, he was a stickler for efficient and courteous service and paid close attention to the people hired in each theatre.

Nathanson printed his full mission statement in major newspapers across the country, including the *Calgary Herald*, where on 6 May 1921 he declared: "You who enjoy the stage, music, or the photoplay will find in this new divertissement a happy blending of the three arts — and yet it is neither a motion picture show, a concert, vaudeville, or spoken drama. It is different and that is why you are going to like it."[36]

Nathanson attended personally to the operation of his theatres, even the smallest, visiting them frequently in order to help employees make a success of their districts. This entailed implementing the Famous Players entertainment policy: providing quality entertainment that combined music, stage productions, and first-run Paramount motion pictures, changing the program three times per week, and creating goodwill among patrons by providing exceptional service.

FAMOUS PLAYERS EXPANDS

Nathanson launched an ambitious construction campaign in the autumn of 1919, challenging the Allens for control of the exhibition business. This involved erecting luxurious venues in major metropolitan centres across Canada, not only offering moviegoers comfortable and safe facilities but also creating an atmosphere that evoked such European venues as the Paris Opera House in such urban centres as (in the order of their opening) Winnipeg, Vancouver, Regina, Montréal, and Calgary, situating these facilities close to Allen theatres.[37] This campaign also involved developing an architectural style that would differentiate "Capitol" theatres from others, especially "Allen" Theatres. In this section, we consider the first three projects.

At a press conference in November, Nathanson announced that Thomas W. Lamb would design and Regal Films would build a deluxe theatre called the Capitol Theatre at 351 Donald Street, Winnipeg, one block north of the newly constructed Allen Theatre.[38] He noted that the site would cost $500,000 and that erecting the 2,200-seat facility would cost another $700,000. Finally, he adopted the language of the booster, predicting that the deluxe venue would be the finest of its kind in Canada, offering the public a weekly program of movies and vaudeville, and an orchestra of thirty-five players to provide musical accompaniment for performances.

Lamb gave the structure two entrances: one was located in the modified western half of Manitoba Hall, a three-storey, brick building on Portage Avenue, near the northeast corner of Donald Street, which had been erected in 1903 by Mark Fortune and housed offices and commercial space. The theatre itself was located at the rear of this building, in a new structure of steel, reinforced concrete, and brick.[39]

Via this configuration, Lamb exploited the frontage, which stood on a major commercial thoroughfare, while using lower-cost property on the Donald Street site. The modifications made to Manitoba Hall included the installation of a large marquee and a box office and the removal of the rear second floor to make way for a marble staircase, the walls of which featured mirrors, silk tapestries, paintings, and heavy brass railings. Patrons crossed a second-storey brick-and-concrete walkway over the alley in order to enter the mezzanine promenade and the balcony. The promenade, with wood and scagliola detailing and cove lighting and featuring silk-cushioned lounge chairs, led to washrooms, a smoking room, and a ladies' "retiring" room. Another marble staircase linked this level with the ground floor and a second entrance, just off Donald Street.

The enormous auditorium featured a highly decorative saucer-like dome with a "sunburst" chandelier, medallions, and sweeping gilt bands which stretched across the ceiling to the balcony and the proscenium arch. Side arches linked up with Ionic and Corinthian columns, and pilasters appeared along the walls of the orchestra floor supporting an entablature at the balcony level. The walls on both sides of the proscenium arch featured tall, gilt round-headed grilles with winged female figures, which concealed the machinery for a pipe organ. One commentator described the seating arrangement as novel, in that loge boxes were situated on both sides of the orchestra and in the balcony; most importantly, the writer pointed out, all seats offered patrons an unobstructed view of the stage and the screen.[40]

Figure 53. The Portage Avenue entrance of the Capitol Theatre, Winnipeg, ca. 1935. Provincial Archives of Manitoba, Peter McAdam 457, negative no. 14238.

The auditorium featured a massive curved stage. John Wenger, a Russian artist who had served as the art director at several theatres and opera houses in New York City and Boston, designed the stage set, scenery, and the drop curtain, upon which a landscape had been painted. Finishing touches included red carpets and arabesque and grotesque details, together with cove lighting and scagliola. Outside, six commercial outlets with large display windows and second-storey office space made up the Donald Street façade.

Ralph Ruffner, the manager, and his staff, which included Jack Arthur, the director of the Capitol Orchestra, implemented the Famous Players' entertainment policy that included screening first-run movies, accompanied by appropriate music-making, and providing "courteous service."[41] The management marked the opening of the Capitol on 14 February 1921 with a gala celebration, thereby setting the pattern for gala celebrations Famous Players would subsequently organize. The inaugural entertainment included *Midsummer Madness* (1920), an adaptation directed by William C. deMille of Cosmo Hamilton's novel *His Friend and His Wife* (1920).

In Regina, W. G. Van Egmond and S. E. Storey, local architects, assisted Thomas W. Lamb in designing the Capitol Theatre at 2031 12th Avenue.[42] In typical "booster" fashion, Famous Players advertised the 1,500-seat facility, which cost $250,000 to build, as "western Canada's finest Photoplay Theatre," replete with the latest luxuries and conveniences. The brick-clad exterior was unusual in offering passersby two contrasting façades.[43] The first, on 12th Avenue, featured a row of twelve single-hung windows on the upper level and a row of six large bays on the street level, together with an arched opening in the middle. The second, on Scarth Street, featured three small single-hung windows on the upper level, just below the cornice, and one door and two very small pseudo-windows on the street level. The façade on the Scarth Street side wrapped around the corner, this section featuring two single-hung windows at the upper level and a box office and two sets of doors, at right angles, at the street level. The curved exterior, accentuated by the cornice and the horizontal lines of the brickwork, anticipated the Art Moderne design of the interior. A wave-shaped horizontal sign, outlined with light bulbs, spelling the name CAPITOL and a disk-shaped marquee, also outlined in light bulbs, extending to the edge of the sidewalk completed the Scarth Street façade.

Figure 54. The Capitol Theatre, Regina, 1921. Archives of Saskatchewan Board, R-B13484.

Figure 55. Interior of the Capitol Theatre, Regina, 1929. Photo courtesy of the City of Regina Archives.

The architects located the box office outside, at the corner of the building, so that patrons would enter the foyer via the doors on either side. The foyer extended the width of the building: Wilton carpets covered the floor, and velour drapes and murals, depicting scenes of a Japanese tea garden, covered the walls. The area was outfitted with tapestry chesterfields and solid walnut chairs of a "Spanish design," as well as writing desks fitted with telephones for patrons' use.

Patrons reportedly found the auditorium "the acme of comfort, safety, and convenience." The ceiling featured a large dome, and eight fluted pilasters divided the side walls (decorated in gold) into three sections, each dominated by what resembled a tall Palladian window. The few photographs that have survived suggest that two of these openings (fitted with elaborate drapery) featured fire escapes. Two wide aisles separated the large upholstered seats (arranged in stadium fashion) into three sections; the orchestra floor and the balcony together featured (as an innovation) 170 loge chairs. The large stage was fitted with an ornately decorated proscenium arch and a medium-sized orchestra pit that accommodated ten players, plus a theatre organ and a baby grand piano. Other technological innovations included a gold-fibre screen, which created a vivid picture without straining viewers' eyes.

Figure 56. Advertisement announcing that Calgary's Capitol Theatre will present films produced by Paramount Pictures. Calgary Herald, *7 May 1921, 13.*

Ann Dornin, an interior decorator at Lamb's New York City company, supervised the installation of the furnishings, focusing on the Canary Room, located on the mezzanine floor, which offered women "a delightful place" to meet before a show. The walls and the furnishings were canary yellow; cretonne draperies, reed chairs, and handmade Chinese rugs completed the space. Live canaries graced the room with their songs. Women sipped tea (prepared on electric elements in the room and served in English china) before taking their seats in the balcony.

Famous Players assembled a staff of enthusiastic showmen to create the requisite "goodwill" among patrons, including Harry Kahn, who served as the manager, and T. Mitchell, who served as the conductor of the Capitol Symphony Orchestra. A gala celebration on 14 March 1921 marked the opening of Regina's Capitol. Invited guests included Henry Newlands, the lieutenant governor of Saskatchewan. The program featured a newsreel called *Capitol News Digest*, Buster Keaton's latest comedy, *Neighbors* (1920), and *The Furnace* (1920), director William D. Taylor's satire on contemporary social relations starring Agnes Ayres, Jerome Patrick, and Theodore Roberts.[44]

In 1920, Famous Players officials announced that the firm was going to build a deluxe theatre called the Capitol Theatre at 230 8th Avenue West in Calgary, a site almost directly opposite that of Allen's Palace Theatre. Executives told the press that the firm would spend more than $275,000 building the 1,800-seat facility, representing the last word in theatre design and construction. Calgary was working its way through an economic downturn at the time, so civic officials applauded news of this project.[45] Calgarians decoded this news as a sign that economic conditions in the city were improving. Thomas W. Lamb designed, and his representative, Paul P. Reuhl, supervised the construction of the facility. Reuhl had assisted Lamb in the construction of the 2,989-seat Strand Theatre in New York City, which had opened in April 1914.

Figure 57. The Capitol Theatre, Calgary, 1921. Glenbow Archives NA-1264-5.

Figure 58. Interior of the Capitol Theatre, Calgary, 1921. Glenbow Archives NA-1264-7.

The builders erected the structure, possibly the largest completed in Calgary in 1921, in a record six months. Three sets of windows separated the brick-clad façade at the upper level into three sections, and four pilasters at the ground level separated the façade into three large bays. A cornice, plus a decorated frieze, stretched across the front, just above the windows.[46] The central bay was crowned by a large, rectangular marquee outlined in light bulbs, extending to the edge of the sidewalk. Interchangeable letters on the sides facing the sidewalk identified the feature attraction, and, on the street side, a sign reading "CAPITOL" identified the theatre. The structure included three shops at the street level.

The vast auditorium reportedly generated in patrons "a feeling of richness and beauty," as well as homely comfort. As a correspondent for the *Calgary Herald* declared on 4 May: "An exclamation of awe and wonder involuntarily escapes us as we lift our eyes to the ceiling and side walls, gazing rapturously upon what is considered by experts to be the most beautiful piece of architectural decorating work in western Canada." An embossed medallion dominated the ceiling, from which hung a massive rock crystal fixture. Pilasters separated the side walls that curved toward the stage and the proscenium into four large sections, each dominated by a Palladian window, together with Greek designs, all executed to great effect by Thomas Edwards, the interior decorator. Heavy silk draperies hung on the walls, and a blue silk velour valance surrounded the stage, which was fitted with all the equipment for hiding scenery and for creating lighting effects. The orchestra pit accommodated fifteen players, a grand piano, and an organ consul. Three wide aisles separated the fifteen hundred "heavily upholstered" pneumatic-cushioned, wine-coloured seats into three sections, without a suggestion of crowding.

According to reports, Famous Players assembled a staff of forty, including John Hazza, who served as the manager of the new theatre.[47] A gala celebration on 7 May 1921 marked the opening of the facility. Dignitaries included Mayor Samuel H. Adams of Calgary and Famous Players executives. The feature film, *The Love Special* (1921), had a railroad theme, telling the story of a railway engineer at work in the mountains who falls in love with the daughter of a railroad magnate.

Famous Players released its annual report on 23 October 1921, indicating that the firm owned or leased twenty-nine theatres and had earned $291,987.91 in the 1920 fiscal year and $380,839.97 the following year. The treasurer indicated that revenue for the year ending August 1922 would show a considerable increase over that for the previous year.[48]

THE ALLEN EMPIRE COLLAPSES

Meanwhile, industry analysts reported that the Allens were in trouble. In February 1921, they announced that Famous Players would acquire the Allen chain, bringing about "the biggest theatrical merger in the history of the Dominion."[49] Nathanson submitted an offer to buy these theatres for between $4 and $5 million, but Jay refused. In July 1921, a correspondent for *Moving Picture World* reported that Empire Palace Theatre, Limited, of London, was suing the Allen brothers for breach of contract: they had secured a site for building a grand theatre on Leicester Square but could not meet the payments.[50]

On 17 May 1922, Jule and Jay announced a personal assignment for the benefit of creditors to the G. T. Clarkson Company, the authorized trustee, seeking an extension of the time needed to pay.[51] J. P. Bickell and Nathanson submitted another offer to buy Allen Theatres, this time for two-fifths of the value of the stock. Again, the Allens rejected his offer. Clarkson declared that the Allen assets were worth $951,618 — as opposed to their liabilities of $687,293. However, over $300,000 of the assets were deemed "nominal equities in pledged securities." The Bank of Commerce held $180,000 of these assets.

On 26 May, several creditors, including Simpson's, Canadian Bank of Commerce, Associated First National Exhibitors, and the Department of Finance, asked the courts to declare the Allens bankrupt. Meanwhile, the Allens asked for more time to pay their debts. At a meeting held on 29 May, the creditors agreed to set up a committee charged with the task of negotiating a sale with Famous Players. The committee judged that Allen Theatres was economically sound and that, in time, the $1.2 million the Allens owed could be repaid; it also rejected Nathanson's offer (made in July) of $1.05 million.[52] The committee thought that they could do better than eighty cents on the dollar, and so continued negotiating. As Cox puts it, independent exhibitors regarded

Figure 59. Advertisement for Allen Theatre Enterprises, an all-Canadian achievement now operating motion picture theatres in the United States and Great Britain. Toronto Globe, 28 August 1920, 4.

the surrender of Allen Theatres to Famous Players as a great disaster. The largest creditor, Associated First National Exhibitors, offered to advance the Allens $100,000 to keep them in business, in order to prevent Zukor from getting his hands on the Allen assets. First National executives asked other creditors to make proportionate advances, but they did not. Some analysts writing for the trade papers predicted that the Allens would survive this crisis. Hedging their bets, members of the Allen family bought up some of the Ottawa Valley movie theatres from Jule and Jay during the winter of 1922–23.

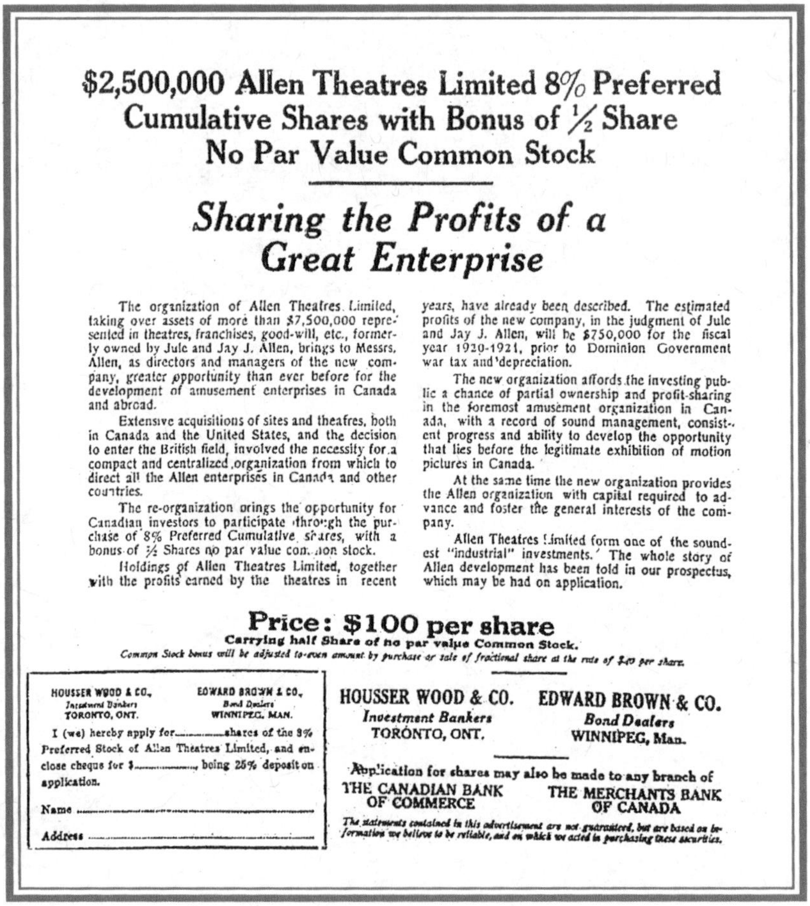

Figure 60. Advertisement for Allen's Calgary Theatre's stock offering of $2.5 million. Toronto Star, *30 September 1920, 29.*

Suddenly, G. T. Clarkson declared Allen Theatres bankrupt. As Cox writes, Nathanson may well have prompted Clarkson to take this action. Clarkson then invited tenders for the Allens' remaining thirty-six theatres, among the best venues in the country. By this time, they owed their creditors $1.25 million. Associated First National decided to buy the Allen theatres, to keep them away from Zukor. Robert Lieber, the president of First National, visited Toronto hoping to effect this transaction, but his effort failed. A correspondent for the *Toronto Star* noted on 8 June, that Famous Players acquired the assets of Allen Theatres — thirty-five large theatres — for $650,000, or less than $19,000 apiece. Clearly, the creditors' committee had failed to get value for the Allens' assets. Instead of Nathanson's highest offer, eighty cents on the dollar, they settled for fifty cents on the dollar, thus giving Famous Players virtual control of the booking situation in Canada. As analysts have pointed out, "the Allen empire collapsed from within," thanks in large part to the effects of losing the exclusive rights to distribute Paramount (and Select) pictures in Canada and of over-expanding.[53] The Allens' exchange then collapsed; Lewis Selznick formed his own company to distribute Select Pictures, and Regal Films, a subsidiary of Paramount Pictures, took over the distribution of Goldwyn pictures. In this way, much of the Allen empire went to the Nathanson group.

CREATING A MADE-IN-CANADA EXHIBITION COMPANY

Throughout these negotiations, Nathanson believed that he was creating a "made-in-Canada" company. He often told reporters that 95 percent of the capital in Famous Players was British and Canadian, representing a total investment of about $15 million.[54] As well, he would point out, his supporters included a British-born financier, Sir William Wiseman, and four major Canadian-born financiers, including Sir Herbert Holt, J. B. Tudhope, J. P. Bickell, and W. D. Ross. Nathanson noted that the great majority of employees were Canadian. He added that, as a matter of policy, Famous Players theatres favoured British and Canadian "road shows," such as the productions of Sir John Martin-Harvey and Matheson Lang, the D'Oyly Carte Opera Company, and the Dumbells' song-and-dance acts.

Meanwhile, on 1 March 1929, Adolph Zukor created a voting trust (he deposited the agreement with the Montreal Trust Company), whereby for a period of ten years voting control was placed in the hands of three trustees, Zukor, Nathanson, and Killam, who exercised equal power.[55] The ostensible object of this pooling of shares was to give the impression that Famous Players was in fact a "Canadian" company, in that two of the trustees were Canadian. Nathanson also believed that, in matters of policy, he and Killam, who acted on behalf of Royal Securities, would in fact form a majority, but he misread the situation. In practice, Zukor retained his position as the head of the board of directors, thereby protecting the agreement ensuring that the major Canadian movie theatres would screen Hollywood movies.[56]

During the summer of 1929, Nathanson travelled to London, planning to convert Famous Players into an important part of an Empire-wide production, distribution, and exhibition organization, linking operations in Great Britain, Canada, South Africa, and Australia. He felt that such an organization would signal to film people everywhere that the movie industries in these countries were no longer spokes in Zukor's wheel.[57] He talked to officials at Gaumont-British Picture Corporation, negotiating what he regarded as the first step in this plan; however, he soon learned that officials from the Fox corporation had preceded him, securing a large block of non-voting Gaumont shares. Nathanson returned to Canada with an offer from Gaumont to buy shares of Famous Players at $75 per share. In September, Zukor and Killam quashed the deal, preventing Canadian shareholders from considering the offer.[58] Nathanson told reporters that he had conducted these talks at the insistence of I. W. Killam, who had approved of the offer. Clearly upset, he resigned from the board of directors on 18 September 1929, stating in his letter of resignation that he could no longer protect Canadian shareholders from the attempts of American interests to take control of the company.[59]

With Nathanson out of the way and with the Gaumont proposal quashed, Zukor quickly secured control over the company's policies and practices. In April 1930, Zukor arranged a stock swap that offered Canadian shareholders four shares of Paramount-Publix Corporation (which was losing money) in return for five shares of Famous Players Canadian Corporation (which was making money and sending remittances to the New York City head office), thereby giving him 93.8

percent of the shares of the Canadian company.[60] Minority Canadian shareholders denounced the deal, describing the stock swap as another example of the Americanization of the company; they were also angry that the New York City office sent J. J. Fitzgibbons to take over as director of theatre operations before the deal was finalized. In addition, shareholders were angry that the deal was closed on 25 May 1930, a Sunday and the day after Victoria Day, evidence that the parties involved acknowledged neither the Canadian national holiday nor the Sunday closing laws, to which Toronto strictly adhered. Shareholders protested throughout the summer.

THE COMBINES INVESTIGATION

In order to appreciate the response of Canadian investors to Adolph Zukor's manoeuvre, which gave him total control of Famous Players, we must consider a number of developments with regard to the monitoring of the American film industry that had an impact on the movie exhibition industry in Canada.[61] We start with the Motion Picture Producers and Distributors of America (the MPPDA), a trade organization that had been formed in 1922 to improve the public image of Hollywood (a series of scandals had rocked the city) and to safeguard the film industry's interests at home and abroad. Will H. Hays, the former postmaster general, became the president of the organization. This public relations genius developed the language of self-regulation, which proved effective in dealing with such matters as the public's concern about the influence of motion pictures and the industry's concern over governments' taxation policies, speaking of common interests and attaching them to high moral and artistic standards in film production.

In 1924, the MPPDA sponsored the formation of the Motion Picture Exhibition and Distributors of Canada (the MPEDC), with a view to promoting "the common interests" of those engaged in the motion picture industry in Canada by maintaining the highest moral and artistic standards in motion picture production, developing the educational and the entertainment value of motion pictures, disseminating accurate information about the industry, reforming practices in the industry that had resulted in abuses, and securing freedom from unjust government regulations.[62] This organization was popularly known as the "Cooper

Organization," named after its first president, James Alexander Cooper. The Hays Organization controlled the Cooper Organization, directing its policies and activities from New York City.[63] Famous Players, vertically integrated with a major American film company, played an important role in the Cooper Organization, providing financial support and personnel (members served as officers on the board of directors). For example, in 1929 American distributors contributed US $21,841.56 to the organization, making up 80 percent of its annual budget. In other words, the Cooper Organization represented no Canadian-owned independent theatres.

During the 1920s, the Cooper Organization engaged in a number of major public relations activities, such as lobbying censor boards, community organizations, religious groups, and government agencies with a view to liberalizing standards of morality and opposing screening quotas. By 1929, many Canadians were again concerned about the content of the motion pictures they saw at theatres; many wanted to see pro-British movies, not to mention Canadian-produced movies, and were prepared to legislate quotas on American films screened. For example, in 1929 and in 1931, the Ontario and the British Columbia legislatures considered bringing in a bill forcing exhibitors to screen 20 percent Canadian pictures.[64]

The Cooper Organization followed the Hays Organization in undertaking these and other public relations activities. In 1925, the latter authorized the former to design a uniform exhibition contract, similar to the Standard Exhibition Contract, which American distributors were using.[65] Under the terms of this agreement, which was introduced in 1926, independent theatre owners paid cash in advance on shipments of films. Distributors refused to sell pictures to "booking combinations," which would have increased the bargaining power of independent theatre owners; the names of theatre owners who breached the contract in any way were put on a blacklist and distributors were instructed not to sell pictures to them. This contract gave distributors in Canada considerable power over independent exhibitors.

In addition, the Cooper Organization followed the Hays Organization in setting up film boards of trade in key urban centres, these self-regulators being another means of reducing competition in the interest of the vertically integrated firms.[66] Via these trade (or marketing) associations, distributors dealt with independent exhibitors according to prescribed rules. The Cooper Organization argued that, in eliminating rivalry among members competing for screen time, it was preserving the long-term interests of all members. Not surprisingly, by 1930 American production and distribution companies controlled about 95 percent of the distribution market.

The government had two reasons for launching an investigation into the grievances of Canadian shareholders in Famous Players.[67] First, independent exhibitors in Canada had long complained about the oppressive market conditions in which they worked. Second, in the United States, the Paramount Famous Players–Lasky Corporation restructured itself, generating turmoil in its Canadian affiliate, Famous Players. On 24 April 1930, the Paramount Famous Players–Lasky Corporation changed its name to the Paramount-Publix Corporation, which was organized as a holding and operating company and comprised of several related enterprises in motion picture production, distribution, and exhibition.[68] Paramount held a 50 percent interest in the William Morris Agency, a theatrical employment agency, and a 50 percent interest in the Columbia Broadcasting System, an emerging radio network. This firm also owned real estate on Broadway in New York City, and its subsidiaries owned film distribution operations in several European countries, such as England, France, Germany, and Spain. Paramount's assets in December 1929 amounted to nearly $236 million.

The majority of Famous Players shareholders endorsed Zukor's manoeuvre, which involved exchanging four Paramount shares for five Famous Players shares, ostensibly to give Canadians the impression that the firm was a Canadian company.[69] As we have seen, however, a number of investors denounced this deal as an example of the Americanization of the company. In response, on 23 September 1930, R. B. Bennett, the recently elected prime minister of Canada, launched an investigation into an alleged combine in the motion picture industry in Canada. The government struck a commission to investigate the motion picture industry in general and Famous Players' business practices in particular, appointing Peter White as the sole commissioner. White gathered evidence in closed hearings over a period of seven months, examining contracts, correspondence, and Famous Players files. He interviewed executives and uncovered evidence indicating that an American monopoly was indeed operating in Canada.[70]

In trying to minimize the damage its member companies would experience as a result of a negative verdict, the Hays Organization sent Edward T. Raftery, counsel and secretary of United Artists Corporation, in New York City, to study the situation and to advise the American distributing companies on a course of action. Raftery engaged the Toronto law firm of Mason, Foulds, Davison, and Kellock to represent the American distributors. He believed that the commissioner would find either a combination between Paramount's two subsidiaries, Famous Players and Regal Films, and Columbia Pictures Corporation, the stock of which was held by individuals associated with Famous Players, or a combination existing among all distributors to the detriment of independent exhibitors. Raftery prepared favourable witnesses, equipped with favourable documents, showing that the independent exhibitors were not treated unfairly and that the Standard Exhibition Contract and the boards of trade protected exhibitors equally. Ultimately, however, Raftery's worst fears materialized. In June 1931, White submitted his report to the minister of Labour in Ottawa, in which he concluded that, since 1926, a combine had existed in the motion picture industry in Canada.[71] He named all the American distributors, Regal Films (a Canadian company), and Famous Players and some of its affiliates, not to mention the Cooper Organization, as parties to the combine.[72]

As the former managing director of Famous Players, Nathanson rejected these findings, namely, that the firm had been under the control of Paramount-Publix even before the exchange of shares. According to a *Toronto Star* reporter who interviewed the movie mogul on his return to the city, Nathanson complained that White had based his report on Killam's evidence only and that, had he (Nathanson) been invited to testify, he could have provided evidence to the contrary.[73] He defended his role as managing director of the company, stressing that he had always acted with the interests of Canadian shareholders and theatregoers in mind; he reiterated that he had agreed to the voting trust because he had Killam's assurance that, as a Canadian, the latter would stand behind the business at all times and that, in fact, he himself had always taken steps to prevent the firm from falling into the hands of foreign investors.

Independent exhibitors waited two years before filing a suit, which, thanks to some confusion about which jurisdiction held the constitutional authority to handle the case, they filed in a provincial court. As Manjunath Pendakur explains, the provinces claimed that the British North America Act gave them the exclusive right to administer the laws, including those of the federal government (an issue that was not resolved until the 1940s).[74] The attorney general of Ontario filed the suit under the Combines Investigation Act against seven distributors, Famous Players, and some of its affiliates, and the Cooper Organization for operating a combine or conspiring to constrain trade in that province. This was the first significant attempt by the state to curb monopoly abuses in the motion picture industry in Canada.

On 18 March 1932, Justice J. Garrow of the Ontario Supreme Court handed down his decision, clearing the accused companies of all charges. Justice Garrow argued that the Standard Exhibition Contract, together with compulsory arbitration, was legal under Canadian law.[75] The Crown had offered a weak case, relying on American antitrust laws and judgments. Quite simply, the prosecution had not proved that a combine existed in Ontario. Famous Players and the American distributors were acquitted on the basis that the prosecution had not been able to establish that the alleged combine was detrimental to the public interest, as ticket prices did not go up during the period under review.

Under Will Hays, the influence of the MPPDA had also increased, in terms of heading off state censorship (under the banner of free speech). The strategy of self-regulation included introducing and maintaining a "production code," a set of ideological and moral principles to which all motion pictures shown commercially in the United States had to subscribe. The production code was formally introduced when "talking pictures" became the norm. Enforcing the code proved difficult, however. Faced with declining attendance, film producers considered sex and violence to be box-office attractions. In 1934, state censors, women's groups, education groups, and religious groups demanded action. The Roman Catholic Church formed the Legion of Decency, and every week millions of Americans recited its "oath of obedience," promising not to attend condemned films. Faced with the possibility of a mass boycott of Hollywood films, the MPPDA implemented the Production Code Administration (PCA) that year, whereby the industry agreed that no film would be distributed in the United States that did not carry a PCA seal.[76]

THE ALLENS RALLY

While they continued to enjoy a comfortable lifestyle following the bankruptcy in 1923, the Allens nevertheless suffered as a result of this traumatic event. Every day at 5:00 p.m., some commentators report, the seemingly easygoing Herbert Allen took a bottle from his desk and drank until he was intoxicated. The cautious Jule Allen suffered a nervous breakdown, which kept him out of the family business for about a year. One day in May 1925, the reliable Barney Allen collapsed in his home in Toronto and died.[77] The risk-taking Jay Allen still lived flamboyantly but undertook a number of unsavoury business ventures (such as rum running) to supplement the family's reduced income. This involved importing cheap scotch from Europe, which was perfectly legal in Ontario, and then exporting it to the United States.[78]

The Allens, ever resourceful, soon rallied. Louis Rosenfeld formed Dominion Films, with a view to resurrecting part of the distribution branch of the family's business, having secured the rights to distribute independent and British pictures.[79] The Allens scored a major triumph when, in 1926, they secured the rights to distribute the movies produced by Columbia Pictures, which Harry Cohn and his brother Jack, together with Joe Brandt, had founded two years earlier. One of the "little two" (including Universal), this studio produced competent co-features and second features, in addition to a number of prestige pictures. For example, Columbia produced Frank Capra's enormously successful romantic comedy *It Happened One Night* (1934), featuring Clark Gable and Claudette Colbert. The Allens formed a new distribution company, Columbia Pictures of Canada, which absorbed the old exchanges, Dominion Films and Independent Films of Canada. Rosenfeld managed this company for the rest of his life.

In addition, Jay and Herbert formed, in January 1928, the Premier Operating Corporation, Limited, hoping to resurrect part of the exhibition branch of the family's business. Gradually, they acquired a number of small theatres located in rural Ontario, stretching from Cobalt in northern Ontario to Leamington near Windsor and along the Ottawa valley from Renfrew to Smiths Falls. Nathanson found the Allen circuit to be more competition than he could tolerate, and formed a fifty-fifty partnership with them.[80] In March 1928, the Famous Players and Premier Operating Corporation formed an umbrella company called the Theatre Holding Corporation, Limited, granting the latter firm independent booking privileges. In this way, the Allen company became a subsidiary of Famous Players and entered a new era of prosperity. As Cox remarks, via this manoeuvre, Nathanson inaugurated a policy of buying out the competition via partnership deals. In 1931, Jule and Jay secured their discharge from personal bankruptcy, and by the time of the Second World War, their Ontario circuit comprised nearly fifty theatres. After Jay died in 1942, at the age of fifty-two; Herb, Louis, and Jule ran the company.[81]

Figure 61. Jule Allen, honorary campaign chairman of the United Jewish Appeal, Toronto, 1949. Ontario Jewish Archives, fonds 28, series 6, file no. 2.

FAMOUS PLAYERS AFFILIATES

Throughout the difficult period that included the Stock Market Crash, much of the Great Depression, and the anti-combines investigation, Nathanson kept a low profile. Industry analysts suggested that he was biding his time, waiting for an opportunity to return. Actually, he was organizing an all-Canadian chain, which would exhibit films made by the Fox Film Corporation, an arrangement that, assuming he secured the franchise, would enable him to compete with Famous Players.[82] Rumours circulated to the effect that prominent Canadian financiers — including Herbert Holt and W. D. Ross — had raised $25 million toward the project.[83] Nathanson told reporters that the new company would build two deluxe theatres in 1930, one in Montréal and one in Toronto, each seating five thousand patrons and featuring a full-width stage, suggesting that operations would probably begin in 1931. Significantly, the circuit would screen "the new type of talkie movie." But negotiations with Fox were abandoned.

Interestingly, however, Nathanson also engineered his return to Famous Players: the board of directors elected him president at the end of May 1933.[84] About this time, according to reports, the supply of

Figure 62. Theatre operator Ken Leach, a Famous Players affiliate, Calgary, n.d. Photo courtesy of Karen Marks.

British films increased in Canada from 4.5 percent in 1930 to 15 percent in 1933. W. D. Ross and Major A. P. Holt, who had resigned when Nathanson did, returned to the board, but the voting trust remained in place, as it was impossible to dissolve the trust without the consent of all the trustees. Many Canadians read his re-election as a sign that, finally, Canadians were taking control of foreign-owned companies like Famous Players. Believing that he and Adolph Zukor had an understanding that control of Famous Players would pass into his hands once the trust voting expired, Nathanson committed himself to promoting among Canadians the broadest taste possible in moving pictures, including British films.[85]

In creating Famous Players, Nathanson had formed an association of movie theatre operators who were eager to access the Paramount franchise.[86] Between 1933 and 1941, he formed partnerships with many exhibitors. Among these were two affiliates located in the prairie West, namely, K. M. (Ken) Leach, who operated three theatres in Calgary, and James Butler and N. C. Bryers, who operated three theatres in Saskatoon.

Ken Leach spent his youth in Hedrick, a farming community in Iowa, but in 1908 the Leach family moved to a homestead in Saskatchewan, near Moose Jaw. Farming never appealed to the young man. Instead, he took a job at a 300-seat nickelodeon owned by a family friend, and developed a passion for show business. In 1912, at the age of twenty-one, he moved to nearby Swift Current in order to manage the Eagle Theatre. At the time, he later recalled, managing a theatre meant fetching films, selling tickets, cranking films through the projector when the projectionist was on a break, securing an ensemble to provide musical accompaniment, closing up at night, and banking the receipts the next day. Leach expanded his operation, acquiring several theatres, starting with the Rose in Regina, which he managed for two years. In 1917, Leach, now married, moved his family to Calgary, where he initially managed the Princess Theatre, an 882-seat facility located at 310 8th Avenue East, and the Regent Theatre, an 800-seat facility

Figure 63. Advertisement for the twenty-fifth anniversary of Famous Players Canadian Corporation. Ottawa Journal, 22 January 1945, 15.

located at 206 8th Avenue West, where the Hudson's Bay Company store now stands. At the time, the Regent included on its program variety acts, such as the Dumbells, the leading Canadian song-and-dance troupe, and country singer Wilf Carter. Between 1918 and 1921, Leach operated a film exchange, the Regent Company, holding the Alberta franchises for United Artists films, which featured the films of Mary Pickford, Charlie Chaplin, and Douglas Fairbanks. In 1926, he became a Famous Players affiliate and over the years operated facilities in Moose Jaw, Regina, Winnipeg, Edmonton, Calgary, and Vancouver.[87]

As we have seen, during the summer of 1923, Famous Players acquired the major Allen theatres. These included the Calgary Allen, at 119 8th Avenue East, originally built in 1913 (see chapter 3). With little fanfare, Famous Players renamed it the Strand Theatre and reopened it in 1924.[88] In March 1926, Leach signed an agreement with Allen Theatres, Limited, the owners of the Allen, agreeing to close the Regent Theatre and to incorporate a new company, the Strand Theatre Company, Limited, for the purpose of operating the Strand at a rental of $6,000 per year and 50 percent of the net profits. In addition, Leach's company signed an agreement with Famous Players to pay "a booking fee of $50 per week for such a period as the theatre does not run at a loss." This agreement allowed him a free hand in selecting and booking movies for the Strand. Leach refurbished the facility and instituted a new policy that offered the public "up-to-date entertainment at moderate prices" and supplied every comfort and convenience possible.[89]

Accordingly, Leach hired staff who pledged to implement the new policy, their motto reading "attention and service to young and old." Later that year, he modernized the marquee, installing "Claude Neon Illumination," regarded as the first "advertising message" of its kind in Calgary.[90] He further demonstrated his progressiveness in September 1929, when he acquired Movietone and Vitaphone equipment so that he could screen talking pictures.[91] He told the press that the new equipment had tested satisfactorily, rendering sound and voice clearly in all parts of the auditorium. Leach launched the new era by screening *Alibi* (1929), an all-talking melodrama about a gangster who, upon his release from jail, feigns honesty, weds a police sergeant's daughter, and is later suspected of killing a policeman. When a number of patrons expressed a concern that talking pictures would prove unsuitable for children, Leach declared that the Strand would cater to patrons of all ages, screening first-run family-oriented movies. He set admission prices at twenty-five cents (for children) and at forty-five cents (for adults) for evening performances.

In 1938, for the sum of $60,250, Leach bought the Princess Theatre, a 1,000-seat facility located at 310 8th Avenue East, not far from the Strand. He renamed it the Variety Theatre, with a view to operating the facility as a Famous Players affiliate.[92] The building dated from 1913, having been constructed by Dr. T. H. (Thomas) Blow, who played an important role in Alberta's economic and political development. Blow had erected a two-storey brick block housing offices and stores, at the rear of which was a three-storey block that housed the theatre's auditorium and balcony.[93]

The auditorium featured a small wooden stage framed by a segmental arch, box seats on either side of the stage, slanting inward, and a balcony sloping down from the third to the second floor over the west half of the theatre. The stage accommodated an ensemble of about thirty actors or musicians, together with simple sets or instruments. The exterior of the two-storey building showed neoclassical influences in design and decoration. Five pilasters separated the façade, which was clad in fire brick, into four bays. Three glass-fronted stores and a doorway dominated the first level, and eight windows (two per bay) dominated the upper level. A terracotta entablature separated the first level from the second, and a cornice ran across the top, lending the design a measure of dignity.

Leach ran the Variety as a Famous Players affiliate from 1947 to 1961, featuring second-run westerns and action films. But business gradually declined, and on 1 July 1961 he closed the Variety, explaining that "the Strand could adequately serve the needs of East Calgary."[94]

In 1949, Leach bought the Empress Theatre, a 480-seat facility built in 1911, at 219 8th Avenue East. Leach had managed the Empress from 1926 to 1930, with his brother (Dale) as his projectionist and John M. Cardell as his house manager. During that period, the Empress featured the latest moving pictures, starring Charlie Chaplin or Douglas Fairbanks or Mary Pickford, and popular vaudeville performers, such as William Hart, a "Black-faced Comedian" from Boston (the other William S. Hart played the hero of silent westerns). Eventually, Leach offered programs that catered to children who had developed a passion for the Saturday matinee: many years later, patrons recalled that, for twenty-five cents, they could ride the streetcar to and from the theatre, purchase a ticket, and buy some popcorn.[95]

Leach refurbished the Empress, hiring builders to "Westernize" the theatre, which had experienced hard times during the Great Depression, including two fires, the second of which seriously damaged the Wright Block (formerly the Co-operative Block), where this facility was located.[96] They covered the façade with logs, designed the box office as a chuckwagon, and constructed a new marquee, topped by a gigantic neon sign constructed in the Western mode, as well as installing the latest theatre fittings: a new screen, new projection and sound equipment, and new carpeting. The management opened the Hitchin' Post on 26 December 1949, marking the occasion by screening Irving Brecher's *Life of Riley* (1949), an adaptation of the popular radio series about Chester A. Riley, "the world's most successful failure," and Lambert Hillyer's *Prairie Express* (1947), a story about a cowboy who recovers a stolen freight wagon. Leach advertised the Hitchin' Post as "Canada's first exclusively western-and-action movie house."[97]

Leach had every reason to be optimistic about this project. After all, Calgary was enjoying a tremendous boom at this time — a correspondent for the *Calgary Herald* reported that permits were issued in Calgary for $21,868,928 during 1949, smashing the record of $20,394,220 set in 1912.[98] The report issued by the city's permit office indicated that home building accounted for the major proportion of the record total, whereas in 1912 the vast majority of permits had been issued for the construction of business buildings. This news suggested that the number of moviegoers would continue to climb.

During the winter of 1928, James Butler and N. C. Bryers, the proprietors of the Empire and the Daylight theatres in Saskatoon (built in 1910 and 1913, respectively), decided to erect a grand facility called the Capitol Theatre on 22nd Street. Like Leach, they deemed an affiliation with Famous Players to be a good business strategy. In fact, they built the first "atmospheric" in western Canada, inaugurating "the era of the talkies" in Saskatoon.[99] As Don Kerr and Stan Hanson explain, 1929 was a good year for Saskatoon. The boom was not as great as the one in 1912, because land speculation was limited by comparison, but it was good for building and town planning, airplane service, public health, and the fine arts.[100] However, storm clouds appeared with the stock market crash in October 1929, checking the city's expansion.

Butler and Bryers hired two architects, the Toronto-based Murray Brown and the Saskatoon-based David Webster, to build a Spanish-style facility at 127 22nd Street at a cost of $400,000.[101] Commentators have pointed out that the exterior of the building concealed the majesty inside. The narrow, two-storey building arched over the alley and extended a city block to 1st Street, with front doors on 2nd Avenue and exits on 1st Avenue. The stuccoed Spanish colonial façade featured a curved-tile, low-pitched roof, a trio of tall, arched, leaded-glass windows on the second floor and at street level an entrance consisting of six leaded-glass doors. The façade also featured two signs: one under the curved tiles and running the width of the front carried the words "CAPITOL ENTERTAINMENT," and the other, a tall sign hanging vertically on the left-hand side (it resembled an arrow pointing downward), carried the words "CAPITOL THEATRE."

Figure 64. The Capitol Theatre, Saskatoon, June 1950. Photograph by Leonard A. J. Hillyard. Saskatoon Public Library, Local History Room, photo A 1263.

Figure 65. Interior of the Capitol Theatre, Saskatoon, June 1950. Photograph by Leonard A. J. Hillyard. Saskatoon Public Library, Local History Room, LH 4180.

The auditorium represented a vast square somewhere in Spain, a space that was canopied by a blue, starlit sky. According to the *Saskatoon Star-Phoenix*, a variety of Spanish-looking houses surrounded the square, each festooned with flowers and equipped with awnings that hung on brackets of iron spear points, all evoking daydreams of sunny days and balmy nights.[102] These faux houses overlooked the crenellated walls that circled the seating area. Wrought-iron balustrades, plain stuccoed walls, small grilled windows, an arch here and an heraldic banner there: these "romantic" details appeared in no particular order. Flat, tiled roofs dominated what appeared to be a vast courtyard or town plaza.

The ceiling offered patrons a spectacular vista, which looked like a sky animated by millions of glittering stars.[103] The architects had imitated the effects American architect John Eberson had created in his "atmospheric" theatres. The projectionist employed the Brenograph, a motor-driven machine capable of "producing a variety of moving visual effects," to create the illusion of stars twinkling and clouds drifting across the sky. The experienced Montréal-based interior decorator Emmanuel Briffa, who had already decorated 150 theatres, managed the painting and the decorating. He supervised the plasterwork, creating the Italianate murals and the "courtyard" that made up the auditorium.

Figure 66. Publicity for Saskatoon's Capitol Theatre, emphasizing the role of Emmanuel Briffa, the celebrated theatre decorator. Saskatoon Star-Phoenix, *9 May* 1929, 21.

The management, including manager Frank Miley and assistant manager Reg Plumb, organized a gala celebration on 11 May 1929 to mark the official opening of the Capitol Theatre. They invited national, regional, and local celebrities, such as the mayor of Saskatoon, and H. M. Thomas and Jack Arthur, the western division manager and the musical director of Famous Players, respectively; Nathanson had planned to attend the celebration, but he was ill. They featured such entertainment as *The Lion's Roar* (1928), Mack Sennett's first talking picture, *The Sidewalks of New York* (1929), a "synchronized singing novelty," a Movietone newsreel, presenting world events "as they occur," and as the main feature, *Close Harmony* (1929), Paramount's first talking picture.

In short, Famous Players expanded rapidly in large part because the firm attracted energetic entrepreneurs who realized that the success of their local and regional enterprises was best served by an affiliation with a national or international organization. By 1929, Famous Players owned or controlled 153 theatres across Canada, with a total seating capacity of 165,000.[104] By late 1945, the firm owned or controlled 311 venues; reports suggest that 2.25 million patrons visited Famous Players theatres every week. Within the walls of the grand theatres operated by these exhibitors, so similar in design to their counterparts throughout Canada and the United States, people in the prairie West participated in the increasingly popular and ritualized mass cultural phenomenon of moviegoing. In this way, they reinforced the region's status as a hinterland to larger metropolitan centres, in central Canada and Great Britain, but most particularly in the United States, while also highlighting the growth and the increasing sophistication of the prairie cities they called home. In the next chapter, we chart the creation of Odeon Theatres, the second half of the duopoly that shaped movie exhibition in Canada for more than five decades.

7

THE STRUGGLE FOR CONTROL: ODEON THEATRES (CANADA) LIMITED

Speaking to reporters in 1931, Nat Nathanson explained that, throughout the years he had managed Famous Players, he had always taken his cue from the interests of shareholders as well as those of moviegoers, offering the public in major urban centres quality entertainment at reasonable prices.[1] After he was elected president of Famous Players for a second time in 1933, he took comfort in the knowledge that he had a verbal agreement with Adolph Zukor to the effect that he (Nathanson) would regain control of the company after the voting trust expired on 8 March 1939.[2] However, in 1936, Barney Balaban replaced Zukor as president of Paramount-Publix Corporation. When Balaban refused to honour the agreement, Nathanson resolved once more to create a nationwide, made-in-Canada chain of movie theatres.[3] Movie attendance was increasing, and the time seemed ripe for undertaking such a project.

MOVIE EXHIBITION AND THE WAR EFFORT

Canadians had entered World War I in August 1914 in a fighting spirit, but they entered World War II in September 1939 jaded by ten years of economic and social crisis. However, the war ultimately lifted Canada out of the Great Depression.[4] The federal government quickly passed a bill to finance the war effort to the extent of $100 million for the fiscal year ending 31 March 1940, defraying such expenses as security, defence, and order, including the promotion of trade, industry, and business.[5] Such wartime policies as food and fuel rationing and wage and price controls kept inflation in check.

From 1939 to 1945, Canada's factories, mines, and fields produced billions of dollars' worth of products to support the war effort.[6] The nation of 11 million people produced more than the country's men and women in uniform needed to fight, and thus sold, or, if Canada's allies could not pay, gave away equipment, food, and minerals in the cause. Workers and entrepreneurs in every sector of the Canadian economy contributed to this astonishing feat of production and organization. Writing in the *Canadian Moving Picture Digest*, Ray Lewis noted that movie exhibitors, big and small, served as a "steadying influence" on society, screening newsreels that reported on the progress of the war, inspirational documentaries, such as *London Can Take It!* (1940), released by Warner Bros. Pictures, and patriotic films, such as *The Long Voyage Home* (1940), released by United Artists.[7] Directed by Humphrey Jennings and Harry Watt and narrated by Quentin Reynolds, *London Can Take It!* depicts the courage and the determination Londoners had demonstrated in coming to grips with a German air raid. Directed by John Ford and starring John Wayne, Thomas Mitchell, Ian Hunter, Ward Bond, and Mildred Natwick, *The Long Voyage Home* tells the story of British merchant marines who survive the loneliness of travelling the sea and the coming of war. In addition, exhibitors contributed to the commonweal by organizing "socials" for men and women in uniform, and generating revenue, directly and indirectly, by (for example) implementing an amusement tax of 20 percent on the price of tickets introduced by the federal minister of Finance in April 1941, organizing rationing and recycling drives, and in general supporting the federal government's systems of price and wage controls.[8] These projects not only contributed to the ultimate success of the war effort but also helped to lay the groundwork for economic growth in the postwar period.

Economic activities of the postwar period built on this momentum. In the prairie provinces, resource-related activities were transforming the region from a rural society into an urban one and fuelling remarkable growth. From 1931 to 1951, the populations of Manitoba and Alberta increased from 700,000 to 777,000 and from 732,000 to 940,000, respectively, and although the population of Saskatchewan declined from

922,000 to 832,000, the population of the region as a whole increased from 2.354 million to 2.548 million.[9]

Attracted by the immense opportunities that the expanding economy offered in the postwar period, over 1.2 million immigrants from Europe settled in Canada between 1946 and 1956, 95,000 settling in Alberta. The population of Winnipeg grew by 17 percent during these years, whereas that of Regina and Saskatoon grew by 34 and 23 percent, respectively. By contrast, the populations of Edmonton and Calgary jumped 124 and 69 percent, respectively. As these figures indicate, Regina and Saskatoon as well as Edmonton and Calgary were becoming the major metropolitan centres of the "new" west. Edmontonians took great pride in the fact that their city was the fastest-growing city in the region.[10] During World War II, the "Gateway to the North" became a centre for military operations and, after Japan's attack on Pearl Harbor, for the construction of the Alaska Highway. To be sure, the discovery of oil and gas after the war accelerated the process of urbanization and industrialization. Calgary developed into the business centre of the oil industry, the headquarters of many hundreds of companies involved in various phases of petroleum exploration, extraction, financing, processing, and marketing, while Edmonton, closer to the major oil fields, became a major refining and petrochemical centre, the base for oil industry contracts and the centre for the transmission of petroleum products.[11] All of these developments affected the business of exhibiting movies not only in western Canada but in the country as a whole.

ODEON THEATRES: MADE IN CANADA

Nathanson had never liked managing a branch plant; thus, it is not surprising to discover that he planned his departure from Famous Players, all the while organizing a Canadian-made, Canadian-run chain of movie theatres that would challenge the company he had created twenty years before.[12] Learning that Zukor's successor, Barney Balaban, did not feel obligated by the "understanding" Nathanson had with Zukor in 1933 that he would gain controlling interest in Famous Players, or by any former verbal agreement between them, Nathanson began "signing up" independent exhibitors who operated regional theatre chains that competed with Famous Players.[13] He probably embarked on this course of action in 1939, when the voting trust expired. Negotiations to renew the trust dragged on for two years; ultimately, it was dissolved.

Still serving as president of Famous Players, Nathanson employed a variety of complex stratagems to create the new chain. As one industry analyst put it, he was the only person in Canada who had the talent, the expertise, and the strategic positioning to realize such a project.[14] On the one hand, he renewed contracts personally, exploiting partnership contracts that contained a clause allowing independent theatre operators to leave the circuit if they served advance notice. On the other, he renewed selected theatre leases for the new chain when they expired. In one case, he signed up a Famous Players subsidiary called Hamilton United Theatres, which owned the Capitol and the Palace theatres in Hamilton, thereby forcing Famous Players out of the centre of the city.[15] Nathanson promised exhibitors that, if they joined his circuit, they could screen the highly prized MGM films. Incorporated as a division of the Loew's Inc. theatre chain, MGM was the only major studio to pay dividends throughout the Great Depression.[16] Reports in the trade papers suggest that Nat's son, P. L. (Paul) Nathanson, and Oscar Hanson — the president and vice-president, respectively, of Empire-Universal Films, Limited, a film distribution company — had spent time in Vancouver trying to acquire theatres for the circuit and that William B. Long had done likewise in Edmonton.[17] Eventually, executives at Famous Players discovered the scheme and forced Nathanson to sell the theatres to Famous Players. Nathanson complied, but nevertheless pressed on with his plan to create a new chain.

What Nathanson had in mind was a chain of movie theatres that offered the public an "enhanced" moviegoing experience, one that would attract a new generation of moviegoers.[18] His plan had three principal components. First, he would need to secure a franchise from a major Hollywood studio. As the Allens' experience had illustrated so clearly, no exhibitor in Canada could operate a national theatre chain without the support of first-run films from a major American studio. Nathanson wanted to screen quality British and American films, accessing these via Empire-Universal Films (which distributed movies made by Universal Pictures, Republic Pictures, Esquire Films, and a group of British producers) and Regal Films, Ltd. (which distributed movies made by MGM Films and Monogram Pictures). Second, Nathanson wanted to operate a chain of distinctive facilities in key locations in major cities across Canada. Among other things, this meant either acquiring and remodelling existing facilities or erecting new ones featuring sleek, streamlined façades of moulded concrete that would contrast with the highly ornamented façades of Famous Players theatres. It also entailed leasing facilities that had been affiliated with Famous Players and affiliating with independent regional chains. Given that Famous Players controlled the central business districts of major cities, Nathanson decided that he should locate his theatres in the largely underserved suburbs that were springing up, thereby signalling a new approach to movie exhibition. Finally, his plan would mean implementing an audience-oriented entertainment policy, one that would include offering the latest motion picture and sound technology.[19]

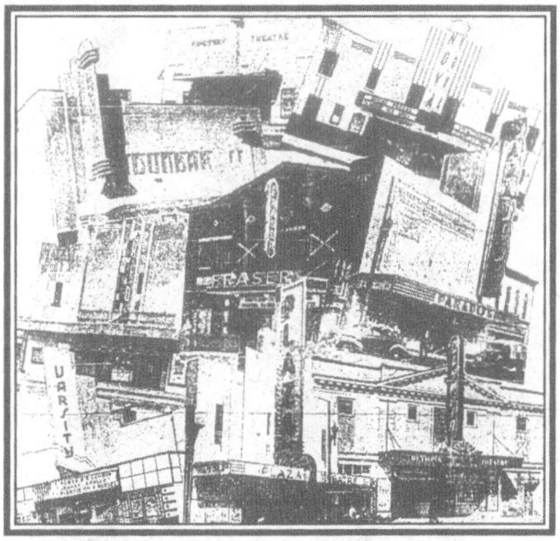

Figure 67. Advertisement for Odeon Theatres Ltd., which operated movie theatres in the suburbs as well as in downtown locations. Vancouver Sun, 12 *April* 1941, 12.

Despite the complex procedures that governed how they booked the films produced by the five major studios, independent exhibitors who owned and operated small chains (defined as two to nineteen facilities operated by one owner) prospered greatly during the 1930s.[20] Two factors account for this. On the one hand, Famous Players had been humbled by the antitrust investigation; on the other, Paramount Pictures, its parent company, was preoccupied with its financial troubles in the United States. As Paul Moore notes, during this period, Famous Players, already in control of most city centres, did not build many new theatres, nor did it take over many independent theatres.[21] Arguably, Famous Players had become complacent about their treatment of the moviegoing public. By contrast, independent exhibitors expanded their circuits, forming cooperative associations and booking services to promote their interests. Moreover, movie attendance went up during the Great Depression. According to Kirwan Cox, the share of theatres operated by independent exhibitors who ran small chains increased from 18 percent to about 50 percent in 1942, when the total number of theatres in Canada reached 1,250. The share of total revenue earned by the chains increased from

Figure 68. Movie impresario Nat Taylor, Toronto, 1965. Photo by Janine Mokrzycki. York University, Clara Thomas Archives and Special Collections, Nat Taylor fonds F0183, ASC-07223, 1999-036/002 (62).

40 percent in 1930 to 75 percent in 1942, when the total reached $38 million.[22] Gradually, bigger and bigger chains controlled more and more of the box-office receipts.

An innovative, Ontario-based movie impresario, N. A. (Nat) Taylor, believed that, even without a guaranteed supply of first-run films, an enterprising exhibitor could turn a small chain into a major force. His model may well have been Barney Balaban and Sam Katz, the Chicago-based exhibitors who had transformed a regional circuit of strategically located movie palaces into an important national chain.[23] Taylor later explained that he had entered the film business in 1918, when he was only twelve years old.[24] He sold advertisements on picture postcards to movie exhibitors along Queen Street, in Toronto. He managed his first theatre at the age of seventeen, all the while acquiring a law degree from Osgoode Hall. In 1935, he went into business for himself, founding Twentieth Century Theatres and building up a chain of second-run theatres in small towns in Ontario. On 16 November 1937, he opened the Elgin Theatre, a 750-seat facility designed in the Art Moderne style, at 216 Elgin Street, in Ottawa. With its modernist, functional, Art Deco styling, the Elgin illustrated the transition from ornate to simple design that was occurring in theatre architecture all across North America at the time.[25] However, while he could certainly point to the success of his original second-run strategy, Taylor succeeded as an exhibitor because United Artists had offered him and other independent exhibitors first-run films.

Nathanson watched Taylor's progress with interest and soon offered him a job, as vice-president and general manager of the company he was creating.[26] The ten-year agreement drawn up by Taylor's lawyers included an annual salary of $15,000 (after the initial year's salary of $10,000), four weeks of vacation every year, an annual payment of 2.5 percent of net operating profits earned by the company, and stock or bonds of the new company allotted in an amount to be agreed upon.

In the meantime, the media circulated notices announcing that Taylor would manage the new company. Famous Players executives then approached Taylor, anxious to prevent him from becoming one of Nathanson's employees. However, Nathanson rejected Taylor's proposed contract, objecting, for example, to the clause giving Taylor the right, upon one month's notice, to terminate his employment with the new company. Ultimately, Taylor accepted the offer from Famous Players, which made him (from 1 July 1941) the manager of a circuit of twenty-five Famous Players "B" theatres in Ontario, over and above the seventeen theatres he already operated. In addition to being very lucrative, this arrangement gave Taylor control over booking films.

News of Nathanson's project surfaced in January 1941, when a correspondent for *Canadian Moving Picture Digest* reported that a movie theatre chain called Odeon Theatres (Canada) Limited planned to build a 1,000-seat facility in Kingston, Ontario, thereby challenging Famous Players, which operated three theatres in the city, namely, the Capitol, the Grand, and the Tivoli.[27] A correspondent for *Canadian Moving Picture Digest* noted in February that Odeon Theatres would become a national chain initially by means of a series of affiliations, starting with Vancouver Owned Theatres, a Vancouver-based independent chain dating from 1935. The writer added that W. J. (Bill) Long, district manager for Odeon Theatres, was supervising the acquisition of theatres in the area as well as supervising the construction of his own theatre. Formerly an Edmonton-based exhibitor, Long told the press that, although allied with the British company of the same name, Odeon Theatres was entirely controlled by Canadian interests.[28] Nathanson's connection to the new chain had not yet been made clear.

Reporters for the *Vancouver Sun* offered the public a more detailed picture of Nathanson's enterprise in April when they ran a feature on Odeon Theatres, profiling the theatres that formed the nucleus of the new chain and the people who managed them. These included Long, who managed the Vogue Theatre, the "flagship" of the new circuit, which opened in 1941.[29] Designed in the Art Moderne style by Kaplan and Sprachman, Toronto-based theatre architects, and built by Long at 918 Granville Street, in Vancouver, the Vogue offered the "perfect" presentation of motion pictures. Inspired by Radio City Music Hall (built in 1932) and often called the "Odeon Style," Art Moderne was characterized by streamlined and curvilinear forms, sharply defined outlines, and bold colours, and featured the use of metals, such as chrome and aluminum, and plastics as construction materials.[30] Odeon Theatres advertised the grand opening of the Vogue as "a patriotic and gala event," thereby tapping into the wartime fervour people in the Vancouver area were feeling.[31] Individuals obtained tickets to the event — the Royal Trust Company managed the finances — by donating a minimum of $5 to the Queen's Canadian Fund for victims of Nazi bombing in London. Pete Barnes, a Texan cattle baron and movie exhibitor in the United States, made the first donation — $300. Paul Nathanson donated $500 to the fund.

According to reporters, opening night featured all the images and the sounds attached to the opening of a Hollywood theatre in the late 1920s: searchlights cut through the sky and floodlights illuminated the façade of the building. A crash of drums and the skirl of bagpipes signalled the beginning of the ceremony: soldiers, naval ratings, and airmen marched into the theatre. Lieutenant R. A. Diespecker, a Vancouver-based radio announcer, served as master of ceremonies. Alderman Halfour D. Wilson congratulated Odeon Theatres, proprietors of the Vogue Theatre. Colonel W. Woodward, a prominent Vancouver entrepreneur and assistant to the minister of Munitions and Supply, spoke about the trials that the people in Great Britain were enduring.[32] The Burrard Male Choir and Dal Richards, music director, led his twenty-five-piece orchestra in patriotic music. The management screened *I See Ice* (1938), an Ealing Studios production featuring George Formby as a photographer who invents a secret camera and winds up trying to evade the police.

Nathanson formed General Theatres Corporation, Limited, a holding company that controlled Odeon Theatres among other concerns, on 18 April 1941, capitalizing it at $5 million, and then opened an office at 20 Carlton Street, in Toronto.[33] He installed H. M. (Haskell) Masters as manager of General Theatre Corporation and his son, Paul, as the managing director. Paul maintained that he was the one responsible for the name "Odeon," having picked the word out of the dictionary, unaware of the existence of Odeon Cinemas in Great Britain — although this seems somewhat unlikely. By 1941, the British chain (founded in 1928 by Oscar Deutsch) ran 258 cinemas in Great Britain.[34]

General Theatres executives announced that Odeon Theatres would expand by buying, leasing, and building theatres in ideal locations across Canada, with a view to producing a chain comprising two hundred theatres. By the end of July, they had reached one hundred, including nineteen theatres in British Columbia.[35] As Moore writes, British Columbia would remain the chain's stronghold well into the 1980s.[36]

Nathanson's contract with Paramount Pictures came up for renewal in 1941, but clearly he had no intention of renewing it. Since returning to Famous Players, he had tried to undo the policies put into effect by J. J. Fitzgibbons, Balaban's protégé at Paramount Pictures.[37] Executives at Paramount had set the selling price of the shares they held at $5 million higher than the figure Canadian interests via Nathanson were prepared to offer, likely to block the sale.[38] Nathanson resigned at a board meeting on 14 May 1941, taking a number of executives with him, including Tom Bragg and Clarence Robson, who had been with him from the beginning. In his letter of resignation, he claimed that Paramount Pictures would not accept his offer to purchase the controlling interests of the company.[39]

Predictably, Famous Players and Odeon Theatres quarrelled over access to producers' films. Balaban, Fitzgibbons, Nathanson, and other executives met in September at the office of Nicholas Schenck, president of Loew's Inc., New York City, to determine who in Canada would hold the MGM franchise. Schenck, the most powerful man in the movie industry at the time, controlled MGM. After deliberating on the matter, he drew up a product allocation policy, whereby Famous Players retained the exclusive rights to show the movies produced by MGM, Paramount, Warner Bros., and United Artists, and Odeon Theatres acquired the rights to screen movies produced by some minor studios, including Columbia, Fox, and Universal. Regal Films, a Paramount subsidiary, retained the right to distribute MGM films in Canada.[40] Odeon Theatres would therefore grow, thanks to the rights to first-run films of mostly minor companies and to a shared part of the Fox supply, but not at the pace that Nathanson had envisioned. Not surprisingly, a number of theatre owners who had joined Odeon Theatres on the understanding that they would be screening MGM films later left, including Biltmore Theatre Ltd., with theatres in Oshawa and Kingston.[41]

EXPANSION: PHASE ONE

Meanwhile, in April 1941, H. A. (Harry) Friedman, the president and the managing director of Odeon-Midwestern Theatres, an affiliate of Odeon Theatres, told the press that negotiations were underway to acquire existing theatres and to build new ones in major urban centres across the prairie West.[42] Friedman noted that Odeon Theatres planned to build two 1,200-seat facilities in Edmonton and one deluxe facility in Lethbridge, the latter at a cost of $150,000. He added that special attention would be given to the air-conditioning systems so that patrons could enjoy their favourite movies in complete comfort, regardless of the weather.

Erecting new theatres during the early 1940s was a challenge, since a Dominion order-in-council had limited the construction of new commercial buildings in Canada, a policy that extended into December 1945. Arguably, this measure prevented an out-and-out war between Famous Players and Odeon Theatres. R. C. Berkinshaw, the head of the Priorities Branch of the Department of Munitions and Supply, told the press in May 1941 that the department would refuse permits for the building of three theatres, one or two of which were to be located in Edmonton. The policy, Berkinshaw added, meant that theatres could not be expanded unless an applicant could show that the building in question was at least half completed at the time of the application.[43] In addition, both building materials and labourers were in short supply.

These formidable challenges notwithstanding, Odeon-Midwestern Theatres executives launched an acquisition and a building campaign in Alberta in 1941. By the end of July, the firm had acquired three facilities, the Rialto in Edmonton and the Crescent and the Plaza in Calgary, bringing the number in the circuit to over one hundred.[44] By the end of August, Odeon-Midwestern Theatres had acquired three more theatres in Edmonton, the Avenue, the Roxy, and the Varscona, and two in Calgary, the Tivoli and the Grand. These acquisitions brought the seating capacity of Odeon Theatres facilities in Alberta to just under eight thousand.

It is instructive to consider the operations of these Calgary and Edmonton theatres and the movie exhibitors who operated them. Their stories illustrate major patterns in the complex interaction between very particular local circumstances and individuals and the larger regional, national, and global dynamics that shaped the competition between Famous Players and Odeon Theatres and defined the evolution of film exhibition in western Canada.

Learning that the directors of Suburban Theatres were building a 780-seat, neighbourhood facility in the Moderne style — the Garneau Theatre, which opened in 1940 at 8712 109th Street, in Edmonton — I. F. (Izzy) Shacker hired Rule, Wynn, and Rule to build a 500-seat, neighbourhood facility, the Varscona Theatre, at 10907 82nd Avenue, not far from the Garneau. Shacker, a Hanna-based entrepreneur and politician, owned and operated theatres in Edmonton, Hanna, Kindersley, and Saskatoon.[45] Graduates of the University of Alberta's architecture program, John Rule, Gordon Wynn, and Peter Rule founded their firm when they were struggling to establish themselves as architects during the Great Depression. One of the leading architectural firms in western Canada, with offices in Edmonton from 1938 and in Calgary from 1945 to 1986, the firm played a crucial role in establishing the Moderne style in western Canada.

Shacker set the architects and the builders two tasks: to erect a more attractive theatre than the Garneau, also in the Moderne style, and to complete it faster. As it happened, all three members of the firm joined the armed forces and fought in the war, and in their absence Peter Rule's father, a building inspector for Alberta Government Telephones (and also named Peter), completed the design and supervised the construction. The design of the Varscona reflects Rule's knowledge of the British Odeon style, gained on his trips to Great Britain. Shacker told reporters that his primary interest in building the Varscona was attending to moviegoers' comfort and convenience, and to this end he insisted on fire-proof construction throughout.[46] Poole Construction workers started the Varscona in April 1940, completing it in July, at a cost of $30,000; Western Canada Construction workers completed the Garneau in October, at a cost of $55,000.

Reporters regarded the Varscona as a striking landmark. Five external pillars supported the sides of the stucco-clad facility, which was finished in gleaming white and black trim.[47] A 35-foot tower (the intake tower for the air-conditioning system) dominated the façade, bisecting five horizontal elements. These elements consisted of fins on the tower; a band just below the roof that stretched across the front, serving as a cornice; two rectangular glass-block windows on the right; a broad band, four feet wide, that extended across the front and wrapped around the corners, serving as the marquee; and a narrower band of vitrolite across the front. At street level, two sets of doors stood on each side of the tower, and a very large circular window dominated the semi-circular section on the right. Neon lights on the fins identified the theatre at night.

Similar features distinguished the auditorium. Buff-coloured acoustic tiles covered the walls and the ceiling. Two pairs of mock pillars adorned the walls near the small stage, which was fitted with bronze drapes, and sienna-and-cream carpeting covered the floors. Three aisles separated the seats, which were covered in deep turquoise mohair, into four sections, arranged in a parabolic design. Reporters observed that Shacker had fitted the auditorium with the latest air-conditioning system.

Figure 69. The Varscona Theatre, Edmonton, 1941. Provincial Archives of Alberta, Alfred Blyth Collection BL 254 1.

The staff, including Izzy's brother, Ralph Shacker, who served as the manager, implemented an entertainment policy that focused on screening quality pictures at the lowest prices. Shacker explained that the goal of a neighbourhood theatre like the Varscona was to show "proved" entertainment, so that visitors would know exactly what kind of show they would be seeing. The moviegoing experience at the Varscona would be first-rate, thanks to the theatre's up-to-date projection and sound equipment. He set admission prices at ten cents for children, while adults paid fifteen cents for matinee performances and twenty-five cents for evening performances. Students received special rates on selected evenings, and families were offered special rates throughout the week. As a special attraction, Shacker offered patrons parking close to the theatre.

The management opened the Varscona on 6 July 1940, marking the occasion with a typical gala celebration. They offered a Dixie cup of ice cream to every child who attended the event, which began at 1:30 p.m. At the evening performance, they screened two family-oriented films, both Universal releases: *The Under-Pup* (1939), directed by Richard Wallace, which tells the story of a shy preteen who wins a scholarship to a music camp, and Lew Landers's *Honeymoon Deferred* (1940), the story of a private investigator who interrupts his honeymoon in order to solve the murder of his boss. Shacker became an Odeon Theatres affiliate in July 1941, an arrangement that enabled him to screen top-notch films made in the United States and in Great Britain.[48]

Meanwhile, in Calgary, Vernon Dixon, a former Warner Bros. employee, announced in December 1934 that the suburb of Hillhurst could support a modern facility, one equipped with the latest projection and sound equipment. He hired an architect to transform a vacant garage, located at 1133 Kensington Road Northeast, into a neighbourhood movie theatre seating 425 patrons: the Plaza Theatre, which opened in 1935. The builders completed the project in three months at a cost of $30,000.[49]

The simply designed façade offered passersby a distinctly Spanish design.[50] Three bays topped with a pediment dominated the white stucco frontage, each featuring a horizontal window at the upper level, while each of the outer bays featured a vertical window. A rectangular marquee extended over the entrance doors, the front of which announced the title of the featured attraction. A narrow door in the left bay (leading to an apartment on the upper level) and a display case in the right bay completed the symmetrical arrangement of the design.

The interior, also simple in design and decoration, impressed commentators very favourably.[51] Grey moulded acoustic tiles covered the ceiling and the walls of the shoebox-shaped auditorium. Mock columns, topped with grotesque figures, dominated the side walls. Two pillars supported the rose-coloured proscenium arch; royal blue curtains covered the screen, which measured 20 feet wide by 12 feet high. The "modernistic" treatment included large, comfortable seats, upholstered with maroon leather, and chromium-and-black fixtures, which provided indirect lighting.[52] The safety features included a cement floor and a cement roof, together with two easily accessible fire exits and a cement projection room.

Figure 70. The Plaza Theatre, Calgary, 2009. Photo by Robert M. Seiler.

Figure 71. Advertisement for the opening of the Plaza Theatre, which later became an Odeon affiliate. Calgary Herald, *9 January 1935, 5.*

Dixon, who served as the theatre's manager, and his staff of six pledged to cater to the family trade exclusively, announcing that "we will make special efforts to furnish a highly entertaining program, representative of the best efforts from the studios of London and Hollywood."[53] This included changing the program twice each week and offering Saturday matinees for children. The opening program on 10 January 1935 consisted of the main feature, *Mr. Skitch* (1933), a comedy about a couple who lose their farm to the bank and embark on a cross-country journey in their "flivver" to Hollywood, followed by a newsreel and a cartoon, and then the second feature. In August 1941, Dixon joined Odeon Theatres as an affiliate exhibitor and programmed first-run movies for the next five years. The sale of the theatre in 1946 seems to have ended its affiliation with Odeon.[54]

In 1936, A. E. Staniland, another entertainment entrepreneur, hired John Russell to build a neighbourhood facility accommodating 480 patrons at 2015 4th Street West, in the heart of Calgary's Mission district. Russell — a member of Green, Blankstein, Russell, and Ham, an architectural firm based in Winnipeg and Calgary, and the former head of the Department of Architecture at the University of Manitoba — championed the Art Moderne movement in building design. Staniland set out to create a "model" theatre, one that utilized every architectural and technological feature available, while meeting moviegoers' demand for comfort and safety.[55] The result was the Tivoli Theatre, completed in 1936 at a cost of $35,000.

One side of the Moderne structure faced 21st Avenue and the other extended along 4th Street.[56] The long wall presented an almost unbroken surface of white stucco, save for a wide band of black ceramic bricks near the flat roof and a narrow band of black and orange ceramic bricks about eight feet from the sidewalk, giving the exterior an Art Deco finish. A tower projected upward from the canopy, resembling a nest of children's blocks and finished in stucco, with a band of black and tango-red vitrolite bricks. A vertical sign attached to the tower flashed the word "TIVOLI" in neon lights. A rectangular marquee located just above the entrance on 4th Street extended over the sidewalk; three rows of 8-inch interchangeable letters announced the current feature film.

Figure 72. The Tivoli Theatre, Calgary, 1978. Glenbow Archives NA-2864-32708.

As commentators noted, every feature of the interior bore witness to a concern for "simplicity" in terms of design and decoration.[57] Buff-coloured acoustic tiles covered the ceiling and the side walls of the auditorium; a rose-coloured carpet covered the floor. Dark bands running horizontally along the side walls served to keep patrons' eyes focused on the screen, and neon tubes forming part of the decorative scheme on the ceiling (they formed a horseshoe) illuminated the space. Two aisles separated the seats, which were upholstered in red mohair and equipped with rubber arm rests, into three sections; a number of the seats featured earphones. Sound equipment had been installed behind the perforated screen.[58] Heerwagen tile covered the rear wall, allowing for the high frequencies of music. Staniland hoped that these features would set new standards in entertainment, offering patrons a truer reproduction of human voices and musical instruments.

A. E.(Allan) Gold, the manager, and his staff, including two usherettes dressed in bellhop uniforms, opened the Tivoli on 7 October 1936, marking the occasion with a gala evening, screening *Rose-Marie* (1936), an MGM picture that tells the story of Marie de Flor, a Montréal opera singer who, in search of her dissolute brother, goes north into the wilds of Canada, where she takes a job singing in a saloon and falls in love with a Sergeant Bruce.[59] Staniland became an Odeon Theatres affiliate in August 1941. In the absence of definitive records, it is impossible to state with certainty how long this affiliation continued; it may well have ended in the mid-1960s.[60]

In June 1937, the Calgary-based theatre impresario Jack Barron acquired the Grand Theatre, at 608 1st Street West, in Calgary. Barron became an Odeon Theatres affiliate in September 1941.[61] The Grand Theatre was originally built in 1912. (On the early days of the Grand, see chapter 3.) The complex negotiations Barron engaged in to acquire the facility illustrate the constraints and the opportunities of the 1930s economy. In addition, they expose the "sharp" methods entertainment entrepreneurs sometimes employed.

Barron was born in Winnipeg in 1888, the son of Joseph S. Barron and Elizabeth Bell Barron, Russian Jews who had settled in the city six years before.[62] At the height of the gold rush, in 1898, Joseph, a jeweller, travelled to Dawson City, hoping to make his fortune, and opened a clothing store. Elizabeth and their two sons, Jack and Abraham, joined him five years later. Jack and his brother, who were among the first graduates of Dawson City High School, moved to Chicago in 1905, where they studied law at the University of Chicago. Elizabeth went with them, working as a seamstress (she made dresses for the leading actresses in vaudeville and Yiddish theatre) to help pay for their education and cooking their meals. After graduating, Jack moved to Calgary in 1911, during the construction boom. Abraham followed soon after, and their parents joined them there in 1913. Jack married Amelia Helman in 1914, and the couple had three sons: William, Robert, and Richard. Jack was admitted to the bar in 1915 and Abraham in 1919; that year, they opened the law firm of Barron and Barron, struggling to make ends meet.

Fascinated by the entertainment business, Jack had served as the Allens' Calgary-based lawyer. In October 1924, after the Allens lost their empire, he leased Allen's Palace Theatre and operated it with success until 1928. He enjoyed the challenge of programming live entertainment and movies, earning a name for himself as an impresario by bringing such celebrities as Nellie Melba, Jascha Heifetz, Sergei Rachmaninoff, Reinald Werrenrath, and Margarete Matzenauer to Calgary.

Figure 73. Jack Barron, Calgary-based lawyer and theatre impresario, n.d. Glenbow Archives NA-5229-1.

When, in the wake of the Allens' bankruptcy, the trust company that was administering the Palace Theatre sold the property to Famous Players, Jack returned to his law practice, all the while keeping an eye open for an opportunity that would allow him to become a theatre manager again. Sometime toward the end of 1935, he found such an opportunity, in the form of a plan to revive legitimate theatres across western Canada that had been dark for a number of years. This meant refurbishing a number of facilities, starting with the Grand, so that they could offer the public a combination of live entertainment, including vaudeville, and movies. This formula had worked well in the past, and he judged that it would work again, once the Great Depression had passed. Acquiring the Grand Theatre from the Lougheed family was the first step in this rather ambitious project.

As historian Donald Smith has observed, the Lougheed family experienced psychological as well as financial hardship after the death of Sir James Lougheed in 1925.[63] Thanks to the Great Depression, which wiped out their investment income, the Lougheeds were forced to depend on their rental properties, which were generating a fraction of the income they once had. In many respects, the Grand Theatre constituted a serious problem. They leased the facility to Famous Players from 1926 to 1931 and then tried for two years to manage it on their own, but they lacked the expertise to make a success of the venture. On 1 October 1933, they leased the theatre to Ken Leach, a seasoned theatre manager and a Famous Players partner (see chapter 6). Leach already operated two movie theatres in Calgary and three in Winnipeg. According to the terms of the lease, which took effect 1 January 1934 and ran for five years and four months, Leach was obliged to pay the Lougheed estate a rental of 50 percent of the net profits from running the theatre. On 20 April, Leach formed the Grand Theatre company for the purpose of operating the facility in accordance with the lease. Because he left the theatre dark for long stretches of time, however, he generated a monthly rental income of only about $100, hardly enough to cover such expenses as upkeep, insurance, and taxes. On 30 November 1935, the property was transferred by Lougheed Buildings (a corporate body that looked after the family's financial interests) to the Royal Trust Company as judicial trustee of the estate of Sir James Lougheed and Edgar Donald Lougheed, surviving executor of his will. In December, the Metropolitan Life Insurance Company, which held a mortgage on the Lougheed Building, started proceedings to foreclose its mortgage.

About this time, Barron approached the Royal Trust Company, offering to lease the theatre. Owing to the existence of the lease to Leach, this was not possible. Barron then asked the trust company to give him a listing of the theatre, arguing that he could form a syndicate to buy it. Under this arrangement, if Barron obtained a purchaser, the trust company would cancel the lease. Familiar with the terms of the lease, he insisted that if the theatre were sold through his efforts, he should receive a commission. He and his associates formed the Grand Theatre Syndicate and made the application on 6 October 1936. Barron and the Royal Trust Company prepared an agreement of sale on 1 February 1937 for $85,000; the trust company informed Grand Theatre on 5 February that it was selling the property to the syndicate and that Leach had thirty days to exercise his option to buy the property. No such application was made. The Lougheed estate and the syndicate completed the agreement on 15 March. They filed a defence of their action on the following day.[64]

On 17 March, Leach launched an action disputing the estate's right to cancel the lease and indicated that Grand Theatre would remain in possession of the building after the expiration of three months, as lessee or purchaser (Action No. 1 in the eventual judgment). On 25 March, the Lougheed estate launched an action against Leach and Grand Theatre (Action No. 2 in the ensuing judgment). Justice S. J. Shepherd of the Supreme Court of Alberta ruled on both actions, handing down his judgment on 16 July. A number of considerations affected this judgment. One involved the complex nature of the premises. They consisted of a portion of the Lougheed Building, some six storeys high and comprising stores, offices, and the Grand Theatre, with entrances and exits accessed by corridors from the street. A party wall and a light well, extending from the ground to the top of the building, separated the theatre from the balance of the building. As well, Shepherd pointed out, the vendors sold the theatre portion of the premises provided that the purchaser spend more than $5,000 refurbishing the facility, install projection and sound equipment necessary for the screening of movies, and operate it for a period of fifteen years, that is, every working day, providing concerts, stage performances, lectures, or movies, thus meeting the competition of other theatres in the city. If these conditions were met, he noted, the sale price would be reduced to $60,000. Ultimately, he concluded, the vendors had in fact sold the theatre properly. The lease to Leach had contained a covenant that the lessee would not keep the theatre closed, meaning that he would operate it at all times that suitable attractions could be secured or that a profit could be realized. Leach could have equipped the theatre for showing movies, but he chose not to, thus reducing the competition he faced as an exhibitor. The judge noted that, from 1 January 1934 to 15 May 1937, the Grand operated for only 239 days (indeed, during the whole of 1936 it operated for only 33 days). Leach admitted to paying a rental fee of $400 for another theatre in Calgary that he kept dark, a practice not uncommon. Justice Shepherd thus dismissed Action No. 1 and judged in favour of the plaintiffs in Action No. 2. This meant that the lease in question terminated on 15 June 1937. In darkening the Grand, the judge indicated, Grand Theatre had failed to fulfil its duty to the Lougheed estate.

Now in control of the Grand, Barron then turned his attention to the enormous task of renovating the 1,500-seat facility, putting every penny he had into the project. C. L. (Clarence) Dowsley, who had served as Barron's assistant at the Palace Theatre and now served as his assistant at Trans-Canada Theatres, supervised the project. Twenty-five craftsmen and labourers worked in two shifts for six weeks. J. S. Bensel, a young Hungarian interior decorator, took charge of the plastering and the painting. Various members of the Barron family, including Dick Barron, Jack's sixteen-year-old son, helped wherever they could, removing wallpaper, replacing light fixtures, painting, or cleaning up. These people together transformed the dark facility into a bright, up-to-date movie theatre.

The builders worked in stages, making major alterations to the building first. They built a new projection room on the balcony (three times the size of the old one), designed to accommodate the latest projection and sound equipment.[65] They covered the ceiling, the walls, and the proscenium with cream-coloured acoustic tiles, enhancing the acoustics. In addition, the builders modified the stage, upgraded the flies, and rewired the auditorium, so that Barron could feature large travelling productions, and installed a large fan in the ceiling above the balcony, so that patrons sitting in the seats there could smoke.

The technicians installed a new screen and the latest projection and sound equipment needed to screen "talkies." A writer for the *Calgary Herald* noted that the new equipment included Brenkert Super X lamps, which illuminated the projectors, and Flexitone amplifiers, which ensured the clearest sound. The same writer noted that the new screen generated hardly any eye strain. In addition, they fitted the proscenium with a new asbestos curtain.

As well, the builders made a number of minor changes to the structure, with a view to offering patrons the "acme of comfort." For example, they renovated the restrooms just off the lobby and built a women's restroom and lounge on the second floor. In addition, they installed cushioned seats in the auditorium and deep chesterfields in the loges on the balcony and covered the hallway leading into the theatre with terrazzo tiles.

Meanwhile, Barron assembled a capable staff to help him operate the new theatre, including Frank Holroyd and Giuseppe Creatore, who had worked with him at the Palace Theatre.[66] Barron implemented the entertainment policy that had served him well at the Palace, namely, combining live performances and movies and charging reasonable prices. He set admission prices at thirty-five cents and fifty-five cents for loge seats until 6:30 p.m. and forty-five cents and sixty-five cents for loge seats after 6:30 p.m.

The management opened the doors to the public on 3 September 1937, presenting a gala program consisting of two films, a comedy, *Meet the Boyfriend* (1937), and a drama, *Beware of Ladies* (1936), as well as a musical performance.[67] Smartly dressed members of the Canadian Corps of Commissionaires escorted patrons to their seats. The stage show that followed featured an ensemble of thirty-five musicians (directed by Giuseppe Creatore) drawn from the Calgary Symphony Orchestra.[68]

Figure 74. The Lougheed Building, in Calgary, featuring the marquee and the sign of the Grand Theatre, 1959. Glenbow Archives NA-5093-688.

Figure 75. The stage of the Grand Theatre, Calgary, 1944. Glenbow Archives PA-3463-15.

Because he liked to program variety entertainment, combining live performances and movies, Barron tried to book vaudeville acts, but this proved to be difficult.[69] He tried to book Sir John Martin-Harvey and his company but had no luck: the celebrated British actor, known as the last of the great Romantic actors, was on the verge of retiring. He succeeded in booking the San Carlo Opera Company, which for thirty years had toured the United States and Canada annually, bringing the standard operatic classics to the mass public at prices average patrons could afford. The company played three engagements at the Grand (4–6 April 1938, 31 January–2 February 1944, and 26–28 February 1945), attracting capacity audiences. Barron also booked animal shows such as the Polack Brothers Circus, which appeared on stage for a week in late May and early June 1938.[70] The circus featured Jumbo, the 9,000-pound elephant. Always ready to try something new, Barron introduced a dance band, Jerry Fuller and His Orchestra, who played Sunday evenings from February 1940 to May 1941 (instead of charging an admission, he asked patrons to make a cash contribution), and "Amateur Nite," a talent contest hosted by Don Mackay, a radio announcer (and the future mayor of Calgary), from September 1940 to June 1941.[71] Significantly, Barron programmed a series of concerts featuring celebrity artists, including Marian Anderson, the acclaimed African-American singer who performed at the Grand on 15 March 1940; Lauritz Melchior, the Danish tenor, who performed on 21 October 1940; Arthur Rubinstein, the acclaimed Polish pianist, who performed on 17 March 1942 (and again on 7 February 1944); and Yehudi Menuhin, the celebrated American violinist, who performed on 4 November 1943.[72] These performances attracted capacity audiences.

Determined to take advantage of the entertainment offered by Odeon Theatres, Barron joined the new circuit as an affiliate in September 1941, thus gaining access to first-run films that featured the top-ranking stars of the era, including (in 1941) Mickey Rooney, Spencer Tracy, Clark Gable, James Cagney, Jeanette MacDonald, Bette Davis, Deanna Durbin, and Judy Garland, as well as those produced by the J. Arthur Rank company.[73]

EXPANSION: PHASE TWO

Few exhibitors built movie theatres in Canada during the Second World War. Industry analysts noted that exhibitors erected only nine theatres, three in 1941, three in 1943, and three in 1944.[74] The major chains nevertheless acquired property, anticipating a time after the war when they could erect new buildings.

As we mentioned earlier, Odeon Theatres executives had announced in April 1941 that Odeon Theatres would build a deluxe facility in Lethbridge. The new theatre was supposed to be completed by 1 December of that year, but no work was done on the project during the war. In May 1946, executives told the press that Odeon Theatres planned to build a total of sixty-four new facilities across the country, including one in Lethbridge. According to the *Lethbridge Herald,* the new theatre would be built on 5th Street South, directly opposite the Capitol

Theatre, which had been in operation since 1929. The report added that the facility would be "modernly equipped with the latest sound features and the design [would] be modernistic. Provision [would be] made for television when such becomes commercially practical." Ultimately, however, this project did not materialize, although many others did.[75]

Exhibitors started building new theatres after December 1945, by which time the federal government had ended its ban on the construction of new entertainment facilities. Odeon Theatres executives decided to buy or to build new theatres in order to catch up with Famous Players; from 1946 to 1948, the number of theatres in the Odeon Theatres circuit jumped from 107 to 180, an increase of 68 percent.[76] Exhibitors across the prairie West, including Jack Barron, Nathan Rothstein, and H. A. (Henry) Mortón, became part of this project. In doing so, they offered moviegoers buildings that looked strikingly modern in architectural design and decoration: often, these facilities featured gleaming white stucco or concrete façades and were highlighted in neon.[77]

Nate Rothstein became an Odeon Theatres affiliate in January 1944; Paul Nathanson marked this propitious arrangement by telling the press that Rothstein's theatres brought the total number of theatres in the Odeon chain to eighty-seven. Rothstein had grown up in Russia, the son of Jewish parents, Jacob and Malka Rothstein. In 1904, at the age of twenty-one, he immigrated to Canada, homesteading in Lipton, Saskatchewan, before entering the hardware business in 1908. In 1912 he established himself in both the motion picture and hotel businesses, founding Rothstein Theatres, a Winnipeg-based organization. He eventually expanded his operation to include eighteen theatres that stretched across Saskatchewan, Manitoba, and Ontario. Many of these facilities bore the name "Roxy" in honour of the Roxy Theatre, the magnificent picture palace in New York City that opened in March 1927.[78]

Located at 320 20th Street West, the Saskatoon Roxy — a brick, stone, concrete, and steel-and-truss structure designed in the Spanish Villa style by architect F. F. (Fred) Le Maistre and built by contractor R. J. Arrand — served as the centrepiece of the Rothstein circuit. This atmospheric theatre, the second to be built in the city, opened in August 1930 and featured vaudeville and cinema. Audiences marvelled at its false gardens, balconies, windows, and parapets, which created the impression of the courtyard of a Spanish mission. The Roxy operated as an Odeon Theatres affiliate until 1995, when it closed. (Rainbow and Magic Lantern Cinemas subsequently restored the facility, reopening it in 2005.) Rothstein Theatres also owned the Skyway Drive-In and the Barry Hotel in Saskatoon, as well as Winnipeg's historic Marlborough Hotel, which first opened its doors on 14 November 1914, on the very eve of World War I. Rothstein died in Winnipeg on 29 April 1969, at the age of eighty-six. According to obituary notices, he had played a major role in many organizations, including the Manitoba Motion Pictures Exhibitors Association, and had made a major contribution to the cultural life of the community.[79]

In January 1940, Barron began negotiating with the City of Winnipeg to acquire the Walker Theatre, at 364 Smith Street. Originally built in 1907, the Walker had been dark for a number of years: the city had seized the facility in lieu of unpaid taxes (see chapter 3). Barron's plan was to establish a chain of theatres that extended across the prairie West, each presenting movies and live entertainment, such as Chicago-based travelling stage shows. The agreement stipulated that National Theatres — the holding company that Barron and his associates were forming for the project — would lease the Walker for three years, starting 1 May 1940, paying a rent of $600 a month for the first year, $700 a month for the second year, and $900 a month for the third year, with an option to purchase. The agreement also stipulated that the holding company would spend $20,000 on improvements before 1 September 1940, when it would start paying taxes. If the purchase option were exercised, the rent already paid would be deducted from the purchase price of $50,000, paid in monthly instalments of $1,100 for the first year and $1,300 for each successive year. Analysts suggested that the holding company would have to pay taxes of $3,657 per year. If the purchase option were not taken up, the improvements made by the lessee would belong to the city. At the time, the building was worth $106,000 and the property $20,350. The unpaid taxes amounted to $70,000. City Council approved the agreement on 23 January 1940, but Barron and his associates dropped the matter, presumably because they found the terms too stringent.[80]

Ultimately, Henry Morton purchased the Walker in 1944 for $35,000, operating the facility, which was now called the Odeon Theatre, as an Odeon Theatres affiliate. Born in Russia, Morton had immigrated to the United States at the age of fourteen and had moved to Winnipeg in 1914, entering the theatre business as a doorman. He went on to manage and acquire several theatres and in 1941 formed Odeon-Morton Theatres. As the firm's president and the managing director, he operated three theatres in Saskatoon and four in Winnipeg, giving Odeon-Morton Theatres a seating capacity of almost 4,000.[81]

Morton commissioned the firm of Green, Blankstein, and Russell to transform the venerable Walker into an up-to-date movie theatre. Clair Appel, the eastern general manager of Odeon Theatres, announced that the venue would be the first of fifteen theatres soon to be built across western Canada (officials were planning to build forty-six theatres across Canada). The builders modified the entrance, the foyer, and the auditorium, renovating the stage (the management planned to feature road companies of major Broadway productions from time to time), removing the orchestra pit, building a new projection room, installing a false ceiling in order to improve the acoustics, and fitting this area with burgundy carpets and opera seats. Technicians installed an up-to-date screen, together with the latest projection and sound equipment, and updated the heating and the air-conditioning systems.

Figure 76. The Odeon Theatre, Winnipeg, 1970, featuring the J. Arthur Rank trademark. Provincial Archives of Manitoba A/S–Winnipeg–Smith Street, AP 6 65-7020.

Morton implemented the Odeon Theatres entertainment policy, which, as we have seen, included screening quality American and British movies, especially J. Arthur Rank releases, and setting competitive admission prices, asking adults to pay thirty cents and children twelve cents for afternoon performances, and adults (on the main floor) fifty cents and children eighteen cents for evening performances. These prices included an amusement tax. The Morton organization advertised widely, offering the public "Screen entertainment at its very best" and "free parking." They opened the Odeon Theatre, now with a capacity of 1,155 seats, on 2 November 1945, marking the occasion with a gala evening. The management screened *Blood on the Sun* (1945), a United Artists melodrama directed by Frank Lloyd that starred James Cagney as a journalist working in Tokyo who runs afoul of the country's imperialist government.[82]

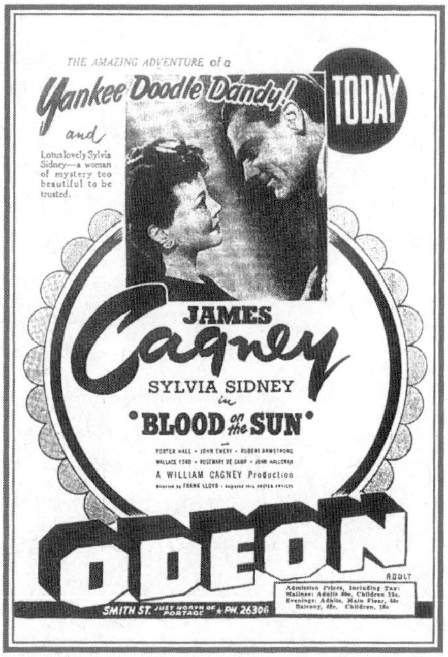

Figure 77. Advertisement for Blood on the Sun *(1945), playing at Winnipeg's Walker Theatre, November 1945.* Winnipeg Free Press, *3 November* 1945, 12.

Not to be outdone, in March 1946, Barron announced that he was planning to build a huge amusement centre in Calgary, including an ultra-modern movie theatre that would rival any facility of its kind on the North American continent.[83] As we noted earlier, the outbreak of World War II had triggered another period of phenomenal growth in Calgary that continued into the postwar era. From 1946 to 1966, the population of the community grew from 100,044 to 330,575, an increase of no less than 230 percent.[84] Construction reached a new high in 1949: building permits issued that year totalled $21.8 million, topping the record set in 1912. The discovery of oil at Leduc in 1947 "propelled Calgary from a branch-plant status to international headquarters status in the petroleum industry."[85] During this period, developers erected many skyscrapers, conveying the city's "progressive attitude."[86] Barron was an early participant in this movement, since his decision to build an office tower predated the Leduc discovery.

Barron proceeded in 1949 with a modified version of the project, to be called the Barron Building, which would cost $1.25 million to erect.[87] Taking his cue from Senator James Lougheed, he insisted that the eleven-storey office tower would meet a variety of needs, housing retail stores and a movie theatre on the ground level, offices on the upper levels, and a residence (a penthouse) on the top floor. To finance the project, he obtained a mortgage of $750,000 from Great West Life and a loan of $250,000 from Odeon Theatres. The building, and the district around it, gradually became known as the "Oil Patch," as a number of oil companies set up their head offices there, including Mobil Oil, Shell Oil, Sun Oil, and TransCanada Pipelines.

Barron researched the project for two years, visiting major movie theatres across the continent. In due course, he commissioned J. A. (Jack) Cawston, of the architectural firm of Stevenson, Cawston, and Dewar, to build a multi-purpose commercial complex, including a "luxurious" theatre, on the property on 8th Avenue, between 5th and 6th Street.

The builders used a variety of fire-resistant materials, steel, and masonry, and employed a number of lightweight techniques to erect the ten-storey building in a Moderne style that exhibited Art Deco and International influences. They clad the exterior in yellow brick, Tyndall limestone, and ornamental aluminium. The stepped-back massing, together with the angled chevron and the scalloped ornamentation on the façade, recall the Art Deco buildings such as the Rockefeller Center and the Chrysler Building that were built in New York City and Los Angeles during the 1920s and the 1930s. The ribbon windows and horizontally projecting roof lines of the penthouse derive from the International style.

The exterior of the Uptown Theatre, built in 1951 at a cost of $900,000, featured a large illuminated marquee that extended over the sidewalk and displayed the word "UPTOWN" in script. At the entrance at 610 8th Avenue Southwest, were two sets of glass doors activated by photoelectric cells, major features of Barron's Grand Theatre.[88] The foyer curved to the left, and neon lights illuminated this space. Slate planting boxes ran along the walls, and a slate fish pond stood in the centre of the foyer. A multitude of blue and orange lights (inserted into the ceiling) created a twilight effect, and nearly two thousand yards of shag carpet, in the autumn-like colours of brown and gold, ran through the theatre. From this space, patrons made their way up to the mezzanine via a marble staircase. They entered the balcony via two doors at the centre of the mezzanine or via two small staircases off the foyer. They then made their way into the narrow auditorium via two sets of doors. Altogether, 1,100 foam-rubber seats offered patrons maximum comfort, with ample leg room, and a clear view of the screen: the floor of the auditorium sloped more steeply than usual. The screen itself was surrounded by a massive fireproof gold damask cloth. Reporters judged the acoustics excellent — because of the plaster that had been applied to the ceiling and the walls. Projection and sound equipment of the latest type was manufactured by a subsidiary of the J. Arthur Rank Organisation.

Figure 78. The Barron Building, in Calgary, with the entrance to the Uptown Theatre, 1956. Glenbow Archives NA-5093247.

Barron told the press that the Uptown would focus on family entertainment, featuring British and American productions on the basis of their merits, and that the Uptown would present "sophisticated" films, while the Grand would present "low-brow" films, such as the popular "Ma and Pa Kettle" movies, starring Marjorie Main and Percy Kilbride. Barron's sons, Dick and Bill, the managers of the Uptown, set admission prices from thirty-five to sixty-five cents for adults and from fifteen to thirty-five cents for children. The Barrons opened the Uptown on 30 March 1951, inviting guests to inspect the facility and to preview Jean Negulesco's *The Mudlark* (1950), an offbeat J. Arthur Rank film. Set in London in 1875, the film chronicled the adventures of a "mudlark," a youth who subsists by scavenging along the banks of the Thames, looking for flotsam and jetsam that might be pawned.

During the 1950s and early 1960s, Odeon-Barron Theatres operated two other facilities in Calgary as Odeon Theatres affiliates, namely, a suburban movie theatre, the Odeon Theatre, built in 1964, and a drive-in, the 17th Avenue Drive-In, one of the nine drive-in theatres in Calgary. Built in 1951 and located at 17th Avenue and 45th Street Southwest, this 500-vehicle facility screened many of the first-run films that were simultaneously screened at the Grand and the Uptown. In March 1964, Barron acquired the Marda Theatre, a 750-seat facility at 2101 33rd Avenue Southwest, Calgary, which was built in 1945 by Mark and Nayda Jenkins. In June 1969, Odeon Theatres (Canada) acquired the Barron family's movie theatre interests, and all of the properties underwent significant changes in the ensuing years.

8

CONSOLIDATION

Over the years, the two national theatre circuits expanded appreciably. The Royal Commission on Corporate Concentration observed in 1976 that Famous Players grew from 196 theatres in 1929 to 342 in 1947 and that the two chains controlled 60.8 percent of the box-office receipts in 1947.[1] Although the number of feature films produced from 1939 to 1945 declined, movie theatre attendance across North America increased dramatically, bringing about a "boom" in the industry.[2] The national circuits prospered, but the small chain and single-theatre operators suffered, thanks to the restrictive practices employed in the movie industry, including block booking and blind booking.[3] Now and then, independent exhibitors complained about their economic situation, but they were unable to take action. In 1935, Nat Taylor formed the Independent Theatres Association (ITA), in Ontario; however, many independent exhibitors lost confidence in the organization when they learned that many of its members and officers had business dealings with Famous Players.

Independent exhibitors organized a lobby group during World War II to protect their interests. This time, the federal and provincial governments took action, presumably because they needed the industry's assistance in producing and exhibiting propaganda films that promoted the war effort. At the outbreak of hostilities, the federal government established the Wartime Prices and Trade Board, with the intention of preventing inflation and social unrest, conditions that had developed during World War I. In a public relations campaign, the board urged

Canadians to restrain their wage and consumer demands. On the face of it, the Theatre and Film section of the board, directed by R. C. McMullen, struck a serious blow against American production-distribution companies, who controlled the Canadian film industry. McMullen invoked a number of measures, ranging from putting severe restrictions on building new movie theatres to setting ceilings on ticket prices. In addition, McMullen cancelled shows in the interest of saving electricity and regulated film rentals, guaranteeing that exhibitors would share films on a pro rata basis.

Over forty non-affiliated exhibitors organized the Independent Motion Picture Exhibitors Association (IMPEA), which met for the first time in Toronto in January 1942. Barnett E. Laxer, who ran the Biltmore theatres in Kingston and Oshawa, Ontario, was elected president.[4] Laxer quickly discovered that McMullen wanted to deal with national organizations only, so the group formed another organization, the National Council of Independent Exhibitors of Canada (NCIEC), with a view to dealing with the board. Laxer produced a pamphlet, dated 26 March 1942, called *Memorandum of the National Council of Independent Exhibitors of Canada to the Wartime Prices and Trade Board and to James Stewart, its Administrator of Services,* in which he attacked the structure of the film industry, alleging that across Canada independent exhibitors were being driven out of business at an unprecedented rate.[5]

Many industry analysts responded to this initiative with hostility. The editor of the *Canadian Moving Picture Digest* attacked the independent exhibitors as unpatriotic: "Why at such a time, when all right-thinking men and women are directing their thinking, their man- and woman-power towards a War effort, [should] a group of motion picture exhibitors spend energy, time, and man-power kicking the Canadian Motion Picture Industry in the pants, instead of Hitler."[6] The editor of the *Canadian Film Weekly* reiterated this sentiment, asserting that Laxer had done more harm to the industry than good.

The two national chains reacted swiftly, setting up a new organization in September 1942, one that included independent exhibitors: the Motion Picture Theatres Association of Ontario (MPTAO). Via this manoeuvre, the chains prevented the independent theatre operators from challenging the status quo. The new association met for the first time on 1 December 1942; the sixty-five members included the major figures in the movie industry, such as Nat Taylor, Herb Allen, Sam Fine, and H. M. Masters. About a hundred delegates, representing over three hundred theatres, including 102 independent theatres, attended the annual meeting in 1946. J. J. Fitzgibbons, president of Famous Players, spoke at this meeting, urging members to resolve their differences in private.[7]

In due course, the IMPEA folded, its effectiveness having been undermined. In the final analysis, the Wartime Prices and Trade Board had no effect on the distribution of films. Another attempt to seek government intervention in dealing with the American control of the Canadian movie industry had failed.

RANK BUYS ODEON THEATRES

During the 1940s, the Rank Organisation, a vertically integrated corporation, tried to break into the North American market. J. Arthur Rank, a member of a Yorkshire flour-milling family, had entered the film industry in the mid-1930s, seeing film as a means of propagating his Methodist faith. Having failed to secure a good distribution for his quasi-religious film, *Turn of the Tide* (1935), which won third place at the Venice Film Festival, he set about acquiring production, distribution, and exhibition firms; by 1941, he controlled two of the major movie theatre circuits in the United Kingdom, together with studios, laboratories, and manufacturers of equipment.[8] Industry analysts often accused him of monopolistic tendencies but admitted that, throughout the 1940s and the 1950s, his influence was positive. Rank served as chairman (1946–62) and president (1962–72) of the Rank Organisation, which during the late 1960s shifted from the film industry to other, more profitable enterprises, including hotels, bowling alleys, ballrooms, bingo halls, and photocopying machines, the most profitable of all.

During the period under consideration, Rank set out to establish an industrial organization that would rival that of Hollywood. He decided to enter the Canadian market first, but thanks to the integration of the two largest Canadian circuits with American production-distribution companies, this proved difficult.[9] Rank remedied the problem by buying a 50 percent interest in Odeon Theatres. On 24 November 1944,

Paul Nathanson and J. Arthur Rank announced that they were fifty-fifty partners in General Theatre Corporation, which controlled Odeon Theatres (Canada) and which operated about a hundred theatres at the time.[10] (Paul had become president and managing director of the Odeon Theatres circuit after his father died in 1943.) This meant that Rank's films would appear on the screens of theatres managed by Odeon Theatres. However, Paul retired in 1946, for health reasons, selling his 50 percent share in the 107-theatre circuit to Rank for a rumoured $2 million.[11] He reasoned that his father had always wanted to set up an empire-wide theatre circuit and that the sale of Odeon Theatres to Rank carried that plan forward.[12] Paul stayed on as a member of the board of directors.

Rank appointed J. Earl Lawson, a former cabinet minister, president of the board of directors in 1946. The plan was to hire a man of influence to run Odeon Theatres, as opposed to an old man of the theatre. He found such a man in Lawson, who had grown up in Hamilton.[13] Of Scottish descent, Lawson studied at Osgoode Hall, was called to the bar in 1916, and became a King's Counsel in 1931. He practised law with the firm of Robinette, Godfrey, Phelan, and later with Godfrey, Lawson, and Corcoran. In the 1920s, he served as the lawyer for the independent exhibitors who fought Nathanson's monopoly. Lawson was elected to the House of Commons for York West in a by-election in 1928 and re-elected in the general election in 1930. He served as national organizer while the Progressive Conservatives, led by R. B. Bennett, were preparing for an election in the fall of 1935; he was appointed minister of National Revenue but served for only a few weeks. Lawson retired from politics in 1939, after standing unsuccessfully for the leadership of the Ontario Progressive Conservative Party at a convention, losing out to George Drew. He developed wide-ranging business interests, and he held the directorships in a number of corporations in Canada and the United States.

By 1948, the Odeon Theatres circuit had grown to 180 theatres, almost doubling in size by integrating with Rank. Canadians sat on the new board of directors, but its policies hardly benefited Canada's struggling film industry, since Rank did not finance the production of any Canadian films. His *Little Kidnappers* (1953) is set partly in Nova Scotia, but it was filmed in Glen Affric, Scotland. Directed by Philip Leacock and starring Jon Whiteley, the film, which takes place around the turn of the century, tells the story of two Scottish orphans who are sent to live with their embittered grandfather. *Campbell's Kingdom* (1957), directed by Ralph Thomas and starring Dirk Bogarde and Stanley Baker, turns on a conflict over the construction of a dam in the Rocky Mountains. Although set in Alberta, it was filmed in Italy and Great Britain. Rank did, however, shoot some films in Canada, often using the Queensborough Studios in Toronto.[14]

After Lawson's death in May 1950, Rank appointed L.W. (Leonard) Brockington president of Odeon Theatres. Born in Cardiff, Wales, Brockington had immigrated to Edmonton in 1912, at the age of twenty-four. He worked as a journalist and as a civil servant, all the while studying law at the University of Alberta.[15] He subsequently moved to Calgary, where he worked as a clerk in the land titles office, continuing his law studies when he could. Upon completing his degree, he joined the law office of Lougheed and Bennett in 1919. Brockington made his mark as a brilliant orator, executive, and public servant. In 1935, he moved to Winnipeg, where he served as counsel for the Northwest Grain Growers' Association, and in 1936 he became chairman of the CBC, then an unpaid office. He championed the principles of non-partisanship and unsponsored broadcasts. During the war, he served as special assistant to Prime Minister Mackenzie King (1939–42) and then as advisor on Commonwealth affairs to the British Ministry of Information (1942–43). From 1947 to 1965, he was the rector of Queen's University. Brockington met Rank when the latter was establishing his reputation in the international film world. Unfortunately, he lacked Lawson's knowledge of the film industry, not to mention the latter's great energy. Lawson's death, together with the collapse of Rank's film production in the United Kingdom and the advent of television, marked the end of the chain's expansive period.[16]

THE PERIOD OF RETRENCHMENT

Movie attendance rose steadily during World War II and then declined sharply. In the United States, attendance went from 85 million weekly in 1942 to 90 million weekly in 1946, an increase of 6 percent. By 1961, however, weekly attendance had fallen to 42 million. During this period, box-office receipts grew from $1.02 billion in 1942 to $1.69 billion in 1946, but fell to $921 million in 1961. Attendance in Canada went from 3.52 million weekly in 1942 to 5.03 million weekly in 1952, an increase of 43 percent, but had dropped to 1.88 million weekly by 1963. During this period, box-office receipts rose from $46,461,097 in 1942 to $104,963,599 in 1952, and then fell to $71,641,505 in 1963.[17]

Clearly, the industry faced many challenges. Service personnel returned from the war, married, and had children, increasing the birth rate dramatically. More and more people moved to the suburbs and focused on their jobs and families. A distinct shift in spending habits accompanied this movement. For example, in the years from 1947 to 1957, the number of television sets in use increased sharply. During this period, about 90 percent of households in the United States and about 25 percent of those in Canada acquired television sets. The American market supported 517 commercial television stations, while 43 served the Canadian market. These figures clearly indicate that television watching was fast becoming the dominant leisure-time activity. Annual box-office receipts in the United States decreased from $1.69 billion in 1946 to $1.30 billion in 1956, a decline of 23 percent. Revenues declined more slowly than attendance, because ticket prices increased nearly 40 percent, roughly from 34 cents to 50 cents. By contrast, during this period annual box-office receipts in Canada increased by 48 percent, going from $55.43 million to $82.21 million, while the average price of admission rose from 35 cents to 52 cents, an increase of 49 percent. In the United States, however, over four thousand movie theatres closed their doors during this period.[18] The introduction of drive-ins offset this loss slightly. In an attempt to improve their financial positions, the studios abandoned their stock-company systems, taking actors, writers, producers, and directors off long-term contracts, and cut back on production.[19]

In addition, in May 1948 the United States Supreme Court handed down its decision in the antitrust action known as the Paramount Case. declaring that such practices as block booking, fixing admission prices, unfair runs and clearances, and discriminatory pricing and purchasing that favoured affiliated theatre circuits were illegal restraints of trade.[20] The court also ordered the major studios to terminate all pooling arrangements and joint interests in theatres belonging to one or another exhibitor. The court called for the divestiture of selected movie theatres and insisted on the complete severance of the affiliated circuits from their production and distribution branches.

The industry faced another assault, this time from the House Committee on Un-American Activities (HUAC), which held hearings from 1947 to 1951 on the alleged Communist infiltration of the motion picture industry. In 1947, J. Parnell Thomas, head of the commission, took testimony from friendly witnesses, including Sam Wood, Ayn Rand, Roy Brewer, Robert Taylor, Mrs. Lela Rogers (the mother of Ginger), and Adolphe Menjou, in an attempt to prove that card-carrying Party members dominated the Screen Writers Guild, that Communists had succeeded in introducing subversive propaganda into movies, and that President Franklin D. Roosevelt had brought improper pressure to bear upon the industry to produce pro-Soviet films during the war. As well, the commission focused on ten political activists (later dubbed the Hollywood Ten) who were leaders of the Hollywood left, including Edward Dmytryk and Ring Lardner, Jr. In 1951, HUAC took testimony from ninety prominent industry figures, with a view to identifying known Communists. These hearings continued sporadically into 1954. HUAC's hold on public opinion had been strengthened by a series of national and international events, including the fall of China to the Communists, the outbreak of the Korean War, and the rise of Joseph McCarthy, which helped the committee in its efforts to eradicate liberalism and radicalism in Hollywood.[21]

In addition to these political developments, as Bruce A. Austin writes, the movement to the suburbs in the 1950s signalled the start of an era of home-bound leisure activities, an era that continues. Suburbanites filled their free time gardening, indulging their hobbies, and taking up do-it-yourself projects. Out-of-home commercial leisure activities also flourished, but this simply expanded the field of possibilities beyond moviegoing.[22] Instead of going to *the* movies, as they had for several decades, people went to *a* movie, if at all. Those who responded to a 1948 *Fortune* survey explained that they were very busy and that the quality of movies had declined sharply.[23] For the moment, an increasing number of North Americans preferred the convenience of staying home to watch television.

THE IMPACT OF TELEVISION

As mentioned above, starting in the later 1940s, the number of television sets in use increased rapidly. In response to this phenomenon, movie moguls in Hollywood decided to distance themselves from the new medium, thinking that the public would soon lose interest in the novelty. After all, most networks operated on shoestring budgets, producing programs that lacked the technical polish of Hollywood productions. These moguls were reluctant to "damage" the theatrical market, one that had produced revenues from the outset.

Many talented people were needed to produce television programs, such as writers, actors, and directors. Most prime-time programs were broadcast live, and to fill out their schedules networks used filmed material, such as old features and shorts, obtained from Republic and Monogram. After 1950, Hollywood developed a subindustry, consisting of small independent companies devoted to producing series of low-budget telefilms, usually thirty minutes in length. Desilu Productions, the creation of Desi Arnaz and Lucille Ball, established the pattern. *I Love Lucy* debuted in the fall of 1951 and soon became an immensely popular series, attracting a weekly audience of 30 million viewers. Arnaz had the foresight to film the program, thereby enabling his company to earn a fortune in residuals from reruns.

As we know, audiences did not lose interest in the new medium, and when the movie moguls realized this, they adopted a new attitude. To draw people back to the theatres, the heads of the major studios resolved to give audiences something television could not.[24] By the late 1950s, television viewing habits had become entrenched, and more and more adults were going to the movies only sporadically. After all, the cost of watching television was negligible compared to that of going to the cinema; television offered an endless variety of programming; and nothing could be more convenient than watching television in the comfort of one's home. As a result, Hollywood tried to distinguish its product from that of its chief competitor.

Hollywood's first line of defence was colour. During the early 1950s, when television networks were broadcasting solely in black and white, the major studios increased the number of features they produced in colour, boosting the percentage from around 20 to more than 50 percent of the total domestic output, thanks to technological advances.[25] For example, in 1950 Eastman Kodak introduced Eastmancolor, which displaced Technicolor, a cinematography system that had dominated the field since 1935. Technicolor utilized a three-strip camera, which was cumbersome and intricate (and thus expensive). Eastmancolor greatly simplified all aspects of colour cinematography. By 1954, the Technicolor camera was a thing of the past; by 1965, television networks themselves were broadcasting in colour.

A second technological revolution was launched in New York on 30 September 1952, with the presentation of *This Is Cinerama*, a spectacular two-hour travelogue featuring scenes ranging from a gripping roller-coaster ride to a plane trip through the Grand Canyon.[26] The Cinerama system achieved a three-dimensional effect through the use of a trio of projectors, which cast an image in three segments on a broad, curved screen. Stereophonic sound enhanced the realism of the viewing experience. Fred Waller, the former head of the special effects department at Paramount, spent a decade developing the system, which he had unveiled well over a decade earlier, at the New York's World's Fair in 1939. Not surprisingly, studio executives viewed the invention as a curiosity. For one thing, converting a single theatre to Cinerama would be an expensive proposition, costing anywhere from $50,000 to $100,000; for another, adopting the three-camera system would mean radically altering production methods.[27]

A related technological revolution was launched two months later, in November 1952, with the screening of Arch Oboler's African adventure picture *Bwana Devil* (1952), a film that featured spears seemingly thrown directly at the audience.[28] Dubbed "Natural Vision," 3-D films required a camera equipped with two lenses, positioned like human eyes, that shot a scene twice, simultaneously, on two separate reels of film. In exhibition, two projectors, each outfitted with a special polarized filter, cast the images on the screen so as to overlap slightly. In viewing the picture, audience members wore spectacles with corresponding filters that fused the images stereoscopically. By 1955, however, the 3-D boom was over. Except for Alfred Hitchcock's *Dial M for Murder* (1954), the majority of 3-D films featured rather puerile horror or adventure plots. The system had at least two drawbacks: dual projectors were difficult to operate in sync, and many people found the spectacles annoying.

By contrast, CinemaScope was the one novelty to make a lasting impact on the movie industry. A major studio was the innovator this time, namely, Twentieth Century–Fox, which screened *The Robe* (1953) at the Roxy in New York on 16 September 1953. After a week of sensational business, the film opened in one hundred other cities with the same result. By February 1955, it had grossed more than $20 million around the world.[29] This was the signal that other companies should jump onto the wide-screen bandwagon. Like Cinerama, CinemaScope grew out of an invention outside the industry, in this case the anamorphic lens perfected in the 1920s by Henri Chrétien, a member of the Paris Optical Institute. With this lens, a camera compresses a wide-angle scene onto a narrow strip of film; this scene is projected through a "compensating" lens, stretching it out to its original shape, thus producing an illusion of depth. In CinemaScope, the screen is curved, and is two and a half times as long as it is high. In due course, United Artists, Columbia, and Warner Bros. signed pacts with Fox. Paramount entered the competition with VistaVision, screening *White Christmas* (1954) at Radio City Music Hall on 20 October 1954.

Thanks to these innovations, movie producers attracted bigger and bigger audiences; increasingly, the "big picture" defined the movie business. Alfred Starr, a Nashville theatre-chain owner and a spokesman for small, independent theatre owners, pointed out that the majors had reduced the number of pictures they produced (405 in 1948, 354 in 1953, and in 1954 fewer than 300), forcing the exhibitor to pay exorbitant percentages and film rentals for the high-budget films the studios were now producing.[30] Via this manoeuvre, Starr argued, the majors also forced the public to watch "quality" films when often audiences would be quite content with low-budget ones, such as the Francis the Talking Mule movies, which appeared from 1949 to 1956. (As it happened, these movies earned Universal Pictures a lot of money.) Y. Frank Freeman, vice-president of Paramount, explained that big pictures were more profitable than little ones for the large studio, because their break-even point was much lower.[31]

According to Freeman, the rule of thumb was that, to break even, a picture had to earn double its investment, whereas a little picture would not "pay out" even if it earned 30 percent more than double the investment In the case of a $700,000 motion picture with a gross of $1,600,000, the distribution cost would be $480,000, prints would run $250,000, and advertising and publicity $260,000, for a total of in additional $990,000 expenses. These costs, added to the cost of the original negative ($700,000), amounted to $1,690,000, representing a $90,000 loss. In the case of a $3 million picture with a $6 million gross, the negative cost ($3 million), plus $1,800,000 for distribution, $300,000 for prints, $400,000 for advertising and publicity, total $5,500,000, a $500,000 profit. Freeman concluded that it made sense for a big studio with $30 million to invest in a year's production to turn out twenty-five pictures at $1,200,000 each, as opposed to forty little pictures that had a high break-even point. From this perspective, one would argue that the beauty of the big picture, such as Paramount's *Ten Commandments* (1956), was that there was no limit to what the box-office returns could be. As Freeman put it, the way to gross big money was to spend big money.

Meanwhile, as movie moguls increasingly realized that television was here to stay, they adopted the adage "If you can't beat them, join them." Collaboration took several forms.[32] One was to produce filmed programming directly for the television market. Columbia moved first, in 1949, converting Screen Gems, a subsidiary that produced theatrical shorts, into a television department, which produced programs for the "Ford Theatre" and, starting in 1954, the hugely popular comedy series, *Father Knows Best*. In 1954, Disney signed a contract with ABC to produce a weekly hour-long series revolving around the Disney theme park. Interestingly, Disney was allowed to devote six minutes of each program to promoting the company's current releases. As Tino Balio points out, other studios found the concept attractive, leading to "The MGM Parade," "The Twentieth Century–Fox Theatre," and "Warner Bros. Presents." By the end of the 1950s, most prime-time television shows emanated from Hollywood. The crossover from live television broadcasting to filmed production offered the possibility of residuals.

Supplying networks with old features and shorts served as another form of collaboration.[33] Monogram and Republic had released their pictures to the networks almost immediately. RKO, deciding to withdraw from motion picture production, sold its film library in December 1955 to a television programming syndicate for $15 million, and Warner Bros. sold its film library in February 1956 to Associated Productions for $21 million. By 1958, television networks had acquired an estimated 3,700 features (mostly of pre-1948 vintage) for an estimated $220 million. In 1961, NBC bought a package from Twentieth Century–Fox to launch the first weekly movie night on a major network, "Saturday Night at the Movies," consisting of pictures from the 1950s, features produced in colour during the CinemaScope period. Via this manoeuvre, NBC promoted colour broadcasting, and RCA (its parent company) promoted the sale of colour television sets.

By this time, television had become a secondary market for theatrical films. Hollywood had considered conventional theatrical exhibition the primary source of revenues, with anything from television as a bonus. As relations between the two industries stabilized, television income was expected — and indeed planned for.[34] New film projects were judged in terms of their potential on television. The demand for feature films increased; ABC signed a co-production deal with MGM, and CBS went into production on its own, forming a subsidiary known as Cinema Center Films. Demand also created a new type of collaboration, the made-for-television movie (MFT), which developed into two formats: the single-night feature and the multi-night miniseries. MCA purchased Paramount's pre-1948 film library, Universal Studios, and Decca Records, thus becoming the biggest producer in Hollywood. As Balio points out, MCA moved into MFTs in 1965. Costs were usually recouped the first time these films were screened, via the sale of commercial spots.

Despite these adaptive strategies, most Hollywood majors lost money during the late 1960s and the early 1970s; only Disney and MCA passed through this period of retrenchment unscathed.[35] After 1972, the majors produced fewer films each year, and by the end of the 1970s the networks' stranglehold on the distribution of mass entertainment had weakened, thanks to the development of such new technologies as pay television, cable television, satellite transmission, and videotape and videodisc, which were designed to distribute entertainment product outside the existing channels.

THE CONGLOMERATES

The motion picture industry survived the turbulence of the immediate postwar era, and the companies that were parties to the Paramount antitrust suit still dominated the movie industry. Starting in the 1950s, North American business as a whole went through a period of consolidation: many firms merged, and in the process they centralized corporate control and decision making. A new type of entity that gradually emerged after World War II, the conglomerate has been defined as a diversified company with interests in several unrelated fields of endeavour. A good example of this new entity was Gulf & Western Industries, which started as a producer of automobile bumpers and spread into such diverse fields as zinc mining, sugar, cigars, real estate, and motion pictures. In 1960, the total assets of the company were $12 million; by 1968, the total came to $3 billion.

This movement increasingly extended to the motion picture industry. In 1966, Gulf & Western absorbed Paramount Pictures; in 1967, TransAmerica, a full-line financial service engaged in insurance and financial activities, took over United Artists; in 1969, Kinney National Company, a conglomerate originally engaged in car rentals, parking lots, building maintenance, and funeral homes, took over Warner Bros.; and in 1969, Kirk Kerkorian, a Los Angeles developer, acquired MGM, moving the studio into the hotel and the casino business. Later, in 1981, United Artists merged with MGM to form MGM/UA, an entertainment Company, Marvin Davis, an oilman, acquired Twentieth Century–Fox, and Coca-Cola acquired (in 1982) Columbia Pictures.[36]

Industry analysts have complained that via this process, motion picture companies moved into the hands of "outsiders" who had no respect for their studio's history or product; they tend to characterize the new industry leaders as finance people, individuals who were more interested in the bottom line than in the quality of their product.[37] Analysts still argue that conglomerization — which has tended toward concentration and centralization — promotes homogenization of the product.[38] Arguably, these criticisms are simplistic. Attendance worldwide has stabilized for all practical purposes: the world can support only a finite number of productions. The majors have cut back on production: in 1969 they released 225 pictures, but by 1977 they were releasing half that number. They learned three lessons. First, although production costs declined briefly, after the huge box-office success of *The Godfather* (1972), production costs for the average movie kept going up, escalating from $2 million in the early 1970s to $11 million in the 1980s. (These days, production costs for a blockbuster with a top-notch cast and state-of-the-art special effects might exceed $200 million.) Second, only a few pictures — perhaps ten a year — will capture most of the box-office dollars. The blockbuster quickly turns the mediocre film into a dud. (Of course, many might argue that blockbusters are, by definition, mediocre.) Third, offsetting the risks of production means cutting operating costs, employing defensive marketing tactics, and diversifying. That is, marketing practices have to go beyond traditional channels of distribution and include generating book tie-ins, novelizations, and soundtracks, not to mention merchandising toys, games, and clothing. Industry leaders argue that, if a blockbuster fails, ancillary income can soften the blow.[39]

RETRENCHMENT IN CANADA

Rank controlled much of the Canadian first-run market, as long as its studios produced films. However, the Rank empire experienced a serious decline in 1948 when it failed to penetrate the American market. Although Rank's position improved somewhat during the 1950s, Odeon had to rely more on American distributors for its supply of films.[40]

Again, movie attendance in Canada increased from 3.52 million weekly in 1942, peaking at 5.03 million paid admissions in 1952. Box-office receipts in Manitoba increased from $2.64 million in 1942 to $5.24 million in 1952, but then dropped to $3.11 million in 1960. In Saskatchewan, revenues increased from $1.83 million in 1942 to $5.35 million in 1952, before dropping to $2.70 million in 1960; in Alberta, they increased from $2.67 million in 1942 to $7.75 million in 1952 and then declined to $5.52 million in 1960. In the same period, the number of movie theatres grew from 1,247 (1942) to 2,749 (1953) and then dwindled to 1,427 (1960). During this crisis, the somewhat veiled co-operative relationship that existed at times between the two chains became very apparent when they set up a joint committee to decide which theatres they would close. Famous Players operated 419 theatres in 1954; by 1965, it had closed 143. The committee was abandoned when attendance increased during the late 1960s.[41]

The growing popularity of television throughout the 1970s and the 1980s created much uncertainty in both the American and the Canadian film industries. The executives at Paramount, for example, decided to keep their hands in the broadcasting industry, which was perceived as a threat to the future of the film industry. During the 1960s, American conglomerates absorbed some major American film production-distribution companies. These business deals affected the Canadian film industry. For example, when Gulf & Western acquired Paramount, Famous Players became a subsidiary of Gulf & Western's holdings in the leisure industry.[42]

Odeon Theatres remained in the Rank Organisation until January 1977, when the British multinational corporation decided to sell it. Rank then completely ceased producing films. The 170 screens that comprised Odeon Theatres carried a price tag of $30 million. Christopher R. B. Salmon, chairman of the board, reported that operations were not as profitable as they had been in the past.[43] Several conditions were imposed on the sale: non-Canadians were discouraged from bidding, and the buyer was required to retain its employees.

Michael Zahorchak, president of Canadian Theatres Group, acquired Odeon Theatres for $31.2 million.[44] Zahorchak was born in eastern Czechoslovakia in 1920, and escaped the Nazi occupation in 1940, immigrating to Canada. He developed an interest in the movie business when friends in Montréal took him to a drive-in. In 1946, he opened a drive-in in St. Catharines, where he and his wife had settled (he made his fortune in real estate). During the 1950s, he operated restaurants and refreshment concessions, eventually focusing on his expanding cinema interests. In 1973, he acquired the American-owned N.G.C. Cinemas, which operated fourteen cinemas from British Columbia to Québec. Zahorchak's Canadian Theatres Group consisted of 47 theatres (66 screens) in Montréal, Winnipeg, Edmonton, and Calgary, not to mention several theatres in Ontario, and in 1977 his company earned $13 million. (By contrast, Odeon Theatres earned $47 million in 1977.) The Bank of Montreal financed the transaction. When he added the 131 theatres (170 screens) of the Odeon circuit to the new chain, Canadian Odeon Theatres, he boasted a circuit of 178 theatres (236 screens).

Salmon retired in December 1983, and Zahorchak became president of the firm. The Zahorchak family sold the chain to Cineplex Corporation on 28 June 1984.

In 1977, Famous Players operated 418 screens in Canada, the total number of single screens in the country, regular theatres and drive-ins, being 1,633, whereas Odeon Theatres operated 236 screens. In short, Famous Players controlled 25.6 percent of the screens in Canada, whereas Odeon Theatres controlled 14.4 percent. The two circuits together controlled 40 percent of the screens in Canada.[45] The key to achieving this pre-eminence in the market was to run theatres that screened first-run American movies in select locations in major urban centres, such as Montréal, Ottawa, Toronto, Winnipeg, Edmonton, Calgary, and Vancouver. Of course, it was important to concentrate on Ontario, the largest motion picture market in the country. In 1976, the seating capacity of theatres in Ontario was greater than that in any other province. Ontario had 480 screens, or 30 percent of the total, that year, and paid admissions amounted to $70,882,000 million, about 37 percent of the total. Famous Players controlled 113 theatres, or 38.7 percent of the 292 theatres in Ontario, whereas Odeon Theatres controlled 55 theatres, or 19 percent of the total. Together, the two chains controlled 57.7 percent of the theatres in the most lucrative market in Canada.

A telling consideration is the amount that the two chains invested in the Canadian film industry. For example, between 1971 and 1975, Famous Players "extracted" $53,433,636 from its Canadian markets on behalf of the American majors yet invested only about $3 million in film production in Canada. In 1971, Odeon Theatres extracted $23,246,000 from its Canadian markets on behalf of UK majors; in 1973, the figure grew to $25,900,000, or 17.2 percent of its total box-office receipts for that year. Between 1975 and 1976, however, Odeon invested only a total of $500,000 in four Canadian feature films.[46] In other words, the major chains felt little obligation to create a genuinely Canadian film industry. Historically, the Canadian film business has been "satisfied to be the middle agent between American producers and Canadian audiences," content to make quick and guaranteed profits.[47]

CONCLUSION: FROM PEEPHOLE PARLOUR TO MULTIPLEX AND BEYOND

Entrepreneurs began organizing commercial leisure-time amusements when they started presenting — on a regular basis and in facilities dedicated to entertainment — performers who, until that point, had appeared at such makeshift venues as taverns and village greens, primarily on local and national holidays.[1] This expanding industry, originating in the United States and moving northward, shaped opportunities in the entertainment business in the Canadian West. In the early twentieth century, the forces of standardization and centralization, pursued in the interests of increased productivity and efficiency, transformed manufacturing and retailing across the continent, creating the template for future development in a wide range of enterprises, including the entertainment industry. Situating our study in the context of commercial leisure-time activities, including legitimate theatre and vaudeville, we have traced the remarkable evolution of theatrical movie exhibition from its humble origins as an amusing novelty to its position as a major commercial leisure-time enterprise, thereby documenting the conditions of moviegoing in prairie Canada during the heyday of the indoor, single-screen facility. We have focused on three organizations, Allen Theatre Enterprises, Famous Players, and Odeon Theatres, and selected theatres they operated, providing an account of the mechanics of commercial entertainment in western Canada, with a view to understanding the social, technological, and economic forces that shaped the practice of movie exhibition and the experience of visiting these theatres. We conclude our study by highlighting our major findings.

CORPORATE ORGANIZATION

The entrepreneurs who formed the organizations we studied were often American and often Jewish in origin; many were second-generation immigrants whose parents had migrated to the United States from eastern Europe. In their efforts to create successful businesses, they transferred the techniques of mass production from manufacturing to commercial leisure-time activities, with a view to attracting the widest audience possible.[2] They tended to hire fellow American immigrants (often family members), with experience in such areas as record keeping, organizing staff, operating and repairing equipment, programming, or marketing, to manage their facilities. As well, they commissioned American architects to design their theatres. For example, C. P. Walker hired Howard G. Stone to design the 1907 Walker Theatre in Winnipeg, and in 1912 Senator Lougheed hired Len Wardrop to design the Sherman Grand in Calgary. The Allens hired C. Howard Crane, the Detroit-based architect, to design a number of theatres for their organization, and Nat Nathanson hired Thomas W. Lamb, the New York City–based architect, to design a number of theatres for his organization. These entrepreneurs also hired American interior decorators, including Theodore Jagmin and Emmanuel Briffa, to complete these facilities. These north-south connections speak to the degree to which the evolution of movie exhibition in Canada is inextricably linked to the evolution of the movie industry in the United States, and contributed to the similarity of the moviegoing experience in both countries.

In 1906, would-be exhibitors with a small amount of capital and a limited amount of technical training could set up a "picture show." Apparently, the Allens chose Brantford as the place to establish themselves under the impression that moving pictures had not yet invaded Canada. When most entrepreneurs regarded motion pictures as a "passing fad," the Allens organized their business activities as a "serious" enterprise: they formed Allen Theatre Enterprises as a single proprietorship, characterized by "unlimited liability" for debts contracted by the business. They were determined to give their customers value for their money, thereby building up a satisfied clientele.[3] This multi-pronged strategy involved, first of all, locating their theatres strategically, preferably in an urban centre's central business district, where people had access to mass transit. Second, it involved building facilities designed specifically to screen movies. As a correspondent for *Construction* noted, the Allens developed a reputation for promoting facilities expressly designed for screening movies, emphasizing comfort and safety.[4] The Allen Theatre built in 1913 in Calgary served as the prototype for all their luxury theatres. Third, it meant providing "a painstaking and courteous service," offering the public more than they expected. Finally, it meant that the above elements must highlight the "show" presented in the auditorium, namely, high-quality films, with the best musicians available providing accompaniment. In this regard, they anticipated the business strategy Balaban and Katz made famous a decade later. Despite their American origins, the Allens set out to create a made-in-Canada exhibition company, and they plowed the profits they earned back into the business. They financed projects by floating shares locally as popular investments, in some cases raising $150,000.[5] However, they found raising investment capital to refit and to build more and more difficult.

By 1916, when Nat Nathanson entered the movie business, small family-run businesses were giving way to joint-stock companies, which were setting up in or relocating to major urban centres. Movie exhibition had quickly become a highly competitive business. Although the Allens had really begun their exhibition and distribution empire in Calgary, it is not surprising that they, like the Nathanson group, eventually located their operations in Toronto, which was well on its way to becoming the biggest market for movies in Canada.[6] Nathanson demonstrated a genius for organizing "big" projects; with the assistance of major financiers, he formed two national movie theatre chains over the course of his career, Famous Players and Odeon Theatres. By definition, these "limited liability" businesses separated the ownership (stockholder) function from the operating (management) function. Nathanson devised a business strategy that included acquiring large, ideally located theatres, establishing affiliations with independent exhibitors, and threatening to build theatres next door to competitors' facilities. In addition, he developed an entertainment policy that stressed quality entertainment, including first-run movies, and exceptional service. In contrast to the

Allens, he found the process of raising investment financing to refit or to build easier and easier.

LEGITIMATION INITIATIVES

Three initiatives undertaken by innovative entertainment entrepreneurs from 1903 to 1908 quickened the transformation of the movies from a sideshow novelty into a legitimate business enterprise: the creation of the film exchange, the shift from travelling exhibitions to permanent facilities for screening movies, and the increased production of the feature-length film, which became the industry standard.[7] The development of the motion picture theatre, in terms of design and decoration as well as programming and presentation, was integral to the development of the movie industry as a whole and to the dramatically expanding role of the movie in North American society.[8] The development of movie exhibition in North America can be divided into two phases.

1905 to 1913

Entrepreneurs in major urban centres across North America sought out empty buildings, such as restaurants, cigar stores, and pawnshops, preferably located in the central business district, with a view to turning them into temporary facilities seating about two hundred people. They hired architects and contractors to prepare these facilities, knowing that if they miscalculated and their business failed, they would have to restore them to their original conditions. They soon realized that the key to success lay in attracting the "family" trade, in terms of the venue and the entertainment presented there, and to this end they made their venues as attractive and comfortable as possible. They focused on the exterior of their buildings, however, designing and decorating the façades so that they attracted attention and also inspired confidence in the product for sale. They also gave their venues exotic or grand names, such as "Dreamland" or "Monarch," as part of their effort to "package" this entertainment as a desirable product.[9] As we have seen, two of the storefront theatres the Allens operated in the prairie West during this period accommodated (on average) 601 patrons. By 1917, this kind of facility had become outmoded.[10]

1914 to 1932

Entrepreneurs erected large, lavishly decorated buildings designed and equipped expressly for screening movies, featuring fan-shaped auditoriums, opulent furnishings, and a myriad of exquisite details, the whole of which constituted the main attraction.[11] During the 1910s, picture palaces accommodated (on average) between 1,000 and 1,800 patrons, and during the 1920s they accommodated (on average) between 1,800 and 2,500 patrons. Entrepreneurs hired theatre architects and interior decorators to complete these structures, with a view to persuading the emerging middle-class patrons of the arts to take moviegoing seriously.[12] Thomas W. Lamb designed the first picture palace in North America, the Regent Theatre, giving it a Venetian palazzo exterior and a Spanish-Moorish interior, which was decorated in gold and blue; Henry Marvin opened this 1,800-seat structure, located in what was then a German-American section of Harlem, in February 1913. James C. Teague designed what was arguably the first picture palace in prairie Canada, Calgary's Allen Theatre, giving it a Venetian palazzo exterior and an Adamesque interior. The Allens opened this grand structure, which accommodated 840 patrons, in November 1913. Generally speaking, architects designed these facilities with an eye on famous buildings of the past, the objective being to obscure the distinction between the "reality" of the theatre and the "illusion" of the movie on the screen, via the stage, the proscenium arch, the furnishings, and the entertainment featured.[13]

Appealing to a middle-class sensibility, exhibitors gave these opulent venues names that evoked exotic times and places, such as "Avalon," recalling the land in the West where King Arthur and the Knights of the Round Table supposedly went after they died. In this way, exhibitors hoped to give their buildings an air of respectability. As we have seen, seven of the deluxe facilities the Allens built in prairie Canada during the 1910s accommodated, on average, 1,036 patrons, and two built during the 1920s accommodated an average of 2,076 patrons. Similarly, one of the deluxe facilities Nathanson built in the region during the 1910s accommodated 2,200 patrons and three built during the 1920s accommodated, on average, 1,633 patrons. Such large and elegantly appointed theatres, modelled primarily on European buildings, were clearly the central piece of visual rhetoric that exhibitors in

Canada employed to present moviegoing as a respectable, indeed an important, cultural activity.

RELIGIOUS AND SECULAR REFORM CAMPAIGNS

Despite the exhibitors' efforts to legitimate moviegoing, the rapid development of commercial entertainment in general and the rapid growth of movies in particular aroused much public concern and opposition.[14] During the Progressive Era, from the 1890s to the 1920s, religious and social reformers urged governments to enact legislation to regulate the new enterprise. Canadian historians have highlighted the considerable influence of social reform movements on Canadian society during the late nineteenth and early twentieth centuries, noting the roots of these movements in the anxieties of middle-class, Anglo-Canadian Protestants about social changes connected with urbanization and immigration.[15] Historians have also remarked on the degree to which the overlapping concerns of the Social Gospel movement — prohibition, women's suffrage, and the Canadianization of immigrants — met with particular favour in prairie Canada.[16] Many middle-class Anglo-Canadian Protestants who lived in the recently founded and rapidly growing towns and cities of Manitoba, Saskatchewan, and Alberta clearly felt threatened by the large numbers of peasant and working-class immigrants who came to the region between 1896 and 1914.[17] Although more research is required to document precisely how ethnic and class tensions played out in particular cultural sites, it seems clear that in spending so much money and effort to create elegant theatre buildings in prairie cities such as Winnipeg, exhibitors like the Allens were responding, at least in part, to the deep class and ethnic cleavages that were arguably that city's defining characteristic and major social problem.[18] In short, the social divisions and tensions in the urban centres of prairie Canada were similar to those in American cities, and the anxieties they generated played a part in the rapid transformation of film exhibition and moviegoing that was taking place in North America during the first two decades of the twentieth century.

Historians (in the United States, especially) remind us that working-class moviegoers engaged in a variety of behaviours that middle-class patrons found objectionable, including eating, drinking, sleeping, and petting or necking. A reporter for *Moving Picture World* noted in 1908 that working-class patrons in New York City sometimes watched the same performance all day and into the night, eating their lunch in the theatre.[19] In fact, for most members of the working class, watching a movie was not a passive experience. Rather than remaining mere spectators, they regarded moviegoing as a social activity, as well as a cultural one, and tended to adopt a participatory approach, interacting volubly not only with the other people in the auditorium but also with the entertainment presented on the screen. Responding to the antics of the hero, for example, might include such "boisterous" behaviour as shouting, whistling, clapping, and stomping.[20] Arguably, as well, the "democratic" pricing at movie theatres fostered an air of informality and communality, and this informality sanctioned a variety of behaviours that middle-class audiences who were accustomed to attending higher-priced entertainment took to be inappropriate. Middle-class observers tended to complain disdainfully about unruly patrons, and very soon one of the jobs of the ticket taker at the nickel theatre was to prevent intoxicated patrons from entering the building.

In addition to complaining about the physical condition of movie theatres and the behaviour of working-class patrons, middle-class commentators and reformers pressed for censorship of the content of movies and legislation to halt the screening of movies on Sunday. In establishing local censorship boards, such as the one that was set up in Chicago in 1907 and the voluntary National Board of Review that was created in New York City in 1909, middle-class reformers achieved their goal of subjecting motion pictures to some sort of surveillance, if not public control.[21] Similar concerns were expressed in Canada, and efforts to censor movies began shortly after the first films were shown. Since censorship has been a provincial responsibility, these efforts took a variety of forms, but, from 1911 to 1913, most provinces — including those on the prairies — established censorship boards that focused on protecting public morality. In due course, movie producers realized that self-censorship would be more prudent and profitable than official, public censorship.

By the outbreak of World War I in 1914, motion pictures dominated commercial entertainment. How, in a few short years, had the middle and the upper classes found their way to the movie theatres they once disdained? Movie exhibitors across the continent had transformed the "shabby" storefront theatres into opulent movie palaces, and movie producers had produced narrative films, thereby persuading the emerging middle-class patrons of the arts that they should rethink their attitude toward moviegoing.[22] These exhibitors did everything in their power to remove the "unease" the middle-class patrons might experience when entering the movie house. In fixing the starting times of their programs, outfitting their ushers with military attire, and fitting the restrooms with expensive furniture, they countered the easygoing atmosphere that characterized such working-class sites as the saloon, the dime museum, and the nickelodeon. The new, deluxe movie theatre mixed the sexes and the classes, and projected an air of comfort and style rather than informality.

THEATRE OPERATION

Operators of picture shows in the prairie West offered the public a leisure-time activity that was becoming increasingly popular across the continent, namely, several kinds of entertainment in programs that ran continuously from morning until night, Monday through Saturday, all at one place and at reasonable admission prices. Anxious to present (silent) motion pictures in an "artistic" way, many early managers looked to Roxy Rothafel for inspiration. This celebrated theatre impresario had made a name for himself by turning entire motion picture theatres, such as the Regent and the Strand, in New York City, into sites for family-oriented, multimedia entertainment.[23] Rothafel published a number of articles in newspapers and trade journals, sharing his insights into giving the public lavish spectacles. In following this advice, prairie exhibitors hoped to offer their patrons a measure of the sophistication associated with the leisure-time activities of eastern American cities. To this end, they focused their energies on five aspects of exhibition.

Programming and Presentation

To some extent, exhibitors took their cue from the managers of vaudeville houses, selecting the items that would make up a program, such as singalongs, vaudeville acts, movies, recitals, slide shows, and illustrated lectures, with an eye on their length and theme and the place they would occupy in a modular arrangement. Initially, they designed short programs that ran from morning until night, and changed them constantly, from three to five times per week during the nickelodeon period, thereby encouraging patrons to return often.[24] The strategy was to appeal to the whole community by offering the public a variety of times and a variety of films. Thus, exhibitors gave the public a rather compelling reason to visit their picture shows: come anytime and stay as long as you like. We think of the Allens, who opened the Monarch Theatre in Calgary on 21 January 1911, offering the public a selection of moving pictures and illustrated songs, charging children and adults admission prices of five and ten cents, respectively. Exhibitors later added inexpensive vaudeville to their programs, when the supply of films failed to meet the demand, and found great financial advantage in establishing themselves as operators of first-run houses.

Exhibitors could be quite creative in programming and presenting their entertainment, blurring the distinction between the setting and the entertainment that was presented there. Taking their cue from Rothafel, operators of large theatres created a desirable atmosphere by employing such extra-filmic techniques as employing a single musician or an ensemble to produce the appropriate musical accompaniment, projecting coloured lights onto the ceiling, spraying the auditorium with exotic perfumes to stimulate the sense of smell, and arranging a variety of stage props related to the action seen on the screen, including potted plants, fountains, and stage sets. They also experimented with projecting films faster or slower than the speed at which the films were photographed.[25] The operators of big houses engaged in product differentiation by offering a form of "entertainment" the operators of small houses could not.

All such exhibitors regarded music as a crucial element in the presentation of entertainment, and so hired musicians (soloists and ensemble players) to accompany the films they screened, thereby enhancing the drama of what was happening on the screen, and to present recitals and concerts in their own right. They distinguished their programs from those of their competitors by installing pipe organs, which were capable of producing a wide variety of sound effects. The Allens set the standard in the prairie West, installing a theatre organ (made by

W. W. Kimball of Chicago, builders of the mammoth organ in the Mormon Tabernacle in Salt Lake City) in the Allen Theatre built in Calgary in 1913. Similarly, Nathanson installed a Casavant concert organ, built in Québec, at the Regent Theatre in Toronto, built in 1916. In time, however, moviegoers complained that the quality of music making had dropped considerably. For example, the house pianist would play the same selections at all the movies, regardless of their subject matter, and would play the pieces rather indifferently at that, thus reducing the quality of the moviegoing experience.[26] The soundtrack, introduced with sound pictures, replaced live musical accompaniment, thereby standardizing screenings and ending the dependency on local musical talent; that is, even operators of small theatres could offer the public quality "shows."[27] Interestingly, Jack Barron, a champion of old-fashioned "variety entertainment," resisted this trend by installing, at the Grand Theatre, a 35-piece ensemble composed of members of the Calgary Symphony Orchestra.

In the early days of cinema, exhibitors preferred to screen short films, believing that the public would not sit through long ones. However, by 1915, the feature film, lasting an hour or so, had defined the industry, as exemplified by the great success of such "spectacles" as D. W. Griffith's *The Birth of a Nation* (1915), which attracted huge audiences. Experience showed that big pictures were more profitable than little ones for major studios, because the break-even point was much lower.

During the 1930s, managers of theatres in prairie Canada typically designed programs that included two feature films, live theatre, such as vaudeville acts, cartoons, and a serial, the whole lasting just over two hours, all at an admission price of ten cents for children and twenty-five cents for adults. Art Evans, who attended programs like this at Calgary's Variety Theatre, recalls that Amateur Nights were especially entertaining. Predictably, he notes, contestants would tell their friends about the event, thereby expanding the audience. By featuring the latest products of North American popular culture as well as local talent, prairie exhibitors were able to tap into their patrons' paradoxical desire to reach beyond as well as to celebrate local culture, and in so doing, they exploited the very rich vein of ambivalence and insecurity that is arguably at the heart of prairie boosterism, if not western sensibility.

Seating Arrangements

Initially, exhibitors sold a special kind of experience, one that varied subtly from theatre to theatre and from chain to chain, depending upon the programming and the presentation, not to mention the comfort and the arrangement of the seats, especially during the movie palace era. They sold seats according to section, namely, the auditorium, the balcony, and loges, some offering patrons social status, that is, over and above an unobstructed view of the stage and the screen. Later, exhibitors differentiated their facilities from those of their competitors by offering patrons the opportunity to reserve their seats and later to smoke in the smoking section, usually in the balcony. In offering such amenities, exhibitors walked a fine line between catering to their patrons' desire to indulge in what Thorstein Veblen famously called "conspicuous consumption" (an urge that was perhaps particularly salient in prairie cities during periods of rapid growth) and valorizing the egalitarianism that many prairie dwellers would see as a defining feature of their regional culture. This highly productive tension between elite and popular culture that has shaped all three branches of the movie industry in a myriad of ways is nowhere more apparent than in the movie theatre itself, particularly the picture palace — grand, opulent, exclusive, and yet available to all, with its varied programming, its reasonable prices, and its unobstructed sightlines.

Customer Service

The Allens pursued a maxim that became the industry standard: offer the public top-notch motion pictures; screen them in comfortable and safe facilities; and provide painstaking service, at whatever the cost. This meant training members of their staff to be courteous at all times, as well as outfitting them with uniforms that lent them both elegance and authority. It also meant equipping theatres with restrooms, many with telephones, check rooms, lost-and-found rooms, and nurseries attached to the women's restroom. In addition, the Allens offered patrons the option of booking their seats in advance. Thus, the customer service strategy of exhibitors like the Allens enabled them to both pamper and discipline their diverse clientele, thereby establishing the framework that would define the practice of moviegoing for decades.

Pricing

The exhibitors we studied offered the public "quality" shows at "competitive" admission prices, that is, with reference to admissions to such venues as legitimate theatres and vaudeville houses. As we suggested in chapter 3, the operators of nickel theatres did not charge adults a five-cent admission fee, as their colleagues in the United States reputedly did. According to newspaper reports, in 1911 adults paid ten cents and children paid five cents to attend the Monarch Theatre, the first storefront theatre the Allens opened in western Canada.

Publicity and Marketing

Initially, the exterior of picture houses "advertised" the novelty of the product offered to the public within. During the first phase of development especially, "boosters" praised every facility in the highest terms. Thus, reporters spoke of the 1917 Allen Theatre in Brandon as the finest photoplay theatre in western Canada and the 1921 Capitol Theatre in Winnipeg as "the most magnificent in western Canada." Exhibitors found it difficult to advertise particular films because they changed programs often, say five times per week. During the nickelodeon era, word-of-mouth publicity had to do. Later, exhibitors employed such techniques as placing small advertisements in newspapers, displaying small cards and colourful posters in the lobbies of their facilities, offering patrons first-night programs as souvenirs, mounting attention-grabbing stunts, such as inviting staff to dress as the characters in the film currently showing, holding in-house competitions and talent contests, and circulating floats calling attention to special features.[28] Throughout the period we studied, exhibitors spoke to the press, stressing that their latest movie house was a locally made project. In employing these strategies, exhibitors used their ability to connect prairie communities with the larger world to construct a place both for themselves and for their enterprises within the structures and discourses of the local community.

BUSINESS ORGANIZATION AND FINANCING

As we noted in chapter 3, the dynamics of big business across North America transformed wholesaling and retailing. In order to reduce expenses and increase profits, managing directors of large corporations employed the principles of "scientific management." Managing directors learned that "rationalizing" their enterprises meant setting up a central office, from which they produced records and controlled inventory, thereby standardizing products and functions; increasing the volume of business; and speeding up the delivery of service. They realized that they could keep their costs low by taking advantage of economies of scale, spreading fixed costs over more and more operations, and by buying in bulk, at lower-than-normal prices.

Influenced by these trends, the managing directors of major movie production companies rationalized their operations, adopting such established business practices as drawing up and maintaining budgets and issuing annual statements, thereby putting their affairs on a sound footing. Industry and financial analysts were encouraged by these developments, which lifted the motion picture business out of the category of "hazardous" speculation, and by 1916 they had ranked the business as fifth among the largest industries in North America, placing it just behind agriculture, transportation, oil, and steel. A correspondent for the *New York Times* estimated that investment bankers were pouring up to $500 million into motion picture production.[29] Analysts debated this ranking, acknowledging that the criteria employed in making such a judgment varied according to point of view taken. By 1924, analysts were ranking the industry as seventh among the leading industries.

Exhibitors also rationalized their operations, depending upon the resources they had to work with. Entering the exhibition business was relatively easy, but surviving, let alone expanding into a chain of theatres, could be difficult. Most businesses, by definition, enjoyed a short life expectancy, six years at the most, especially if they were undercapitalized and employed unorthodox business practices. Many exhibitors, including John Schuberg, Paul LeMarquand, and the Allens, chose to operate as a single proprietorship (family business) because they wanted to own as well as control their business. The Allens "rationalized" their operation very early on, managing their affairs in a businesslike fashion, plowing the profits they earned back into the business and raising capital to refurbish existing theatres or build new ones. For example, to defray part of the cost of a project, they raised capital by floating shares as popular investments, believing that investors would value local theatres highly as a result.[30] However, this form of business organization soon gave way to the joint-stock company. Initially, operating as a single proprietorship might have been an advantage, but as the organization grew, operating under the rubric of "unlimited liability" became a handicap. As we have seen, by 1923 the Allen organization was forced to declare bankruptcy.

Such entrepreneurs as Nathanson formed joint-stock corporations, capitalizing them at a very high level, and located them in such major financial metropolitan centres as Montréal and Toronto, settling for a separation of functions, that is, ownership and control. As we noted, Nathanson and a group of financiers formed Famous Players early in 1920, capitalizing the company at $15 million. A number of prominent Canadians — Sir Herbert Holt, J. P. Bickell, W. D. Ross, and I. W. Killam — became members of the board of directors. Armed with the most lucrative franchise of the day and supported by national and international capitalists, Nathanson turned his attention to building a chain of movie theatres that stretched from one coast to the other. He, too, "rationalized" the operations of the corporation, promising investors greater stability than managers of family-run operations could offer, since joint-stock, limited-liability companies could raise large sums of capital fairly easily.

CORPORATE EXPANSION

Given its rather shaky origins as an amusing, somewhat tawdry novelty, the movie business evolved surprisingly quickly into a global entertainment industry, propelled by converging social, economic, and technological forces.[31] We have focused on one branch of that industry, noticing that the industrial developments at work in theatrical movie exhibition from 1910 to 1970 mirrored those at work in other domains of retailing. The history of movie exhibition in the prairie West can thus be viewed as an economic history of technological change that can be traced through the effort exhibitors put into designing and equipping the nickel theatre, developing regional and national chains, and designing and equipping the multiplex. We do not chart the history of moviegoing as such, because few documents describing the experience have survived; instead, we suggest some of the social implications of the industrial foundation for the practice of going to the movies during this period. Understanding the growth of movie exhibition has meant considering such matters as supply and demand, corporate structure, and corporate behaviour. As we have seen, innovative entertainment entrepreneurs opened family-operated nickel theatres, established regional and national chains, and (as the final step) exploited economies of operation, taking the first steps in the direction of vertical and horizontal integration. Our study has highlighted a series of key players in this historical narrative.

The Nash Chain

John Schuberg, a Winnipeg-based exhibitor, opened some of the first permanent exhibition sites in western Canada, eventually operating, with Frederick Burrows, a chain of movie theatres in Manitoba, North Dakota, Minnesota, and Wisconsin. In this regard, his story illustrates the longitudinal, cross-border dynamics of the entertainment industry. In 1917, he partnered with W. P. deWees to secure the exclusive rights to distribute First National Pictures throughout western Canada. Suffering financial losses at the box office, as a result of the flu epidemic in 1918 and the Winnipeg general strike in 1919, Schuberg sold his distribution and exhibition interests to the Allen organization for approximately $1 million.

The Starland Chain

Paul LeMarquand, a Winnipeg-based exhibitor, managed Starland Theatre Company, which operated a chain of fifteen theatres in the West, including the Empress Theatre in Calgary, built in 1911.[32] Very little is known about this organization, although we do know that the Allens challenged Starland's monopoly of the movie exhibition market by opening the Monarch Theatre in 1911, which became the nucleus of the Allens' chain of theatres. Arguably, the Allens drove LeMarquand out of business by building deluxe theatres in the vicinity of Starland theatres and offering the public a more attractive moviegoing experience, in terms of the films exhibited, the luxurious and safe venues, and the courteous service.

Allen Theatre Enterprises

The Allens established their enterprise not in Winnipeg, the metropolitan centre of western Canada at the time, but in Calgary, organizing their activities, a distribution company and an exhibition company, as a "serious" business venture. In this booming community, they developed business strategies and programming policies geared to offering customers value for their money, thereby building up a satisfied middle-class clientele.[33] In December 1915, they consolidated the nine theatres they operated and their film exchanges, and moved their headquarters to Toronto, which had become the largest market for commercial entertainment in the country.[34] By 1920, the Allens operated a Canada-made chain of sixty theatres in twenty-one urban centres, many having a seating capacity of over two thousand. As industry analysts have pointed out, "the Allen empire collapsed from within," thanks in large part to the effects of losing the exclusive rights to distribute Paramount Pictures and over-expanding, as they planned to open theatres in the United States, Great Britain, and the USSR.[35] On 23 June 1923, Famous Players acquired the assets of Allen Theatres Limited, that is, thirty-five of the largest theatres, for $650,000.

Famous Players

One of the most remarkable figures in the history of the Canadian entertainment business, Nat Nathanson stands apart as the creator of two national movie theatre chains. The belief that Canadians themselves should control the Canadian movie industry shaped Nathanson's business strategies.

Nathanson demonstrated an uncanny ability to organize "big" projects. He entered the movie business in 1916 when, with a number of major financiers, he formed an exhibition company that would exploit (he argued) a number of new strategies for presenting picture shows to great effect. By the fall of 1919, the Nathanson group (including his brother Henry) controlled a chain of sixteen theatres, and in January 1920 they formed Famous Players. For all practical purposes, Famous Players won the race to build the first "big" theatre in Canada in 1921, when the company opened the Capitol Theatre in Calgary five months before the Allens opened the Allen's Palace Theatre. By 1929, Famous Players owned or had a substantial interest in no fewer than 153 theatres, with a capacity of 165,000 seats. Nathanson told a writer for the *Toronto Star* that 95 percent of the capital in Famous Players was British and Canadian. He resigned as managing director of Famous Players in September 1929, arguing that he could no longer protect Canadian shareholders from the attempts of American interests, as represented by Adolph Zukor, to seize control of the company.[36]

Odeon Theatres

In May 1933, Nathanson engineered his return to Famous Players, as the board elected him president. Believing that he and Zukor had an understanding that eventually Famous Players would pass into his hands, Nathanson committed himself to promoting the widest range of tastes possible among Canadians, especially for British films.[37] When he realized that whatever agreement he had with Zukor would not be honoured, he began acquiring, through an agent, second-run theatres that were operating in small towns in Ontario, with a view to establishing a movie theatre chain that would compete with Famous Players in all respects.[38] He incorporated Odeon Theatres on 18 April 1941, while he was still the managing director of Famous Players, installing his son, Paul, as managing director.

Nathanson championed a new style of facility in design and decoration, streamlined and curvilinear in form, bold in colour and utilizing metal, and he also designed a new programming policy, with a predilection for British movies, hoping to attract a new generation of moviegoers. He intended the moviegoing experience at Odeon Theatres to be distinctive, in terms of up-to-date projection and sound equipment, family-oriented programming changed three times per week, and low admission prices. He resigned from Famous Players in May 1941, unhappy playing the role of branch-plant manager. Sadly, he died in May 1943 and thus never saw a made-in-Canada chain of movie theatres in operation. In December 1944, Paul Nathanson, as managing director of Odeon Theatres, formed a fifty-fifty partnership with the J. Arthur Rank Organisation. At this time, Odeon Theatres owned or controlled one hundred movie theatres across Canada. In 1946, Paul retired for health reasons, selling his share of Odeon Theatres to the Rank organization for about $2 million.[39] Paul reasoned that the sale advanced his father's ambition to create a worldwide chain, one that promised to set the movie industry among Commonwealth countries on an equal basis with Hollywood.[40] In founding two national movie theatre chains, Nat Nathanson had created a "duopoly," one that would dominate movie exhibition in Canada for decades.[41] However, his efforts to establish a Canadian-owned chain of theatres ultimately failed: Famous Players was eventually subsumed by American interests, and Odeon Theatres by British interests.

THE BIRTH OF THE MULTIPLEX: CINEPLEX ODEON

In the decades following World War II, movie exhibitors across Canada faced a number of challenges. Not only did those interested in operating national, Canadian-owned theatre chains continue to confront the virtually insurmountable barriers created by metropolitan influences and economies of scale, but also, like exhibitors elsewhere, they faced massive technological and social changes that threatened to topple moviegoing from its position as the most popular of mass entertainments and render their grand motion picture palaces virtually obsolete. In the discussion that follows, we consider the final era of the period we have chosen to examine, with a view to providing the perspective required to illuminate major patterns of persistence and change: continuities and discontinuities between the business strategies and the social practices that shaped film exhibition during the first half of the twentieth century and those that shaped its evolution during the second half and beyond.

As we have seen, despite some encouraging developments here and there, the 1950s and 1960s brought declining audiences and the transformation or demise of a great number of movie theatres. During the late 1970s, Nat Taylor, a film producer, distributor, and exhibitor, and Garth Drabinsky, a movie producer and entertainment lawyer, resolved to revitalize exhibition practices and enhance the experience of going to the movies.[42] Like the Allens before them, they believed that the future of moviegoing would depend upon "the distinctiveness of the event and the site" and that the "upgrading" of the cinema experience would in fact benefit all exhibitors. Drabinsky pointed to the need to create "the most felicitous motion picture viewing ambience that the present technology and the most creative architectural designs will permit."[43] He looked to the motion picture palaces as "inspired solutions to the problem of how to attract audiences," also recommending that exhibitors create "a superbly educated and prepared work force."[44] In terms of a basic strategy, Taylor and Drabinsky decided to fill an important "gap" in movie exhibition that had so far gone unnoticed. As they had observed, by the late 1970s the bottom had essentially fallen out of the second-run market.[45] Hollywood studios rarely re-released even their most successful films; instead, films were put on the shelf virtually upon the completion of their first run, even though they might still have substantial box-office life. Taylor and Drabinsky also realized that the answer to the problem of serving an increasingly fragmented audience lay in building multi-screen theatre complexes. Their efforts along these lines, while originally centred in Ontario, soon affected exhibition practices in prairie Canada.

Taylor experimented with the concept of the multi-screen facility during the 1940s. Annoyed by the fact that he had to replace films that were still making money with new releases, in 1957 he added a 400-seat art-film theatre, the "Little Elgin," to the 750-seat Elgin Theatre in Ottawa, which he ran for Famous Players. Originally built in 1937, the Elgin stood on the corner of Lisgar and Elgin streets, in what was then a mixed commercial and residential area. Mandel Sprachman, a Toronto-based theatre and cinema architect, designed and supervised the renovations.[46]

Taylor explained that, when operating a "multiplex" (the name he gave the facility) located in a shopping plaza and featuring multiple screening rooms rather than one large auditorium, an exhibitor could reduce the overhead by consolidating a number of functions, such as film projection, customer service, and concessions, and by showing one picture on as many screens as warranted or by moving a film from a small auditorium to a large one, or vice versa, depending upon demand.[47] He upheld this principle when he moved United Artists' *Witness for the Prosecution* (1957) out of the big auditorium, where it was still making money, to make way for a film that had just become available, Columbia Pictures' Oscar-winning *The Bridge on the River Kwai* (1957), which proved to be a tremendous success. For years, Taylor moved films from one auditorium to the other, depending upon conditions. However, attendance dropped throughout the 1970s and the 1980s, and the Elgin closed late in 1994.[48] Shortly after he had remodelled the Elgin in 1970, Taylor had similarly rebuilt Loew's Uptown Theatre in Toronto, which had been damaged by fire. This seven-storey, 3,000-seat theatre, designed by Lamb and originally built in 1920, had served as a venue for vaudeville and movies. Again, Taylor hired Sprachman as project architect. They installed five auditoriums — a main theatre (seating 1,000 people), with two smaller ones below and another two backstage — thereby giving the old cinema a new lease on life.

Following the example set first by the Allens and then by the Nathansons, Taylor, Drabinsky, and H. S. (Harry) Mandel formed Pan-Canadian Film Distributors and Cineplex Corporation to distribute and to exhibit motion pictures in a chain of multi-screen complexes in Canada.[49] They began operations on 19 April 1979, when they opened a $2.5 million multiplex at the north end of the Eaton Centre shopping mall in Toronto. Designed by Sprachman, the Eaton Centre Cineplex represented the perfect marriage of culture, commerce, and technology.[50] In its design and decoration, the facility testified to the increasing dominance of film over the other arts, signalling the growing appetite for "visual spectacle." The facility also enabled the exhibitors to pack more patrons into one building, minimizing the overhead per film. The facility comprised eighteen theatres of varying capacity, seating from 58 to 168 customers, for a total capacity of 2,000, and distinguished from one another by a colour-coded decor, as well as an "international" restaurant, a cinema-themed bookstore, and an "art gallery."[51] In addition, the facility featured the latest in sound-system technology, rear projection (without any loss of quality), a computerized box office, and colour-coded tickets to match the decor of particular theatres. During the Christmas and Easter seasons, Cineplex offered daytime children's movies, inviting parents shopping at the centre to leave their children with "matrons" on the staff who acted as babysitters. The management promised that the staff would clean the auditoriums after every show.[52]

Drabinsky took his cue from Rothafel, the flamboyant movie theatre impresario who had built his career on catering to his audience's every need. As Drabinsky reminds us, Rothafel — who, at the peak of his career, managed the 6,200-seat Roxy on Broadway — felt that the key to customer loyalty lay in "service cheerfully given."[53] Most importantly, Drabinksy and Taylor committed themselves to programming contemporary foreign films, second runs of recent Hollywood hits, and repertory hits from the past. Initially, they equipped Cineplex theatres with 6-by-12-foot glass screens (for rear projection) and 16 mm projectors. At the time, building codes did not permit the use of 35 mm projectors in such auditoriums, but the major studios did not provide 16 mm prints of their films until a year after their initial release in 35 mm, that is, until the films had completed their theatrical runs. For the next two decades, the Eaton Centre Cineplex served as the chain's flagship movie complex; it closed its doors with little fanfare on 12 March 2001. The story of its trajectory is instructive.[54]

At first, distributors and industry analysts declared that Cineplex was moving in the wrong direction, suggesting that pay television and video discs would kill the multiplex.[55] Experience proved otherwise. Drabinksy and Taylor targeted their audiences carefully, so as to fill all possible seats: they showed reggae films to the Caribbean community, Yiddish films to the Jewish community, and Italian films to the Italian community. Their prediction that "move-over" pictures (that is, those that had completed their first run) could generate box-office revenue proved correct.[56] These included *Midnight Express* (1978) and *Life of Brian* (1979), which ran for sixty-eight and eighty-five weeks, respectively. They were forced to screen Rainer Werner Fassbinder's riveting film *The Marriage of Maria Braun* (1979) in more than one auditorium. By the end of its second year, the Eaton Centre Cineplex was grossing an average of $50,000 per week.[57] Drabinsky believed that the success of the move-over proved that reaching specialty audiences with mass-appeal films, even as second-runs, was going to yield profits.

Some of Canada's major capitalists, including HCI Holdings, a Toronto investment company, the Cadillac Fairview Corporation, which was controlled by Charles Bronfman's CEMP Investments, and Max Tanenbaum, owner of Tanenbaum Investments, financed Cineplex's expansion.[58] In addition, Drabinsky secured a $1 million line of credit from the Toronto-Dominion Bank. By late 1981, the firm was operating 124 screens in sixteen locations, including Montréal, Ottawa, Toronto, Winnipeg, Calgary, Edmonton, and Vancouver, with a box office revenue of $20 million.

Three years after launching the firm, Drabinsky and Taylor transferred their Cineplex formula to West Los Angeles, where on 16 July 1982 they opened a fourteen-screen, 1,650-seat complex on the eighth floor of a high-end shopping mall, the Beverly Center, located at the corner of La Cienega and Beverly boulevards. The facility cost them US$3 million. Three projectionists ran fourteen projectors, employing a platter system with a continuous loop. The Beverly Centre Cineplex, the largest complex of its kind at the time, was an immediate success.[59] Here, they screened a mixture of first-run art films and timely "move-overs," such as *Chariots of Fire* (1982). They also refined their "formula," opening with a well-advertised film on three or four screens and then manoeuvring auditoriums as the popularity of the film decreased or increased. Soon, Cineplex operated 146 auditoriums in thirteen cities in Canada, as well as fourteen auditoriums in Los Angeles. Manjunath Pendakur writes that Drabinsky and Taylor leased all of their theatres, "with terms ranging from ten to fifteen years with options to renew, essentially the same policy that Nathanson had employed in building the Odeon Theatres in the 1940s."[60]

Encouraged by their success, Drabinsky and Taylor resolved to turn Cineplex into a premier movie theatre circuit. This meant converting to 35 mm and shifting to first-run status. In doing so, of course, they would clash with Famous Players and Odeon Theatres.[61] Cineplex based its expansion on lease agreements worked out with operators in urban and suburban shopping malls and in locations near universities, focusing on Odeon's weaknesses.[62] Odeon had the right of first refusal for films distributed by Columbia, Universal, and Fox. These leases had to be secured for operations in urban and suburban centres because operations in small towns could not support a large number of screens, especially if these operations screened art and specialty pictures.

Cineplex prospered. The company started the process of vertical integration by acquiring concession stands (an important source of revenue) for its theatres. Nevertheless, Cineplex faced two major problems during the fall of 1982. First, they wrestled with the branch-plant mentality.[63] As Drabinsky put it, Famous Players and Odeon Theatres were preventing the company from obtaining first-run films, and "blockbusters" were the key to establishing its presence in the marketplace. Accordingly, on 22 December 1982 he filed a complaint with the

Restrictive Trade Practices Commission (RTPC), charging that seven distributors — Astral Films, Columbia Pictures, Paramount Productions, Universal Films (Canada), Warner Bros. Distributing (Canada), the United Artists Corporation, and the Twentieth Century–Fox Film Corporation — supplied movies to Famous Players and Odeon Theatres to the "exclusion of Cineplex and other exhibitors."[64] The Combines Investigation Act had been amended in 1976 to include business practices that restricted access to the supply of goods as well as services. In May 1983, the commission handed down its judgment in Cineplex's favour, and from 1 July the distributors dropped all practices favouring Famous Players and Odeon Theatres.[65] As Drabinsky declared, market forces would now determine which theatres played which pictures; that is, the distributor would ask all eligible exhibitors in a geographic region to submit bids for a film and then license it on a zone-by-zone, theatre-by-theatre, basis, thereby putting all exhibitors on an equal footing.[66] To take advantage of this new "playing field," Cineplex badly needed an infusion of capital, and to this end Drabinsky pursued Leo Kolber at CEMP Investments, securing an investment of $2.5 million.

As Drabinsky put it, Cineplex "boomed" during the fiscal year 1983–84. The net income for the year was $760,000 on revenue of $29.5 million, compared to a loss of $15 million on revenues of $20 million for 1982. Cineplex expanded very quickly. On 28 June 1984, Drabinsky acquired the Odeon Theatres chain, paying $22 million in cash and assuming the $35 million in debt Odeon had accumulated. This acquisition gave the new circuit, the Cineplex Odeon Corporation, 297 screens in 164 locations.[67] In February 1985, Cineplex obtained a lease agreement with Landmark Cinemas of Canada, thereby adding another twenty-two screens in western Canada.

Turning Cineplex Odeon into a premier movie theatre chain meant making sure that patrons knew they were in a Cineplex theatre. This entailed equipping theatres with exceptionally comfortable chairs, covering the foyer floors with marble, installing cafés and restaurants, providing each facility with a colour scheme designed to reflect the culture of the region, and, as a final touch, offering patrons the very best service.[68] In addition, Drabinsky hired David Burnett, then art historian and curator of contemporary Canadian Art at the Art Gallery of Ontario, to organize an art program for the theatres. Cineplex ended the year 1984 on an upbeat note: the asset base had increased to $103 million, shareholders' equity had increased to $39 million, and revenues had tripled to $87 million.

Buoyed by this success, in November 1985, for the sum of US$136 million, Cineplex Odeon acquired the vast Plitt circuit, including Plitt Theatres and Plitt Theatre Holdings, the fourth-largest motion picture theatre circuit in the United States.[69] Plitt had taken over the theatres that were spun from Adolph Zukor's Paramount chain when it was broken up by the consent decree in 1948; it operated 574 screens in 209 locations in twenty-one states, serving such key cities as San Francisco, Los Angeles, Minneapolis, Atlanta, and Houston. The Cineplex Odeon Corporation now controlled 1,060 screens in 391 locations in North America.[70]

Also in 1985, Drabinsky and Sidney (Sid) Sheinberg, president of MCA, an American multimedia producer of movies, television shows, and recorded music, decided to build an 18-screen, 6,000-seat multiplex in the parking lot of Universal Pictures. They commissioned David K. Mesbur, a Toronto-based architect who specialized in multiplex design, to plan what was at the time the largest movie palace in the world. The massive complex featured a glassed-in atrium-cum-lobby, 80 feet wide, with a 50-foot ceiling, marble columns, and a grand floating staircase, "complete with twinkling stars," reminiscent of John Eberson's atmospheric theatres. Within it were eighteen theatres, each seating between 250 and 800 people, equipped with the latest projection and sound technology. Should patrons grow hungry, they could visit the two-storey greenhouse food fair, featuring four massive concession stands, or one of two continental cafés serving espresso, sandwiches, and pastries. The complex also housed an art gallery and a six-storey parking structure that could hold 2,000 cars.[71] Costing US$18 million to build, Cineplex Odeon Universal City Cinemas opened on 4 July 1987. Later, Jon Jerde, the innovative "mall architect," incorporated the facility into a four-acre entertainment and retail complex called Universal CityWalk, which opened in May 1993. The goal of mixing a shopping mall and a city street, in this case comprised of retail shops, restaurants, simulated games, and high-tech movie theatres, was to generate the excitement of a grand thoroughfare, such as Hollywood Boulevard, but with none of the problems associated with contemporary urban life, such as mugging, panhandling, soliciting, and so on. CityWalk quickly became a major entertainment destination, attracting over 8 million people every year.

During 1985, Drabinsky negotiated a second major investment, US $219 million from MCA, giving the conglomerate a 50 percent equity interest in Cineplex Odeon and one-third of the votes. This deal, which entitled MCA to nominate four members to the board of fourteen, was completed on 15 January 1986. Sheinberg announced that this investment indicated MCA's confidence in the economic future of theatrical exhibition in North America and their belief that the management of Cineplex Odeon will "lead the industry to a new era of growth and resurgence" in Canada as well as in the United States.[72] Like Nathanson, Drabinsky had invited an American firm to turn his burgeoning business into another branch plant. By the end of 1985, Cineplex Odeon's revenues had doubled to $162 million, and the net income had tripled to $12.5 million.

The firm expanded quickly, extending its control over a number of key exhibition markets.[73] During the course of 1986, it acquired the Loew's circuit, which operated 222 screens in prime locations throughout metropolitan New York City and New Jersey, paying US $325 million, and the RKO circuit, which operated 97 screens, paying US $169 million outright and assuming RKO's debt of US $97.3 million. In the same year, Cineplex Odeon also purchased the Septum chain, which operated 48 screens at twelve locations in Atlanta, for US $7.5 million; the Essaness circuit, which operated 41 screens at thirteen locations in Chicago (the second-largest theatrical market), paying US $14.5 million; and, for US $21 million, the Neighborhood chain, which operated 67 screens in Washington DC. By the end of May 1986, Cineplex Odeon operated 1,350 screens in 460 locations.[74]

During 1987, the firm acquired the Walter Reade chain, Manhattan, paying US $32.5 million. Altogether, from 1984 to 1987, the circuit grew from 143 screens in twenty-one locations to a network of 446 screens in 185 locations.[75] However, Drabinsky paid dearly for this tumultuous expansion; during this period, the debt-to-assets ratio increased to 2-to-1. Industry analysts claimed that, generally speaking, Drabinsky was too willing to pay far above prevailing prices for a multiplex he considered vital to his vision of a national chain.[76] Drabinsky and Sheinberg struggled for the control of Cineplex Odeon for most of 1989; critical of the firm's financial reporting practices and management procedures, a number of MCA board members charged Drabinsky with betraying his "fiduciary duty" to the shareholders.[77] Unable to raise the US$1.1 billion needed to secure control of the firm, he submitted his letter of resignation on 1 December 1989, settling for a multi-million dollar buyout and control of the Pantages Theatre in Toronto.

THE MULTIPLEX AND GLOBALIZATION

During the late 1980s, the multiplex, which turned exhibition space into a major part of a "location-based entertainment centre," served as the model for movie exhibition.[78] With a view to stimulating demand, exhibitors across North America followed the example set by Cineplex Odeon and built bigger and more expensive facilities in major movie markets, bundling together a variety of leisure activities and attempting to restore a sense the elegant and upscale to the experience of moviegoing.[79] Typically, the theatres in these facilities featured state-of-the-art film projection and sound equipment, floor-to-ceiling, wall-to-wall curved screens, and stadium seating. In addition, the spaces housed high-tech video-game arcades, party rooms (for children), and restaurants, all designed to add excitement to the big-screen experience. Industry analysts complained that the new "dream palace," dull in design and ornamentation and in some cases resembling a carpet warehouse, had in fact given way to the "retail outlet."[80] From 1990 to 1999, the number of screens increased by 56 percent; however, attendance increased by only 24 percent, resulting in the serious problem of "overscreening."[81] Market analysts judged that exhibitors would have to close as many as a third of their screens in order to return to profitability.

Predictably, in the face of this downturn, Famous Players and Cineplex Odeon squared off, each determined to produce the biggest, the grandest, facility. Their activities in the fast-growing city of Calgary provide an interesting case study. In 1997 Cineplex Odeon opened a 12-screen, 2,471-seat complex in the city's northwest called Crowfoot Crossing Cinemas, offering customers all the latest services and amenities. In 2000, Famous Players opened a 16-screen, 3,870-seat complex called Paramount Chinook, at Chinook Shopping Centre in the southwest, offering patrons a variety of services, plus an IMAX theatre, a large food fair, and an array of state-of-the-art video games, all wrapped up in a dramatic ancient Egyptian architectural style, complete with an impressive laser-light show beamed through the eyes of the Egyptian mummy that dominated the lobby.

In addition, however, during the 1990s the industry built multiplexes across western Europe, Southeast Asia, and South America, with a view not merely to attracting audiences but to stimulating the demand for American entertainment in general and Hollywood movies in particular. Hollywood had entered the age of globalization.[82] Executives and analysts were rethinking the multiplex as the model for movie exhibition and considering digital distribution and projection as the alternative.[83] According to a 1989 report from Time Warner, the largest media company in the world, globalization demanded that top players in the movie business develop long-term strategies if they wanted to establish "a major presence in all of the world's important markets."[84] At the same time, though, by intensifying their efforts to dominate global markets, producers, distributors, and exhibitors further deflected attention from local concerns, thereby permitting the moviegoing experience in western Canada, as elsewhere, to deteriorate appreciably. The construction of multiplexes indeed seemed to go hand-in-hand with the rise of the global box office.[85] Daniel Pruzin reported in 1991 that "U.S. films now account for over 50 percent of the box office in every major Western European country, with the share in Great Britain and West Germany well above 70 percent."[86]

Figure 79. Announcement of the tenth anniversary of Cineplex Odeon, 1989. Variety, 26 April–2 May 1989 (double issue), 93. Courtesy of Reed Business Information.

In other words, the exportation of the multiplex paved the way for the globalization of distribution and exhibition. According to Tino Balio, those in the movie industry were convinced that, outside the United States, every market was underscreened, and a great many were underdeveloped.[87] Exhibitors in western Europe operated about one-third the number of screens per capita as exhibitors in the United States, despite having about the same population. In due course, the

Figure 80. The Paramount Chinook Theatre, Calgary, 2003. Photo by Robert M. Seiler.

American majors and their partners launched a campaign to upgrade moviegoing in western Europe, Asia, and South America. Millard Ochs, of United Cinemas International, argued that the internationalization of exhibition followed the saturation of the domestic market.[88] The development of international movie theatre chains thus represented an extension of previous arrangements, as when, during the 1930s, Paramount and Loew's operated movie theatres in Great Britain and France.[89] American Multi-Cinemas (AMC) declared that it would build and buy three thousand screens in Europe, Asia, and South America.[90] In 1990, *Variety* described "a multiplex building boom throughout Europe, with U.S. majors providing the capital (and guidance) for much of the expansion."[91] The writer was thus pointing to the "Americanization" of moviegoing, which, among other things, involved intensifying the relationship between shopping and watching movies. American interests shaped cinema construction and renovation in most European countries. For example, Warner Bros. International announced in 1991 that the firm hoped to establish a 500-screen global circuit by 1995, and Cineplex Odeon announced in 1998 that the firm planned to build twelve multiplexes in Turkey between 1998 and 2002.[92] Although industry analysts equated multiplexing with growth in attendance, this was not necessarily the case. Interestingly, UK exhibitors operated 1,242 screens in 1988 and 2,454 in 1998, although, during this period, the number of sites rose only from 655 to 748.[93] This proliferation in the number of screens generated concerns about "overscreening." In addition, international corporations inevitably clashed with local organizations over such matters as preserving historical sites.

Accounting for the "multiplex revolution" in Europe is no easy matter. It can be argued that the restructuring of distribution and exhibition arrangements that resulted from this expansion in fact shaped the moviegoing experience.[94] Film historians remind us that the tales of growth conceal the tales of the closure, demolition, and transformation of facilities, reinvigorating some zones of moviegoing and obliterating others.[95] Without a doubt, they also speak to the impact of economic forces on the social practice of going to the movies, both locally and globally.[96]

STAYING HOME TO WATCH THE MOVIES

For the sake of discussion, we can distinguish three periods of moviegoing.[97] During the first, which extended from the opening of the first movie theatres to the early 1950s, people were fascinated by the new medium's capacity to tell stories. At the same time, religious reformers, social activists, and government censors, concerned about the impact of movies on the attitudes and the actions of viewers, devoted considerable effort to curtailing the power of film. Undeterred by these concerns, audiences flocked to the movies during the 1920s, 1930s and 1940s, making "the picture show" the dominant artifact of North American popular culture.

Moviegoing went into a decline during the second period, which extended from the early 1950s to the mid-1970s. People migrated to the suburbs (a mass movement that began in the 1930s but was interrupted by the Depression and World War II) and turned their attention to their homes and children. Analysts point out that although suburban families accounted for less than one-fifth of the population in the United States during the 1950s, they possessed one-third of the disposable income. The suburbs gave rise to a distinctive lifestyle, as well as new spending habits: suburban dwellers focused on a variety of home-centred leisure activities, including do-it-yourself-projects, such as making home movies and building short-wave radios and hot rods.[98] In addition, for reasons of cost and convenience, people in the suburbs increasingly regarded television as the medium for family-oriented entertainment.[99] A survey conducted in 1948 suggested that storytelling media, such as books, movies, and radio, had fallen on hard times; 38 percent of the respondents claimed that the movies had declined in quality, and 50 percent noted that a variety of activities got in the way of moviegoing.[100]

During the third period, which began in the mid-1970s, attendance at movies declined even further, thanks to the diffusion of television-related media, starting with the introduction of Betamax and VHS video-recording systems in 1975 and 1976, respectively. New media offered consumers a wider range of home-centred entertainment options than ever before. According to contemporary surveys of attitudes toward leisure-time pursuits, an increasing number of people across North America pursued home-centred activities, especially watching television and playing video games.[101] Significantly, many respondents indicated that they made no distinction whatsoever between watching movies on television screens and watching movies on large, movie theatre screens. Clearly, the proliferation of videocassette recorders had blurred the lines separating television and cinema. By the end of the 1980s, Bruce Austin could write that "among younger people the movie and television experience may be virtually indistinguishable."[102] The trend was, of course, reinforced by the advent of DVDs, which often include supplementary materials that purport to give audiences — seated not in theatres but in front of television sets — an insider's view of how movies are made.

As we have suggested, the multiplex served to sustain moviegoing for more than a decade, attracting at the peak of its popularity 1.57 billion admissions in the United States in 2002 and, in 1998–99, 112.8 million admissions in Canada. But then attendance dropped off, with consumers complaining that moviegoing was losing its magic.[103] As industry analyst Howard Lichtman, president of the Lightning Group, a Toronto-based marketing consulting firm, observed in 2007, attendance across Canada had been edging downward steadily over the previous decade, a trend that has continued.[104] Movie industry websites, such as natoonline.org, indicate that movie theatres across North America sold 1.52 billion tickets in 2010. More specifically, in 2010, movie theatres in the United States sold 1.35 billion tickets, a decrease of 9.5 per cent from 1.42 billion tickets in 2009, whereas movie theatres in Canada sold 112.20 million tickets, a drop of 1.9 per cent from 114.40 tickets in 2009.[105] The downward turn may be less dramatic in Canada, where the recent recession has not been as severe, but it is obvious nevertheless. Industry analysts explain this overall decline in terms of an increase in ticket prices, especially for 3-D screenings, and an increase in the number of entertainment alternatives.

Other factors have had an impact on attendance, however. Critics have pointed to the carnival-like atmosphere that characterizes the "new" multiplex, complaining about the garish lighting, the pervasive odour of fast foods, and the noise emanating from the video games arcade, not to mention the volume at which the sound system in the auditorium is pitched.[106] In addition, during the early 1990s, exhibitors in Canada and elsewhere began screening commercials before the main attraction, in another effort to increase revenue. Not surprisingly, as commentators have noted, audiences regarded commercials "as a discourteous intrusion and considered it a duty to hiss at them."[107]All the same, the number of commercials has increased over the years, and the volume has gone up, intensifying the frustration of even the most enthusiastic movie buffs.

In addition, some commentators claim that the quality of movies has been deteriorating over the years. To some extent, they argue, the major Hollywood studios have lost touch with audiences, to the point that, as Robert Fulford asserts, any list of newly released movies reads like a recipe for "creative bankruptcy." They claim that the MBAs who run the studios may have studied the art of separating customers from their money, but they seem to have missed the lectures on product. To a great extent, the argument goes, studios now produce sequels, prequels, and adaptations that have a built-in audience (or so they hope), displaying a clear preference for films based on "safe" material, such as best-selling books, popular television shows, and comics. The formula for producing a sequel is simple: duplicate the original experience without being obvious. That is, find a way to give the audience more of what they liked the first time but with a slightly new twist. Critics blame this lack of originality on the high cost of producing movies, the budgets of which often exceed US$100 million — price tags that do not promote a willingness to take risks.[108]

Critics have also taken to complaining about the behavior of some moviegoers, especially their tendency to talk, text, and tweet during movies. Some argue that this behaviour has become ever more pronounced, prompting an increasing number of moviegoers to stop visiting the cinema altogether.[109] A number of explanations for this allegedly boorish behavior have been offered. First, people have been conditioned by watching movies at home, where they can do whatever they please. Second, going to the movies has become a multimedia event. Multiplexes have become huge indoor amusement parks, offering the public a variety of entertainments, over and above movies. This somewhat raucous environment, in which the overriding goal is to have fun, further promotes a lack of restraint, an attitude that can easily be transported from the video arcade into the theatre. Third, the big movie theatre chains appear to have abandoned any serious efforts to "manage" or "discipline" audiences. One could argue that, for exhibitors, creating an atmosphere that encourages patrons to find an acceptable balance between self-indulgence and self-restraint has become an ongoing challenge. After all, a paradox lies at the centre of the moviegoing experience — a social activity that is nonetheless basically solitary. As Adam Sternbergh notes, operators of multiplexes address this paradox by infusing the site with an intensity that some amusement seekers perceive as part of having a good time.[110] In doing so, however, exhibitors may risk encouraging the kinds of behaviours that some moviegoers find offensive.

Finally, commentators complain about the exorbitant cost of going to the movies, noting that two adults can easily spend $50 on tickets, popcorn, and soft drinks.[111] One might say that to the degree that such critiques are accurate, they highlight a fascinating irony in the evolution of moviegoing. That is, one can see in the amusement park approach to film exhibition a return to the popular, working-class roots of this pastime — a development driven by technological and social changes and the economic imperatives that accompany them, in much the same way that such factors earlier drove the effort of exhibitors to legitimate and gentrify moviegoing by building elaborate palaces for screening films. That the cost of moviegoing has arguably become "exorbitant" heightens this irony: while early exhibitors, many of whom came from a working-class background, made every effort to appeal to the middle class, they also kept prices quite low in order to attract as many patrons as possible. Clearly, negotiating the contradictions that converge on the site where entertainment is consumed is more complex than at first it may appear to be.

Quite apart from possible deterrents related to the quality of the moviegoing experience itself, the decline in attendance no doubt also reflects the attractions of ever-expanding amusement options. These days, not only can consumers choose from a wide selection of commercial leisure-time activities, but they also have many options for how and when to watch movies, thanks to the proliferation of delivery systems. The movie theatre is now only one of many venues for consuming movies. Cable and satellite television, especially the services devoted exclusively to the screening of movies, enable people to watch movies at any time they choose. Similarly, the Internet has made films available to an increasing number of consumers. The development of video-on-demand (VOD) interactive technology during the late 1990s allowed consumers to view programming in real time or to download programs and view them later.[112] Solutions Research Group (SRG) analysts reported in 2005 that about 1.8 million Canadians had downloaded at least one feature-length film. SRG analysts also noted that few young Canadians subscribe to the argument that downloading illegally can be equated to the theft of physical objects: many regard this practice as a victimless crime, arguing that, in the greater scheme of things, stealing from wealthy pop stars and Hollywood actors is no big deal.[113]

Over the years, media services have become increasingly digitized and interactive, and advances in compression technology have reduced bandwidth requirements. Streaming is now faster than downloading, and consumers can watch movies on a variety of devices. A Bloomberg report suggests that, in 2012, online viewing across North America will exceed DVD and Blu-Ray use. The report notes that legal online viewing of movies will more than double in 2012, rising to 3.4 billion from 1.4 billion in 2011; by the same token, the instances of viewing DVDs and Blu-Ray discs will shrink to 2.4 billion from 2.6 billion. In 2011, unlimited-streaming subscription plans, including those offered by Netflix Inc. and Amazon.com's Prime Service, accounted for 94 percent of all paid online movie consumption in the United States. Established in 1997, Netflix was offering a subscription-based digital distribution service by 1999, and by 2009 it boasted a collection of some hundred thousand titles. This leading Internet subscription service announced in the spring of 2010 that it would expand into forty-five countries in Latin America, Europe, and Asia. It launched its Canadian service in July of that year, enabling consumers to watch movies on a variety of devices, including the PS3, Wii, Xbox, PC, Mac, and Apple Television, for a monthly fee of about $7.99. The Bloomberg report also indicated that five major studios have an agreement with Wal-Mart Stores Inc. that may re-ignite home-video purchases by giving consumers the option to store copies in the cloud. Wal-Mart announced in April 2012 that it would expand into thirty countries; it launched its disc-to-digital program on an à la carte basis, enabling sales associates to digitize consumers' DVDs and consumers to access the streaming through VUDU (the content delivery and media technology company owned by the retailer) on supported devices, including computers, tablets, smart phones, or game consoles.[114] What issues, legal as well as technological, the media services just mentioned will experience when setting up in Canada remains to be seen.

The optical disc, epitomized by the DVD, has, of course, had a dramatic impact on moviegoing. DVD technology, introduced in 1995, swiftly penetrated most North American homes. After only six years, 80 percent of households owned DVD players, which is to say that people adopted this technology faster than they adopted the CD player, the computer, or the VCR. Spending on rentals and sales of VHS cassettes and DVDs grew from US$12.8 billion in 1999 to US$24.5 billion in 2004.[115] DVD releases can be divided into two categories: films that run first in theatres and are subsequently made available on DVD (initially, six months after their theatrical release, although now three months is the average) and direct-to-DVD releases. At first, the latter category included low-budget erotic thrillers, cheap comedies, and adventure stories — films that were deemed not good enough for movie theatres. Thus, direct-to-DVD releases essentially replaced the made-for-television category of film. Increasingly, however, A-list producers and actors have joined these projects, and the direct-to-DVD market now infuses billions of dollars into a maturing business that is gaining legitimacy in terms of creativity and revenue. In May 2005, 20th

Century Fox Home Entertainment released *Sandlot 2* (2005), the first title from its division dedicated to direct-to-DVD category, selling more than one million units. The studio indicated that it would release four or five DVD premieres annually. At that time, the best-selling movie in this category, *The Lion King 2: Simba's Pride* (2004), earned US $464.5 million worldwide in sales and rentals.[116]

For a number of years, the major studios regarded the DVD as a major source of revenue. Analysts, including Price Waterhouse Coopers, note that many buyers of DVD players have built up a substantial library of DVDs. However, the industry has not been able to sustain this growth in sales and rentals. Analysts observed a drop in the sales of *Shrek 2* (2004), which was produced by DreamWorks SKG, and *The Incredibles* (2005), which was produced by Pixar Animation Studios, a decline that prompted retailers to return unsold copies. This trend has continued, highlighted by such events as the bankruptcy of Blockbuster Video, the video retail and sales giant, in the United States (2010) and in Canada (2011).

Not surprisingly, the proliferation of venues for watching movies has had a negative impact on moviegoing. Consumers can watch movies anywhere at any time, not only on high-definition flat-screen televisions but on their home computers, as well as portable electronic devices, including cellphones, Blackberrys, iPods, iPhones, iPads, and other electronic tablets. As well, a sophisticated home entertainment system can rival the movie theatre in terms of movie-watching experience.[117] Moreover, movies must increasingly compete with video games. In 2005, industry analysts noted the interest in *Halo 2*, which was designed for the Xbox system, and *Grand Theft: San Andreas*, which was designed for the Playstation 2 system: *Halo 2* racked up US $125 million in the first twenty-four hours after its release, more than many movies earned during the same period.[118] The video game industry had a banner year in 2004: video games and console sales went up 5 percent to a record high of US $766 million.[119] Analysts have predicted that video games and game equipment will play an ever bigger role in consumer entertainment, with the global video game market expanding exponentially. Understandably, major multimedia corporations have considered tapping into this lucrative industry, which ranks in popularity just behind the music industry.

The merger of Cineplex Galaxy LP and Famous Players in 2005 promised to have a positive impact on moviegoing in Canada.[120] In fact, it would seem that the merger has had the opposite effect, limiting the choice of venues even further. In October 2004, Viacom — the New York City–based multimedia conglomerate, parent of two television channels, CBS and MTV, one movie studio, Paramount Pictures Corporation, and a publishing house, Simon and Schuster — announced that it was selling its Canadian cinema arm, Famous Players, a non-core operation worth US$400 million. In June 2005, Cineplex Galaxy LP, the Toronto-based movie theatre chain, announced its plan to buy Famous Players, its long-time archrival, for US$500 million. Cineplex Galaxy, which had grossed $354 million in 2004, ran or had an interest in eighty-six theatres, with a total of 775 screens in six Canadian provinces, operating under the Cineplex Odeon and Galaxy brands.[121] Famous Players, which had grossed $250 million in 2004, operated eighty-four theatres, with a total of 787 screens across the country, including theatres in joint ventures with IMAX and with Alliance Atlantis. The deal gave American interests 132 theatres, with more than 1,300 screens, and a share of 61 percent of the Canadian market. As part of the deal, the Competition Bureau of Canada required Cineplex Galaxy to sell a number of theatres across the country to resolve "competition concerns" arising out of the merger. Cineplex agreed to sell about thirty-five theatres, with 284 screens and annual box office revenues of $100,000, in seventeen cities in which the two chains had formerly competed.[122] Ben Mogil, an analyst at Westwind Partners, called the marriage of Cineplex and Famous Players "the deal of a lifetime." Mogil noted that Cineplex would be able to sell pre-movie digital advertisements nationally, pointing out that cinema owners across North America are eager to sell more advertising because of the high margins and potential growth, which outstrip the traditional business of showing movies. Cineplex was already the ad agency for AMC and Landmark Theatres in Canada. Mogil also predicted that Cineplex's distribution income per unit would rise by at least 10 to 15 percent.[123] Clearly, this prognostication ignored some of the dynamics driving movie enthusiasts from multiplexes.

NEW FRONTIERS: THE DIGITAL REVOLUTION

As we have seen, the business of exhibiting movies and the social practice of going to the movies have both evolved from era to era, propelled by social, economic, and technological forces. Acknowledging that box office revenues had become stagnant and that DVD sales and rentals were becoming more important financially than theatrical releases, industry executives across North America recently implemented another innovation: digital cinema. This paradigm shift includes digital projection, which produces a brighter, crisper image but, like the introduction of "talkies" in the late 1920s, requires exhibitors to invest in expensive technology. Advances in digital technology also drive the growing interest in video-on-demand and interactivity, all in the context of the global economic downturn that began in late 2008.[124]

In addition, digital technology has made possible ever more spectacular cinematic effects, which many in the industry view as a way to attract audiences. To some extent, of course, filmmakers have always employed special effects, such as double exposure in telling their stories, but the digital revolution has vastly increased the range and complexity of such techniques. Over the past three decades, a growing number of filmmakers — especially makers of science-fiction thrillers — have utilized computer graphics (CG) to create characters, settings, and effects. Generally speaking, computer-generated effects are more efficient and reliable than, for example, physically constructing miniatures for special-effects shots or hiring dozens of extras for crowd scenes. During the 1970s, technicians employed raster wireframe graphics to represent 3-D or physical objects or sequences.[125] For example, Michael Crichton's *Westworld* (1973) featured representations of a robot gunslinger's point of view, an effect managed by John Whitney, Jr., and Gary Demos. For George Lucas's *Star Wars* (1977), Larry Cuba created a 3-D simulation for the "trench run" sequence, Luke Skywalker's climactic attack on the Death Star. (Industrial Light and Magic, a visual effects studio founded by Lucas, created 3-D graphics for all the *Star Wars* films.) The famous scene in Ridley Scott's *Alien* (1979), in which the alien creature "explodes" out of John Hurt's chest, was the work of special effects wizard Berand Lodge.

With the development of computer processing, storage, and memory capacity, plus the growing sophistication of CG software during the 1980s, it became possible to create even more complex special effects. For example, for Nicholas Meyer's *Star Trek 2: The Wrath of Khan* (1982), Pixar (a division of LucasFilm at the time) created CG representations of the rebirth of a once-dead planet. Steven Lisberger's *Tron* (1982), produced for the Walt Disney Company, featured a 15-minute animated depiction of the 3-D world of a video game inside a computer, while Nick Castle's *The Last Starfighter* (1984) included a 25-minute animated sequence of spaceships, spacecapes, and battle scenes. The poor performance of the last two films at the box office might have encouraged some directors to rethink the viability of films that rely chiefly on spectacular CG effects.

Nevertheless, computer-generated imagery has become a major form of special effects, thanks to the huge success of *Jurassic Park* (1993), based on Michael Crichton's novel of the same title. In this science-fiction thriller, Steven Spielberg integrated real people and computer-generated dinosaurs into a live-action film, representing the transition from stop-motion animation to digital animation. Industrial Light and Magic produced the visual effects for the film (and many others). From 1995 to 2005, the average visual effects budget jumped from US$5 million to US$40 million. In *Toy Story* (1995), John Lasseter created the first fully computer-animated feature movie, producing a "buddy film," in the time-honoured Disney tradition, that appealed to children as well as adults. Completed on a budget of US$30 million, *Toy Story*, a Pixar-Disney Animation production, earned three Academy Award nominations and eight Annie Awards, including Best Animated Feature. In *Titanic* (1997), James Cameron used scale models and computer-generated imagery to re-create the sinking of the Titanic. The film was enormously expensive (US$200 million) but was also an enormous critical and commercial success, receiving eleven Academy Awards, including that for Best Picture. In *The Polar Express* (2004), Robert Zemeckis employed a technique known as "performance capture," whereby the movements of actors are captured digitally and used as the basis for animated characters.

In the eyes of filmmakers such as these, digital 3-D technology is poised to turn cinema into "the ultimate immersive medium," a revolution comparable to those of sound and colour.[126] Many industry analysts believe that *Avatar* (2009), Cameron's science-fiction epic that combines live action, performance capture, and digital animation, will serve as the model for mainstream filmmaking. As it happens, 3-D films have earned more revenue than 2-D films, thanks to high ticket prices and longer runs. Not surprisingly, Cameron decided to re-release *Titanic* in 3-D on 12 April 2012, to coincide with the one-hundredth anniversary of the disaster. Jeffrey Katzenberg, the chief executive officer at DreamWorks Animation and executive producer of the immensely successful *Shrek 2* (2004), has committed his company to producing digital 3-D films only. According to industry statistics, only three 3-D films were produced in 2008, followed by twelve in 2009, and then more than thirty in 2010. The long-term effects of this development are, of course, not entirely clear. For example, whether this digital revolution, which has tempted many filmmakers to re-release previous works in the 3-D format, will serve the best interests of narrative is still a matter of debate.

Exhibitors across the prairie West, like their colleagues elsewhere, have been diversifying their operations, offering the public such alternative forms of entertainment as high-definition video simulcasts of sports events, rock concerts, operas, plays, and video-game competitions, over and above movies, in order to supplement their revenue. Early in the twentieth century, entrepreneurs across North America turned their vaudeville houses and legitimate theatres into movie theatres, taking advantage of the new medium; these days, entrepreneurs are turning their movie theatres into "entertainment destinations," taking advantage of new technology and the increasing appetite for variety entertainment. Live performances from the Metropolitan Opera in New York City have been a great success. During the 2006–7 season, 113 theatres in the United States and sixty in Canada carried the simulcasts; in the following season, the numbers rose to three hundred theatres in the United States and a hundred in Canada. The practice has continued, along with similar simulcasts of live theatrical productions from London and New York City.

The digital revolution is affecting all branches of the movie industry: production, distribution, and exhibition. The developments just discussed speak to a reconfiguration of movie exhibition and moviegoing that is taking place in prairie Canada, as elsewhere. Over the past century, unique local realities have both resisted and embraced the many metropolitan and global influences that have arguably made towns and cities across North America and the social and cultural experiences of their inhabitants more and more alike. However, the local seems to persist, if perhaps in muted form, in the geographic, social, and cultural particularities that define it in any given place and time. At some times, the local has been expressed tangibly, in the decorative features of a particular theatre; at others, less tangibly but just as importantly, it has found expression via the sensibility that members of an audience bring to the viewing of films — films made elsewhere by and about people with whom they have much, but not everything, in common. In a perceptive discussion of how Canadians consume American films, Charles Acland reminds us that signs are polysemic, that is, open to many interpretations, and that an individual's "reading" of a film is not determined by where the film originates or by the economic structures that enable its consumption. In fact, audiences have great freedom in making sense of the films they see and, one might add, in making sense of the entire experience of going to the movies. One's interpretation is "influenced by context, personal history, and one's association with particular cultures and knowledge."[127] Place thus seems to be an important influence on perception. Although metropolitan and global influences are powerful, indeed dominant, and seem to be growing more so everyday, the local has never and will never simply disappear.

What of movie theatres themselves? Will they persist, or will they gradually vanish, pushed aside by the juggernaut of technological change that seems to be turning movie watching into a private pursuit? As streaming increasingly becomes the dominant mode of delivery, and the movie theatre becomes increasingly irrelevant, will film exhibition as we know it simply disappear? Clearly, the movie industry is going through another period of change, indeed a revolution, driven by transformations in consumer behaviour and, of course, by digital technology. After a tough recession, people are spending their money on home entertainment, buying and renting fewer DVDs, and downloading and streaming via such services as Netflix. The convergence of the developments discussed above suggests that movie exhibition will become a highly competitive niche industry and that exhibitors will have to balance the global and the local with even greater ingenuity to survive.

NOTES

Introduction

1. As Bruce Austin puts it, the process of organizing commercial spectator amusement or entertainment, which should be understood as a function of industrialization and urbanization, dates from the last decade of the nineteenth century, when entrepreneurs began presenting scheduled programs at facilities purpose-built for performers, such as acrobats, actors, jugglers, and magicians, who had to that point travelled widely and performed (primarily on holidays) in such makeshift venues as taverns and village greens. In other words, the standardization of commercial entertainment mirrored the standardization of industrial production. Until they discovered how best to market the new form of entertainment, exhibitors screened movies in theatres and vaudeville houses. These entrepreneurs specialized in a particular line of entertainment, consolidating their activities and seeking control of their field. Typical were the impresarios who, in 1895, formed the Theatrical Syndicate (discussed in chapter 3) with a view to establishing a monopoly over theatrical production and presentation. Gregory Waller highlights the pressure impresarios felt to standardize the moviegoing experience, on the one hand, and to distinguish their product from that of other impresarios, on the other. See Bruce A. Austin, *Immediate Seating: A Look at Movie Audiences* (Belmont, CA: Wadsworth, 1989), 25–28; and Gregory A. Waller, *Main Street Amusements: Movies and Commercial Entertainment in a Southern City, 1896–1930* (Washington, DC: Smithsonian Institution Press, 1995), xiii–xx, 191–221; see also Roy Rosenzweig, *Eight Hours for What We Will: Workers and Leisure in an Industrial City, 1870–1920* (New York: Cambridge University Press, 1983), 172; and Charles R. Acland, *Screen Traffic: Movies, Multiplexes, and Global Culture* (Durham, NC: Duke University Press, 2003), 42–44.
2. For an analysis of the fundamental economic forces that arguably underlay centralization and standardization, and also determined the position of Canadian

exhibitors in the North American film industry, see Wallace Clement, "Uneven Development: A Mature Branch-Plant Society," in Wallace Clement, *Class, Power, and Property: Essays on Canadian Society* (Toronto: Methuen Publications, 1983), 55–84, and "Introduction: Whither the New Canadian Economy?" in *Understanding Canada: Building on the New Canadian Political Economy,* ed. Wallace Clement (Montreal and Kingston: McGill-Queen's University Press, 1997), 3–18. Clement explains that foreign domination has distorted the Canadian economy (and hence its class structure). He points out that the manufacturing sector is underdeveloped, while the resource sector is geared to external requirements, and both are vulnerable to the whims of metropolitan capitalists. British capitalists began the process in the nineteenth century, using Canada as an outlet for their surplus capital and manufactured products and as a source for important resources, including grain. Later, American capitalists similarly used Canada as a market for their surplus production. Canada set up tariffs, but American capitalists established branch-plant operations. After World War I, foreign-owned branch plants dominated the sphere of production.

3. Frederick J. Turner, "The Significance of the Frontier in American History" (1893), repr. in *One West, Two Myths II: Essays on Comparison,* ed. C. L. Higham and Robert Thacker (Calgary: University of Calgary Press, 2006), 165–92.
4. See Gerald Friesen, "Prairie West," in *The Canadian Encyclopedia,* 3 vols., ed. James H. Marsh (Edmonton: Hurtig, 1985), vol. 3, 1464–65.
5. J. M. S. Careless promoted "the "metropolitan thesis" in a number of texts, including "Frontierism, Metropolitanism, and Canadian History" (1954), which was reprinted in *A Passion for Identity: Introduction to Canadian Studies,* ed. Eli Mandel and David Taras (Toronto: Methuen, 1987), 51–63; "Metropolis and Region: The Interplay Between City and Region in Canadian History Before 1914," *Urban History Review* 3 (February 1979): 99–118; and *Frontier and Metropolis: Regions, Cities, and Identities in Canada Before 1914* (Toronto: University of Toronto Press, 1989).
6. Many historians have challenged the validity of the frontier thesis, and many have debated the impact it has had on American and Canadian historiography. See George F. G. Stanley, "Western Canada and the Frontier Thesis," in *Canadian Historical Association Report* (Toronto: University of Toronto Press, 1940), 105–14; Michael S. Cross, ed., *The Frontier Thesis and the Canadas: The Debate on the Impact of the Canadian Environment* (Toronto: Copp Clark, 1970); Michael Steiner, "The Significance of Turner's Sectional Thesis," *Western Historical Quarterly* 10, no. 4 (October 1979): 437–66; Robert Irwin, "Breaking the Shackles of the Metropolitan Thesis: Prairie History, the Environment, and Layered Identities," *Journal of Canadian Studies* 32, no. 3 (Fall 1997): 98–118; William J. Cronon, *Nature's Metropolis: Chicago and the Great West* (New York: W. W.Norton, 1991); Richard White, *It's Your Misfortune and None of My Own: A History of the American West* (Norman: University of Oklahoma Press, 1991); and Donald Worster, "Two Faces West: The Development Myth in Canada and the United States," in *One West, Two Myths: A Comparative Reader,* ed. C. L. Higham and Robert Thacker (Calgary: University of Calgary Press, 2004), 23–45.

7. See Careless, "Frontierism, Metropolitanism, and Canadian History," 59.
8. Ibid., 62–63; Gilbert A. Stelter, "The City-Building Process in Canada," in *Shaping the Urban Landscape: Aspects of the Canadian City-Building Process,* ed. Gilbert A. Stelter and Alan F. J. Artibise (Ottawa: Carleton University Press, 1982), 1–29; and Gilbert A. Stelter, "A Regional Framework for Urban History," *Urban History Review* 13 (February 1985): 193–206.
9. Vernon C. Fowke, *The National Policy and the Wheat Economy* (Toronto: University of Toronto Press, 1957), 5–8.
10. See Gerald Friesen, *The Canadian Prairies: A History* (Toronto: University of Toronto Press, 1984), 162–63; Fowke, *The National Policy and the Wheat Economy,* 4–5; Donald Swainson, "Canada Annexes the West: Colonial Status Confirmed," in *Readings in Canadian History: Post-Confederation,* ed. R. Douglas Francis and Donald B. Smith (Toronto: Holt, Rinehart, and Winston of Canada, 1986), 64–82.
11. Fowke, *The National Policy and the Wheat Economy,* 5.
12. See Stelter, "The City-Building Process in Canada," 18, and "A Regional Framework for Urban History."
13. Friesen, *The Canadian Prairies,* 185. The challenges that the Canadian government faced in attempting to attract settlers to the prairie West are well known. See, for example, Howard Palmer, "Patterns of Immigration and Ethnic Settlement in Alberta," in *Peoples of Alberta: Portraits of Cultural Diversity,* ed. Howard Palmer and Tamara Palmer (Saskatoon: Western Producer Prairie Books, 1985,) 1–5. See also Roberto Perin and Harold Troper, "Immigration Policy," in *Encyclopedia of Canada's Peoples,* ed. Paul Robert Magosci (Toronto: University of Toronto Press, 1999), 700–713; Robert Bothwell, *The Penguin History of Canada* (Toronto: Penguin Canada, 2006), 225–32.
14. Max Foran, *Calgary: An Illustrated History* (Toronto: James Lorimer, and Ottawa: National Museum of Man, 1978), 12, 16; Friesen, *The Canadian Prairies,* 237; Hugh Dempsey, *The Golden Age of the Canadian Cowboy: An Illustrated History* (Saskatoon: Fifth House, 1995), 11–12; Simon M. Evans, *The Bar U and Canadian Ranching History* (Calgary: University of Calgary Press, 2004), 37–38.
15. See D. J. Hall, "Clifford Sifton: Immigration and Settlement Policy, 1896–1905," in *The Settlement of the West,* ed. Howard Palmer (Calgary: University of Calgary Comprint, 1977), 60–85; and Friesen, *The Canadian Prairies,* 245–48. See also Harold Troper, *Only Farmers Need Apply* (Toronto: Griffin Press, 1972); and Roberto Perin and Harold Troper, "Immigration Policy."
16. See Hall, "Clifford Sifton," 70.
17. Fowke, *The National Policy and the Wheat Economy,* 72.
18. Friesen, *The Canadian Prairies,* 249.
19. See Alan F. J. Artibise, "City-Building in the Canadian West: From Boosterism to Corporatism," *Journal of Canadian Studies* 17, no. 3 (Fall 1982): 35–44; "Canada as an Urban Nation," *Daedalus* 117 (Fall 1988): 237–64; and "Boosterism and the Development of Prairie Cities, 1871–1913," in *The Prairie West,* 2nd ed., ed. R. Douglas Francis and Howard Palmer (Edmonton: University of Alberta Press, 1992), 515–43.

20. Artibise, "City-Building in the Canadian West," 36.
21. Artibise, "Boosterism and the Development of Prairie Cities, 1871–1913," 517–18.
22. Artibise, "City-Building in the Canadian West," 36–37.
23. Friesen, *The Canadian Prairies*, 291–92.
24. Ibid., 296.
25. Artibise, "City-Building in the Canadian West," 38.
26. Ibid.
27. Ibid., 41–42.
28. See, for example, David Jones, *Empire of Dust* (Edmonton: University of Alberta Press, 1987).
29. Friesen, *The Canadian Prairies*, 272–73.
30. Waller, *Main Street Amusements,* xiii. See also Maria Tippett, "The Writing of English Canadian Cultural History, 1970–1985," *Canadian Historical Review* 67 (1986): 560–61; Donald G. Wetherell and Irene Kmet, *Useful Pleasures: The Shaping of Leisure in Alberta, 1896–1945* (Regina: Canadian Plains Research Center, 1990), xxiv; Robert C. Allen and Douglas Gomery, *Film History: Theory and Practice* (New York: Alfred A. Knopf, 1985), 193–212; Rosenzweig, *Eight Hours for What We Will,* 172.
31. See, for example, Austin, *Immediate Seating*, 28; Miriam Hansen, *Babel and Babylon: Spectatorship in American Silent Film* (Cambridge: Harvard University Press, 1991), 94–95; and Waller, *Main Street Amusements,* xvii.
32. See Ben Hall, *The Best Remaining Seats: The Story of the Golden Age of the Movie Palace* (New York: Bramhall House, 1961). In 1969, concerned by the ongoing destruction of what he described as "those picture pagodas of fragrant memory," Hall circulated a letter announcing the founding of the Theatre Historical Society of America (available on the Theatre Historical Society of America's website at http://www2. Hawaii.edu/~angell/thsa/founding.html). See also Tino Balio, ed., *The American Film Industry*, rev. ed. (Madison: University of Wisconsin Press, 1985); Charlotte Herzog, "The Motion Picture Theatre and Film Exhibition, 1896–1932" (PhD diss., Northwestern University, 1980); and Maggie Valentine, *The Show Starts on the Sidewalk: An Architectural History of the Movie Theatre, Starring S. Charles Lee* (New Haven, CT: Yale University Press, 1994).
33. Douglas Gomery, "Film and Business History: The Development of an American Entertainment Industry," *Journal of Contemporary History* 19, no. 1 (January 1984): 89–103; Waller, *Main Street Amusements,* xiii–xx; David Bordwell, Janet Staiger, and Kristin Thompson, *The Classic Hollywood Cinema: Film Style and Production to 1960* (New York: Columbia University Press, 1985), iv; Allen and Gomery, *Film History*, 193–212; Robert C. Allen, "From Exhibition to Reception: Reflections on the Audience in Film History," *Screen* 31 (Winter 1990): 354–55; Douglas Gomery, "Thinking About Motion Picture Exhibition," *Velvet Light Trap* 25 (Spring 1990): 3–11; Douglas Gomery, *Shared Pleasures: A History of Movie Presentation in the United States* (Madison: University of Wisconsin Press, 1992), xix, 3; Ina Rae Hark, ed., *Exhibition: The Film Reader* (London and New York: Routledge, 2002).

34. See Fredric Jameson, *Postmodernism: Or the Cultural Logic of Late Capitalism* (Durham, NC: Duke University Press, 1997), 1–54.
35. See Peter Morris, *Embattled Shadows: A History of Canadian Cinema, 1895–1939* (Montreal and Kingston: McGill-Queen's University Press, 1978); Manjunath Pendakur, *Canadian Dreams and American Control: The Political Economy of the Canadian Film Industry* (Detroit: Wayne State University Press, 1990); Charles R. Acland, "National Dreams, International Encounters: The Formation of Canadian Film Culture in the 1930s," *Canadian Journal of Film Studies* 3 (Spring 1994): 3–26, "IMAX in Canadian Cinema: Geographic Transformation and Discourse of Nationhood," *Studies in Cultures, Organizations, and Societies* 3 (1997): 289–305, "Popular Film in Canada: Revisiting the Absent Audience," in *A Passion for Identity: Introduction to Canadian Studies*, 3rd. ed., ed. David Taras and Beverly Rasporich (Scarborough, ON: ITP Nelson, 1997), 281–96, "Cinemagoing and the Rise of the Megaplex," *Television and New Media* 1, no. 4 (2000): 375–402, and *Screen Traffic*, 1–22; and Paul S. Moore, "Nathan L. Nathanson Introduces Canadian Odeon: Producing National Competition in Film Exhibition," *Canadian Journal of Film Studies* 12, no. 2 (Fall 2003): 22–45, "Movie Palaces on Canadian Main Streets: Montréal, Toronto, and Vancouver," *Urban History Review* 32, no. 2 (Spring 2004): 3–20, and *Now Playing: Early Moviegoing and the Regulation of Fun* (New York: State University of New York Press, 2008). See also Kirwan Cox, "Canada's Theatrical Wars: The Indies vs. the Chains," *Cinema Canada* 56 (1979): 47–53; Ted Madger, *Canada's Hollywood: The Canadian State and Feature Films* (Toronto: University of Toronto Press, 1993), 62–66; and Charles Tepperman, "The Perfect Order of a Canadian Crowd: Cinema in Ottawa, 1894–1896" (MA thesis, Carleton University, 2000).
36. For a discussion of possible research strategies and sources, see Allen and Gomery, *Film History*, 38–42, 207–11.
37. We take our cue from such scholars as Nicholas Garnham, "Concepts of Culture: Public Policy and Cultural Industries," *Studies in Culture: An Introductory Reader*, ed. Ann Gray and Jim McGuigan (London: Arnold, 1997), 54–61. See also Manjunath Pendakur, *Canadian Dreams and American Control*; Mike Gasher, "The Myth of Meritocracy: Ignoring the Political Economy of the Canadian Film Industry," *Canadian Journal of Communication* 17 (1992): 371–78: and Jameson, *Postmodernism: Or the Cultural Logic of Late Capitalism*.
38. In analyzing the impact of architectural design on social function, we follow the example set by Herzog, "The Motion Picture Theatre and Film Exhibition, 1896–1931," v–viii; and Valentine, *The Show Starts on the Sidewalk*, 163–82. See also Mark Jancovich and Lucy Faire, with Sarah Stubbins, *The Place of the Audience: Cultural Geographics of Film Consumption* (London: British Film Institute), 67–80.
39. In this case, media texts as "texts" relate to and interact with a variety of practical, social activities. See, for example, Don H. Zimmerman and Melvin Pollner, "The Everyday World as a Phenomenon," *Understanding Everyday Life*, ed. Jack Douglas (Chicago: Aldinem 1970), 80–103: Alec McHoul, *Telling How Texts Talk*

(London: Routledge and Kegan Paul, 1982); Dorothy E. Smith, *The Everyday World as Problematic: A Feminist Sociology* (Toronto: University of Toronto Press, 1987); Ien Ang, *Desperately Seeking the Audience* (New York: Routledge, 1991); Janet Staiger, *Perverse Spectator: The Practice of Film Reception* (New York: New York University Press, 2000); Charles Acland, "Haunted Palace: Montréal's Rue St. Catherine and its Cinema Spaces," *Screen* 44, no. 2 (Summer 2003), 133–53; Acland, *Screen Traffic*, 50–51, 61–62, 67–69, 230.

Chapter 1: Pioneers

1. We base this discussion on a number of sources, including the website of *The History of Edison Motion Pictures: The Kinetoscope*, http://memory.loc.gov/ammem/edhtml/edmvhist.html, part of the Library of Congress's Inventing Entertainment educational website; Charles Musser, *The Emergence of Cinema: The American Screen to 1907* (New York: Charles Scribner's Sons, 1990); Steven Higgins and Charles Musser, curators, *Edison: The Invention of the Movies*, DVD, produced by Bret Wood (New York: Kino International Corp., 2005).
2. Gordon Hendricks, *The Edison Motion Picture Myth* (Berkeley: University of California Press, 1961), 11–12.
3. David Robinson, *From Peepshow to Palace: The Birth of American Film* (New York: Columbia University Press, 1997), 23.
4. Musser, *The Emergence of Cinema*, 63.
5. Marta Braun, *Picturing Time: The Work of Etienne-Jules Marey, 1830–1904* (Chicago: University of Chicago Press, 1992), 188.
6. See Hendricks, *The Edison Motion Picture Myth*, 48–53; Robinson, *From Peepshow to Palace*, 27.
7. Neil Baldwin, *Edison: Inventing the Century* (Chicago: University of Chicago Press, 2001), 208–9.
8. See Braun, *Picturing Time*, 189; Deac Rossell, *Living Pictures: The Origins of the Movies* (Albany: State University of New York Press, 1998), 21.
9. See Hendricks, *The Edison Motion Picture Myth*, 48; Robinson, *From Peepshow to Palace*, 27.
10. Braun, *Picturing Time*, 155; Paul C. Spehr, "Unaltered to Date: Developing 35 mm Film," in John Fullerton and Astrid Söderbergh Widding, eds., *Moving Images: From Edison to the Webcam* (Sydney: John Libbey, 2000), 23.
11. Musser, *The Emergence of Cinema*, 66.
12. Ibid.; Richard W. Burns, *Television: An International History of the Formative Years* (London: Institution of Engineers, 1998), 73; Baldwin, *Edison*, 208–9.
13. See Robinson, *From Peepshow to Palace*, 31–34.
14. Hendricks, *The Edison Motion Picture Myth*, 130–37.
15. See Gordon Hendricks, *The Kinetoscope: America's First Successful Motion Picture Exhibitor* (New York: Government Printing Office, 1966), 9–17; A. R. Fulton, "The Machine," in, *The American Film Industry*, rev. ed., ed. Tino Balio (Madison: University of Wisconsin Press, 1985), 38–41.

16. Robinson, *From Peepshow to Palace*, 38.
17. Hendricks, *The Kinetoscope*, 17–39.
18. These films included *Sandow* (6 March 1894), *Carmencita* (10–16 March 1894), *Leonard-Cushing Fight* (14 June 1894), *The Boxing Cats* (mid-July 1894), *Annie Oakley* (1 November 1894), and *Robetta and Doretto* (26 November 1894). See Hendricks, *The Kinetoscope*, 56–69; Douglas Gomery, *Shared Pleasures: A History of Movie Presentation in the United States* (Madison: University of Wisconsin Press, 1992), 5; Musser, *The Emergence of Cinema*, 86–156. Many of the moving pictures Dickson and Heise made for the Edison Manufacturing Company can be viewed at the Library of Congress's "Edison Motion Pictures" website, http://memory.loc.gov/ammem/edhtml/edmvhm.html.
19. Hendricks, *The Kinetoscope*, 35–36.
20. Ibid., 40–45.
21. See Library and Archives Canada, Thomas Edison fonds, MG 29-B8, R 7330-0-2-E; George C. Holland, "My Ottawa Memories," *Maclean's Magazine*, 1 June 1922, 22, 49; obituary notice, *Ottawa Journal*, 27 February 1923, 7; Terry Ramsaye, *A Million and One Nights: A History of the Motion Picture* (New York: Simon and Schuster, 1926; repr. London: Frank Cass, 1964), 87–88; Balio, *The American Film Industry*, 3–4; Hendricks, *The Kinetoscope*, 56, 64–65; Peter Morris, *Embattled Shadows: A History of Canadian Cinema, 1895–1939* (Montreal and Kingston: McGill-Queen's University Press, 1978), 6–7; Bruce S. Elliott, *The City Beyond: A History of Nepean, Birthplace of Canada's Capital, 1792–1990* (Nepean: City of Nepean, 1991), 182–90; Bruce S. Elliott, *Irish Migrants in the Canadas: A New Approach*, 2nd ed. (Montreal and Kingston: McGill-Queen's University Press, 2004), 90, 153, 362; Charles Tepperman, "The Perfect Order of a Canadian Crowd: Cinema in Ottawa, 1894–96" (MA thesis, Carleton University, 2000).
22. Morris, *Embattled Shadows*, 6–7.
23. See, for example, *Ottawa Citizen*, 2 November 1894, 8; 3 November 1894, 7; 2 November 1895, 7.
24. Musser, *The Emergence of Cinema*, 81–89.
25. Hendricks, *The Kinetoscope*, 126–43.
26. See Ramsaye, *A Million and One Nights*, 104–36, 290–98, 553–61; Fulton, "The Machine," 34–35. Prizefight films comprised an important genre during the first twenty years of cinema; the success of these films helped to modernize and legitimize the practice of boxing. See Dan Streible, *Fight Pictures: A History of Boxing and Early Cinema* (Berkeley: University of California Press, 2008).
27. Ramsaye, *A Million and One Nights*, 139–46, 193–201, 218–25.
28. See *New York Times*, 24 April 1896, 7; Ramsaye, *A Million and One Nights*, 226–34; Garth S. Jowett, *Film: The Democratic Art* (Boston: Little, Brown, 1976), 26–28; Balio, *The American Film Industry*, 5–7; Hendricks, *The Edison Motion Picture Myth*, 91, 97; Robert C. Allen, "The Movies in Vaudeville: Historical Context of the Movies as Popular Entertainment," in Balio, *The American Film Industry*, 67–69; Musser, *The Emergence of Cinema*, 109–31; and Gomery, *Shared Pleasures*, 2, 7–8.

29. *New York Times*, 24 April 1896, 5.
30. Ramsaye, *A Million and One Nights*, 262.
31. Balio, *The American Film Industry*, 5–6.
32. See Ramsaye, *A Million and One Nights*, 163–67, 318–21; Balio, *The American Film Industry*, 5–6, 7; Musser, *The Emergence of Cinema*, 135, 137–45; Richard Abel, ed., *Encyclopedia of Early Cinema* (London: Routledge, 2005), 398–99.
33. For a discussion of the first screening of motion pictures in Canada, see Gary Evans, "The First Films in Canada," *Cinema Canada* 26 (March 1976): 17; Peter Morris, "The First Films in Canada: The True Story (1)," *Cinema Canada* 29 (June–July 1976): 18–19; Léon Bélanger, *Les Ouimetoscopes: Léo-Ernest Ouimet et les débuts du cinéma québécois* (Montreal: VLB, 1978); Germain Lucasse, "Cultural Amnesia and the Birth of Film in Canada," *Cinema Canada* 108 (June 1984): 6–7; André Gaudreault and Germain Lucasse, "The Introduction of the Lumière Cinématographe in Canada," *Canadian Journal of Film Studies* 5, no. 2 (Fall 1996): 113–23; Robert W. Gutteridge, "The Vitascope" and the "Lumière Cinématographe," in *Magic Moments: The First 20 Years of Moving Pictures in Toronto, 1894–1914* (Toronto: Gutteridge-Pratley, 2000), 7–18, 23–32; Tepperman, "The Perfect Order of a Canadian Crowd."
34. See Balio, *The American Film Industry*, 7; Allen, "The Movies in Vaudeville," 69.
35. Balio, *The American Film Industry*, 7–8; Musser, *The Emergence of Cinema*, 176–77; Arthur Frank Wertheim, *Vaudeville Wars: How the Keith-Albee and Orpheum Circuits Controlled the Big Time and Its Performers* (New York: Palgrave Macmillan, 2006), 90.
36. See Ramsaye, *A Million and One Nights*, 210–17, 322–32; Balio, *The American Film Industry*, 10–13; Musser, *The Emergence of Cinema*, 145–57, 176–77; Abel, *Encyclopedia of Early Cinema*, 71–72.
37. Musser, *The Emergence of Cinema*, 176–77.
38. Ibid., 150–52.
39. See Ramsaye, *A Million and One Nights*, 453–58; Edward Wagenknecht, *The Movies in the Age of Innocence* (Norman: University of Oklahoma Press, 1962), 62; Robert M. Henderson, *D. W. Griffith: The Years at Biograph* (London: Secker and Warburg, 1970), 32–59; Richard Schickel, *D. W. Griffith: An American Life* (New York: Simon and Schuster, 1984), 90–93, 103–7, 112, 162, 203.
40. See Ramsaye, *A Million and One Nights*, 444–45, 518, 661; Balio, *The American Film Industry*, 141, 248; Abel, *Encyclopedia of Early Cinema*, 503–4.
41. Musser, *The Emergence of Cinema*, 488–89.
42. Douglas Gomery, *The Hollywood Studio System: A History* (London: British Film Institute, 2005), 8–9.
43. See Ramsaye, *A Million and One Nights*, 302–7, 386–88, 442–43, 519–22, 532–34, 652–63, 677–78; Balio, *The American Film Industry*, 108, 118, 134, 141; Musser, *The Emergence of Cinema*, 167–68, 288–93; Abel, 581.
44. See Musser, *The Emergence of Cinema*, 288–93; Ramsaye, *A Million and One Nights*, 286–88.
45. We base our discussion on Ramsaye, *A Million and One Nights*, 274–76, 330–32,

384–93; Charles Musser, "American Vitagraph: 1897–1901," *Cinema Journal* 22, no. 3 (Spring 1983): 4–46; Balio, *The American Film Industry*, 16, 22, 141, 149; Musser, *The Emergence of Cinema*, 253–55, 260–61, 271–74, 406–12, 466–74; Abel, *Encyclopedia of Early Cinema*, 679–81.

46. Musser, *The Emergence of Cinema*, 254–55.
47. See Ramsaye, *A Million and One Nights*, 269–72, 288–89, 377–81, 419–22; Balio, *The American Film Industry*, 16, 22, 25, 134, 141; Musser, *The Emergence of Cinema*, 36, 168–69; 177, 200–208, 234–36, 284–88, 329–33, 393–98; Abel, *Encyclopedia of Early Cinema*, 395–96.
48. Musser, *The Emergence of Cinema*, 167–70.
49. Encouraged by the great popularity of *The Corbett-Courtney Fight* (1894), a fight film featuring James Corbett, the reigning world heavyweight champion (he won the title when he defeated John L. Sullivan in 1892), and Peter Courtney, an up-and-coming boxer, in a contest of six rounds, Otway Latham, Grey Latham, Samuel Tilden, and Enoch Rector (who founded the Kinetoscope Exhibition Company with the express purpose of making boxing films for the Kinetoscope) signed a contract with Dan Stuart, a Dallas-based fight promoter, the objective of which was to film Corbett, the San Francisco-born world champion, and Robert Fitzsimmons, a Cornwall-born challenger, in a prizefight. For the history of the making of the *Corbett-Fitzsimmons Fight* (1897), see, for example, Ramsaye, *A Million and One Nights*, 281–89; Musser, *The Emergence of Cinema*, 193–200; and Streible, *Fight Pictures*, 52–67, 72–73.
50. Musser, *The Emergence of Cinema*, 478–84.
51. See Ramsaye, *A Million and One Nights*, 264; Lewis Jacobs, *The Rise of the American Film: A Critical History* (New York: Harcourt, Brace, 1939), 5–7; Albert F. McLean, *American Vaudeville as Ritual* (Lexington: University of Kentucky Press, 1965); Balio, *The American Film Industry*, 6–7; Allen, "The Movies in Vaudeville," 71–72; Gomery, *Shared Pleasures*, 13–14, 17.
52. Allen, "The Movies in Vaudeville," 80–81; Wertheim, *Vaudeville Wars*, xvii.
53. See Douglas Gilbert, *American Vaudeville: Its Life and Times* (New York: Dover Publications, 1940), 124–25, 146–55, 197–207, 212–17; McLean, *American Vaudeville as Ritual*, 19–22, 53–60, 110–11, 193–96, 201–10; Charles W. Stein, *American Vaudeville: As Seen by Its Contemporaries* (New York: Alfred Knopf, 1984), 3–5, 100–102, 124–30, 336; Robert W. Snyder, *The Voice of the City: Vaudeville and Popular Culture in New York* (New York: Oxford University Press, 1989), 26–29, 34–35, 73–81, 140–42; Anthony Slide, *The Encyclopedia of Vaudeville* (Westport and London: Greenwood Press), 278–80; Wertheim, *Vaudeville Wars*, 18–34, 72–75, 81–86.
54. See *New York Times*, 17 November 1940, 49; Gilbert, *American Vaudeville*, 210–15; McLean, *American Vaudeville as Ritual*, 21–24; Stein, *American Vaudeville*, 124–30, 312–14; Snyder, *The Voice of the City*, 37, 65, 73, 80, 158–59; Slide, *Encyclopedia of Vaudeville*, 30–31, 381–83; Wertheim, *Vaudeville Wars*, 35–66, 151–56, 197–208.
55. Wertheim, *Vaudeville Wars*, 206–7.

56. See *New York Times*, 13 February 1943, 11; Gilbert, *American Vaudeville*, 219, 313, 367; McLean, *American Vaudeville as Ritual*, 2; Theodore Saloutos, "Alexander Pantages, Theatre Magnate of the West," *Pacific Northwest Quarterly* 57 (October 1966): 140–41; Stein, *American Vaudeville*, 284; Slide, *Encyclopedia of Vaudeville*, 112; Wertheim, *Vaudeville Wars*, 156.
57. See *New York Times*, 18 February 1936, 23; Gilbert, *American Vaudeville*, 218–20, 367; McLean, *American Vaudeville as Ritual*, 2; Saloutos, "Alexander Pantages," 142–43; Stein, *American Vaudeville*, 125–30; Slide, *Encyclopedia of Vaudeville*, 387–90; Wertheim, *Vaudeville Wars*, 244–46, 248, 277.
58. Allen, "The Movies in Vaudeville," 62, 71; Gomery, *Shared Pleasures*, 14.
59. See Allen, "The Movies in Vaudeville," 71–76.
60. Ibid., 71–72; Wertheim, *Vaudeville Wars*, 56.
61. Gomery, *Shared Pleasures*, 7–8.
62. Ibid., 9.

Chapter 2: Introducing Cinema to Prairie Canada

1. Charles Musser, *The Emergence of Cinema: The American Screen to 1907* (New York: Charles Scribner's Sons, 1990), 122–32.
2. Charles Musser, "Introducing Cinema to the American Public: The Vitascope in the United States, 1896–97," in *Moviegoing in America: A Sourcebook in the History of Film Exhibition*, ed. Gregory A. Waller (Malden, MA: Blackwell, 2002), 13–26.
3. For biographical information on Hardie and Wall, see, for example, *Manitoba Free Press*, 17 February 1892, 7; 16 April 1892, 3; 25 April 1892, 8; 1 June 1895, 7.
4. See W. L. Morton, *Manitoba: A History*. 2nd ed. (Toronto: University of Toronto Press, 1967), 171–72; Alan F. J. Artibise, *Winnipeg: A Social History of Urban Growth, 1874–1914* (Montreal and Kingston: McGill-Queen's University Press, 1975), 14–16; Alan F. J. Artibise, *Winnipeg: An Illustrated History* (Toronto: James Lorimer, and Ottawa: National Museum of Man, 1977), 16–18; George A. Nader, *Cities of Canada*, 2 vols. (Toronto: MacMillan of Canada, 1975–76), vol. 2, 266–67, 286; Gerald Friesen, *The Canadian Prairies: A History* (Toronto: University of Toronto Press, 1984), 274–76.
5. Artibise, *Winnipeg: A Social History of Urban Growth, 1874–1914*, 93–94; and *Winnipeg: An Illustrated History*, 143–44.
6. Nader, *Cities of Canada*, 270–71.
7. Morton, *Manitoba*, 192–93.
8. J. S. Woodsworth, quoted in Artibise, *Winnipeg: An Illustrated History*, 52.
9. See, for example, *Winnipeg Tribune*, 18 July 1896, 4; 20 July 1896, 5; 23 July 1896, 5; 25 July 1896, 2.
10. See *Manitoba Free Press*, 22 July 1896, 5; *Winnipeg Tribune*, 24 July 1896, 4, 5.
11. *Manitoba Free Press*, 25 July 1896, 4; 27 July 1896, 2; *Winnipeg Tribune*, 27 July 1896, 4.
12. *Winnipeg Tribune*, 18 July 1896, 4; 20 July 1896, 5; and 24 July 1896, 5.

13. Nader, *Cities of Canada*, 163–89; John H. Taylor, *Ottawa: An Illustrated History* (Toronto: James Lorimer, and Ottawa: Canadian Museum of Civilization, 1986), 75–117.
14. See *Ottawa Journal*, 28 June 1938, 1, 12; Taylor, *Ottawa*, 75–81; Charles Tepperman, "The Perfect Order of a Canadian Crowd: Cinema in Ottawa, 1894–1896" (MA thesis, Carleton University, 2000), 12–35.
15. See, for example, Peter Morris, *Embattled Shadows: A History of Canadian Cinema, 1859–1939* (Montreal and Kingston: McGill-Queen's University Press, 1978), 5–6; Musser, *The Emergence of Cinema*, 81–82; Hilary McLaughlin, "Inventor Brought Light to Ottawa: Thomas Ahearn," *Ottawa Citizen*, 20 September 1999, D3; Tepperman, "The Perfect Order of a Canadian Crowd," 16–18.
16. Tepperman, "The Perfect Order of a Canadian Crowd," 14–18.
17. Ibid., 16–18.
18. See, for example, *Ottawa Journal*, 18 July 1896, 7; 23 July 1896, 7; 24 July 1896, 5; 25 July 1896, 7.
19. See, for example, *Ottawa Journal*, 5 November 1895, 8; 1 May 1896, 5; 31 May 1896, 6; 18 July 1896, 7; 22 July 1896, 1; *Ottawa Free Press*, 15 July 1896, 3; 25 July 1896, 1; 1 August 1896, 1. West End Park became Victoria Park in 1897 in honour of Queen Victoria's Diamond Jubilee.
20. Tepperman, "The Perfect Order of a Canadian Crowd," 112–16.
21. See, for example, *Canadian Film Weekly* (hereafter cited as CFW), 26 July 1944, 5.
22. *Ottawa Journal*, 22 July 1896, 8.
23. See Tepperman, "The Perfect Order of a Canadian Crowd," 101–11.
24. Andrew declared that their rental was low. Quoted in Tepperman, "The Perfect Order of a Canadian Crowd," 110–11. See Morris, *Embattled Shadows*, 3, 243–44, 275; Paul S. Moore, *Now Playing: Early Moviegoing and the Regulation of Fun* (New York: State University of New York Press, 2008), 21–22, 85, 94–96.
25. Morton, *Manitoba*, 201–3, 239; G. F. Barker, *Brandon: A City, 1881–1961* (Brandon: Privately Published, 1977), 1–24; Pierre Berton, *The Last Spike: The Great Railway, 1881–1885* (Toronto: McClelland and Stewart, 1971), 23–32; T. S. Mitchell, "Introduction," in *Brandon: A Prospect of a City*, ed. Mary Hume (Brandon: City of Brandon, 1981), 13–25; *Brandon: An Architectural Walking Tour* (Winnipeg: Department of Cultural Affairs and Historical Resources, 1982); Friesen, *The Canadian Prairies*, 321–22; Gary D. Palmer, *The Way We Were: A Look at Life in Brandon as It Used to Be* (Brandon: Brandon Books, 1997), 1–6, 70–71.
26. *The Canadian Year Book 1912* (Ottawa: King's Printer, 1913), 9.
27. *Brandon in the Year 1913* (Brandon: Brandon Board of Trade, 1913), 21–23.
28. We base our discussion on *Manitoba Free Press*, 25 July 1896, 7; 30 July 1896, 2; 31 July 1896, 2; *Winnipeg Tribune*, 28 July 1896, 1; 29 July 1896, 1; 30 July 1896, 1; and *Brandon Sun*, 30 July 1896, 5; 6 August 1896, 4.
29. See *Brandon Sun*, 30 July 1896, 5.
30. *Manitoba Free Press*, 31 July 1896, 2; *Brandon in the Year 1913*, 15–16.
31. *Winnipeg Tribune*, 29 July 1896, 1.
32. *Brandon Sun*, 30 July 1896, 5.

33. For a discussion of the premiere of the Vitascope in Toronto, Halifax, and Montréal, see, for example, *Toronto World*, 22 August 1896, 5; *Globe and Empire*, 22 July 1933, 1, 4; Morris, *Embattled Shadows*, 3–14; Andrew Johnson, "The History of Film Exhibition in Toronto, 1894 to 1932" (MA thesis, University of Toronto, 1982), 1–16; Robert W. Gutteridge, *Magic Moments: The First 20 Years of Moving Pictures in Toronto, 1894–1914* (Toronto: Gutteridge-Pratley, 2000), 7–18; Paul S. Moore, *Now Playing: Early Moviegoing and the Regulation of Fun* (New York: State University of New York Press, 2008), 21–22, 85, 94–96.
34. Morris, *Embattled Shadows*, 243–44, 275; Musser, *The Emergence of Cinema*, 81, 113, 130; Musser, "Introducing Cinema to the American Public," 21–25.
35. Morris, *Embattled Shadows*, 8, 10, 244; Musser, *The Emergence of Cinema*, 167; Gutteridge, *Magic Moments*, 41–44.
36. See *Toronto World*, 14 November 1896, 2; 5 December 1896, 2; 8 December 1896, 3; 10 December 1896, 5; 25 December 1896, 3, 4.
37. *Manitoba Free Press*, 17 May 1897, 3; 24 May 1897, 8; 26 May 1897, 5.
38. See Charles Musser, *Edison Motion Pictures, 1890–1900: An Annotated Filmography* (New York: Smithsonian Institution Press, 1997), 206, 232, 257.
39. See *Regina Leader*, 16 February 1886, 2–3; 19 August 1897, 8; May Neal, "First Town Hall Returned Handsome Profit," *Regina Leader-Post*, 18 June 1963, Jubilee Edition, first section, 7–8; "Dewdney Opened the First Town Hall in 1886," *Regina Leader-Post*, 11 June 1976, 16; P. B. O'Neill, "Regina's Golden Age of Theatre: Her Playhouses and Players," *Saskatchewan History* 28, no. (1975): 29–37; E. Ross Stuart, *The History of Prairie Theatre* (Toronto: Simon and Pierre, 1984), 34–35.
40. See *Regina Leader*, 9 February 1896, 1; 16 February 1886, 2–3; *Regina Leader-Post*, 18 June 1963, Jubilee Ed., first sec., 16; 11 June 1976, 16.
41. Berton, *The Last Spike*, 113–25; Nader, *Cities of Canada*, 296–313; J. William Brennan, *Regina: An Illustrated History* (Toronto: James Lorimer, and Ottawa: Canadian Museum of Civilization, 1989), 21–54.
42. *Regina Leader*, 19 August 1897, 8.
43. *Manitoba Free Press*, 11 September 1897, 8; 15 September 1897, 2.
44. See Pierre Véronneau, Peter Morris, and Piers Handling, who claim in their article, "The History of Film in Canada," that J. S. Freer, an Oxfordshire-born newspaper reporter, produced the very first motion pictures in Canada. With his family, Freer settled in the Brandon Hills district of Manitoba in 1887 and in 1888 made films depicting life on the Canadian prairies. Under the auspices of the CPR, he toured Great Britain in 1898–99 and in 1902, screening the films and lecturing on the attractiveness of life in the prairie West. Available on *The Canadian Encyclopedia* website, http://thecanadianencyclopedia.com/articles/film-history. See also "James S. Freer, Pioneer Manitoban and Veteran *Free Press* Employee, Dies," *Winnipeg Free Press*, 23 December 1933, 1, 9; Gene Walz, "100 Years of Moviemaking," *Winnipeg Real Estate News*, 28 November 1997, 3.
45. *Manitoba Free Press*, 11 September 1897, 8.
46. *Edmonton Bulletin*, 18 October 1897, 1.
47. Clifford Sifton, the new minister of the interior, proclaimed that settling the West

was a national enterprise, akin to building an all-Canadian transportation system. The first train crossed the North Saskatchewan River on 20 October 1902. See *Edmonton Bulletin*, 23 December 1897, 2; Friesen, *The Canadian Prairies*, 217–18, 245–46; J. G. MacGregor, *Edmonton: A History*, 2nd ed. (Edmonton: Hurtig, 1975), 107–25.

48. We base our discussion on John Orrell, *Fallen Empires: The Lost Theatres of Edmonton* (Edmonton: NeWest, 1981), 8, 11–27; Stuart, *The History of Prairie Theatre*, 40–42; Lawrence Herzog, "Home to a Sheriff, a Builder, and a Vaudeville King," *Our Heritage* 21, no. 11 (20 March 2003), and "The Stages That Built Edmonton Theatre," *Our Heritage* 25, no. 20 (8 March 2007).
49. Orrell, *Fallen Empires*, 11–13; Stuart, *The History of Prairie Theatre*, 40–43; David Mittelstadt, *Foundations of Justice: Alberta's Historic Courthouses* (Calgary: University of Calgary Press, 2005), 75–78.
50. See *Edmonton Bulletin*, 9 November 1893, 4; 28 December 1893, 4; 20 December 1894, 4; 3 February 1896, 4.
51. See *Nebraska State Journal*, 8 April 1894, 13; *Edmonton Bulletin*, 2 August 1894, 4; Orrell, *Fallen Empires*, 18.
52. *Edmonton Bulletin*, 18 October 1897, 1.
53. *Calgary Herald*, 16 October 1897, 3.
54. James G. MacGregor, *A History of Alberta* (Edmonton: Hurtig, 1972), 134–39; Max Foran, *Calgary: An Illustrated History* (Toronto: James Lorimer, and Ottawa: National Museum of Man, 1978), 45; Nader, *Cities of Canada*, 333–53; Howard Palmer and Tamara Palmer, *Alberta: A New History* (Edmonton: Hurtig, 1990), 50–51.
55. See, for example, *Calgary Herald*, 21 March 1884, 2; Alan F. J. Artibise, "Boosterism and the Development of Prairie Cities, 1871–1913," in *The Prairie West*, 2nd ed., ed. R. Douglas Francis and Howard Palmer (Edmonton: University of Alberta Press, 1992), 515–43.
56. Foran, *Calgary*, 30.
57. Ibid., 36, 40; Palmer and Palmer, *Alberta*, 56.
58. See Stuart, *The History of Prairie Theatre*, 47–48;
59. See the obituary notice, *Calgary Herald*, 4 April 1925, 1, 28; Henry C. Klassen, *Eye on the Future: Business People in Calgary and the Bow Valley, 1870–1900* (Calgary: Calgary University Press, 2002), 247–51; Warren M. Elofson, "William Charles Roper Hull," in *Dictionary of Canadian Biography*, http://biographi.ca/009004-119.01-e.php?id_nbr=8203; Donald B. Smith, *Calgary's Grand Story: The Making of a Prairie Metropolis from the Viewpoint of Two Heritage Buildings* (Calgary: University of Calgary Press, 2005), 275.
60. The management marked the occasion by organizing a school children's music festival, directed by Frank B. Fenwick, a local music teacher. Commentators admired the building and praised the children for their performances. See *Calgary Herald*, 13 March 1893, 4; 23 March 1893, 4.
61. See, for example, *Calgary Herald*, 16 October 1897, 3.
62. See *Calgary Herald*, 26 October 1897, 1.

63. Presumably, these films included *Fire Rescue Scene* (1894), showing smoke and the effects of uniformed men in action; *The Burning Stable* (1896), showing a barn in flames, from which four horses and a burning wagon are rescued by firemen and stable hands; *Black Diamond Express, No. 1* (1896), showing the locomotive bowling along at a speed exceeding 70 mph; and *Cavalry Passing in Review* (1897), a troop of American cavalry coming toward the camera in columns of four, all of which were produced by the Edison Manufacturing Co. See Musser, *Edison Motion Pictures*, 163, 251, 259–60, 286–87. A. W. Paul produced *Queen Victoria's Jubilee* (1897), showing the procession passing through Pall Mall, Westminster, London.
64. *Calgary Herald*, 27 October 1897, 4.
65. *Saskatoon Phoenix,* 2 October 1904, 5.
66. See "The Saskatoon District," *Saskatoon Phoenix*, 23 October 1903, 1, 4, 8; Nader, *Cities of Canada*, 314–32; Don Kerr and Stan Hanson, *Saskatoon: The First Half-Century* (Edmonton: NeWest, 1982), 37–68.
67. Kerr and Hanson, *Saskatoon*, 45–54; John Gilpin, "The Dark Side of the 'Saskatoon Spirit': James F. Cairns and Power, Street Railway, and Land Development in Saskatoon, 1908–1914," *Saskatchewan History* 45, no. 2 (1993): 15–23; Don Cameron Kerr, "James Frederick Cairns," *Dictionary of Canadian Biography Online*, http://www.biographi.ca/009004-119.01-e.php?&id_nbr=8056.
68. Kerr and Hanson, *Saskatoon*, 274–75.
69. Nader, *Cities of Canada*, 314–17.
70. William DeLainey and William A. S. Sarjeant, *Saskatoon: The Growth of a City* (Saskatoon: Saskatoon Environmental Society, 1974), 23.
71. Nader, *Cities of Canada*, 317.
72. See *Saskatoon Phoenix*, 2 October 1903, 1, 4, 8; 2 October 1903, 5.
73. *Saskatoon Phoenix*, 23 October 1903, 7.
74. Travelling exhibitors brought movies to new audiences—and energized the cinema during the early years. See Morris, *Embattled Shadows*, 11–18; Douglas Gomery, *Shared Pleasures: A History of Movie Presentation in the United States* (Madison: University of Wisconsin Press, 1992), 11; Pierre Véronneau, "The Creation of a Film Culture by Travelling Exhibitors in Rural Québec Prior to World War II," *Film History* 6, no. 2 (1994): 250–61.
75. See Musser, *The Emergence of Cinema*, 444–47; Gomery, *Shared Pleasures*, 7–18.
76. Kathryn H. Fuller, *At the Picture Show: Small-Town Audiences and the Creation of Movie Fan Culture* (Washington, DC: Smithsonian Institution Press, 1996), 7.
77. Gomery, *Shared Pleasures*, 11.
78. See Morris, *Embattled Shadows*, 11–14; Fuller, *At the Picture Show*, 25–26.
79. See *Canadian Moving Picture Digest* (hereafter cited as CMPD), 2 March 1940, 3; Hye Bossin, "Canada and the Film: The Story of the Canadian Motion Picture Industry," *Canadian Film Weekly Year Book of the Canadian Motion Picture Industry, 1951* (Toronto: Film Publications of Canada, 1951), 27; CFW, 8 October 1952, 8, and 24 April 1963, 4–5; *Manitoba Free Press*, 27 February 1960, 19–20; F. W. Ackery, *Fifty Years in Theatre Row* (Vancouver: Hancock House, 1980), 55; *Vancouver Sun*, 15 December 1953, 16; Hilary Russell, "All That Glitters: A Memorial

to Ottawa's Capitol Theatre and its Predecessors," *Canadian Historic Sites: Occasional Papers in Archaeology and History*, no. 13 (Ottawa: Parks Canada, National Parks, and Sites Branches, 1975), 12–14; Morris, *Embattled Shadows*, 14–17.

80. See *Calgary Albertan*, 21 September 1963, 12.
81. See CMPD, 1 May 1940, 10; *Vancouver Sun*, 15 December 1953, 16; Ackery, *Fifty Years in Theatre Row*, 55.
82. Quoted in *Vancouver Sun*, 15 December 1953, 16.
83. See Russell, "All That Glitters," 12–13. See also *Moving Picture World* (hereafter cited as *MPW*), 15 July 1916, 368–69.
84. Quoted in CMPD, 1 May 1940, 11.
85. Russell, "All That Glitters," 4.
86. Morris, *Embattled Shadows*, 19.
87. See CMPD, 1 May 1940, 11; Russell, "All That Glitters," 17; Morris, *Embattled Shadows*, 19.
88. Quoted in Terry Ramsaye, *A Million and One Nights: A History of the Motion Picture* (New York: Simon Schuster, 1926; repr. London: Frank Cass, 1964), 425.
89. See CFW, 26 April 1963, 4; Ackery, *Fifty Years in Theatre Row*, 56.
90. Russell, "All That Glitters," 16; Morris, *Embattled Shadows*, 19.
91. CFW, 24 April 1963, 4–5; see also CMPD, 2 March 1940, 3.
92. Ibid.
93. See CMPD, 1 May 1940, 11; 3 January 1953, 3; Ackery, *Fifty Years in Theatre Row*, 57.
94. We base our discussion of block booking and the development of First National on Howard T. Lewis, *The Motion Picture Industry* (New York: D. Van Nostrand, 1933), 142–80; Lewis Jacobs, *The Rise of the American Film: A Critical History* (New York: Harcourt, Brace, 1939), 165–67; Tino Balio, ed., *The American Film Industry*. rev. ed. (Madison: University of Wisconsin Press, 1985), 120–21; Neal Gabler, *An Empire of their Own: How the Jews Invented Hollywood* (New York: Crown, 1988), 11–46; Richard Koszarski, *An Evening's Entertainment: The Age of the Silent Feature Picture, 1915–1928* (New York: Charles Scribner's Sons, 1990), 69–80.
95. Quoted in *Vancouver Sun*, 15 December 1953, 16.
96. Jacobs, *The Rise of the American Film*, 8; Balio, *The American Film Industry*, 16–17.
97. See Balio, *The American Film Industry*,17; Musser, *The Emergence of Cinema*, 365–68; Fuller, *At the Picture Show*, 20–24.

Chapter 3: Movie Exhibition During the Nickelodeon Era

1. Lewis Jacobs, *The Rise of the American Film: A Critical History* (New York: Harcourt, Brace, 1939), 52–55.
2. For critical accounts of the business dynamics at work during the "nickelodeon" period, see Robert C. Allen, "Vaudeville and Film, 1895–1915: A Study in Media Interaction" (PhD diss., University of Iowa, 1977), 192–273; Robert C. Allen, "The Movies in Vaudeville: Historical Context of the Movies as Popular Entertainment," and Russell Merritt, "Nickelodeon Theatres, 1905–1914: Building an Audience for the Movies," in *The American Film Industry*. rev. ed., ed. Tino

Balio (Madison: University of Wisconsin Press, 1985), 57–78 and 83–102 respectively; Charles Musser, *The Emergence of Cinema: The American Screen to 1907* (New York: Charles Scribner's Sons, 1990), 417–89; Eileen Bowser, *The Transformation of Cinema, 1907–1915* (New York: Charles Scribner's Sons, 1990), 1–20, 37–40, 121–36; Douglas Gomery, *Shared Pleasures: A History of Movie Presentation in the United States* (Madison: University of Wisconsin Press, 1992), 18–23.

3. See *Moving Picture World* (hereafter cited as MPW), 15 July 1916, 405.
4. Robert C. Allen and Douglas Gomery, *Film History: Theory and Practice* (New York: Alfred A. Knopf, 1985), 202–3; Gregory A. Waller, *Main Street Amusements: Movies and Commercial Entertainment in a Southern City, 1896–1930* (Washington, DC: Smithsonian Institution Press, 1995), 69.
5. See MPW, 4 May 1907, 140; *Saturday Evening Post*, 23 November 1907, 10–11, 38; Merritt, "Nickelodeon Theatres, 1905–1914," 85–86.
6. Harold M. Faulkner, *Decline of Laissez Faire, 1897–1917* (New York: Rinehart and Co., 1951), 22; Allen, "Vaudeville and Film, 1895–1915," 205; Allen, "The Movies in Vaudeville," 77–78; Roy Rosenzweig, *Eight Hours for What We Will: Workers and Leisure in an Industrial City, 1870–1920* (New York: Cambridge University Press, 1983), 194–95.
7. Sebastian de Grazia, *Of Time, Work, and Leisure* (New York: Twentieth Century Fund, 1962), 441.
8. John Higham, *Strangers in the Land: Patterns of American Nativism* (New York: Athenaeum, 1973), 110, 114; Allen, "Vaudeville and Film, 1895–1915," 206; Merritt, "Nickelodeon Theatres, 1905–1914," 86–87.
9. Rosenzweig, *Eight Hours for What We Will*, 194–95.
10. Hilary Russell, "All That Glitters: A Memorial to Ottawa's Capital Theatre and its Predecessors," *Canadian Historic Sites: Occasional Papers in Archaeology and History*, no. 13 (Ottawa: Parks Canada, National Parks and Sites Branch, 1975), 21–22; Charlotte Herzog, "The Motion Picture Theatre and Film Exhibition, 1896–1932" (PhD diss., Northwestern University, 1980), 35.
11. For a discussion of the architectural design and the social function of the movie theatre, see MPW, 11 April 1911, 762; Benjamin B. Hampton, *A History of the Movies* (New York: Covici, Friede, 1931); repr. and retitled *History of the American Film Industry* (New York: Dover, 1970), 45; Russell, "All That Glitters," 14–16; Jacobs, *The Rise of the American Film*, 54–55; Herzog, "The Motion Picture Theatre and Film Exhibition," 30–43, 54–66, 103–30; Maggie Valentine, *The Show Starts on the Sidewalk: An Architectural History of the Movie Theatre, Starring S. Charles Lee* (New Haven, CT: Yale University Press, 1994), 20–21.
12. See MPW, 22 October 1910, 918–19.
13. MPW, 5 November 1910, 1051.
14. See *Saturday Evening Post*, 23 November 1907, 10–11; Jacobs, *The Rise of the American Film*, 55–56; Carl Laemmle, "This Business of Motion Pictures," *Saturday Evening Post*, 27 August 1927, 10–11, 130, 133–34, 136; 3 September 1927, 18–19, 86, 88, 91–92; 10 September 1927, 28–29, 94, 97, 103; repr., ed. Richard

Koszarski, in *Film History* 3, no. 1 (1989): 51–52; Abel Green and Joe Laurie, Jr., *Show Biz: From Vaudeville to Video* (New York: Henry Holt, 1951), 30–32.

15. See MPW, 19 December 1925, 710–11.
16. See *Harper's Weekly*, 24 August 1907, 1246–47; Terry Ramsaye, *One Million and One Nights: A History of the Motion Picture* (New York: Simon and Schuster, 1926; repr. London: Frank Cass, 1964), 267–68; Jacobs, *The Rise of the American Film*, 56; Allen, "Vaudeville and Film, 1895–1915," 56–57; Herzog, "The Motion Picture Theatre and Film Exhibition, 1896–1932," 24–35: Merritt, "Nickelodeon Theatres, 1905–1914," 85–86; Kathryn M. Fuller, *At the Picture Show: Small-Town Audiences and the Creation of Movie Fan Culture* (Washington, DC: Smithsonian Institution Press, 1996), 64–65.
17. Allen, "Vaudeville and Film, 1895–1915," 244–45; Allen, "The Movies in Vaudeville," 79–80.
18. By 1907, many exhibitors were thinking that the storefront theatre might not be such a suitable venue after all. For a sampling of the early debates, see "The Fire Risk," *MPW*, 2 November 1907, 555; Joseph Medill Patterson, "The Nickelodeons," *MPW*, 11 January 1908, 21–22; William B. Ely, "The Safety of Moving Picture Theatres," *MPW*, 2 May 1908, 390–92; W. Stephen Bush, "The Coming Ten and Twenty Cent Moving Picture Theatre," *MPW*, 29 August 1908, 152–53; F. H. Richardson, "What Is the Future?" *MPW*, 28 August 1909, 280; Robert Grau, "The Theatre of Cinematography," *MPW*, 29 April 1911, 936; "The Motion Picture Theatre," *Architecture and Building*, May 1911, 319–22; George Rockhill Craw, "Swelling the Box Office Receipts," *MPW*, 6 May 1911, 998–99; 13 May 1911, 1059–60; 20 May 1911, 1117; and Epes Winthrop Sargent, "Buying a Theatre," *MPW*, 12 March 1912, 1047. See also Herzog, "The Motion Picture Theatre and Film Exhibition, 1896–1932," 17, 43, 52, 59. Eventually, as the number of purpose-built theatres increased, exhibitors (as well as legislators) across North America took their cue from the legislators who revised the Chicago Building Code of March 1911 and the New York City Building Code of August 1913 with a view to applying improved standards of seating, ventilation, and sanitation to these new buildings.
19. See *MPW*, 29 August 1909, 152–53; 9 October 1909, 494; 8 January 1910, 13; 29 July 1911, 199.
20. See Roxy Rothafel, *MPW*, 12 February 1910, 202–3; 26 February 1910, 289; 12 March 1910, 373; 9 April 1910, 16 April 1910, 593; 15 November 1913, 714–15; 20 December 1913, 1041–42. He refined his position in subsequent publications. Rothafel went on to manage other opulent picture palaces in New York, including the Strand (1914), the Rialto (1916), the Rivoli (1917), the Capitol (1919), and the Roxy (1927), where he offered the public elaborate, multimedia stage presentations. We base our discussion on a number of sources, including Ramsaye, *A Million and One Nights*, 674–77, 723–35; obituary notice, *New York Times*, 14 January 1936, 21; Ben Hall, *The Best Remaining Seats: The Story of the Golden Age of the Movie Palace* (New York: Bramhall House, 1961), 26–36, 53–55, 80–88; Herzog, "The Motion Picture Theatre and Film Exhibition, 1896–1932," 163–85; Bowser, *The*

Transformation of Cinema, 131–32; Ross Melnick, "Rethinking Rothafel: Roxy's Forgotten Legacy," *The Moving Image* 3, no. 2 (Fall 2003): 62–95.

21. See *Variety*, 13 March 1913, 19; 20 June 1913, 8. For an analysis of the attempts of theatre managers to control the behaviour of (working-class) patrons, see Rosenzweig, *Eight Hours for What We Will*, 210–12; Waller, *Main Street Amusements*, 40, 54, 85, 88, 150, 158; Fuller, *At the Picture Show*, 98–99.
22. See *Canadian Film Weekly* (hereafter cited as CFW), 28 October 1942, 2; CFW, 1 May 1963, 4; *Calgary Albertan*, 21 September 1963, 13; Kirwan Cox, "The Rise and Fall of the Allens: The War for Canada's Movie Theatres," *Lonergan Review* 6 (2000): 44.
23. Floyd S. Chalmers, "The Story of the Allens," *Maclean's*, 15 February 1920, 14.
24. Actually, three Russian-born Allens settled in the United States during the 1880s: Barney, his brother Philip and his wife, Leona, who settled in Rochester, New York, and a second brother, who settled in the West. Apparently, the latter vanished without a word of explanation (personal communication, Mrs. Ethel Allen, 28 November 2003).
25. Cox, "The Rise and Fall of the Allens," 45.
26. See CFW, 13 July 1960, 6.
27. Chalmers, "The Story of the Allens," 14.
28. See Lary May, *Screening Out the Past: The Birth of Mass Culture and the Motion Picture Industry* (Chicago: Chicago University Press, 1980), 169–73; Neal Gabler, *An Empire of their Own: How the Jews Invented Hollywood* (New York: Crown Publishers, 1988), 5–6.
29. George A. Nader, *Cities of Canada*, 2 vols. (Toronto: Macmillan of Canada, 1975–76), vol. 2, 250; *Brantford Expositor*, 12 September 1908, 1; CFW, 28 October 1942, 2; Chalmers, "The Story of the Allens," 14.
30. We base this discussion on Hye Bossin, "Canada and the Film," *Yearbook of the Canadian Motion Picture Industry* (Toronto: Film Publications of Canada, 1951), 21–42; Russell, "All That Glitters," 17–21; Peter Morris, *Embattled Shadows: A History of Canadian Cinema, 1895–1939* (Montreal and Kingston: McGill-Queen's University Press, 1978), 21; Robert W. Gutteridge, *Magic Moments: The First Twenty Years of Moving Pictures in Toronto, 1894–1914* (Toronto: Gutteridge-Pratley, 2000), 37, 124, 128–30, 160, 208; Paul S. Moore, *Now Playing: Early Moviegoing and the Regulation of Fun* (New York: State University of New York Press, 2008), 34, 76–83, 87–97.
31. Quoted in Chalmers, "The Story of the Allens," 14.
32. See *Canadian Moving Picture Digest* (hereafter cited as CMPD), 1 May 1940, 8.
33. Quoted in Chalmers, "The Story of the Allens," 14.
34. Cox, "The Rise and Fall of the Allens," 46–47.
35. Ibid., 47.
36. *Brantford Expositor*, 4 March 1915, 1; Philip Dombowsky, "Emmanuel Briffa Revisited" (MA thesis, Concordia University, 1995), 30.
37. *Brantford Expositor*, 23 June 1960, 18.
38. See CMPD, 1 May 1940, 8; CFW, 13 July 1960, 6.

39. Commentators have debated the effect movies may or may not have on young people since films were first screened. Many middle-class vice crusaders regarded the movies with horror and struggled to regulate the new medium. The editorial board of *Chicago Daily Tribune* (13 April 1907) threw its weight against movies, denouncing nickelodeons as firetraps and movies as "corrupters" of children. See MPW, 18 September 1909, 369; 18 September 1909, 369; Garth S. Jowett, *Film: The Democratic Art* (Boston: Little, Brown, 1976), 108–15.
40. Quoted in Cox, "The Rise and Fall of the Allens," 48–49.
41. See CMPD, 3 January 1953, 11; CFW, 13 July 1960, 6; Morris, *Embattled Shadows*, 22; Cox, "The Rise and Fall of the Allens," 48. Interestingly, W. M. Gladish, in MPW for 15 September 1916, 410–11, describes the Allen brothers as "the oldest exchangemen" in the business. During 1910–11, Laemmle placed (in MPW) advertisements for the Universal Film Manufacturing Company announcing that the Canadian Film Exchange was the sole agent for the entire Universal Program, thereby ensuring that exhibitors across Canada would get "the finest films and the finest service ever known to the trade." See, for example, the issues for 7 September 1910, 555; 17 September 1910, 611; 3 December 1910, 1295; 24 December 1910, 1447; 20 May 1911, 1107; and 15 July 1911, 21.
42. Cox, "The Rise and Fall of the Allens," 44.
43. Laemmle led the independent producers' struggle against Edison's Trust. See MPW, 17 April 1909, 472–73; 5 June 1909, 750; 10 July 1909, 48; 23 October 1909, 563; and 27 November 1909, 764. For a discussion of his business strategies, see Laemmle, "This Business of Motion Pictures," 51–52; "Carl Laemmle Sr., Film Pioneer, Dies," *New York Times*, 25 September 1939, 19; Gabler, *An Empire of their Own*, 47–78; Douglas Gomery, *The Hollywood Studio System: A History* (London: British Film Institute, 2005), 57–60, 205–6.
44. Ramsaye, *A Million and One Nights*, 495–97.
45. It has been suggested that, by 1925, the Soviet Union, a country of just under 147 million (according to the 1926–27 census), boasted about 2,000 movie theatres. See Paxton Hibben, "The Movies in Russia," *Nation*, 11 November 1925, 539–40; CFW, 13 July 1960, 6.
46. See *Brantford Expositor*, 22 June 1910, 7.
47. Quoted in MPW, 18 December 1909, 877.
48. See *Calgary News-Telegram*, 15 May 1911, 1.
49. See CFW, 13 July 1960, 6; CFW, 1 May 1963, 4.
50. See Manjunath Pendakur, *Canadian Dreams and American Control: The Political Economy of the Canadian Film Industry* (Detroit: Wayne State University Press, 1990), 53; Cox, "The Rise and Fall of the Allens," 50–52.
51. Ramsaye, *A Million and One Nights*, 580–84.
52. Ibid., 612. Via a number of mergers in 1915, Laemmle formed an ensemble of studios in the San Fernando Valley in southern California called Universal City. A leading studio during the 1920s and 1930s, Universal produced many horror films, including James Whale's *Frankenstein* (1931) and Tod Browning's *Dracula* (1931). Universal handled the films of such directors as Erich von Stroheim and

such stars as Lon Chaney and Rudolph Valentino. See Gomery, *The Hollywood Studio System*, 57–60.

53. See MPW, 27 August 1910, 469.
54. See Gerald Friesen, *The Canadian Prairies: A History* (Toronto: University of Toronto Press, 1984), 186–90; Howard Palmer and Tamara Palmer, *Alberta: A New History* (Edmonton: Hurtig, 1990), 151–53; Reg Skene, "C. P. Walker and the Business of Theatre: Merchandising Entertainment in a Continental Context," in *The Political Economy of Manitoba*, ed. James Silver and Jeremy Hull (Regina: Canadian Plains Research Center, University of Regina, 1990), 128–30.
55. We base this discussion on a variety of biographical materials, including those provided by *Winnipeg Free Press*, 23 December 1942, 1, 5; E. Ross Stuart, *The History of Prairie Theatre: The Development of Theatre in Alberta, Manitoba, and Saskatchewan, 1833–1982* (Toronto: Simon and Pierre, 1984), 31–32; Reg Skene, "Corliss Powers Walker," in *The Oxford Companion to Canadian Theatre*, ed. Eugene Benson and L. W. Conolly (Toronto: Oxford University Press, 1989), 585–86; Skene, "C. P. Walker and the Business of Theatre," 129–31.
56. See *Winnipeg Free Press*, 13 February 1940, 6; 22 February 1940, 8.
57. *Manitoba Free Press*, 11 September 1897, 3.
58. Skene, "C. P. Walker and the Business of Theatre," 130–31.
59. Skene, "Corliss Powers Walker," 586; Skene, "C. P. Walker and the Business of Theatre," 136–37; Joan Mattie, "Walker Theatre," Agenda Paper (Winnipeg: Historic Sites and Monuments Board of Canada, 1991), 9–22, 1991-19A, Archives of Manitoba.
60. See Mattie, "Walker Theatre," 13.
61. See George C. Izenour, *Theatre Design* (New York: McGraw-Hill, 1977), 82–85.
62. Ibid., 85.
63. Stuart, *The History of Prairie Theatre*, 32.
64. In providing these details, we take our cue from *Manitoba Free Press*, 5 December 1906, 1; 6 December 1906, 1, 10, 42; 15 December 1906, 9; 19 February 1907, 1, 10; the Walker Theatre Program, 18 February 1907, P 2184-A, Archives of Manitoba; "Walker Theatre," n.d., Historical Buildings Committee, City of Edmonton, 1–11; "Walker Theatre," in *1990: The Year Past* (City of Winnipeg Historical Buildings Committee, 1990), 59–64; R. R. Rostecki and D. M. Lyon, "A Description of the Interior Appointments and Decor of the Walker Theatre, 1906–07" (City of Winnipeg Planning Department, 1991), 1–8; Mattie, "Walker Theatre," 14–18; R. R. Rostecki, "Walker Theatre Lobby" (City of Winnipeg Historical Buildings Committee, 1998), 1–5; James B. Hartman, "On Stage: Theatre and Theatres in Early Winnipeg," *Manitoba History* 43 (Spring–Summer 2002): 15–24.
65. See *Manitoba Free Press*, 19 February 1907, 1, 10.
66. Stuart, *The History of Prairie Theatre*, 168–69.
67. Skene, "Corliss Powers Walker," 586.
68. See Mattie, "Walker Theatre," 12; Nader, *Cities of Canada*, 271–72; Skene, "C. P. Walker and the Business of Theatre," 145–46.
69. We are indebted to Reg Skene for this information. Actually, Skene points out,

Walker screened films from the time he opened the Winnipeg Theatre, in 1897. Walker booked a variety of films, starting with Enoch J. Rector's *Corbett-Fitzsimmons Fight* (1897), which he screened at the Winnipeg Theatre on 1 and 2 November 1897 and programmed them at most if not all the theatres in his chain (personal communication, 10 September 2008). Skene has compiled a list of the movies Walker screened for the period 1 November 1897 to 26 December 1927. We base our discussion here on the accounts offered in *Manitoba Free Press*, 1 November 1897, 4, 5. See, for example, *Manitoba Free Press*, 3 May 1915, 2.

70. We base this discussion on a variety of sources, including "Lougheed Was the First Lawyer When Calgary Was Mushroom Town," *Calgary Herald*, Jubilee Ed., 2 June 1925, 14; "Senate Loses Notable Figure [in] Sir J. Lougheed," *Ottawa Evening Journal*, 2 November 1925, 1, 2; "Sir James' Funeral Will Be Held in Calgary," *Calgary Herald*, 2 November 1925, 1, 13; "Sir James Lougheed Passes After [a] Long Career," *Toronto Globe*, 2 November 1925, 1; Marian C. McKenna, "Calgary's First Senator and City Builder," in *Citymakers: Calgarians After the Frontier*, ed. Max Foran and Sheilagh S. Jameson (Calgary: Historical Society of Alberta, Chinook Country Chapter, 1987), 96; Donald B. Smith, *Calgary's Grand Story: The Making of a Prairie Metropolis from the Viewpoint of Two Heritage Buildings* (Calgary: University of Calgary Press, 2005), 21–64, 81–95.
71. McKenna, "Calgary's First Senator and City Builders," 99.
72. Tom Ward, *Cowtown: An Album of Early Calgary* (Calgary: City of Calgary Electric System and McClelland and Stewart West, 1975), 456, 458.
73. See *Calgary Albertan*, 28 October 1911, 13; Anthony Slide, *The Encyclopedia of Vaudeville* (Westport and London: Greenwood Press, 1994), 112.
74. See Ward, *Cowtown*, 454–59; Alan Hustak, "The Grand Lady of First Street," *City Scope*, September 1985, 53–54; Smith, *Calgary's Grand Story*, 4, 6. For contemporary accounts of Bill Sherman, see *Calgary Herald*, 27 January 1905, 7; 30 January 1905, 5; 31 January 1905, 4–5; *Calgary News-Telegram*, 3 May 1911, 5; 20 March 1912, 3; *Calgary Albertan*, 5 November 1906, 2; 3 May 1911, 15; 2 November 1912, 9; 7 February 1925, 15, 18.
75. Smith, *Calgary's Grand Story*, 60–61.
76. Izenour, *Theatre Design*, 85. See Jacqueline Mary Durrie, "Come to the Cabaret: Adaptive Re-Use of the Lougheed Building" (MA thesis, University of Calgary, 2003), 35–40.
77. Smith, *Calgary's Grand Story*, 74.
78. In providing these details, we follow *Calgary Albertan*, 28 October 1911, 13; *Calgary Herald*, 7 February 1912, 9; *Calgary News-Telegram*, 27 January 1912, 4; Jeffrey Goffin, "Canada's Finest Theatre: The Sherman Grand," *Theatre History in Canada* 8, no. 2 (Fall 1987): 193–203; Durrie, "Come to the Cabaret," 35–40; Smith, *Calgary's Grand Story*, 1–19.
79. *Calgary Albertan*, 6 February 1912, 1; *Calgary News-Telegram*, 7 February 1912, 9. See the Sherman Grand Theatre Program, 5 February 1912, 792.097123 S553P Pam, Glenbow Library.
80. Ward, *Cowtown*, 460.

81. See *Calgary News-Telegram*, 1 May 1912, 20; *Calgary Herald*, 6 September 1912, 5; *Calgary Albertan*, 11 October 1912, 11; 17 December 1912, 1.
82. *Calgary Herald*, 6 September 1912, 5.
83. *Calgary Herald*, 9 October 1912, 7; *Calgary Albertan*, 11 October 1912, 11.
84. See *Calgary Herald*, 4 December 1915, 8. We base our discussion of the kinetophone on the accounts provided in *Calgary News-Telegram*, 21 April 1913, 5; *Calgary Herald*, 24 April 1913, 17; 26 April 1913, 10; 15 November 1913, 10; 4 December 1915, 8; 9 December 1915, 14; 27 January 1917, 14; 30 January 1917, 12; 17 April 1917, 7; 24 February 1917, 15; 28 April 1917, 10; 28 December 1918, 8; 2 January 1919, 20; 11 January 1919, 8; 15 January 1919, 17; 16 January 1919, 13; 17 January 1920, 10; 2 December 1924, 7; 3 December 1924, 6. See also Smith, *Calgary's Grand Story*, 210.
85. Smith brought this information to our attention (*Calgary's Grand Story*, 138, 140). See *Calgary News-Telegram*, 7 February 1914, 1; *Calgary Albertan*, 26 March 1912, 5; *Calgary Herald*, 6 June 1914, 1; *Calgary News-Telegram*, 8 August 1914, 8; 26 December 1914, 9.
86. Jule Allen, quoted in *Winnipeg Tribune*, 25 January 1913, 17.
87. Quoted in Chalmers, "The Story of the Allens," 64.
88. Quoted in *Brantford Expositor*, 3 January 1920, 20.
89. See *Calgary News-Telegram*, 12 July 1913, 1; Chalmers, "The Story of the Allens," 15; CMPD, 3 January 1953, 11.
90. Chalmers, "The Story of the Allens," 15.
91. *Edmonton Journal*, 30 November 1918, 19.
92. See *Calgary News-Telegram*, 12 July 1913, 25; Chalmers, "The Story of the Allens," 15; *Calgary Herald*, 19 March 1920, 31; MPW, 7 May 1921, 42.
93. We base our discussion of "modern" management on Frederick W. Taylor, *The Principles of Scientific Management* (New York: Harper Bros., 1911), 5–29; May, *Screening Out the Past*, 169–78; Richard S. Tedlow, *New and Improved: The Story of Mass Marketing in America* (New York: Basic Books, 1990), 1–12; Gomery, *Shared Pleasures*, 33–36. For a discussion of the impact of these changing practices on Alberta businesses generally, see Henry C. Klassen, *A Business History of Alberta* (Calgary: University of Calgary Press, 1999), 150–53.
94. Gomery, *Shared Pleasures*, 33.
95. To paraphrase Gomery, the Allens differentiated their corporate product along five dimensions. See *Saturday Night*, 19 July 1919, 7; Jule, quoted in *Brantford Expositor*, 3 January 1920, 20. Arguably, they anticipated Balaban & Katz. See Barney Balaban and Sam Katz, *The Fundamental Principles of Balaban & Katz Theatre Management* (Chicago: Balaban & Katz Corporation, 1926). Compare Gomery, *Shared Pleasures*, 43–56.
96. See Gomery, *Shared Pleasures*, 47–48.
97. See, for example, Russell, "All That Glitters," 47; Herzog, "The Motion Picture Theatre and Film Exhibition, 1896–1932," 35; David Naylor, *American Picture Palaces: The Architecture of Fantasy* (New York: Van Nostrand Reinhold, 1981), 20; Valentine, *The Show Starts on the Sidewalk*, 1994, 9.

98. Quoted in *Opening Program*, Allen Theatre, Toronto, 12 November 1917.
99. Quoted in *Brantford Expositor*, 3 January 1920, 20.
100. See *Opening Program*, Allen Theatre, Toronto, 12 November 1917.
101. See Morris, *Embattled Shadows*, 104.
102. Chalmers, "The Story of the Allens," 15; John C. Lindsay, *Turn Out the Lights Before Leaving: The Story of Canada's Theatres* (Erin, ON: Boston Mills Press, 1983), 132; Pendakur, *Canadian Dreams and American Control*, 53; Cox, "The Rise and Fall of the Allens," 57–58.
103. We base our discussion on *Calgary Herald*, 2 June 1905, 4; 23 September 1905, 10; 19 December 1905, 3; *Calgary Albertan*, 2 January 1906, 4; 31 March 1906, 4; 18 April 1906, 4; 18 May 1906, 4; 29 May 1906, 4; 5 July 1906, 3.
104. *Calgary Albertan*, 1 November 1906, 1; 5 November 1906, 1; 9 November 1906, 1; *Calgary Herald*, 18 November 1906, 6; *MPW*, 5 October 1912, 49; Morris, *Embattled Shadows*, 46; Cox, "The Rise and Fall of the Allens," 50.
105. *Calgary Herald*, 26 June 1906, 4; 3 July 1906, 4; 5 July 1906, 1; 9 July 1906, 5; 19 July 1906, 3; *Calgary Albertan*, 22 June 1906, 3; 4 July 1906, 3, 8; 14 July 1906, 2; 19 July 1906, 3.
106. See the advertisement, *Calgary Albertan*, 4 July 1906, 5; 5 July 1906, 3; 19 July 1906, 3.
107. We base our discussion of the Starland group on *Calgary Herald*, 15 November 1909, 5; 16 November 1909, 5; 19 November 1909, 5; 23 November 1909, 5.
108. See *Calgary Herald*, 14 May 1910, 5; 2 July 1910, 5; 13 July 1910, 5.
109. In providing these details, we draw on the accounts in *Calgary Herald*, 25 February 1911, 5; 3 March 1911, 7; 6 March 1911, 10; 7 March 1911, 7; 8 March 1911, 10; 14 March 1911, 8; 28 March 1911, 4; *Calgary News-Telegram*, 3 March 1911, 4; 7 March 1911, 4.
110. James C. Teague built at least four theatres for the Allens from 1911 to 1913, during the time he operated an architectural firm in Calgary. His drawings of the Bijou Theatre and the Rex Theatre, both constructed in 1912, appeared in the *Provincial Standard*, 30 September 1911, 7, and 14 September 1912, 4, and in *Construction* 6, no. 10 (October 1913): 371. The drawings represent variations on the same design. Each theatre featured a mammoth Coney Island façade.
111. Our description of the Monarch, built in 1911, is based on the accounts that appeared in *Calgary News-Telegram*, 21 January 1911, 5; 23 January 1911, 4; 27 January 1911, 4; 29 January 1911, 4; 31 January 1911, 4; 28 February 1911, 4; 15 May 1911, 4.
112. Edwards refers to the Monarch as a "death trap" a number of times: see *Eye Opener*, 16 September 1911, 1; 23 March 1912, 1; 5 October 1912, 4. As to the fire in Canonsburg, Pennsylvania that Edwards refers to, see *New York Times*, 27 August 1911, 1.
113. *Calgary Herald*, 6 March 1911, 10; 7 March 1911, 7.
114. See *Calgary Standard*, 14 September 1912, 4; *Calgary News-Telegram*, 12 July 1913, 25; *Construction* 6, no. 10 (October 1913): 371–79; *Regina Leader*, 18 October 1917, 12; *Calgary Herald*, 24 October 1921, 14.

115. We base our discussion of the architectural design and the social function of the deluxe Allen theatre on the accounts that appeared in *Western Standard*, 22 May 1913, 11; *Calgary News-Telegram*, 7 November 1913, 5; 14 November 1913, 18–19; 15 November 1913, 30; *Calgary Albertan*, 10 November 1913, 9; 14 November 1913, 7; 15 November 1913, 10; 17 November 1913, 10; *Calgary Herald*, 10 November 1913, 7; 14 November 1913, 7; 15 November 1913, 11, 13, 17; 18 November 1913, 13; *Eye Opener*, 22 November 1913, 2; 6 December 1913, 4.
116. See *Calgary News-Telegram*, 12 July 1913, 25.
117. The Allens formed many companies, renaming them as circumstances dictated. As Cox writes, in naming their firms, the Allens often looked to the corporate names Adolph Zukor gave his companies. For example, Famous Players Film Service resembles Zukor's Famous Players–Lasky Corporation and Canadian Paramount Pictures Corporation resembles Zukor's Paramount Pictures. See Cox, "The Rise and Fall of the Allens," 79.
118. Pendakur, *Canadian Dreams and American Control*, 53–54.

Chapter 4: Reforms and Regulations

1. See *Moving Picture World* (hereafter cited as MPW), 23 January 1909, 92; Terry Ramsaye, *A Million and One Nights* (New York: Simon and Schuster, 1926; repr. London: Frank Cass, 1964), 486–98; Lewis Jacobs, *The Rise of the American Film: A Critical History* (New York: Harcourt, Brace, 1939), 81–84; Garth Jowett, *Film: The Democratic Art* (Boston: Little, Brown, 1976), 51–54; Tino Balio, ed., *The American Film Industry*. rev. ed. (Madison: University of Wisconsin Press, 1985), 23–25, 103–6; Robert Anderson, "The Motion Picture Patents Company: A Revaluation," in Balio, *The American Film Industry*, 134–52; and Douglas Gomery, *Shared Pleasures: A History of Movie Presentation in the United States* (Madison: University of Wisconsin Press, 1992), 33.
2. Jacobs, *The Rise of the American Film*, 82–83.
3. Lary May, *Screening Out the Past: The Birth of Mass Culture and the Motion Picture Industry* (New York: Oxford University Press, 1980), 43–59. See Howard Palmer and Tamara Palmer, "Reformers, War, and the Liberals," in *Alberta: A New History* (Edmonton: Hurtig, 1990), 173–87.
4. May, *Screening Out the Past*, 51.
5. See *Chicago Tribune*, 13 April 1907, 3; MPW, 11 May 1907, 147; 29 May 1907, 263; 1 June 1907, 195, 198; Jane Addams, *Twenty Years at Hull House* (New York: Macmillan, 1909), 75–76, 107–9, 384–86; *New York Times*, 22 May 1935, 1, 16; 23 May 1935, 23; Jill Conway, "Jane Addams: An American Heroine," *Daedalus* 93 (Spring 1964): 761–80; Kathleen D. McCarthy, "Nickel Vice and Virtue: Movie Censorship in Chicago, 1907–1915," *Journal of Popular Film* 5, no. 1 (1976): 43–44; May, *Screening Out the Past*, 52–53.
6. See Frederic C. Howe, *The Confessions of a Reformer* (New York: Charles Scribner's Sons, 1925; repr. Chicago: Quadrangle Books, 1967), 75–84, 240–51; obituary notice, *New York Times*, 4 August 1940, 33; Robert Fisher, "Film Censorship

and Progressive Reform: The National Board of Censorship of Motion Pictures, 1909–1922," *Journal of Popular Film* 4, no. 2 (1975): 143–46: May, *Screening Out the Past*, 46–47.

7. *New York Times*, 1 January 1904, 1, 3; 2 January 1904, 1–2.
8. Boyd Fraser, "The Regulation of Motion Picture Theatres," *American City* 7 (1912): 520–21.
9. MPW, 4 August 1913, 526–27; Gregory A. Waller, *Main Street Amusements: Movies and Commercial Entertainment in a Southern City, 1896–1930* (Washington, DC: Smithsonian Institution Press, 1995), 123.
10. MPW, 21 November 1914, 1061–62; 16 January 1915, 357.
11. During the year 1914–15, *Moving Picture World* ran a series of articles on how the authorities in various states were dealing with such matters as safety, licensing fees, the qualifications needed to operate a theatre, and censorship practices. See MPW, 21 November 1914, 1061–62; 5 December 1914, 1372; 19 December 1914, 1167; 5 June 1915, 1610; 24 July 1915, 664. See also Charles Musser, *The Emergence of Cinema: The American Screen to 1907* (New York: Charles Scribner's Sons, 1990), 443–44.
12. Waller, *Main Street Amusements*, 129. As early as 1907, reformers in Brooklyn insisted that exhibitors observe the Sabbath. See MPW, 26 October 1907, 539.
13. See, MPW, 23 December 1911, 969; 24 February 1912, 658–59; 2 March 1912, 759; 9 March 1912, 845; 15 May 1915, 1232; and 5 February 1916, 825.
14. Quoted in Gordon Hendricks, *The Kinetoscope: America's First Commercially Successful Motion Picture Exhibitor* (New York: Government Printing Office, 1966), 77–78; Waller, *Main Street Amusements*, 129.
15. Waller explains that reformers realized they would have to challenge motion picture theatres on matters over and above those of physical design and safety. See Waller, *Main Street Amusements*, 125. Eileen Bowser writes that, in *Moving Picture World* (26 August 1911), W. Stephen Bush praised movie exhibitors for forming in August 1911 their first national organization, called the Moving Picture League of America, guided by the policy of raising the standards of moving picture films, securing the recognition of the National Censor board, regulating prices for film service, preventing breaches of contract, securing the appropriate insurance rates, and protecting members against adverse legislation. He argued that the control of the industry had actually passed from the hands of the exhibitors to the hands of the producers. See MPW, 26 August 1911, 522, 530; Eileen Bowser, *The Transformation of Cinema, 1907–1915* (New York: Charles Scribner's Sons, 1990), 48–52.
16. Jowett, *Film: The Democratic Art*, 108.
17. The literature on film censorship, especially in the United States, is vast. Some recent studies include Richard Corliss, "The Legion of Decency," *Film Comment* 4 (Summer 1968): 24–61; Fisher, "Film Censorship and Progressive Reform," 143–56; McCarthy, "Nickel Vice and Virtue," 37–55; Jowett, *Film: The Democratic Art*, 108–35, 166–71, 203–5, and 404–13; Roy Rosenzweig, *Eight Hours for What We Will: Workers and Leisure in an industrial City, 1870–1920* (New York:

Cambridge University Press, 1983), 285; Nancy J. Rosenbloom, "Between Reform and Regulation: The Struggle over Film Censorship in Progressive America, 1901–22," *Film History* 1 (1987): 307–25; Waller, *Main Street Amusements*, 134–48, 232–37, 301.

18. Ramsaye, *A Million and One Nights*, 117–18; Jowett, *Film: The Democratic Art*, 42–43, 109–10; Hendricks, *The Kinetoscope*, 55, 77.
19. Quoted in Jowett, *Film: The Democratic Art*, 109.
20. Cited in Ramsaye, *A Million and One Nights*, 474.
21. See Jowett, *Film: The Democratic Art*, 110.
22. See, for example, *New York Times*, 24 December 1908, 5; 25 December 1908, 1–2, 6; Ramsaye, *A Million and One Nights*, 478; see Jowett, *Film: The Democratic Art*, 112–13.
23. See, for example, *New York Times*, 26 December 1908, 2, 6; 27 December 1908, 1–2; 28 December 1908, 1–2; *MPW*, 2 January 1909, 3.
24. See *MPW*, 12 June 1909, 797; 26 June 1909, 867; 10 July 1909, 43; 16 October 1909, 524–25; *World Today*, January 1909, 175, 476; *Century Illustrated Monthly Magazine*, April 1910, 850–63; Jowett, *Film: The Democratic Art*, 126.
25. See *Harper's Weekly*, 30 July 1910, 12–13.
26. Ramsaye, *A Million and One Nights*, 480–81.
27. Fisher, "Film Censorship and Progressive Reform," 146; May, *Screening Out the Past*, 55; Rosenbloom, "Between Reform and Regulation," 311, 312, 314; Bowser, *The Transformation of Cinema*, 48–49.
28. *MPW*, 4 September 1915, 1625; Fisher, "Film Censorship and Progressive Reform," 146; Rosenbloom, "Between Reform and Regulation," 319.
29. See *New York Times*, 15 May 1921, 1, 18; Jowett, *Film: The Democratic Art*, 167–68; Waller, *Main Street Amusements*, 232.
30. See *Calgary Herald*, 2 January 1912, 1; 20 March 1913, 4; 22 March 1922, 17; *Edmonton Journal*, 5 April 1919, 1; D.H. Bocking, "The Saskatchewan Board of Censors, 1910–1935," *Saskatchewan History* 24, no. 2 (Spring 1971): 51–52; Malcolm Dean, *Censored! Only in Canada* (Toronto: Virgo Press, 1981), 20, 51; David C. Jones, "The Reflective Value of Movies and Censorship on Interwar Prairie Society," *Prairie Forum* 10, no. 2 (1985): 384; Donald G. Wetherell and Irene Kmet, *Useful Pleasures: The Shaping of Leisure in Alberta, 1896–1945* (Regina: Canadian Plains Research Center, 1990), 43–44, 262, 273.
31. See, for example, Gerald Friesen, *The Canadian Prairies: A History* (Toronto: University of Toronto Press, 1984), 339–81; Jones, "The Reflective Value of Movies and Censorship on Interwar Prairie Society," 392.
32. Richard Allen, *The Social Passion: Religion and Social Reform in Canada, 1914–28* (Toronto: University of Toronto Press, 1971), 3–17; Friesen, *The Canadian Prairies*, 250–55; Ramsay Cook, "Ambiguous Heritage: Wesley College and the Social Gospel Reconsidered," *Manitoba History* 19 (Spring 1990): 2–11.
33. Allen, *The Social Passion*, 16.
34. Friesen, *The Canadian Prairies*, 350.
35. Ibid., 365.

36. Ibid., 351–81.
37. See *Calgary Herald*, 14 February 1902, 1; 2 January 1912, 1; Wetherell and Kmet, *Useful Pleasures*, 252.
38. See *Calgary Albertan*, 1 May 1911, 7; *Calgary Herald*, 24 November 1911, 1; 30 October 1912, 6; *Calgary News-Telegram*, 30 October 1912, 6; T. H. Mawson, "The City of the Plain: Calgary," *Construction* 6, no. 10 (November 1913): 380–82; Henry Vivian, "How to Apply Town Planning to Calgary," *Construction* 6, no. 10 (November 1913): 383–86; Frederick Law Olmsted, "The Town-Planning Movement in America," *Housing and Town Planning* 51 (January 1914): 172–81; T. H. Mawson, *The City of Calgary, Past, Present, and Future: A Preliminary Scheme for Controlling the Economic Growth of the City* (London and New York: T. H. Mawson City Planning Experts, 1914). For a discussion of urban planning, see J. P. Dickin McGinnis, "Birth to Boom to Bust: Building in Calgary, 1875–1914," in *Frontier Calgary: Town, City, and Region, 1875–1914*, ed. Anthony W. Rasporich and Henry C. Klassen (Calgary: University of Calgary and McClelland and Stewart West, 1975), 6–19; Max Foran, *Calgary: An Illustrated History* (Toronto: James Lorimer, and Ottawa: National Museum of Man, 1978), 98; Bryan Peter Melnyk, "Calgary Buildings, 1905–1914: The Emergence of an Urban Landscape" (MA thesis, University of Calgary, 1980), 13–34, 125–49, 164–68; Trevor Boddy, *Modern Architecture in Alberta* (Regina: Canadian Plains Research Center, University of Regiona, 1987), 29–30; Anthony W. Rasporich, "The City Yes, the City No: Perfection by Design in the Western City," in *The Prairie West as Promised Land*, ed. R. Douglas Francis and Chris Kitzan (Calgary: University of Calgary Press, 2007), 177–97.
39. For details, see *Calgary Herald*, 3 October 1912, 6; *Calgary Albertan*, 9 October 1912, 1, 8; *Calgary Herald*, 24 October 1912, 1, 14; *Calgary Albertan*, 28 February 1913, sec. 3, 17.
40. *Calgary Albertan*, 28 February 1913, section 3, 17.
41. See *Toronto Globe*, 9 August 1897, 8; Robert W. Gutteridge, *Magic Moments: The First Twenty Years of Moving Pictures in Toronto, 1894–1914* (Toronto: Gutteridge-Pratley, 2000), 73–74; Paul S. Moore, *Now Playing: Early Moviegoing and the Regulation of Fun* (New York: State University of New York Press, 2008), 137–47.
42. *Toronto Mail and Empire*, quoted in Dean, *Censored! Only in Canada*, 13.
43. *Toronto News*, 7 May 1907, 4.
44. *Regina Leader*, 13 July 1910, 4, citing the Pittsburgh report.
45. See *Regina Leader*, 12 July 1910, 1; *MPW*, 16 July 1910, 133.
46. S. D. Chown to the Hon. W. Scott, 12 July 1910, *Scott Papers*, p. 31708, Archives of Saskatchewan (hereafter cited as AS): cited in Bocking, "The Saskatchewan Board of Censors, 1910–1935," 51.
47. Quoted in *Regina Leader*, 12 July 1910, 1.
48. *Regina Leader*, 15 July 1910, 4.
49. Bocking, "The Saskatchewan Board of Censors, 1910–1935," 52.
50. Ibid.; Dean, *Censored! Only in Canada*, 230.

51. See MPW, 7 October 1911, 25; Dean, *Censored! Only in Canada*, 135, and Moore, *Now Playing*, 138–39, 148, 217.
52. Dean, *Censored! Only in Canada*, 135–36.
53. See MPW, 24 January 1920, 549; Dean, *Censored! Only in Canada*, 137.
54. Quoted in Dean, *Censored! Only in Canada*, 137.
55. The CFW, 22 May 1946, 1, 3. See Dean, *Censored! Only in Canada*, 138–40.
56. Quoted in Dean, *Censored! Only in Canada*, 140.
57. See *Globe and Mail*, 7 May 1963, 3; 27 January 1968, 1; 28 March 1969, 4; 26 May 1973, 3.
58. See *Manitoba Free Press*, 6 November 1915, 19; 30 November 1915, 7.
59. Dean, *Censored! Only in Canada*, 125.
60. Cited in MPW, 10 March 1919, 807; 15 March 1919, 1450.
61. Dean, *Censored! Only in Canada*, 126.
62. Dean, *Censored! Only in Canada*, 126. See also James A. Skinner, "Clean and Decent Movies: Selected Cases and Responses of the Manitoba Film Censor Board, 1930 to 1950," *Manitoba History* 14 (Autumn 1987): 2–9; Locksley D. McNeill, "Reminiscences of a Manitoba Film Censor," *Manitoba History* 17 (Spring 1989): 19–21, and "A Leap in the Dark: The Transition from Film Censorship to Classification in Manitoba, 1970–72," *Manitoba History* 25 (Spring 1993): 2–8.
63. Dean, *Censored! Only in Canada*, 127–28; see *Globe and Mail*, 26 May 1973, 3.
64. Bocking, "The Saskatchewan Board of Censors, 1910–1935," 53; Dean, *Censored! Only in Canada*, 165.
65. Chapter 28 of the 1913 Statutes of Saskatchewan, cited by Bocking, "The Saskatchewan Board of Censors, 1910–1935," 52–53; Dean, *Censored! Only in Canada*, 165–66.
66. See *Regina Leader*, 23 January 1914, 14.
67. Saskatchewan, Department of Labour, Theatres, and Public Halls Branch, E. J. Wright, Deputy Provincial Secretary, to B. L. Baldwinson, 5 February 1914, SA: cited in Bocking, "The Saskatchewan Board of Censors, 1910–1935," 54.
68. Bocking, "The Saskatchewan Board of Censors, 1910–1935," 60–61.
69. See *Calgary Herald*, 26 October 1911, 1; 28 October 1911, 6; 15 December 1911, 6.
70. *Calgary Herald*, 25 October 1910, 5.
71. See *Calgary Herald*, 2 January 1912, 1; 20 March 1913, 14; *Calgary Albertan*, 3 January 1912, 5; MPW, 22 March 1913, 1208. We build on the work of Dean, *Censored! Only in Canada*, 109–15, Terry L. Chapman, "Film Censorship in Lethbridge, 1918–1920," *Alberta History* 33, no. 1 (Winter 1985): 1–9, and Wetherell and Kmet, *Useful Pleasures*, 262–78, who examined the files of the Alberta Board of Censors, located at the Provincial Archives of Alberta.
72. *Calgary Herald*, 20 March 1913, 14.
73. Gerald Pelton, "Some Causes and Remedies for Juvenile Delinquency," 30 September 1927, 3, Premiers' Papers (hereafter cited as PP), File 235, Provincial Archives of Alberta (hereafter cited as PAA): cited in Wetherell and Kmet, *Useful Pleasures*, 263–64.

74. *Calgary Herald*, 28 October 1911, 6.
75. *Calgary Herald*, 2 January 1912, 1, 6.
76. See Bocking, "The Saskatchewan Board of Censors, 1910–1935," 59–60. During the first two decades of the twentieth century, reformers across North America campaigned to eradicate a variety of social evils, including "White Slavery," widely understood as the trafficking in women for immoral purposes, namely, prostitution. As Lary May observed in *Screening Out the Past*, the rapid changes that the Industrial Revolution brought to the New World, in terms of industrialization and urbanization, were seen as a threat to the Victorian family, society's core institution. Anxieties generated by the changing role of women, who were moving to cities and entering the workforce, were combined with those generated by the growing presence of diverse immigrants who were settling in the United States and Canada. Muckraking journalists fuelled the hysteria by writing stories of "foreigners" who allegedly kidnapped young girls and forced them to work in brothels. In the United States, the White-Slave Traffic Act (1910) banned the interstate transport of females for immoral purposes. See, for example, Jane Addams, *The Spirit of Youth and the City Streets* (New York: Macmillan, 1909), and Clifford G. Rose, *The Great War on White Slavery, or Fighting for the Protection of our Girls* (Chicago: Clifford G. Rose, 1911). In western Canada, the public focused on Chinese, Japanese, and black immigrants, regarding the Chinese in particular as "White Slavers." Anti-Chinese rhetoric, as exemplified in Emily Murphy's *The Black Candle* (Toronto: Thomas Allen, 1922), linked the evils of gambling, drug trafficking, and prostitution, which were thought to thrive in the largely male "Chinatowns" that had grown up not only in Vancouver but also in the largest communities of the prairies. In Canada, as in the United States, a number of discriminatory laws were enacted in response to the "Chinese problem," including legislation (enacted in Saskatchewan in 1908, in Ontario in 1914, and in British Columbia in 1923) that prevented white women from working in Chinese-owned establishments. See Peter S. Li, "The Chinese," in *An Encyclopedia of Canada's People*, ed. Robert Magosci (Toronto: University of Toronto Press, 1999), available online at http://multiculturalcanada.ca/Encyclopedia/A-Z/c10. See also Howard Palmer, *Patterns of Prejudice: A History of Nativism in Alberta* (Toronto: McClelland and Stewart, 1982), 32–37, 82–86.
77. Dean, *Censored! Only in Canada*, 109–10.
78. Alberta, Department of the Provincial Secretary, "Theatres and Amusements Tax Branch," *Annual Report*, 1922, 61: cited in Wetherell and Kmet, *Useful Pleasures*, 265.
79. "Censorship in Alberta," [1933], 73.347/37, PAA: quoted in Wetherell and Kmet, *Useful Pleasures*, 265.
80. Reply to Communication from the Calgary Board of Trade re. Censorship, [June 1932], PP, file 366, PAA: cited in Wetherell and Kmet, *Useful Pleasures*, 265. See CFW, 5 September 1945, 1–2; 19 September 1945, 1, 12; 9 April 1946, 1, 16.

81. Reply to Communication from the Calgary Board of Trade re. Censorship, [June 1932], PP, file 366, PAA: cited in Wetherell and Kmet, *Useful Pleasures*, 266.
82. Vangro to Pearson, 31 October 1934, 73.347/37, PAA: cited in Wetherell and Kmet, *Useful Pleasures*, 267.
83. Cooper to Blankstein, 14 December 1934, 73.347/28, PAA: cited in Wetherell and Kmet, *Useful Pleasures*, 267.
84. Hardy to Pearson, 22 September 1937 and 27 October 1937, 73.347/37, PAA: cited in Wetherell and Kmet, *Useful Pleasures*, 267.
85. *Edmonton Journal*, 5 April 1919, 1.
86. Petition by Calgary Council on Child Welfare, 13 January 1927, PP, file 365, PAA: cited in Wetherell and Kmet, *Useful Pleasures*, 273.
87. Douglas to Trowbridge, 9 February 1927, PP, file 365, PAA: cited in Wetherell and Kmet, *Useful Pleasures*, 274.
88. Minutes, 25 October 1928, M6466, box 1, Glenbow Archives: cited in Wetherell and Kmet, *Useful Pleasures*, 274.
89. Circular Letter, 15 May 1935, PP, file 862, PAA: cited in Wetherell and Kmet, *Useful Pleasures*, 274.
90. Fleming to Arthurs, 21 March 1949, 71.170/1, PAA: cited in Wetherell and Kmet, *Useful Pleasures*, 274.
91. Pearson to L'Ami, 14 March 1935, 73.347/37, PAA: cited in Wetherell and Kmet, *Useful Pleasures*, 270.
92. Communication from the Censor to the Premier, 3 March 1930, PP, File 366, PAA: cited in Wetherell and Kmet, *Useful Pleasures*, 269.
93. Pearson to Wingate, 30 December 1932, 73.347/37, PAA: cited in Wetherell and Kmet, *Useful Pleasures*, 269.
94. Cooper to Brownlee, 2 June 1926, PP, File 364, PAA: cited in Wetherell and Kmet, *Useful Pleasures*, 272; Peter Morris, *Embattled Shadows: A History of Canadian Cinema, 1895–1939* (Montreal and Kingston: McGill-Queen's University Press, 1978), 179–81.
95. Morris, *Embattled Shadows*, 179–81.
96. Pearson to Brownlee, 23 February 1932, and Pearson to Brownlee, 31 January 1924, PP, files 366 and 190 respectively, PAA: cited in Wetherell and Kmet, *Useful Pleasures*, 268–69.
97. Brownlee to Greenfield, 5 December 1924, PP, file 364, PAA: cited in Wetherell and Kmet, *Useful Pleasures*, 268.
98. Russell Merritt, "Nickelodeon Theatres, 1905–1914: Building an Audience for the Movies," in Balio, *The American Film Industry*, 96.
99. Quoted in *Canadian Film Weekly* (hereafter cited as CFW), 13 March 1946, 1, 3. See also CFW, 22 January 1947, 1, 10; 28 June 1950, 1, 14; Dean, *Censored! Only in Canada*, 111.
100. See *Canadian Moving Picture Digest* (hereafter cited as CMPD), 14 July 1954, 1, 4.
101. See *Toronto Globe and Mail*, 7 November 1972, 47.
102. See Dean, *Censored! Only in Canada*, 173, 187.
103. Ibid., 21–22.

104. See, for example, MPW, 11 November 1911, 461; 9 December 1911, 795; Morris, *Embattled Shadows* 55–56; Jones, "The Reflective Value of Movies and Censorship on Interwar Prairie Society," 384–85; Manjunath Pendakur, *Canadian Dreams and American Control: The Political Economy of the Canadian Film Industry* (Detroit: Wayne State University Press, 1990), 49–51.
105. See MPW, 13 December 1913, 1259.
106. See MPW, 28 November 1914, 1236.
107. Dean, *Censored! Only in Canada*, 22–25.
108. See *Toronto Telegram*, 21 January 1916, 4; 27 January 1916, 9.
109. See MPW, 1 May 1920, 719.
110. See *Maclean's*, 1 November 1925, 28–29, 49; 15 June 1940, 10, 38–40.
111. Dean, *Censored! Only in Canada*, 31.
112. We take our cue from the reports printed in CFW for 27 February 1946, 1, 3; 13 March 1946, 1, 3; 23 October 1946, 1, 5; 25 December 1946, 14, 29, 31; 18 August 1948, 1, 8; 27 April 1949, 1, 5; 4 October 1950, 1, 3; 11 October 1950, 1, 2; 25 December 1950, 1, 5.
113. CFW, 25 December 1946, 14, 29, 31; 27 April 1949, 1, 5.
114. See C. A. Dawson and Eva R. Younge, *Pioneering in the Prairie Provinces: The Social Side of the Settlement Process* (Toronto: Macmillan of Canada, 1940), 243; Allen, *The Social Passion*, 13, 21–22; Wetherell and Kmet, *Useful Pleasures*, 22–25.
115. See *Toronto Globe*, 12 July 1905, 1, 4; *Brandon Sun*, 27 February 1906, 3; *Toronto Globe*, 11 July 1906, 8; *Calgary Herald*, 8 February 1944, 1; *Vancouver Sun*, 24 April 1963, 1.
116. *Calgary News-Telegram*, 17 July 1913, 4.
117. See *Globe and Mail*, 26 April 1985, 6.
118. See, for example, *Globe and Mail*, 7 May 1963, 11; Dean, *Censored! Only in Canada*, 67.
119. Concerned about the impact of motion pictures on the young, pro-censorship forces, such as the social and moral reform associations, tended to emphasize the contribution censors made to the progress of society, whereas the anti-censorship forces raised questions about the abuse of power and the matter of freedom of expression. See Dean, *Censored! Only in Canada*, 60.
120. See, for example, CFW, 27 February 1946, 1, 3; 13 March 1946, 1, 3; 23 October 1946, 1, 5; 25 December 1946, 14, 29, 31; 18 August 1948, 1, 8; 27 April 1949, 1, 5; 4 October 1950, 1, 3; 11 October 1950, 1, 2; 25 December 1950, 15; *Toronto Star*, 19 May 1960, 37; *Globe and Mail*, 17 January 1962, 9; 22 May 1962, 42; Dean, *Censored! Only in Canada*, 51, 214.
121. Dean, *Censored! Only in Canada*, 88–89.
122. Quoted in CMPD, 14 July 1956, 1, 4; see Dean, *Censored! Only in Canada*, 112–13.
123. Dean, *Censored! Only in Canada*, 127.
124. *Star Weekly*, 8 August 1964, 2–3.
125. Jones, "The Reflective Value of Movies and Censorship on Interwar Prairie Society," 395.

Chapter 5: Grand Entertainment

1. Kirwan Cox, "The Rise and Fall of the Allens: The War for Canada's Movie Theatres," *Lonergan Review* 6 (2000): 52–53; Paul S. Moore, *Now Playing: Early Moviegoing and the Regulation of Fun* (Albany: State University of New York Press, 2008), 33–43.
2. See George A. Nader, *Cities of Canada*, 2 vols. (Toronto: Macmillan of Canada, 1975–76), vol. 2, 203; James Lemon, *Toronto Since 1918: An Illustrated History* (Toronto: James Lorimer, and Ottawa: National Museum of Man, 1985), 13–17; Hilary Russell, *Double Take: The Story of the Elgin and Winter Garden Theatres* (Toronto: Dundurn Press, 1989), 18–19.
3. According to *The Canada Year Book 1913* (Ottawa: King's Printer, 1914), a typical family in Toronto in 1913 lived on an income of $800 per year, or about $15.40 per week. The cost of living rose steadily, as rents had risen an astonishing 35.9 percent since 1910; that is, the typical family spent on average $7.70 on food, $4.08 on rent, and $2.03 on fuel, lighting, and so on per week, for a total of $13.81, leaving little indeed for purchasing theatre tickets. See *The Canada Year Book 1913*, 503.
4. Patricia McHugh, *Toronto Architecture: A City Guide* (Toronto: Mercury Books, 1985), 8–13.
5. Russell, *Double Take*, 17.
6. See Manjunath Pendakur, *Canadian Dreams and American Control: The Political Economy of the Canadian Film Industry* (Detroit: Wayne State University Press, 1990), 54; Cox, "The Rise and Fall of the Allens," 52.
7. See Pendakur, *Canadian Dreams and American Control*, 54; Cox, "The Rise and Fall of the Allens," 53–56.
8. See *Calgary Albertan*, 6 December 1918, 3.
9. See, for example, *Canadian Moving Picture Digest* (hereafter cited as CMPD), 3 January 1953, 17.
10. *Regina Leader-Post*, 13 October 1917, 13; Cox, "The Rise and Fall of the Allens," 53–56.
11. See *Edmonton Journal*, 30 November 1918, 17; CMPD, 3 January 1953, 17.
12. *Edmonton Bulletin*, 30 November 1918, 20.
13. Pendakur, *Canadian Dreams and American Control*, 55.
14. See *Edmonton Bulletin*, 15 February 1919, 15; *Edmonton Journal*, 15 February 1919, 19, 21; *Calgary Albertan*, 1 March 1919, 10; *Calgary Herald*, 1 March 1919, 11.
15. See *Calgary Albertan*, 22 February 1919, 10; *Calgary Herald*, 21 March 1919, 14; 18 November 1921, 21; CMPD, 1 May 1940, 9; Peter Morris, *Embattled Shadows: A History of Canadian Cinema, 1895–1939* (Montreal and Kingston: McGill-Queen's University Press, 1978), 74.
16. See CMPD, 3 January 1953, 17; Morris, *Embattled Shadows*, 71–78.
17. See *Construction* 11, no. 2 (February 1918): 39; *Construction* 13, no. 4 (April 1920): 123; *Calgary Albertan*, 26 March 1919, 2; *Calgary Herald*, 18 March 1920, 20; 19 March 1920, 31.
18. Nader, *Cities of Canada*, 297.

19. *Moose Jaw Daily News*, 19 August 1916, 8.
20. *Moose Jaw Daily News*, 19 August 1916, 8, 9; 10 April 1919, 5.
21. G. F. Barker, *Brandon: A City, 1881–1961* (Brandon: G. F. Barker, 1977), 97, 129, 174, 178, 256.
22. Barker, *Brandon*, 174, 195, 264.
23. Very little material about the theatre made its way into the Winnipeg or the Brandon archives. We base our remarks on the information provided by Iona Fraser, Arthur Osborne, and Jack Stothard, who worked at the facility starting in the late 1940s; they provided us with photographs of the interior and the exterior respectively. See *Brandon Sun*, 11 July 1917, 6; 14 July 1917, 1; 16 July 1917, 1, 6; Barker, *Brandon*, 191, 202, 227, 256, 264, 402.
24. See *Brandon Sun*, 14 July 1917, 1; 16 July 1917, 1, 6.
25. See *Brandon Sun*, 14 September 1918, 6; Edward Wagenknecht, *The Movies in the Age of Innocence* (Norman: University of Oklahoma Press, 1962), 116–171, 215, 224, 253; Richard Schickel, *D. W. Griffith: An American Life* (New York: Simon and Schuster, 1984), 340–60.
26. For more information about the Spanish flu pandemic, see *Brandon Sun*, 11 October 1918, 1, 2; 12 October 1918, 3; 14 October 1918, 1; 19 October 1914, 3; 22 October 1918, 1, 3; 6 November 1918, 1; 11 November 1918, 4; 15 November 1918, 3; 19 November 1918, 3; 11 December 1918, 1, 2; Barker, *Brandon*, 191; Fred McGuinness, *The Wheat City: A Pictorial History of Brandon* (Saskatoon: Western Producer Prairie Books, 1988), 12.
27. See *Manitoba Free Press*, 26 October 1918, 23; 2 November 1918, 20; 28 November 1918, 4.
28. See, for example, *Construction* 13, no. 4 (April 1920): 123–26.
29. Hilary Russell, "All That Glitters: A Memorial to Ottawa's Capitol Theatre and its Predecessors," *Canadian Historical Sites: Occasional Papers in Archaeology and History*, no. 13 (Ottawa: Parks Canada, National Parks and Sites Branch, 1975), 45–46.
30. C. Howard Crane, "Observations on Motion Picture Theatres," *Architectural Forum* 42 (June 1925): 381–84; obituary notice, *New York Times*, 17 August 1952; 76; Russell, "All That Glitters," 39–40; Geoffrey Beard, *The Works of Robert Adam* (London: Bloomsbury Books, 1978), 1–26; David Naylor, *Great American Motion Picture Theatres* (Washington, DC: Preservation Press, 1987), 39–40; Lisa Maria DiChiera, "The Theatre Designs of C. Howard Crane" (MSc thesis, University of Pennsylvania, 1992), 15–23.
31. We build on the discussions presented in *Toronto World*, 8 November 1917, 7; 10 November 1917, 7; Toronto *Daily News*, 10 November 1917, 7, 18; *Moving Picture World* (hereafter cited as *MPW*), 29 December 1917, 1952; 26 January 1918, 553; 21 June 1919, 1782; *Construction* 11, no. 2 (February 1918): 39–44; Hye Bossin, "The Cinema Comes to Toronto," *Canadian Film Weekly* (hereafter cited as CFW), 22 May 1963, 12–13; 28 May 1963, 6; Russell, "All That Glitters," 41–43; John C. Lindsay, *Turn Out the Stars Before Leaving* (Erin, ON: Boston Mills Press, 1983), 40–41, 78, 131–38; John C. Lindsay, *Palaces of the Night: Canada's Grand*

Theatres (London: Lynx Images, 1999), 57–60; Philip Dombowsky, "Emmanuel Briffa Revisited" (MA thesis, Concordia University, 1995), 53.

32. Quoted in Floyd S. Chalmers, "The Story of the Allens," *Maclean's*, 15 February 1920, 15.
33. Terry Ramsaye, *A Million and One Nights: A History of the Motion Picture* (New York: Simon and Schuster, 1926; repr. London: Frank Cass, 1964), 822.
34. In discussing Adolph Zukor, we draw on the following sources: "$12,500,000 Merger of Film Companies," *New York Times*, 29 June 1916, 9; "Europe the Field for Its Pictures," *New York Times*, 16 May 1919, 13; "Zukor Proclaims his Principles, Promising to Correct All Evils," *MPW*, 2 July 1921, 26, 27, 36, 38; "Attacks Big Firm as Monopoly," *New York Times*, 1 September 1921, 1; Adolph Zukor, "Origin and Growth of the Industry," in *The Story of Films*, ed. Joseph P. Kennedy (Chicago: A. W. Shaw, 1927), 55–76; Tino Balio, ed., *The American Film Industry*. rev. ed. (Madison: University of Wisconsin Press, 1985), 116–22; Neal Gabler, *An Empire of Their Own: How the Jews Invented Hollywood* (New York: Crown Publishers, 1988), 11–46.
35. Ramsaye, *A Million and One Nights*, 629–33.
36. See *MPW*, 15 July 1916, 415–16.
37. Balio, *The American Film Industry*, 118.
38. See Balio, *The American Film Industry*, 120–22; Gabler, *An Empire of Their Own*, 41–44; Garth Drabinsky, *Closer to the Sun* (Toronto: McClelland and Stewart, 1995), 64; Cox, "The Rise and Fall of the Allens," 64; Paul S. Moore, "Nathan L. Nathanson Introduces Canadian Odeon: Producing National Competition in Film Exhibition," *Canadian Journal of Film Studies* 12, no. 2 (Fall 2003): 26.
39. See Howard Lewis, *The Motion Picture Industry* (New York: Van Nostrand, 1933), 15–19, 22–23; Douglas Gomery, *Shared Pleasures: A History of Movie Presentation in the United States* (Madison: University of Wisconsin Press, 1992), 60–61.
40. Quoted in *Manitoba Free Press*, 29 November 1919, 5; *Brantford Expositor*, 3 January 1920, 20.
41. Russell, "All That Glitters," 40; Pendakur, *Canadian Dreams and American Control*, 55; Dombowsky, "Emmanuel Briffa Revisited," 34.
42. Chalmers, "The Story of the Allens," 15.
43. See *Cleveland Sunday-Leader*, 3 April 1921, Allen Theatre sec., 2–4; I. T. Frary, "The Allen Theatre," *Architectural Record* 50 (November 1921): 358–69.
44. *MPW*, 19 June 1920, 1577.
45. See *Edmonton Bulletin*, 30 November 1918, sec. 3, 17. Harry Allen's brother, Max Allen, served as the caretaker of the Gem in 1914 and, according to *Henderson's Edmonton City Directory*, managed the Monarch from 1914 to 1927.
46. See *Edmonton Bulletin*, 30 November 1918, sec. 3, 17–20; 2 December 1918, 8; 3 December 1918, 8; *Edmonton Journal*, 30 November 1918, 19–20; 2 December 1918, 8. The architectural plans, dated 17 June 1918, plus detailed instructions for building the facility, "Specifications for Motion Picture Theatre to Be Erected on Jasper Avenue" (28 June 1918), can be found in City of Edmonton Archives, RG 17 78/17, box 3.

47. Quoted in *Edmonton Bulletin*, 30 November 1918, 17.
48. Quoted in *Edmonton Journal*, 30 November 1918, 19.
49. See *Edmonton Bulletin*, 3 December 1918, 18.
50. See *Edmonton Journal*, 30 November 1918, 19.
51. See *Edmonton Bulletin*, 30 November 1918, 17.
52. J. William Brennan, *Regina: An Illustrated History* (Toronto: James Lorimer, and Ottawa: Canadian Museum of Civilization, 1989), 191. For the drought and recession of the early 1920s, see Friesen, *The Canadian Prairies*, 329–36; see also Palmer and Palmer, *Alberta: A New History*, 198–202.
53. See *Regina Leader*, 21 December 1918, 14; 27 December 1918, 5; 28 December 1918, 11, 12, 13, 14; 30 December 1918, 9; *Construction* 13, no. 4 (April 1920): 123–26.
54. See *Regina Leader*, 21 December 1918, 14.
55. Ibid., 30 December 1918, 9.
56. See *Manitoba Free Press*, 5 October 1918, 8; 10 October 1918, 1, 2; 12 October 1918, 1, 4; 18 October 1918, 5; 29 October 1918, 5; 26 October 1918, 1, 3; 5 November 1918, 5.
57. See *Manitoba Free Press*, 12 May 1919, 8.
58. For an overview of the Winnipeg General Strike, see Alan F. J. Artibise, *Winnipeg: An Illustrated History* (Toronto: James Lorimer, and Ottawa: National Museum of Man, 1977), 109–14.
59. Cox, "The Rise and Fall of the Allens," 61.
60. See *Manitoba Free Press*, 12 June 1919, 8.
61. We base our discussion on *Manitoba Free Press*, 29 November 1919, 5; 4 December 1919, 10; 13 December 1919, 1; 27 December 1919, 23; 29 December 1919, 4; 30 December 1919, 4; 31 December 1919, 6; 2 January 1920, 8–9, 14–15; *Winnipeg Tribune*, 3 January 1920, 4; *Construction* 13, no. 4 (April 1920): 123–26.
62. See *Winnipeg Tribune*, 2 January 1920, 14; *Winnipeg Free Press*, 2 January 1920, 8.
63. Quoted in *Winnipeg Tribune*, 1 January 1920, 10. With the release of *The Birth of a Nation*, producers and exhibitors realized that adding particular musical scores to particular movies intensified the viewing experience.
64. *Winnipeg Tribune*, 2 January 1920, 14; *Construction* 13, no. 4 (April 1920): 123.
65. *Manitoba Free Press*, 21 June 1919, 21; 3 January 1920, 20.
66. For reports on the movie industry becoming the fifth largest industry in the United States, if not on the North American continent, see "At Least $500,000,000 Invested in Movies," *New York Times Magazine*, 2 January 1916, sec. 8, 20; *Calgary Herald*, 18 March 1920, 20; *Barron's*, 14 April 1924, 10; *Forbes*, 1 March 1927, 13; *New York Times*, 7 November 1926, section 8, 7. The Allens reiterated this claim in their advertisements inviting Calgarians to invest in their projects. See, for example, *Calgary Herald*, 19 March 1920, 31.
67. See Ramsaye, *A Million and One Nights*, 751.
68. See *Edmonton Journal*, 7 December 1918, 9.
69. See Ramsaye, *A Million and One Nights*, 768.
70. For details of the Allens' mortgage, see *Calgary Herald*, 5 January 1928, 9; *Calgary Albertan*, 10 January 1928, 2.

71. Quoted in *Calgary Herald*, 18 March 1920, 20. See also *Calgary Herald*, 19 March 1920, 31.
72. We base our remarks on the details provided by the correspondents for *Calgary Albertan*, 20 October 1921, 16, 17; 25 October 1921, 11, 15; *Calgary Herald*, 24 October 1921, 13–17. In addition, we draw on the comments provided by Russell, "All That Glitters," 41–43; Elise A. Corbet, "The Palace Theatre," unpublished manuscript (Calgary, 1982), 5–9; Lorri Dauncey, "The Palace Theatre: A Case Study in Heritage Resource Preservation" (MA thesis, University of Calgary, 1993), 45–51; Harry M. Sanders, *Historic Walks of Calgary* (Calgary: Red Deer Press, 2005), 93–95.
73. See the "Inaugural Program," Allen's Palace, 25 October 1921, repr.. in *Calgary Albertan*, 25 October 1921, 10; *Calgary Herald*, 24 October 1921, 12.
74. Quoted in Corbet, "The Palace Theatre," 10.
75. See *MPW*, 21 June 1919, 1782; *MPW*, 2 August 1919, 647–48; *CMPD*, 3 June 1920, 21.
76. Quoted in *Toronto Mail and Empire*, 28 August 1920, 20; *Toronto Globe*, 28 August 1920, 4.
77. See "$400,000 Suit Opens Battle for Palace Theatre Properties," *Calgary Herald*, 5 January 1928, 9. We provide biographical sketch of Jack Barron in chapter 7.

Chapter 6: Famous Players Canadian Corporation Limited

1. See *Globe and Mail*, 28 May 1943, 5; Peter Morris, *Embattled Shadows: A History of Canadian Cinema, 1895–1939* (Montreal and Kingston: McGill-Queen's University Press, 1978), 176–77; Manjunath Pendakur, *Canadian Dreams and American Control: The Political Economy of the Canadian Film Industry* (Detroit: Wayne State University Press, 1990), 56–57; Garth Drabinsky, *Closer to the Sun* (Toronto: McClelland and Stewart, 1995), 63; Paul S. Moore, "Nathan L. Nathanson Introduces Canadian Odeon: Producing National Competition in Film Exhibition," *Canadian Journal of Film Studies* 12, no. 2 (Fall 2003): 24.
2. Quoted in *Toronto Daily Star*, 19 September 1929, 5. See Drabinsky, *Closer to the Sun*, 63; Kirwan Cox, "The Rise and Fall of the Allens: The War for Canada's Movie Theatres," *Lonergan Review* 6 (2000): 15.
3. See *Canadian Moving Picture Digest* (hereafter cited as CMPD), 16 March 1929, 10; Pendakur, *Canadian Dreams and American Control*, 61; Moore, "Nathan L. Nathanson Introduces Canadian Odeon," 27.
4. We draw on a number of sources for providing these biographical details, including the obituary notices in *Globe and Mail*, 28 May 1943, 5, 6; *Canadian Film Weekly* (hereafter cited as CFW), 2 June 1943, 1–2, 6–7; 5 June 1943, 2, 10; 9 June 1943, 2: 15 December 1943, 1; and *Canadian Moving Picture Digest* (hereafter CMPD), 5 June 1943, 2, 10. Genealogical research conducted in 2007 by Irene Theodore Heinstein, of El Cerrito, California, has shown that Nathan Louis (Nat) Nathanson was in fact born on 24 May 1886 in Taurage, Lithuania, which at the time was part of Russia, and that Henry Nathanson, his younger brother,

was born on 18 August 1890 in Minneapolis. Heinstein consulted the 1900 US census for Minneapolis, World War I draft registrations (available in the Ancestry.com database), and an S.S. *Aquitania* passenger list dated 31 August 1929, when the Nathanson family travelled to Europe (Irene Heinstein, email message to authors, 28 May 2007).

5. Quoted in CFW, 2 June 1943, 6.
6. Ibid.
7. See *Toronto Star*, 21 August 1926, 52.
8. Quoted in *Globe and Mail*, 28 May 1943, 5; CFW, 2 June 1943, 1–2; 9 June 1943, 1–2.
9. Quoted in *Calgary Herald*, 7 May 1921, 13.
10. See *Moving Picture World* (hereafter cited as MPW), 10 June 1916, 1927; *Toronto Globe*, 24 August 1916, 2; *Toronto World*, 25 August 1916, 7; *Toronto Daily News*, 26 August 1916, 2; *Toronto World*, 26 August 1916, 4; *Toronto Star*, 26 August 1916, 3; *Toronto Mail and Empire*, 26 August 1916, 38; Peter White, *Investigation into an Alleged Combine in the Motion Picture Industry in Canada* (Ottawa: King's Printer, 1931), 16–20.
11. Quoted in *Toronto World*, 26 August 1916, 4.
12. Quoted in *Toronto World*, 24 August 1916, 7.
13. See CMPD, 1 August 1919, 21; Drabinsky, *Closer to the Sun*, 64–65; Cox, "The Rise and Fall of the Allens," 64. See also Moore, "Nathan L. Nathanson Introduces Canadian Odeon," 26. As to the renaming of Nathanson's company, see *Calgary Herald*, 7 May 1921, 13.
14. See CMPD, 3 January 1956, 6.
15. See Moore, "Nathan L. Nathanson Introduces Canadian Odeon," 26.
16. We follow Kirwan Cox in outlining the decline of the Allen Empire. See Cox, "The Rise and Fall of the Allens," 65.
17. See Tino Balio, ed., *The American Film Industry*, rev. ed. (Madison: University of Wisconsin Press, 1985), 119–21; Neal Gabler, *An Empire of Their Own: How the Jews Invented Hollywood* (New York: Crown Publishers, 1988), 42–44.
18. See MPW, 21 June 1919, 1782.
19. See Cox, "The Rise and Fall of the Allens," 65–67.
20. Ibid.
21. Quoted in CMPD, 1 May 1940, 9.
22. See CMPD, 1 May 1940, 9; 3 January 1956, 6.
23. *Toronto Star*, 3 December 1920, 10; Cox, "The Rise and Fall of the Allens," 66–67.
24. Ernest Shipman, the Ottawa-born theatre impresario, and James Oliver Curwood, the American novelist who wrote outdoor adventure tales, in the tradition of Jack London and Zane Grey, about the Canadian North, formed a production company in 1918 for the express purpose of making films based on the latter's stories—featuring Shipman's wife, Nell Shipman, the Victoria-born actress, writer, and director. They chose "Wapi, the Walrus," which had just appeared in *Good Housekeeping*; the story, set in the wilds of northern Canada, contained the elements typical of Curwood narratives: a heroine, a hero, and a villain—with a dog as a

co-hero. Nell took on the task of adapting the story, expanding the heroine's role and that of the Great Dane. Shipman raised money in Calgary to make the film, and the crew shot part of the picture at Faust, a summertime fishing village on Lesser Slave Lake. The Allens screened the movie, *Back to God's Country* (1919), at the Allen Theatre (1913) in Calgary during the third week of February 1920. See *Calgary Albertan*, 16 February 1920, 7; 17 February 1920, 2; 18 February 1920, 2; *Calgary Herald*, 19 February 1920, 16; 20 February 1920, 22. For information about Nell Shipman and the making of the film, see Nell Shipman, *The Silent Screen and My Talking Heart: An Autobiography*, ed. Tom Trusky (Boise, ID: Boise State University, 1987), 70–83.

25. See *Toronto Star*, 21 July 1920, 20; *MPW*, 13 August 1921, 708.
26. See *Toronto Star*, 18 September 1920, 23; 21 September 1920, 27; 23 September 1920, 27; 28 September 1920, 22; 30 September 1920, 29. See also Cox, "The Rise and Fall of the Allens," 68.
27. Mrs. Herb Allen, quoted in Cox, "The Rise and Fall of the Allens," 70. See also *New York Times*, 18 September 1921, sec. 2, 1, 6.
28. See Cox, "The Rise and Fall of the Allens," 70. In the wake of the First World War, thousands of Americans invested in the German mark, buying when the mark was selling for about 8 cents US. These investors and speculators believed that German industry would quickly recover and that the mark would return to its pre-war value of 23.8 cents. Instead, it collapsed in September 1921, falling to a value of under a cent for the first time in financial history. Investors and speculators lost millions of dollars.
29. See *CMPD*, 3 May 1919, 4; 15 September 1919, 1, 4; 1 December 1919, 1; 20 February 1920, 11; *MPW*, 14 February 1920, 1071; 11 June 1921, 568–69; 16 March 1929, 10; White, *Investigation into an Alleged Combine in the Motion Picture Industry in Canada*, 16.
30. *CMPD*, 1 May 1940, 9; See also *CFW*, 14 July 1954, 3.
31. See *MPW*, 14 February 1920, 1071.
32. See *MPW*, 7 May 1921, 42; 25 June 1921, 843. See also Pendakur, *Canadian Dreams and American Control*, 53, 61; Drabinsky, *Closer to the Sun*, 65; Moore, "Nathan L. Nathanson Introduces Canadian Odeon," 27.
33. Quoted in Drabinsky, *Closer to the Sun*, 65.
34. See, for example, *Winnipeg Tribune*, 10 February 1921, 14; *Manitoba Free Press*, 11 February 1921, 15; 12 February 1921, 11; *Regina Leader*, 6 March 1921, 8; 16 March 1921, 8; *Calgary Herald*, 6 May 1921, 10; *Vancouver Sun*, 10 March 1921, 7; 11 March 1921, 7; 12 March 1921, 7.
35. See Douglas Gomery, *Shared Pleasures: A History of Movie Presentation in the United States* (Madison: University of Wisconsin Press, 1992), 34, 40–56.
36. See the *Calgary Herald*, 6 May 1921, 10, and 7 May 1921, 12.
37. See, for example, Hilary Russell, "All That Glitters: A Memorial to Ottawa's Capitol Theatre and its Predecessors." *Canadian Historical Sites: Occasional Papers in Archaeology and History*, no. 13 (Ottawa: Parks Canada, National Parks and Sites Branch, 1975), 43–50; Pendakur, *Canadian Dreams and American Control*, 59;

Dane Lanken, *Montreal Movie Palaces: Great Theatres of the Golden Era, 1884–1938* (Waterloo, ON: Archives of Canadian Art, 1993), 169.

38. See *Manitoba Free Press*, 9 December 1919, 1, 3.
39. In describing the building, we draw on the reports that appeared in *Winnipeg Free Press*, 14 February 1921, 11; 17 February 1921, 17; 18 February 1921, 6; 19 February 1921, 28; *Winnipeg Tribune*, 10 February 1921, 14.
40. *Manitoba Free Press*, 15 February 1921, 17.
41. See the advertisements Nathanson placed in the local newspapers, including the *Winnipeg Tribune*, 10 February 1921, 14; *Manitoba Free Press*, 11 February 1921, 15; 12 February 1921, 11.
42. *Regina Leader*, 12 March 1921, 16.
43. We follow the *Regina Leader*, 19 March 1921, 24–27, in providing these architectural details.
44. See *Regina Leader*, 19 March 1921, 23.
45. See George A. Nader, *Cities of Canada*, 2 vols. (Toronto: Macmillan of Canada, 1975–76), vol. 2, 336–37; Max Foran, *Calgary: An Illustrated History* (Toronto: James Lorimer, 1978), 79–82; Howard Palmer and Tamara Palmer, *Alberta: A New History* (Edmonton: Hurtig, 1990), 76–79.
46. In providing these details, we draw on the descriptions supplied by the reporters for *Calgary Herald*, 4 May 1921, 12; 7 May 1921, 12–13, 15; 9 May 1921, 11.
47. See *Calgary Herald*, 28 January 1946, 7; Ivan Ackery, *Fifty Years in Theatre Row* (Vancouver: Hancock House, 1980), 63–67.
48. Quoted in *Toronto Star*, 24 October 1921, 5.
49. See *Toronto Star*, 6 February 1922, 2; 8 February 1922, 1; MPW, 7 May 1922, 42.
50. See MPW, 16 July 1921, 42.
51. See *Toronto Star*, 18 May 1922, 24; 22 May 1922, 15.
52. See *Toronto Star*, 21 July 1921, 10.
53. We base our discussion on *Toronto Star*, 8 June 1923, 19; *Saturday Night*, 16 June 1923, 18; MPW, 30 May 1925, 525; CMPD, 26 March 1938, 10; 3 January 1953, 3, 6, 11; CFW, 1 May 1963, 4–5; Russell, "All That Glitters," 115; Morris, *Embattled Shadows*, 92, 310–11; Pendakur, *Canadian Dreams and American Control*, 61; Cox, "The Rise and Fall of the Allens," 70–73; Moore, "Nathan L. Nathanson Introduces Canadian Odeon," 27.
54. See, for example, *Calgary Albertan*, 7 December 1929, 1; *Toronto Star*, 11 July 1931, 3.
55. White, *Investigation into an Alleged Combine in the Motion Picture Industry in Canada*, 16.
56. Ibid., 16–18; Pendakur, *Canadian Dreams and American Control*, 61.
57. See CMPD, 16 March 1929, 1, 10; 30 March 1929, 1; 21 September 1929, 1; *Toronto Star*, 19 September 1929, 5, 9.
58. CFW, 2 June 1943, 6.
59. *Toronto Star*, 19 September 1929, 5, 9; *Toronto Globe*, 19 September 1929, 1; *Calgary Herald*, 21 September 1929, 2; CMPD, 21 September 1929, 1; 9 November 1929, 10–11; 1 July 1933, 21.
60. See *Toronto Star*, 11 July 1931, 3; Pendakur, *Canadian Dreams and American*

Control, 60–61; Drabinsky, *Closer to the Sun*, 66; Moore, "Nathan L. Nathanson Introduces Canadian Odeon," 28.

61. In providing this overview, we follow White, *Investigation into an Alleged Combine in the Motion Picture Industry in Canada*; Garth Jowett, *Film: The Democratic Art* (Boston: Little, Brown, 1976), 164–82; Balio, *The American Film Industry*, 125–25, 199–200; Pendakur, *Canadian Dreams and American Control*, 79–100; Douglas Gomery, *The Hollywood Studio System: A History* (London: British Film Institute, 2005), 64–68.
62. White, *Investigation into an Alleged Combine in the Motion Picture Industry in Canada*, 211–12.
63. Pendakur, *Canadian Dreams and American Control*, 80–81.
64. Ibid., 84–85.
65. White, *Investigation into an Alleged Combine in the Motion Picture Industry in Canada*, 164–74; Pendakur, *Canadian Dreams and American Control*, 85.
66. Pendakur, *Canadian Dreams and American Control*, 85–86.
67. See *Calgary Albertan*, 24 September 1930, 1; Pendakur, *Canadian Dreams and American Control*, 87–88.
68. Gomery, *Shared Pleasures*, 57–61; Gomery, *The Hollywood Studio System*, 25–26.
69. Quoted in Pendakur, *Canadian Dreams and American Control*, 60.
70. Pendakur, *Canadian Dreams and American Control*, 88–89; Moore, "Nathan L. Nathanson Introduces Canadian Odeon," 28.
71. Pendakur, *Canadian Dreams and American Control*, 90.
72. White, *Investigation into an Alleged Combine in the Motion Picture Industry in Canada*, 230–34.
73. *Toronto Star*, 11 July 1931, 3.
74. Pendakur, *Canadian Dreams and American Control*, 90–91.
75. CFW, 2 June 1943, 6.
76. Balio, ed., *The American Film Industry*, 124–26, 199–200, 238, 268, 286; Pendakur, *Canadian Dreams and American Control*, 78–82.
77. *MPW*, 30 May 1925, 525. See also Cox, "The Rise and Fall of the Allens," 73–77.
78. Mrs. Herb Allen, quoted in Cox, "The Rise and Fall of the Allens," 81. In the United States, prohibition was a federal matter and extended from 1920 to 1933. In Canada, prohibition was a provincial matter, so regulations, enforcement, and the length of time that prohibition laws were in effect varied from province to province. The Ontario Temperance Act was repealed in 1924 and replaced by the Liquor Control Act, which permitted the sale of liquor through government-run stores. See Herald Holowell, "Prohibition," *The Canadian Encyclopedia*, vol.3 (Edmonton: Hurtig, 1985), 1491.
79. See CFW, 5 October 1955, 3; White, *Investigation into an Alleged Combine in the Motion Picture Industry in Canada*, 139; Cox, "The Rise and Fall of the Allens," 74.
80. White, *Investigation into an Alleged Combine in the Motion Picture Industry in Canada*, 20–21, 23–25.
81. *Globe and Mail*, 19 October 1942, 5.

82. See *Toronto Star*, 5 December 1929, 21; 11 July 1931, 3; *Calgary Herald*, 7 December 1929, 1.
83. Cox, "The Rise and Fall of the Allens," 48.
84. *Toronto Star*, 1 June 1933, 11; CMPD, 1 July 1933, 21–22; Moore, "Nathan L. Nathanson Introduces Canadian Odeon," 28–29.
85. See CMPD, 1 July 1933, 2; CFW, 5 June 1943, 2, 10.
86. Moore, "Nathan L. Nathanson Introduces Canadian Odeon," 27.
87. We base our discussion on a variety of sources, including "Strand Theatre, Calgary, 1939–1952," the Kenneth McLure Leach fonds, M2354, S897, Glenbow Archives; *Calgary Herald*, 7 September 1929, 5; CFW, 15 November 1948, 1; 28 June 1950, 1, 14; Ralph Melnychuk, "K. M. (Ken) Leach: Personality of the Week," *Calgary Herald*, 26 March 1971, 4; Jack Peach, "Movies Source of Wonderment for Early Calgary Theatre-Goers," *Calgary Herald*, 29 June 1985, G7; obituary notice, *Calgary Herald*, 1 December 1985, D4.
88. *Calgary Albertan*, 25 February 1924, 7.
89. See *Calgary Herald*, 1 May 1926, 13.
90. See *Calgary Herald*, 24 November 1928, 36.
91. See *Calgary Herald*, 21 September 1929, 9.
92. Leach, quoted in *Calgary Albertan*, 2 March 1970, 13.
93. In providing these details, we follow the Dominion Appraisal Company, who produced a report on the building, *Variety Theatre: Appraisal for Famous Players Canadian Corporation Limited, Toronto, Ontario* (31 March 1945), M2354, box 1, file folder 4, Glenbow Archives; *Calgary Herald*, 14 March 1914, 5; 18 March 1914, 12; *Calgary News-Telegram*, 14 March 1914, 14; 17 March 1914, 3; 19 March 1914, 5; 21 March 1914, 14; *Calgary Albertan*, 17 March 1914, 2.
94. Quoted in Jamie Portman, "Three City Cinemas Deserted as 'Progress' Dims Lights," *Calgary Herald*, 9 April 1962, 22.
95. Quoted in *Calgary Herald Sunday Magazine*, 19 May 1991, 12.
96. See *Calgary Herald*, 22 September 1930, 4; *Calgary Albertan*, 18 July 1932, 1, 7.
97. See *Calgary Herald*, 31 December 1949, 18; 24 December 1949, 21; 31 December 1949, 18; *Calgary Albertan*, 29 December 1949, 7; 31 December 1949, 18; Portman, "Three City Cinemas Deserted as 'Progress' Dims Lights," 22.
98. See *Calgary Herald*, 31 December 1949, 1.
99. Ruth Millar, "Architectural Influences in the Capitol Theatre, Saskatoon's Lost Palace of Illusion," *Saskatoon History Review* 16 (2002): 21.
100. Don Kerr and Stan Hanson, *Saskatoon: The First Half Century* (Edmonton: NeWest, 1982), 292–93.
101. See *Saskatoon Star*, 7 January 1928, 3; *Saskatoon Star-Phoenix*, 9 May 1929, 15–22; 11 May 1929, 3, 4, 18; Millar, "Architectural Influences in the Capitol Theatre, Saskatoon's Lost Palace of Illusion," 21–38.
102. Quoted in *Saskatoon Star-Phoenix*, 9 May 1929, 17.
103. Millar, "Architectural Influences in the Capitol Theatre, Saskatoon's Lost Palace of Illusion," 24.
104. *Saskatoon Star*, 7 January 1928, 3; *Saskatoon Star-Phoenix*, 9 May 1929, 18.

Chapter 7: The Struggle for Control

1. See *Toronto Star,* 11 July 1931, 3.
2. Nathanson, quoted in *Canadian Moving Picture Digest* (hereafter cited as CMPD), 5 June 1943, 5.
3. For more information about the origins of Odeon Theatres (Canada) Limited, see Kirwan Cox, "Hollywood's Empire in Canada: The Majors and the Mandarins through the Years," *Cinema Canada* 22 (October 1975): 18–22; Kirwan Cox, "The Indies vs. the Chains: Canada's Theatrical Wars," *Cinema Canada* 56 (June–July 1979): 47–53; Manjunath Pendakur, *Canadian Dreams and American Control: The Political Economy of the Canadian Film Industry* (Detroit: Wayne State University Press, 1990), 95–100; Paul S. Moore, "Nathan L. Nathanson Introduces Canadian Odeon: Producing National Competition in Film Exhibition," *Canadian Journal of Film Studies* 12, no. 2 (Fall 2003): 28–45.
4. Arthur R. M. Lower, *Colony to Nation: A History of Canada* (Toronto: Longmans, Green, 1961), 551–52. For early impressions of the development of World War II, see Clifton Daniel, ed., *Chronicle of the Twentieth Century* (Mount Kisco, NY: Chronicle Publications, 1987).
5. *Globe and Mail,* 11 September 1939, 1; *Calgary Herald,* 11 September 1939, 1.
6. We follow Granatstein in producing this overview of the war effort. See J. L. Granatstein, "Arming the Nation: Canada's Industrial War Effort, 1939–1945," 1–16. Granatstein gave this paper at a roundtable on foreign policy and defence that was organized by the Canadian Council of Chief Executives and held at the Canadian War Museum in Ottawa on 27 May 2005. Available online at http://www.ceocouncil.ca/publication/arming-the-nation-canadas-industrial-war-effort-1939-1945-by-j-l-granatstein.
7. See CMPD, 30 September 1939, 1; *Canadian Film Weekly* (hereafter cited as CFW), 5 January 1942, 2. John Grierson, Canada's Film Commissioner at the time, discussed some of these films in his talk, on 30 December 1940, to the movie industry, which was reprinted in CMPD, 4 January 1941, 1, 7.
8. See CMPD, 3 May 1941, 1; 17 May 1941, 1.
9. Gerald Friesen, *The Canadian Prairies: A History* (Toronto: University of Toronto Press, 1984), 511, 513.
10. See, for example, *Edmonton Bulletin,* 4 July 1940, 1.
11. See J. G. MacGregor, *Edmonton: A History* (Edmonton: Hurtig, 1967), 259–71; Friesen, *The Canadian Prairies,* 427–28; Howard Palmer and Tamara Palmer, *Alberta: A New History* (Edmonton: Hurtig, 1990), 285–88, 304–7.
12. Cox, "The Indies vs. the Chains," 49; Pendakur, *Canadian Dreams and American Control,* 95–96; Moore, "Nathan L. Nathanson Introduces Canadian Odeon," 28–29.
13. CFW, 5 June 1943, 2, 10.
14. Ray Lewis, CMPD, 26 April 1941, 3, 7; 3 May 1941, 3, 5; 17 May 1941, 3, 7; 21 June 1941, 5. See also Cox, "The Indies vs. the Chains," 49; Moore, "Nathan L. Nathanson Introduces Canadian Odeon," 31, 43.
15. Cox, "The Indies vs. the Chains," 49.

16. See, for example, Douglas Gomery, *The Hollywood Studio System: A History* (London: British Film Institute, 2005), 27–36.
17. See, for example, CMPD, 22 February 1941, 2; 8 March 1941, 3; 17 May 1941, 3, 7; *Boxoffice*, 6 December 1941, 134.
18. CMPD, 22 February 1941, 2; 3 May 1941, 3, 7; 17 May 1941, 3; CFW, 12 January 1944, 1, 2.
19. Cox, "The Indies vs. the Chains," 49.
20. See Pendakur, *Canadian Dreams and American Control*, 75–77, 95–105; Moore, "Nathan L. Nathanson Introduces Canadian Odeon," 30–31. At this time, exhibitors contracted with distributors in advance to lease a selection of pictures, most likely for a complete season, regardless of their technical quality and box-office appeal, a practice known as "block booking," and to lease a selection of films, sight unseen, a practice known as "blind booking." In addition, exhibitors who held a franchise with a major studio enjoyed the privilege of leasing new, first-run features, whereas independent exhibitors, holders of no franchise, were obliged to pick films that the franchise holders had not selected.
21. Moore, "Nathan L. Nathanson Introduces Canadian Odeon," 30.
22. Cox, "The Indies vs. the Chains," 48, 50–51; Moore, "Nathan L. Nathanson Introduces Canadian Odeon," 30.
23. Douglas Gomery, *Shared Pleasures: A History of Movie Presentation in the United States* (Madison: University of Wisconsin Press, 1992), 40–56; Gomery, *The Hollywood Studio System*, 24–25.
24. See Sid Adilman, "Unique Aspects of Toronto Venture," *Variety*, 18 April 1979, 5, 32; Sid Adilman, "The Man Behind the Multiplex and Cineplex," *Variety*, 26 April and 2 May 1981 (double issue), 50, 84; Garth Drabinsky, *Closer to the Sun* (Toronto: McClelland and Stewart, 1995), 67–73; Michael Posner, "N. A. (Nat) Taylor: The Father of the Cineplex," *Globe and Mail*, 8 March 2004, R5; David Schultz, "Nathan Aaron Taylor," *Globe and Mail*, 29 April 2004, A24.
25. Alain Miguelez, *A Theatre Near You: 150 Years of Going to the Show in Ottawa-Gatineau* (Ottawa: Penumbra Press, 2004), 226.
26. See the "Proposed Agreement" (n.d.) between Taylor and General Theatres Limited and "Interview with Nat Taylor" (1990) conducted by Bronwyn Drainie, Nat Taylor fonds, 1999-036, box 001, file 30, and box 006, file 10, Clara Thomas Archives, York University. See also Ray Lewis, CMPD, 26 April 1941, 3; 21 June 1941, 5; Cox, "The Indies vs. the Chains," 49; Pendakur, *Canadian Dreams and American Control*, 96; Moore, "Nathan L. Nathanson Introduces Canadian Odeon," 30–31.
27. CMPD, 25 January 1941, 5.
28. Long, quoted in CMPD, 22 February 1941, 2.
29. See *Vancouver Sun*, 8 April 1941, 11; 12 April 1941, 10, 12, 13; 16 April 1941, 12.
30. See Patricia McHugh, *Toronto Architecture: A City Guide* (Toronto: Mercury Books, 1985), 20; Trevor Boddy, *Modern Architecture in Alberta* (Regina: Canadian Plains Research Center, University of Regina, 1987), 59–61, 65, 70; Kenneth Frampton, *Modern Architecture: A Critical History*, 4th ed., rev., expanded, and updated (London: Thames and Hudson, 2007), 248–61.

31. See, for example, the advertisement in the *Vancouver Sun*, 9 April 1941, 16.
32. In providing these details, we draw on the descriptions provided in the *Vancouver Sun*, 15 April 1941, 10; 16 April 1941, 12.
33. CMPD, 22 February 1941, 2; 3 May 1941, 3, 7; 17 May 1941, 3; CFW, 12 January 1944, 1, 2.
34. See Thom Gorst, *The Buildings Around Us* (London: Taylor and Francis, 1995). The British Odeon theatres were distinguished by their marine-inspired Art Deco architecture.
35. See *Vancouver Sun*, 30 April 1941, 11; *Edmonton Journal*, 2 August 1941, 9.
36. Moore, "Nathan L. Nathanson Introduces Canadian Odeon," 33.
37. Cox, "The Indies vs. the Chains," 49; Pendakur, *Canadian Dreams and American Control*, 97–98.
38. See Ray Lewis, "Ray Presents," CMPD, 3 May 1941, 3, 7; 17 May 1941, 3, 7.
39. CMPD, 3 May 1941, 3; 17 May 1941, 3, 7.
40. Pendakur, *Canadian Dreams and American Control*, 98–100.
41. See, for example, Moore, "Nathan L. Nathanson Introduces Canadian Odeon," 43.
42. See CMPD, 25 January 1941, 5; 22 February, 1941, 2; 26 April 1941, 7; *Edmonton Bulletin*, 28 April 1941, 1; *Vancouver Sun*, 30 April 1941, 11; *Edmonton Journal*, 2 August 1941, Section 2, 9; *Boxoffice*, 16 August 1941, 40; CFW, 25 December 1948, 24; Pendakur, *Canadian Dreams and American Control*, 287.
43. *Calgary Albertan*, 20 May 1941, 1; *Boxoffice*, 16 August 1941, 49; CFW, 5 June 1943, 2.
44. *Edmonton Bulletin*, 2 August 1941, 9; CFW, 12 October 1949, 1, 5.
45. *Edmonton Journal*, 6 July 1940, 7.
46. Quoted in *Edmonton Bulletin*, 6 July 1940, 15.
47. In describing the structure, we take our cue from the Rule, Wynn, and Rule (Edmonton) drawings, Varscona Theatre RUL(E) 4012, Accession 6A/77.07 in the Canadian Architectural Archives, MacKimmie Library, University of Calgary, and we follow *Edmonton Bulletin*, 9 May 1940, 2; 6 July 1940, 15; *Edmonton Journal*, 6 July 1940, 7; Boddy, *Modern Architecture in Alberta*, 65–72; Harold Kalman, *A History of Canadian Architecture*, 2 vols. (Toronto: Oxford University Press, 1994), vol. 2, 773–74.
48. *Edmonton Bulletin*, 8 July 1940, 5; *Edmonton Journal*, 6 July 1940, 7; 2 August 1941, sec. 2, 9.
49. On the Plaza Theatre, see *Calgary Herald*, 3 November 1934, 13; *Calgary Albertan*, 3 November 1934, 12.
50. *Calgary Herald*, 9 January 1935, 14; *Calgary Albertan*, 9 January 1935, 5; 10 January 1935, 12.
51. *Calgary Albertan*, 9 January 1935, 5.
52. Ibid.
53. *Calgary Albertan*, 9 January 1935, 5; *Calgary Herald*, 10 January 1935, 14.
54. *Edmonton Journal*, 2 August 1941, sec. 2, 9; Susan Warrender, *Behind the Marquee: A History of Alberta's Motion Picture Theatres* (Calgary: Alistair Bear Enterprises, 2007), 147–48.

55. *Calgary Albertan*, 6 October 1936, 2.
56. Quoted in *Calgary Albertan*, 6 October 1936, 2. In offering these descriptions, we take our cue from the writers for the *Calgary Herald*, 6 October 1936, 14–15; 8 October 1936, 5, and the *Calgary Albertan*, 6 October 1936, 2.
57. *Calgary Albertan*, 6 October 1936, 15.
58. Quoted in *Calgary Herald*, 6 October 1936, 15.
59. See, for example, Pierre Berton, *Hollywood's Canada: The Americanization of our National Image* (Toronto: McClelland and Stewart, 1975), 127–32.
60. *Edmonton Journal*, 2 August 1941, sec. 2, 9; Warrender, *Behind the Marquee*, 90, 93.
61. *Edmonton Journal*, 2 August 1941, sec. 2, 9.
62. In producing this sketch, we draw on a number of sources, including Grace Lydiatt Shaw's interview with Jack Barron for the CBC, Calgary, 3 July 1963, tape RCT-950, Glenbow Archives; obituary notice, *Calgary Herald*, 29 September 1965, 30; Tom Keyser, "Golden Years of Theatre Are Gone Forever," *Calgary Herald*, 13 February 1990, B1; Richard (Dick) Barron, interview with the authors, Calgary, 21 January 2004; Donald B. Smith, *Calgary's Grand Story: The Story of a Prairie Metropolis from the Viewpoint of Two Heritage Buildings* (Calgary: University of Calgary Press, 2005), 228–32; Deborah Yedlin, "Barron Building Stands Firm," *Calgary Herald*, 5 August 2001, B10–B11; Irena Karshenbaum, "J. B. Barron: A Renaissance Man for All Ages," *Jewish Free Press*, 15 February 2007, 28, 20; obituary notice, Robert H. Barron, *Calgary Herald*, 16 May 2008, B6.
63. Smith, *Calgary's Grand Story*, 232.
64. See Smith, *Calgary's Grand Story*, 232–35. Justice J. S. Shepherd of the Supreme Court of Alberta heard the case, and the local press reported on it. See *Calgary Herald*, 17 March 1937, 11; 2 June 1937, 9; 16 July 1937, 1; *Calgary Albertan*, 18 March 1937, 3. Justice Shepherd's judgment, Grand Theatre Limited v. Royal Trust Company et al., dated 16 July 1937, can be found in [1937] 2 W.W.R. 615.
65. See *Calgary Herald*, 28 July 1937, 11; 1 September 1937, 14; 3 September 1937, 5, 20–21; and the *Calgary Albertan*, 3 September 1937, 11.
66. *Calgary Herald*, 7 April 1938, 8; 29 January 1944, 15; 2 February 1944, 11; 28 February 1945, 13.
67. *Calgary Herald*, 4 September 1937, 10; and *Calgary Albertan*, 4 September 1937, 10.
68. *Calgary Herald*, 4 September 1937, 10.
69. See Smith, *Calgary's Grand Story*, 235–39. Barron may have been influenced by talk of the revival of road shows. See, for example, Ted Farah, "Revival of Road Shows in Canada Likely," *Calgary Herald*, 4 June 1938, 9. The Dominion Bureau of Statistics reported that the number of theatres in Canada offering "professional" vaudeville programs had declined from 141 in 1937 to 99 in 1939. The report also noted that ten theatres in Manitoba offered vaudeville programs, as did two in Saskatchewan and one in Alberta. See, for example, *CMPD*, 9 December 1939, 3.
70. *Calgary Herald*, 30 May 1938, 15; 1 June 1938, 1; Tom Primrose, "Old Grand Theatre Holds Memories," *Calgary Herald*, 17 September 1960, 5.
71. See, for example, *Calgary Herald*, 5 April 1941, 8; 2 June 1941, 5; 17 April 1941, 5.

72. See, for example, *Calgary Herald*, 16 March 1940, 9; 22 October 1940, 5; 16 March 1942, 11; 18 March 1942, 11; 4 November 1943, 9; 5 November 1943, 13.
73. *Calgary Herald*, 4 January 1941, 5; 13 January 1941, 9.
74. See *Globe and Mail*, 26 July 1944, 8; CFW, 6 October 1948, 1, 3; 12 October 1949, 5; 25 December 1948, 24.
75. *Lethbridge Herald*, 11 May 1946, 7. See also CMPD, 26 April 1941, 7; *Boxoffice*, 7 June 1941, 89, 92; George Adolf Mann, *Theatre Lethbridge: A History of Theatrical Production in Lethbridge, Alberta* (Calgary: Detselig, 1993).
76. See *Calgary Albertan*, 10 May 1946, 11; 11 May 1946, 15; *Globe and Mail*, 26 July 1944, 8; CFW, 6 October 1948, 1, 3; 25 December 1948, 24; Cox, "The Indies vs. the Chains," 51; Pendakur, *Canadian Dreams and American Control*, 100, 107–8.
77. Moore, "Nathan L. Nathanson Introduces Canadian Odeon," 32.
78. On Rothstein Theatres, see *Saskatoon Star-Phoenix*, 28 August 1930, 3, 7; 30 August 1930, 2; CFW, 12 January 1944, 1, 2; *Winnipeg Free Press*, 30 April 1969, 41; Winnipeg *Jewish Post*, 1 May 1969, 15; Pendakur, *Canadian Dreams and American Control*, 95–96; *Jewish Post and News*, 18 February 1998, 10; George Kovalenko, "The Roxy: Saskatoon's Last Historic Theatre," *Saskatoon History Review* 13 (1998): 8–23.
79. Winnipeg *Jewish Post*, 1 May 1969, 15. After Nathan Rothstein's death, David Rothstein, who had been involved in the family's theatre business from an early age, continued his father's work. For additional information about the Rothstein family, contact the Jewish Heritage Centre of Western Canada, Winnipeg, and the Local History Room (LHR) of the Saskatoon Public Library.
80. *Winnipeg Tribune*, 20 January 1940, 5; *Winnipeg Free Press*, 20 January 1940, 4; *Calgary Herald*, 24 January 1940, 5; *Calgary Albertan*, 25 January 1940, 3.
81. For more information about the Morton family, see *Winnipeg Free Press*, 30 August 1951, 14; *Jewish Post*, 30 August 1951, 1; CFW, 12 September 1951, 1, 3; 16 January 1952, 5; *Winnipeg Free Press*, TAB, 15 February 2007, 14. Over the years, Henry Morton became very active in community and professional organizations. He died on 29 August 1951, at the age of sixty.
82. *Winnipeg Free Press*, 3 November 1945, 13. On the transformation of the Walker into the Odeon, see *Winnipeg Tribune*, 2 November 1945, 4; *Winnipeg Free Press*, 3 November 1945, 13; Joan Mattie, "Walker Theatre," n.d., Historic Sites and Monuments Board of Canada, Agenda Paper, 1991-19a, Archives of Manitoba.
83. On Barron's project, see *Calgary Herald*, 28 March 1946, 1, 8; 10 May 1946, 11; 10 February 1949, 13; *Calgary Albertan*, 11 February 1949, 7.
84. Max Foran, *Calgary: An Illustrated History* (Toronto: James Lorimer, 1978), 163–64.
85. Robert M. Stamp, "Suburban Modern: Searching for an Aesthetic in Post-War Calgary," in the Nickel Arts Musuem's exhibit catalogue *Calgary Modern, 1947–1967* (Calgary: Nickel Arts Museum and the University of Calgary, 2000), 13.
86. Foran, *Calgary*, 157–58; Jane Kondo, "Workplace," in Nickel Arts Museum, *Calgary Modern, 1947–1967*, 26–31.
87. The plans for the Barron Building, PROJ RUL (E) 4012, can be found in the Canadian Architectural Archives, McKimmie Library, University of Calgary. See

Boddy, *Modern Architecture in Alberta*, 77–79; Deborah Yedlin, "Barron Building Stands Firm in City's Downtown Core," *Calgary Herald*, 5 August 2001, B10, B11; Douglas Bell, "Cowtown's Diamond in the Rough," *Toro*, August–September 2003, 54–57; Mario Toneguzzi, "Barron Building to Get Platinum Touch," *Calgary Herald*, 14 August 2007, C3.

88. In providing these details, we take our cue from the correspondents for the *Calgary Albertan*, 11 February 1949, 7; 29 March 1951, 9; *Calgary Herald*, 30 March 1951, 24.

Chapter 8: Consolidation

1. Manjunath Pendakur, *Canadian Dreams and American Control: The Political Economy of the Canadian Film Industry* (Detroit: Wayne State University Press, 1990), 100.
2. Tino Balio, ed., *The American Film Industry*. rev. ed. (Madison: University of Wisconsin Press, 1985), 281–84.
3. Pendakur, *Canadian Dreams and American Control*, 102.
4. Kirwan Cox, "The Indies vs. the Chains: Canada's Theatrical Wars," *Canada Cinema* 56 (June–July 1979): 50.
5. Ibid., 51.
6. *Canadian Moving Picture Digest* (hereafter cited as CMPD), 22 August 1942, 3.
7. Quoted in Pendakur, *Canadian Dreams and American Control*, 105.
8. For a glimpse into the Rank Organisation, see *Canadian Film Weekly* (hereafter cited as CFW), 25 December 1943, 11; 15 November 1944, 1–2; 29 November 1944, 1; 30 May 1945, 1–2; 6 June 1945, 1–2; 13 June 1945, 1; 17 March 1948, 1; Geoffrey Macnab, *J. Arthur Rank and the British Film Industry* (London: Routledge, 1993).
9. Pendakur, *Canadian Dreams and American Control*, 105–6.
10. CFW, 29 November 1944, 1.
11. CFW, 27 February 1946, 1; 27 November 1946, 1, 3.
12. Quoted in Cox, "The Indies vs. the Chains," 52.
13. CFW, 27 February 1946, 4; 27 November 1946, 1, 3; 25 December 1948, 24; 24 May 1950, 1, 3; *Globe and Mail*, 15 May 1950, 13.
14. See CFW, 25 December 1948, 24; Pendakur, *Canadian Dreams and American Control*, 107–8.
15. For more information about Brockington, see CFW, 14 June 1950, 1, 3; Eric Hutton, "And Now, a Few Words from Leonard Brockington," *Maclean's*, 15 April 1953, 65; "L. W. Brockington," *Globe and Mail*, 17 September 1966, 6; A. M. Laverty, "Leonard W. Brockington, 1888–1966," *Queen's Review*, September–October 1966, 120–22; Edward M. Bredin, "Calgary's Silver Tongued City Solicitor: Leonard W. Brockington C.M.G. LL.D. D.C.L. K.C.," in *City Makers: Calgarians after the Frontier*, ed. Max Foran and Sheilagh S. Jameson (Calgary: Historical Society of Alberta, Chinook Chapter, 1987), 91–93.
16. Cox, "The Indies vs. the Chains," 53.

17. For the American figures, see U.S. Bureau of the Census, *Statistical Abstract of the United States* (Washington, DC: Government Printing Office, 1968), Tables 11 on 203, and 12 on 208; Garth Jowett, *Film: The Democratic Art* (Boston: Little, Brown, 1976), 475. For the Canadian figures, see *The Canada Year Book* for the years discussed; CFW, 11 September 1946, 1, 3; 6 September 1950, 1, 3; Hye Bossin, ed., *Canadian Film Weekly Year Book of the Canadian Motion Picture Industry, 1957–58* (Toronto: Film Publications of Canada, 1958), 25–27.
18. Freeman Lincoln, "The Comeback of the Movies," *Fortune* 51 (February 1955): 127–31, 155–58.
19. Balio, *The American Film Industry*, 401–2. MGM continued operating on the stock-company system, keeping its big stable of stars, producers, directors, writers, and technical people, all under long-term contract. See Lincoln, "The Comeback of the Movies," 130.
20. Lincoln, "The Comeback of the Movies," 128.
21. Balio, *The American Film Industry*, 408–12.
22. Bruce A. Austin, *Immediate Seating: A Look at Movie Audiences* (Belmont, CA: Wadsworth, 1989), 35–38. 23.
23. For an overview of this period, including explanations for the decline in attendance, see "The Fortune Survey: The People's Taste in Movies, Books, and Radio," *Fortune* 39 (March 1949): 39–40, 43–44; Eric Johnson, "Movies: End of an Era?" *Fortune* 39 (April 1949): 99–102, 135–50; Jowett, *Film: The Democratic Art*, 333–63, 472–86; Balio, *The American Film Industry*, 401–47; Pendakur, 105–8.
24. Balio, *The American Film Industry*, 422–33.
25. Ibid., 425–27.
26. Ibid., 427–29.
27. Lincoln, "The Comeback of the Movies," 129.
28. Balio, *The American Film Industry*, 429–30.
29. Lincoln, "The Comeback of the Movies," 129.
30. Quoted in Lincoln, "The Comeback of the Movies," 121.
31. Lincoln, "The Comeback of the Movies," 131.
32. Balio, *The American Film Industry*, 433–34.
33. Ibid., 434–36.
34. Ibid., 436–38.
35. Ibid., 438–39.
36. For a discussion of how the studios reinvented themselves, see Douglas Gomery, *The Hollywood Studio System: A History* (London: British Film Institute, 2005), 226–37, 238–51, 252–56, 276–87, 309–10.
37. Quoted in Balio, *The American Film Industry* 440.
38. See, for example, Robert Fulford, "The Death Wish of Cinema," *National Post*, 19 July 2005, AL1–AL2.
39. Quoted in Balio, *The American Film Industry* 442.
40. Pendakur, *Canadian Dreams and American Control*, 108.
41. Ibid., 109. See *The Canada Year Book* for the years discussed.

42. Pendakur, *Canadian Dreams and American Control*, 110.
43. Quoted in Robert Martin, "Odeon Sale: Chance to Seize Distribution," *Globe and Mail*, 1 August 1977, 12. See *Winnipeg Free Press*, 4 August 1977, 21; Carol Hogg, "Odeon Chain Acquisition Means Better Movie-going," *Calgary Herald*, 6 December 1977, D12.
44. *Maclean's*, "Business," 23 January 1978, 47–48; *Toronto Star*, 13 May 1982, A17; *Cinema Canada*, June 1982, 12.
45. Pendakur, *Canadian Dreams and American Control*, 111.
46. Ibid., 117.
47. Ibid.

Conclusion

1. Roy Rozenzweig, *Eight Hours for What We Will: Workers and Leisure in an Industrial City, 1870–1920* (New York: Cambridge University Press, 1983), 171–72; Bruce A. Austin, *Immediate Seating: A Look at Movie Audiences* (Belmont, CA: Wadsworth, 1989), 28–29; Gregory A. Waller, *Main Street Amusements: Movies and Commercial Entertainment in a Southern City, 1896–1930* (Washington, DC: Smithsonian Institution Press, 1995), xviii.
2. See Rozenzweig, *Eight Hours for What We Will*, 172–73.
3. Quoted in Floyd S. Chalmers, "The Story of the Allens," *Maclean's*, 15 February 1920, 64.
4. "New Allen Theatre, Winnipeg," *Construction* 13, no. 4 (April 1920): 123.
5. Chalmers, "The Story of the Allens," 15; *Moving Picture World* (hereafter cited as MPW), 7 May 1921, 42.
6. "Nathanson Arrayed Empire Film Forces," *Toronto Daily Star*, 19 September 1929, 5; Garth H. Drabinsky, *Closer to the Sun* (Toronto: McClelland and Stewart, 1995), 63.
7. Lewis Jacobs, *The Rise of the American Film: A Critical History* (New York: Harcourt, Brace, 1939), 52–55.
8. Charlotte Herzog, "The Motion Picture Theatre and Film Exhibition, 1896–1932" (PhD diss., Northwestern University, 1980), 186.
9. Ibid., 186–92.
10. See Jacobs, *The Rise of the American Film*, 168.
11. Barney Balaban and Sam Katz, *The Fundamental Principles of Balaban and Katz Theatre Management* (Chicago: Balaban and Katz, 1926), 77; Ben Hall, *The Best Remaining Seats* (New York: Bramhall House, 1961), vii, 251; Herzog, "The Motion Picture Theatre and Film Exhibition, 1896–1932," 74–75.
12. Rozenzweig, *Eight Hours for What We Will*, 210.
13. Herzog, "The Motion Picture Theatre and Film Exhibition, 1896–1932," 191–92.
14. See, for example, "At Least $500,000,000 Invested in Movies, *New York Times*, 2 January 1916, 4; Richard Koszarski, *An Evening's Entertainment: The Age of the Silent Feature Picture, 1915–1928* (New York: Charles Scribner's Sons, 1990), 91–93.

15. See Richard Allen, *The Social Passion: Religion and Social Reform in Canada, 1914–1928* (Toronto: University of Toronto Press, 1971).
16. See, for example, Gerald Friesen, *The Canadian Prairies: A History* (Toronto: University of Toronto Press, 1984); Alison Prentice et al., *Canadian Women: A History* (Toronto: Harcourt, 1988).
17. Howard Palmer, *Patterns of Prejudice: A History of Nativism in Alberta* (Toronto: McClelland and Stewart, 1982); Donald H. Avery, *Reluctant Host: Canada's Response to Immigrant Workers, 1896–1994* (Toronto: McClelland and Stewart, 1995).
18. See, for example, Alan F. J. Artibise, *Gateway City: Documents of the City of Winnipeg, 1873–1913* (Winnipeg: Manitoba Record Society in association with the University of Manitoba Press, 1979), 19–20.
19. MPW, 27 April 1908, 140.
20. Rozenzweig, *Eight Hours for What We Will*, 201–2.
21. See, for example, MPW, 25 May 1907, 179.
22. Rosenzweig, *Eight Hours for What We Will*, 210, 217; Lary May, *Screening Out the Past: The Birth of Mass Culture and the Motion Picture Industry* (New York: Oxford University Press, 1980), 148.
23. See Horace Fuld, editorial, *New York Dramatic Mirror*, 14 January 1914, 54; S. L. Rothafel, "What the Public Wants in the Picture Theatre," *Architectural Forum* 42 (June 1925): 361–64; obituary notice, *New York Times*, 14 January 1936, 21.
24. Jacobs, *The Rise of the American Film*, 57; Herzog, "The Motion Picture Theatre and Film Exhibition, 1896–1932," 168–69; Koszarski, *An Evenings's Entertainment*, 34–35.
25. See "Regulating the Speed of Pictures," MPW, 4 December 1909, 792; Kevin Brownlow, "Silent Films: What Is the Right Speed?" *Sight and Sound*, Summer 1980, 164; Koszarski, *An Evening's Entertainment*, 56–61.
26. "Leopold Godowsky Criticizes Music in Small Cinemas," *New York Times*, 16 November 1924, Section 8, 5.
27. See Benjamin B. Hampton, *A History of the Movies* (New York: Covici, Friede, 1931), 399; Herzog, "The Motion Picture Theatre and Film Exhibition, 1896–1932," 172–73; Waller, *Main Street Amusements*, 256.
28. Koszarski, *An Evening's Entertainment*, 36–38.
29. "At Least $500,000,000 Invested in Movies," *New York Times Magazine*, 2 January 1916, 20; *Calgary Herald*, 19 March 1920, 31; "Movies as Investments," *Barron's*, 24 April 1924, 4, 15; Richard W. Saunders, "Finance and Pictures," *New York Times*, 7 November 1926, sec. 8, 7; Koszarski, *An Evening's Entertainment*, 91–93.
30. See *Calgary Herald*, 19 March 1920, 31; Chalmers, "The Story of the Allens," 15; MPW, 7 May 1921, 42.
31. See Douglas Gomery, *Shared Pleasures: A History of Movie Presentation in the United States* (Madison: University of Wisconsin Press, 1992), xvii–xx.
32. Kirwan Cox, "The Rise and Fall of the Allens: The War for Canadian Movie Theatres," *Lonergan Review* 6 (2000): 5.
33. See Chalmers, "The Story of the Allens," 64.

34. Drabinsky, *Closer to the Sun*, 63.
35. Ibid.
36. See *Toronto Daily Star*, 19 September 1929, 5, 9; Nathanson's letter to the *Toronto Globe*, 19 September 1929, 1; *Canadian Moving Picture Digest* (hereafter cited as CMPD), 21 September 1929, 1.
37. See CMPD, 1 July 1933, 2.
38. See Cox, "The Rise and Fall of the Allens," 48.
39. Ibid., 52.
40. *Canadian Film Weekly* (hereafter cited as CFW), 2 June 1943, 6.
41. See Manjunath Pendakur, *Canadian Dreams and American Control: The Political Economy of the Canadian Film Industry* (Detroit: Wayne State University Press, 1990), 68–79; Drabinsky, *Closer to the Sun*, 93–95; and Charles R. Acland, *Screen Traffic: Movies, Multiplexes, and Global Culture* (Durham, NC: Duke University Press, 2003), 171.
42. See Sid Adilman, "Cineplex 18: Haven of 'Fragmented' Biz," *Variety*, 18 April 1979, 5, 32; Sid Adilman, "The Man Behind the Multiplex and the Cineplex," *Variety*, 26 April and 2 May 1981 (double issue), 50, 84, 86; Michael Posner, "N. A. (Nat) Taylor: The Father of the Cineplex," *Globe and Mail*, 8 March 2004, R3, R5; David Schultz, "Nathan Aaron Taylor," *Globe and Mail*, 29 April 2004, A24; Drabinsky, *Closer to the Sun*, 172–73, 253–54.
43. Garth H. Drabinsky, "New Strategies for the Future: Two Challenges Facing Exhibition, Part 1," *Boxoffice*, February 1988, 10, 11.
44. Garth H. Drabinsky, "New Strategies for the Future: Two Challenges facing Exhibition, Part 2," *Boxoffice*, March 1988, 82.
45. Drabinsky, *Closer to the Sun*, 141–42.
46. See *Ottawa Journal*, 17 November 1937, 7.
47. Drabinsky, *Closer to the Sun*, 142.
48. See *Ottawa Citizen*, 18 November 1994, B3.
49. See *Variety*, 26 April and 2 May 1981 (double issue), 50, 84, 86.
50. Posner, "N. A. (Nat) Taylor: The Father of the Cineplex," R3.
51. Drabinsky, *Closer to the Sun*, 141–42.
52. Jay Scott, "Cineplex First in National 'Dream' Plan," *Globe and Mail*, 18 April 1979, 13. At a basic level, "front" projection is the method of bouncing an image off a reflective surface and back to the viewer. In this case, the projector is located behind the viewer. By contrast, "rear" projection is the method of throwing an image through a translucent screen to the viewer. In this case, the projector is located behind the special screen. Filmmakers use both methods to achieve a variety of cinematic effects.
53. Quoted in Drabinsky, *Closer to the Sun*, 61–62.
54. See Andrew H. Malcolm, "Toronto Movie Bazaar," *New York Times*, 22 November 1981, travel sec., 11; Betsy Powell, "Eaton Centre Cineplex Suddenly Fades to Black," *Toronto Star*, 13 March 2001, A1.
55. See "Cineplex Expands on Multiscreen Theatres, but Some Say Its Future Is Doomed by TV," *Wall Street Journal*, 9 November 1981, 31.

56. The term refers to a film that has completed its first run at a major theatre chain and then is moved over to another theatre in the market, often an independent, because it could still attract an audience. See Douglas Gomery, "Building a Movie Theatre Giant," in *Hollywood in the Age of Television*, ed. Tino Balio (Boston: Unwin Hyman, 1990), 379; Gomery, *Shared Pleasures*, 106.
57. "Toronto's Cineplex Seeks to Construct New 10-Unit House," *Variety*, 21 November 1979, 51.
58. Adilman, "The Man Behind the Multiplex and the Cineplex," 84, 86.
59. See Aljean Harmetz, "Largest Movie Complex in US Opens on Coast," *New York Times*, 21 July 1982, C15; Drabinsky, *Closer to the Sun*, 181–92, 201–6.
60. Quoted in Pendakur, *Canadian Dreams and American Control*, 227.
61. Adilman, "The Man Behind the Multiplex and the Cineplex," 84; Drabinsky, *Closer to the Sun*, 142, 150–51, 172–73.
62. Drabinsky, quoted in Pendakur, *Canadian Dreams and American Control*, 228–29.
63. See, for example, Pendakur, *Canadian Dreams and American Control*, 133–34, 188, 215–16, 248.
64. Drabinsky, *Closer to the Sun*, 209–10.
65. "Hollywood Gives the Small Fry a Chance," *Maclean's*, 20 June 1983, 24.
66. Sid Adilman, "US Majors to Go Pic-by-Pic in Canada, *Variety*, 15 June 1983, 5.
67. "Cineplex to Buy Odeon," *Calgary Herald*, 29 May 1984, D2; "Canada Plans Talks to Increase Markets for Domestic Movies," *Wall Street Journal*, 30 May 1984, 10; Gomery, "Building a Movie Theatre Giant," 381–82; Gomery, *Shared Pleasures*, 107.
68. Drabinsky, *Closer to the Sun*, 230–31.
69. Gomery, "Building a Movie Theatre Giant," 382; Gomery, *Shared Pleasures*, 108.
70. Cineplex Odeon Corporation, News Release, 8 February 1985.
71. See Anne Thompson, "L.A. Clips Velvet Seats for a Grounding," *Globe and Mail*, 3 October 1986, D3; Gomery, "Building a Movie Theatre Giant," 111; Drabinsky, *Closer to the Sun*, 250, 313–14.
72. Sid Sheinberg, quoted in Cineplex Odeon Corporation, News Release, 15 January 1986, 3; Drabinsky, *Closer to the Sun*, 235–38, 267; Acland, *Screen Traffic*, 91–92.
73. Drabinsky, *Closer to the Sun*, 302–5.
74. Harvey Enchin, "Cineplex Purchases RKO Chain," *Globe and Mail*, 31 July 1986, B1, B4; Thompson, "L.A. Clips Velvet Seats for a Grounding," D3.
75. *Los Angeles Times*, 16 June 1987, sec. 6, 1, 8; 7 July 1987, sec. 6, 1, 10.
76. Gomery, "Building a Movie Theatre Giant," 388; Gomery, *Shared Pleasures*, 112.
77. Quoted in Drabinsky, *Closer to the Sun*, 367.
78. See, for example, Susan Bourette and Michael Grange, "Mega-Complex Coming to a Theatre Near You," *Globe and Mail*, 28 August 1995, B1, B5.
79. Gomery, "Building a Movie Theatre Giant," 389; Gomery, *Shared Pleasures*, 113, 115; Michael Posner, "A Really big Show," *Maclean's*, 11 August 1997, 38–39; Acland, *Screen Traffic*, 103–4; Stuart Hanson, "Spoilt for Choice? Multiplexes in the 90s," in *British Cinema in the 90s*, ed. Robert Murphy (London: BFI Publishing, 2000), 50–51.

80. See Gary R. Edgerton, *American Film Exhibition and an Analysis of the Motion Picture Industry's Market Structure, 1963–1980* (London: Garland, 1983), 138–43; John Izod, *Hollywood and the Box Office, 1895–1986* (New York: Columbia University Press, 1988), 195–98; Hanson, "Spoilt for Choice? Multiplexes in the 1990s," 53.
81. Exhibitors in Canada closed 23 theatres (comprising 94 screens) in 2000 and 41 theatres (comprising 231 screens) in 2001. See "Theatre of the Overextended," *Globe and Mail*, 30 August 2000, A12; Daniela Deane, "Multiplexes Glut the American Marketplace," *Montreal Gazette*, 30 September 2000, D3; "EDI Box Office News: Inventory Falls for Big Screens," *Variety*, 15–21 January 2001, 34; Acland, *Screen Traffic*, 72–73, 104–5, 212–17, 224.
82. See Thomas M. Pryor, "The New Exhibition Mania," *Variety*, 6 August 1986, 5, 31; Richard W. Stevenson, "Lights! Camera! Europe!" *New York Times*, 6 February 1994, Section 3, 1; Adam Dawtrey, "Euros Go on Screen-building Spree," *Variety*, 6–12 February 1995, 1, 15; Leonard Klady, "Locals Boost B.O.," *Variety*, 9–15 February 1998, 9, 30; Tino Balio, "The Globalization of Hollywood in the 1990s," in *Contemporary Hollywood Cinema*, ed. Steve Neale and Murray Smith (London: Routledge, 1998), 58.
83. Lawrence Cohn, "Fewer Plexes but More Multi: Sites Down, Screens Up as Boom Fades," *Variety*, 29 October 1990, 1, 76; Acland, *Screen Traffic*, 18–19, 212–28.
84. Balio, "The Globalization of Hollywood in the 1990s," 58.
85. See "MPEA, Studios Promote Big-Screen Film-Watching," *Variety*, 9–15 February 1989, 48; Don Groves, "New Multiplex Building Boom May Reshape Euro Film Biz," *Variety*, 13 June 1990, 1, 20, 21.
86. Daniel R. Pruzin, "The Americanization of Europe. Part 1: How Hollywood Dominates the European Film Market," *Boxoffice*, February 1991, SW-56, SW-57; Daniel R. Pruzin, "The Americanization of Europe. Part 2: The Old World Fights Back," *Boxoffice*, February 1991, SW-58, SW-61.
87. Balio, "The Globalization of Hollywood in the 90s," 60.
88. See Millard L. Ochs, "Cost Considerations in Developing the International Market," *Boxoffice*, February 1992, SW-16, SW-18.
89. Thomas Guback has described the difficulties the Motion Picture Export Association (MPEA) had in establishing theatres in West Germany after World War II. See Thomas Guback, *The International Film Industry* (Bloomington: Indiana University Press, 1969), 129–32.
90. "AMC Goes Global," *Boxoffice*, January 1993, 40.
91. Don Groves, "New Multiplex Building Boom May Reshape Euro Film Biz," *Variety*, 13 June 1990, 1, 20, 21; Kim Williamson, "A Small World After All," *Boxoffice*, July 1994, 26, 28, 30, 32.
92. John Nadler, "Cineplex Enters Turkey," *Variety*, 27 April–3 May 1998, 16.
93. Allen Eyles, "The Last Remaining Sites for U.K. Plexes," *Variety*, 15–21 June 1998, 49–50; Hanson, "Spoilt for Choice? Multiplexes in the 90s," 48–49.
94. Richard Gold, "U.S. Pix Tighten Global Grip," *Variety*, 22 August 1990, 1, 96.
95. Acland, *Screen Traffic*, 142–43.

96. See, for example, Anne Friedberg, *Window Shopping: Cinema and the Postmodern* (Berkeley: University of California Press, 1993); Kevin Robins, *Into the Image: Culture and Politics in the Field of Vision* (London: Routledge, 1996); James Hay, "Piecing Together What Remains of the Cinematic City," in *The Cinematic City*, ed. David B. Clark (London: Routledge, 1997), 209–29.
97. See Austin, *Immediate Seating*, 27–43.
98. See, for example, Margaret Mead, "The Patterns of Leisure in Contemporary American Culture," *Annals of the American Academy of Political and Social Science* 313 (September 1975): 11–15.
99. See, for example, Austin, *Immediate Seating*, 38.
100. See "The Fortune Survey: The People's Taste in Movies, Books, and Radio," *Fortune*, March 1949, 39–40, 43–44.
101. See *Gallup Opinion Index*, report no. 146, September 1977, 14–15; U.S. Bureau of the Census, *Statistical Abstract of the United States: 1984* (Washington, DC: Government Printing Office, 1983), 238.
102. Austin, *Immediate Seating*, 40.
103. See, for example, Sean Daly, "Has Hollywood Run Out of New Ideas?" *National Post*, 25 August 2001, W2; Rick Groen, "The Magic of Moviegoing," *Globe and Mail*, 4 January 2002, R1–R2; Russell Smith, "The Films Stink More Than the Greasy Audience," *Globe and Mail*, 13 January 2005, R3; Robert Fulford, "The Death Wish of Cinema," *National Post*, 19 July 2005, B1–B2; "Canadians Are Skipping the Trip to the Big Screen," *Globe and Mail*, 4 August 2007, R2; Claudia Eller and Richard Verrier, "Hollywood Braces for Hard Times," *Los Angeles Times*, repr. *Calgary Herald*, 4 January 2009, E3.
104. Howard Lichtman, quoted in James Adams, "Our Box Office Not So Boffo," *Globe and Mail*, 3 February 2007, R1, R5.
105. See the National Association of Theatre Owners (NATO) website, http://www.natoonline.org/statisticsadmissions.htm; "Motion Picture Theatres," *The Daily*, http://www.statscan.gc.ca/dai-quo.
106. See Acland, *Screen Traffic*, 71–81, 144–46; Smith, "The Films Stink More Than the Greasy Audience," R3; Jamie Portman, "What's the Real Reason for the Decline in Movie Attendance?" *Vancouver Sun*, 13 July 2005, D5.
107. Fulford, "The Death Wish of Cinema," B2.
108. See, for example, Daly, "Has Hollywood Run Out of New Ideas?" W2; Fulford, "The Death Wish of Cinema," B1–B2; "Bad Films Blamed for Slump," *Calgary Sun*, 20 August 2005, 40.
109. See Adam Sternbergh, "The Last Quiet Movie Theatre," *National Post*, 22 March 2003, SP1, SP5; Smith, "The Films Stink More Than the Greasy Audience," R3.
110. See Sternbergh, "The Last Quiet Movie Theatre," SP5. Sternbergh quotes Charles Acland and Paul Moore, respectively, on exhibitors' reluctance to "manage" or "discipline" audiences.
111. See, for example, Michael White, "Higher Ticket Prices Rescue Hollywood," *National Post*, 29 December 2007, FP7.

112. See, for example, Frank Segers, "Say VCR Effect on Tix Sales Peaking," *Variety*, 15 January 1986, 5, 36; Thomas Guback, "The Evolution of the Motion Picture Business in the 1980s," *Journal of Communication* 37 (Spring 1987): 60–77; Saul Hansell, "Downloading Goes Hollywood," *National Post*, 5 July 2005, FP7; Richard Blackwell, "The DVD's Star Status Starting to Wane," *Globe and Mail*, 16 July 2005, B4; John Greenwood, "Wal-Mart Kicks Off Web Movie Downloads," *National Post*, 7 February 2007, FP3; Ian Harvey, "The Movie Industry's Changing Picture," *Globe and Mail*, 21 February 2008, B9.
113. See Carol Pickering, "At a Theatre Near You?" *Financial Post*, 22 October 2001, IT2; Hansell, "Downloading Goes Hollywood," FP7; Blackwell, "The DVD's Star Status Starting to Wane," B4.
114. See, for example, Cliff Edwards, "Online Film Viewing in U.S. to Top Discs in 2012, IHS Says," report posted on http:/www.bloomberg.com/news on 22 March 2012. For additional statistics regarding online streaming across North America, see the National Association of Theatre Owners (NATO) website, http://natoonline.org, and "Motion Picture Theatres," *The Daily*, http://www.statscan.gc.ca/dai-quo. For more details about Netflix and Wal-Mart and their plans to expand, see Matt Peckham, "Wal-Mart Launches VUDU Disc-to-Digital Store Program: Here's How It Works," *PC World*, 16 April 2012, http://www.pcworld.com/article/253873/walmart_launches_vudu_disctodigital_store_program_heres_how_it_works.html; Andrew Wallenstein, "Walmart's VUDU Plans Big International Expansion: Streaming Service to Compete with Netflix, Local Players," *Variety*, 19 April 2012, http://www.variety.com/article/VR1118052866.
115. See Blackwell, "The DVD's Star Status Starting to Wane," B4; Frank Ahrens, "DVDs Were Supposed to Turn TV Upside Down," *Calgary Herald*, 5 September 2006, D3.
116. Elaine Dutka, "Direct-to-DVD Films Find Legitimacy," *Calgary Herald*, 15 August 2005, E1–E2.
117. See, for example, Barrie McKenna, "YouTube Goes Legit, Signs Deal with Warner," *Globe and Mail*, 19 September 2006, B1; Catherine McLean, "Apple's iPhone Shakes Rivals to the Core," *Globe and Mail*, 19 January 2007, B1, B6; Randall Stross, "Pass the Popcorn. But Where's the Movie?" *New York Times*, 19 August 2007, BU3; Matt Hartley, "Silver Screen in the Palm of Your Hand," *Globe and Mail*, 20 January 2009, B3.
118. See, for example, Evelyn Nussenbaum, "Video Game Makers Go Hollywood. Uh-Oh," *New York Times*, 22 August 2004, BU5; Malcolm Kelly, "New Game Will Blow Past Anything Hollywood Has," *National Post*, 9 November 2004, A1–A2; Marc Saltzman, "Halo 2 Gets Down to Earth," *National Post*, 10 November 2004, B7; Michel Marriott, "Hollywood Would Kill for Those Numbers," *New York Times*, 14 November 2004, 2; Marc Saltzman, "A Full-Scale Assault," *National Post*, 1 December 2004, B6; Laura Rich, "The Teeming Crowd in Video Games," *New York Times*, 5 December 2004, BU7; Greg Hughes, "Video Games Shoot to Record on Popular Titles," *Globe and Mail*, 3 March 2005, B10; Simon Avery, "Telefilm Plugs into Video Game Funding," *Globe and Mail*, 8 November 2006, B3.

119. Hughes, "Video Games Shoot to Record on Popular Titles," B10.

120. See Richard Bloom, "Movie Theatre Industry Poised to Reel in Canadian Operations," *Globe and Mail*, 22 February 2005, B7; Barbara Shecter, "Cineplex Snaps Up Rival," *National Post*, 14 June 2005, FP1, FP6; Richard Blackwell, "Alliance Eyes Spinoffs from Cineplex Deal," *Globe and Mail*, 15 June 2005, B3; Richard Blackwell, "Cineplex Plans Real Estate Sale to Pay for Blockbuster Takeover," *Globe and Mail*, 30 June 2005, B7; "Cineplex Buys Famous Players Theatre Exhibition Business," *National Post*, 23 July 2005, FP4.

121. See Bloom, "Movie Theatre Industry Poised to Reel in Canadian Operations," B7.

122. Richard Blackwell, "From Paperbacks to Popcorn: Power Couple Strikes Again," *Globe and Mail*, 14 June 2005, A1, A12.

123. Quoted in Shecter, "Cineplex Snaps Up Rival," FP1, FP6.

124. See, for example, Acland, *Screen Traffic*, 212-28; Guy Dixon, "Cineplex Looks to Broadway After Opera Hit," *Globe and Mail*, 31 January 2007, R1, R3; Shirley Won, "Cineplex Sees Past the Big Picture," *Globe and Mail*, 8 February 2007, B9; Scott Valentine, "Interactive TV-Watching Has Advertisers Sitting Up," *Globe and Mail*, 24 January 2008, B8; Brooks Barnes, "At Cineplexes, Sports, Opera, Maybe a Movie," *New York Times*, 23 March 2008, 1, 15; Ben Kaplan, "Dramatic Development," *National Post*, 17 January 2009, A3, A5.

125. See, for example, Xan Brooks, "Is the Future of Cinema Three-Dimensional?" *Globe and Mail*, 29 August 2009, R3; John Anderson, "Alternate World, Alternate Technology," *New York Times*, 13 December 2009, AR20, AR22; Mark Medley, "Can Avatar Bring 3-D Back from Its Lengthy Exile?" *National Post*, 16 December 2009, B1, B3; Manohla Dargis, "Floating in the Digital Experience," *New York Times*, 3 January 2010, AR1, AR9; Janet Whitman, "Hollywood's Got a Smash Hit," *National Post*, 16 January 2010, FP9.

126. See, for example, Brooks, "Is the Future of Cinema Three-Dimensional?" R3.

127. Acland, "Popular Film in Canada: Revisiting the Absent Audience," 286.

INDEX